West of Jim Crow

West of Jim Crow

The Fight against California's Color Line

LYNN M. HUDSON

UNIVERSITY OF
ILLINOIS PRESS
Urbana, Chicago, and Springfield

Publication supported by a grant from the Howard D.
and Marjorie I. Brooks Fund for Progressive Thought.

Portions of chapter 1 appeared in "Entertaining
Citizenship: Masculinity and Minstrelsy in Jim Crow
San Francisco," *The Journal of African American History*
93, no. 2 (Spring 2008): 174–197. © Association for the
Study of African American Life and History.

Portions of chapter 2 appeared in "'This is Our Fair and
Our State': African Americans and the Panama Pacific
International Exposition," *California History* 87, no. 3
(July 2010): 26–45. © California Historical Society.

Library of Congress Cataloging-in-Publication Data
Names: Hudson, Lynn M. (Lynn Maria), 1961– author.
Title: West of Jim Crow : the fight against California's
    color line / Lynn M. Hudson.
Description: Urbana : University of Illinois Press, 2020.
    | Includes bibliographical references and index.
Identifiers: LCCN 2020006503 (print) | LCCN
    2020006504 (ebook) | ISBN 9780252043345
    (hardcover) | ISBN 9780252085253 (paperback) |
    ISBN 9780252052224 (ebook)
Subjects: African Americans—Segregation—
    California—History. | African Americans—Civil
    rights—California—History. | Racism—California—
    History. | California—Race relations—History.
E185.93.C2
Classification: LCC E185.93.C2 H83 2020 (print) | LCC
    E185.93.C2 (ebook) | DDC 323.1196/0730794—dc23
LC record available at https://lccn.loc.gov/2020006503
LC ebook record available at https://lccn.loc.gov/
    2020006504

For my mother,
Antonette M. Hudson

Contents

Acknowledgments

The journey of this book has been a long one. It has taken me up and down the state of California, to public libraries in Visalia and Riverside, to special collections at the Bancroft Library, UCLA, and the California Historical Society, and to the offices of the NAACP in Pasadena, my hometown. During the research and writing of *West of Jim Crow*, I have taught at four institutions and was encouraged and supported by innumerable colleagues, students, and friends. A journey like this requires sensible shoes and at least a village on your side, but several villages are best.

I was fortunate to be the recipient of generous support from the Newberry Library (in the form of a fellowship from the Associated Colleges of the Midwest) while I was employed by Macalester College. This was the perfect place to think about the significance of world's fairs. Several grants from Macalester College's Wallace Foundation made it possible for me to advance the project in its early stages. Since I arrived at the University of Illinois at Chicago (UIC), the Department of History and the Dean of the College of Liberal Arts and Sciences have been stalwart supporters of my research, and I thank them for this. A fellowship from the Huntington Library allowed me to benefit from their rich collections in western history and the company of a great cohort.

Sometimes support comes from unexpected places. A retreat for historians organized by Annette Atkins, professor emeritus of Saint Benedict and Saint John's University, provided a quiet sanctuary for writing and reflection. I benefitted tremendously from the suggestions I received from my fellow historians. A big thanks also to the writing coaches from the Loft Literary

Center in Minneapolis. A wonderful circle of women in Cambridge, Massachusetts, sustained my body and soul during a sabbatical in 2015, and to them I remain forever grateful. Thanks to Daisy Hay, Lydia Diamond, Katherine Ibbett, and Tsitsi Jaji. While in Chicago, I had the good fortune to attend Write Out!, a writing retreat at the Institute for Research on Race and Public Policy at UIC, where I met amazing colleagues and felt truly lucky to be in the company of such fierce and committed scholars. To also receive editorial advice and support from editor extraordinaire Jill Petty seemed an embarrassment of riches.

My deep thanks to friends and colleagues who read all or part of the manuscript and offered invaluable suggestions: Julia Trimmer, Choi Chatterjee, Karin Vélez, Lisa Park, Mary Murphy, Charise Cheney, Jayna Brown, Mérida Rúa, Jeff Sklansky, Kevin Schultz, Sue Levine, Marina Mogilner, and Jane Rhodes. A special thanks to Richard Blackett, whose job as advisor is, apparently, never-ending. His skills as a historian are unmatched, and I will always consider myself lucky to have landed in his orbit.

Other friends and colleagues sent sources, asked questions, challenged me, or let me bounce ideas around in their company. Thanks to Alexandra Stern, Albert Broussard, Jason Ruiz, Regina Kunzel, Dara Strolovitch, David Pellow, Amy Glass, Peter Geoffrion, Keith Glidewell, Scott Nelson, Cindy Hahamovitch, Susan Larsen, Cynthia Chris, Jill Randerson, Johanna Eager, Erica Doss, Tiya Miles, Michelle Mitchell, Becky Nicolaides, Martin Schiesl, Laura Ackley, Jamie Monson, Andrea Robertson, Chris Wells, Catherine Jacquet, Leon Fink, Keely Stauter-Halsted, Gosia Fidelis, Cynthia Blair, Jennie Brier, Barbara Ransby, Lisa Lee, Laura Hostetler, Elizabeth Todd-Breland, Chris Boyer, Rod Ferguson, Quintard Taylor, Leslie Harris, Robin D.G. Kelley, Jacquelyn Hall, and Bob Korstad.

Librarians at the following institutions offered their expertise and guidance: the Bancroft Library, Special Collections at UCLA, Pasadena Public Library, Pasadena History Museum Research Library and Archives, Riverside Public Library, Tulare County Library, (including volunteers Bobbie Levine and Sheryll Strachan), California Polytechnic State University, the Newberry Library, and the Huntington Library. A special thanks to the California Historical Society, especially Alison Moore and Debra Kaufman for their patience and deep knowledge of the archives; and to Lorraine Perrotta and Peter Blodgett of the Huntington Library for alerting me to sources that delighted and surprised.

Acknowledgments

My students at California Polytechnic State University San Luis Obispo, University of California San Diego, Macalester College, and UIC kept me on my toes and inspired me to tell a bigger and better story. Molly Brookfield offered assistance with chapter 3. At UIC my research assistant Stephanie Smith applied her razor-sharp research skills and legal acumen to several of the chapters.

I could never have written this book without a team of California supporters. The following people provided shelter and love on endless visits to the Golden State: Michael Gorman, Patrick Patterson, Gary Phillips, Choi Chatterjee, Omer Sayeed, Ellen Seiter, Stevie Ruiz, Brenda and Darryl Henriques, Leslie Henriques, Ray Riegert, Alice Riegert, Jadson Souza de Jesus, Toni Hudson, Patrick Gaganidze, and Mignon Henriques. Alma Stokes, my junior high school teacher, showed me at an early age why history mattered and what racial injustice in California looked like.

Special thanks to members of my extended family who provided joy and encouragement during what must have seemed like an interminable journey: Kris, Kyr, Isabel and Skye Gaganidze, the Rhodes family, and my amazing aunties Debbie Wier and Sandra Clark and the whole Ciunci clan. I am especially grateful to my mother, Toni Hudson, for her unwavering support and faith in my abilities. If not for her admonition to "enjoy the ride," I would never have been able to complete this book. Big thanks to my sister, Kim Hudson, who has been a friend, assistant, mentor, technical wizard, and so much more. Jane Rhodes has been with me on every part of this journey. She has read drafts, discussed evidence, listened to my rambling, shared her vast knowledge of African American history, and in every way possible made this a better book. I am truly grateful that she is by my side.

My editor at the University of Illinois Press, Dawn Durante, is truly a gem. This project would not exist without her careful guidance through every step of the process. I thank my anonymous readers for their excellent advice and suggestions.

Finally, my cousin Billie Anne Stoerzer did not live to see this book in print, but I thank her for the many gifts she gave me, not least of which was a love of history, including my own.

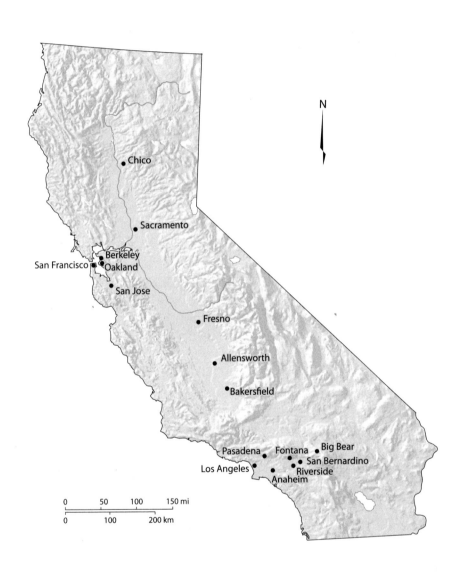

N

Chico

Sacramento

Berkeley
Oakland
San Francisco
San Jose

Fresno

Allensworth

Bakersfield

Pasadena • Fontana • Big Bear
• San Bernardino
Los Angeles • Riverside
Anaheim

| 0 | 50 | 100 | 150 mi |

| 0 | 100 | 200 km |

West of Jim Crow

Introduction

In the early years of the Great Depression, Ruby McKnight Williams left Kansas for California planning to become a schoolteacher. Having earned her credential from the Kansas State Teachers College, she wanted to make a difference in the lives of young Californians. But her dreams were derailed in a few short months when she found that her new home, Pasadena, did not hire black teachers. Only ten miles from downtown Los Angeles, Pasadena had been declared the wealthiest city in the nation in the 1920s. Williams found that black people were unwelcome at most public facilities, including the public pool. Tuesday, the day known as Negro Day, was the only day of the week she was allowed to swim. On Tuesday evenings the city drained the pool and refilled it with fresh water for white swimmers to enjoy on Wednesdays. The rigid color line in Pasadena took Williams by surprise. Segregation was common in Kansas in the years before World War II, but Williams and other African American migrants had moved to California to evade them. This was not the West that Williams had imagined. As she later recalled, "I didn't see any difference in Pasadena and Mississippi except they were spelled differently."[1] *West of Jim Crow* tells the story of Californians like Williams who, disarmed by economic and social discrimination in the promised land, mobilized against western segregation.

Fantasies of western freedom drove thousands of African Americans from their homes during the second half of the nineteenth and first half of the twentieth centuries in successive waves of migration to California. Since the 1849 gold rush, the state had drawn black migrants from every region of the country. They left behind sharecropper shacks in Piedmont North

Carolina, dust bowl towns of Oklahoma, and the swampy backwaters of Louisiana. Whether families of nineteenth-century southern farmers or twentieth-century teachers from Topeka like Ruby McKnight Williams, these migrants shared the same dream of finding in California a haven from Jim Crow. African Americans sought to escape the discrimination they encountered back home. Driven by stories in the black press, letters from friends in Los Angeles, or a burgeoning film industry that pictured sunny orange groves and picket fences, black men and women understood the West to be a place of possibility, and therefore a place they belonged. For many, California was where they planned to reinvent themselves outside of the harsh—and dangerous—racial climate of segregated America.

According to historian Douglas Flamming, "such optimism was neither inappropriate nor misleading."[2] The stories of home ownership, high-paying jobs, and a vibrant social and cultural scene were well-founded. An astounding 36 percent of African Americans in Los Angeles owned homes in 1910, a rate far higher than other western cities and most eastern ones as well.[3] African Americans, by the early twentieth century, had already created impressive enclaves in Northern and Southern California, causing easterners to wax poetic about their accomplishments. In W. E. B. Du Bois's 1913 profile of Pasadena and Los Angeles in the *Crisis*, he famously proclaimed that "nowhere in the United States is the Negro so well and beautifully housed, nor the average efficiency and intelligence in the colored population so high."[4] Black Californians built homes, enjoyed picnics at the beach, raised families, published newspapers, played music in nightclubs, voted, and ran for public office. The markers of social mobility abounded. The bustling businesses on Central Avenue, Los Angeles's black main street, included Charlotta Bass's the *California Eagle*, which began publication in 1879 and continued for over seven decades. Golden State Mutual Life Insurance Company, the first black-owned insurance company in the state, opened its office on Central Avenue in 1925. (Ruby McKnight Williams would take the Pacific Electric Red Cars from Pasadena to work there in the 1930s.) Duke Ellington and Billie Holiday played the jazz clubs on Central Avenue, and the area's boisterous night life would later become the stuff of novels by Walter Mosley.[5] Black musicians like Dexter Gordon received a stellar education at South Central's Jefferson High School and brought the West Coast sound of bebop to the world.[6] African Americans around the country saw these achievements as indicators of progress and equality in the Golden

State. Black migrants hoped and expected California would provide equal treatment in jobs, employment, and housing. Perhaps no one embraced the West's "culture of expectation" as eagerly as black Californians.[7]

For Ruby McKnight Williams, stories about Central Avenue fueled her desire to leave Kansas; she imagined a place where she could live free of Jim Crow and thrive. Her dreams of a good life in the Golden State did not begin with Central Avenue, however: California was already part of her family history. In 1849 Williams's great-grandfather left Kansas as a cook on a wagon train bound for the gold rush. "When he came back, he told the children about the oranges growing on trees," she remembered. "And, of course, they couldn't imagine that. But grandmother kept it in mind that she was going to California to see these oranges grow on trees."[8] In 1906, Williams's grandmother, Eliza Overr, did just that. Taking her youngest son, Oscar, to California, they settled in Pasadena, in the neighborhood where most African Americans, including baseball legend Jackie Robinson's family, would live. Ruby, her mother, and her three siblings would follow in 1930 and live in a house on Vernon Avenue, near her grandmother and uncle. But their dreams of orange groves and equal opportunities quickly dissipated.

In Pasadena, Williams found that jobs were scarce and segregation common. California had been separating white from nonwhite bodies for nearly a century and was adept at limiting black mobility in a state otherwise rife with opportunities. Williams's experiences negotiating Jim Crow in Kansas provided a road map, but she and other black Californians found themselves off the map. Their new state would require new methods of navigation and new ways of contesting and acquiring power.

West of Jim Crow traces California's history of segregation from statehood to the beginning of the long civil rights movement in order to better understand the ways African Americans operated in this terrain. This particular temporal frame both highlights Jim Crow's long history and its roots in slavery and state formation and also foregrounds the unusual methods African Americans used to combat inequality, methods that fall outside those traditionally associated with the black freedom struggle. This book considers what came *before* the better-known struggles of the 1950s and 1960s. The Golden State became home to the first nineteenth-century civil rights movement in the West and organized resistance to black codes and antiblack practices that put black Californians at the center of the state's—and sometimes the nation's—contestations over Jim Crow. No other western state had such an active black press from the nineteenth century forward. Further, as Mark Brilliant, Douglas Flamming, Scott Kurashige, Josh Sides, and others have shown, California became a "civil rights frontier" again in the twentieth century, providing the staging ground for innumerable challenges to segregation in schools, workplaces, and neighborhoods.

Focusing on the long span from Reconstruction to the Great Migration reveals the surprising places black Californians inhabited as they carved out freedom in the far West. Post-emancipation societies, as Thomas Holt argues, were "dependent on keeping blacks and other racialized groups in their place."[9] This book follows the black bodies that refused to stay in their place. They crossed color lines in terrain familiar to the historical narrative: in schools, on streetcars, on buses. But they also crossed lines in places that are not central to our understanding of Jim Crow: in pools on white-only days, on public fairgrounds amid displays on eugenics, and in Arts and Crafts homes in wealthy suburbs. A focus on these spaces where African Americans collided with Jim Crow helps expand our understanding of the reach of white supremacy and the ways African Americans forced post-emancipation society to grapple with their presence.

West of Jim Crow presents stories that highlight the diverse forms of racial restrictions, containment, and antiblack violence in the Golden State. The aim here is to follow the shape of segregation—and the pushback against it—as it changes over time. The forces of white supremacy manifest themselves in myriad disguises across the state; color lines were drawn differently in wealthy cities and in rural farming communities. Responses to California's segregation were never static. From letter-writing campaigns to the governor, to the establishment of a vibrant free press, to creating an all-black town, black women and men in the West were agile and astute adversaries in the fight against Jim Crow. Many of their inventive, creative strategies arose as a response to the unique conditions in places like Los Angeles or Riverside.

California proved to be an innovator of methods to control, contain, and restrict people of color. From theaters in San Francisco to pools in Pasadena, the impetus to contain and control black bodies remained a constant from the late nineteenth to the mid–twentieth century. Armed with the wealth of a rapidly expanding economy and the ideological weapons of scientific racism, California invested millions of dollars to bolster the infrastructure of segregation: city attorneys were hired, separate schools and playgrounds were built, and research labs were funded. From the political upheavals of Reconstruction to the massive influx of African Americans during the Great

Migration, California seemed determined to track the place and status of its black citizens. But why was blackness seen as such a threat? Compared to southern states, California's black population during the era of Jim Crow seemed miniscule. In 1870, during Reconstruction, only 4,272 black men and women lived in the state, whereas Mississippi was home to 444,201 African Americans, a hundred times more people in less than a third of the total area.[10] By 1920, the numbers were less stark but significant nonetheless: 935,184 African Americans lived in Mississippi and 38,763 in California.[11] Indeed, from the Civil War to the 1880s, the Chinese population in California was roughly ten times that of the African American population. Despite their relatively low numbers, black Californians were subjected to the material and ideological imperatives of Jim Crow. Segregationists were haunted by a blackness they felt but could not always see.[12] Just as Ruby Williams imagined California as a place free from Jim Crow, defenders of white supremacy imagined a place free of African Americans. Indeed, for these protectors of whiteness, the presence of African Americans rendered California untenable. The size of the African American population was beside the point; what worried white supremacists was what black bodies represented and where they went.

The physical and social boundaries that separated the races loomed large for the state's gatekeepers of white supremacy. These boundaries were meant to ensure that white men—not Chinese, African American, Native American, Mexican, or other nonwhite men—were omnipotent authority figures and that white women stayed within the dictates of their roles in a binary gender system. Women and men of color were meant to serve, disappear, or perform symbolic functions that fed the social or emotional needs of the elite. As black men and women acquired a modicum of social, economic, or political power, however, the state began to police those boundaries ever more vigilantly. Black power increased as African Americans became taxpayers, voters, homeowners, reformers, and consumers. When black men voted during Reconstruction, black Californians found themselves increasingly hemmed in by Jim Crow laws and mocked nightly on the minstrel stage. When men and women bought houses in middle-class neighborhoods, the full force of white supremacy bore down on them. At the same time, black activists hammered away at the material and ideological foundations of Jim Crow: as early as 1868, Jeremiah Sanderson delivered a scathing indictment of the tenets of scientific racism at an emancipation celebration in San Francisco.

When African American women claimed their rights as citizens they undermined foundational beliefs of Jim Crow. As Sarah Haley shows, ideas about black women were central to the creation and maintenance of Jim Crow modernity.[13] In the Golden State, beginning in the antebellum era, black women challenged slavery and black codes, insisting on making space for African Americans where they were least welcome. African American women fought against segregated streetcars and took their fight to court as soon as it was legally possible for them to do so. Women had long worked on California's Underground Railroad hiding slaves and helping to secure their freedom. By the end of the century, clubwomen were campaigning for gender justice: marching in parades, organizing boycotts, petitioning segregated institutions, and establishing clinics, schools, and hospitals to serve black Californians. All of these acts threatened white supremacy.

Most of the women whose lives are chronicled in this book—Delilah Beasley, Josephine Allensworth, Charlotta Bass, Ruby Williams, and Edna Griffin—were pioneers for racial and gender justice, but they were also professional journalists, doctors, and teachers. Despite their similar middle-class backgrounds, their methods were far from monolithic. They pushed against the racial and gender restrictions in ways that defy the conventional stories often told about race women and freedom fighters.[14] Bass, for example, challenged racism and white supremacy from her vantage point as a journalist, editor, and socialist; she waged war against the Ku Klux Klan when they arrived in the state in the 1920s. Beasley, an indefatigable defender of racial uplift, embraced a patriotic fervor unmatched by her male or female cohorts as she championed the Panama Pacific International Exposition and led the state's protests against lynching and the screening of D. W. Griffith's *The Birth of a Nation*. This book shows that women's efforts were central to the movements, practices, and ideologies that challenged Jim Crow. Contemporary assumptions about the insignificance of black women's presence made their interventions unexpected and often successful.

The project of maintaining the privileges of whiteness seemed especially precarious in a state that was carved out of Mexico and balanced on the edge of the Pacific Rim. The color lines in California were ever-changing, targeting different populations and communities at different times. African Americans, Asians, Latina/os, and Native Americans were subject to laws and customs meant to restrict, exclude, and contain them. Ideologies of racial purity and fears of race mixing undergirded such restrictions. Historians of the state have documented the ways color lines were drawn to keep nonwhites from owning property, attending school, and marrying whites.[15] As they have shown, we must study the ways different groups of Americans are racialized and how that process shapes their possibilities for freedom and citizenship if we are to understand segregation.[16] Blackness in the Golden State was never constructed in a vacuum, and the meanings attached to it were never fixed. Scholars Stacey Smith, Natalia Molina, Najia Aarim-Heriot, and others have reminded us that what it meant to be black in California was constantly in flux, interwoven with ideas and imagery about other racialized groups including Native Americans, Mexicans, and Asians. This book highlights the experience of black Californians and their own process to define and protect their status as citizens in the midst of rapidly changing racial configurations. From the height of the anti-Chinese movement to the Zoot Suit Riots, *West of Jim Crow* considers how black people created movements for racial justice in a place where Jim Crow was never solely directed at African Americans. Multiracial color lines did not always result in the formation of multiracial coalitions.

As African Americans voted in previously all-white elections, marched in patriotic parades, bought houses in restricted neighborhoods, established black towns and institutions, and swam in forbidden pools, they became the focus of the enforcers of segregation. Their physical and mental capacities were consistently found lacking, and what this meant for black Californians is the centerpiece of this book. The stories contained herein demonstrate that ideas about black citizens were significant in both the creation and destruction of Jim Crow practices. Well aware of the arsenal of white supremacist beliefs at work in the United States, African Americans placed body and mind in the service of racial equality. We have much to learn from women like Ruby McKnight Williams, who studied the California color line and devised ways to resist it, only to see it materialize somewhere else in another form.

✳ ✳ ✳

To understand the entrenched segregation that Ruby Williams encountered, we must look to the history of California's commitment to Jim Crow, a history that begins during the state's earliest years. Chapter 1 delineates the origins of California's Jim Crow laws and practices, rooting them in the complex process of establishing white supremacy on land that moved from the domain of Native Americans to Mexicans to Anglos. By the time the first California Constitutional Convention met to hammer out the details of a new state government in 1849, the gold rush had already pulled thousands of hopeful seekers from all over the world to the towns, valleys, streams, and mountains of the Golden State. The population included a diverse mix of South and Central Americans, Europeans, Australians, Pacific Islanders, Chinese, South Asians, Native Americans, African American slaves, and about a thousand free African Americans, among many others.[17] Despite African Americans accounting for roughly one percent of the state's population throughout most of the nineteenth century, they loomed large in the minds of California's earliest legislators and politicians. So-called black codes became a prominent feature of the state's legal system.

Restricting black testimony in the court of law became a priority for many early lawmakers. First passed in 1850, when California entered the Union as a "free" state, the anti-testimony laws disallowed Africans Americans, mulattos, and Native Americans from testifying against a white person, making it necessary to determine the boundaries of whiteness. Toward that end, the law specified that a person with one-eighth or more "Negro blood" would be considered mulatto and anyone with "one half Indian blood" would be considered an Indian.[18] Members of the state's legal apparatus applied tests in order to determine the racial makeup and therefore viability of a witness. California's history of applying the "science" of biological difference—or scientific racism—developed in tandem with black codes. Scientific racism would become a central and embedded feature in the state's arsenal of discriminatory laws and practices. Black bodies as a site of difference became a staple of the public discourse of citizenship.

As soon as the anti-testimony law was revised to allow African American witnesses in 1863, black San Franciscans filed charges against streetcar drivers who refused to pick up riders or harassed them on the cars. Public transportation represented a grave concern for segregationists, as black and white bodies could easily mingle on trains and streetcars. African American women led the effort to desegregate horse-drawn cars and were some of the first women in the country to challenge segregated public transportation.[19] Their insistence on equal treatment and respect countered the claims of racial pseudoscience that argued that African Americans did not deserve such treatment due to their natural and biological inferiority.

African Americans pushed the state to make good on the promises of freedom, equality, and citizenship during and after the Civil War. Black Californians dominated discussions about inequality in the state legislature as they fought for four decades to amend the legal mandate for educational segregation. After the Civil Rights Act of 1875 guaranteed the right of African Americans to enjoy public amusements, including theaters, black Californians embraced the opportunity to enter the best venues in the state. The resulting lawsuits would, once again, force the state and the nation to take notice of the workings, and failures, of racial justice and democracy.

Black Californians were not of one mind when it came to devising strategies to defeat Jim Crow. During Reconstruction, discord erupted among African American men in the state as they formulated new definitions of citizenship and masculinity in an era of tenuous freedoms, shrinking civil rights, and rampant antiblack stereotypes. In this volatile environment, elite black men policed the behavior of black workers, finding them uncomfortably close to the caricatures of black manhood offered up nightly on San Francisco's many minstrel stages. While African Americans agreed that they were fully prepared for the responsibilities of citizenship, its boundaries were always under negotiation, especially as black freedom became threatened. Men *and* women would manipulate the definitions of respectable behavior in ways that pushed and pulled at racial and gender constructions.

In 1915, California produced two events that showcased white anxieties about black freedom. Chapter 2 chronicles the release of *The Birth of a Nation,* which coincided with the opening of the Panama Pacific International Exposition (PPIE) in San Francisco. The PPIE celebrated both San Francisco's recovery from the 1906 earthquake and fire and the building of the Panama Canal. For African Americans, this fair, like the 1893 Columbian Exposition in Chicago, provided the opportunity to demonstrate their contributions to the nation. The fairs also presented possibilities for black citizens to critique discrimination within and outside the fairgrounds. Delilah Beasley, a black journalist for the *Oakland Tribune* and the *Oakland Enquirer,* knew that the exposition offered a rare chance to garner a wide audience for her writing about black Californians and black history. At the same time, she knew that *The Birth of a Nation,* made in southern California and previewed in Riverside, reached millions of viewers with the message that African Americans were unfit for citizenship and that violence against them was justified if not necessary. In spite of an organized protest to ban the showing of the film in the state, it played in California theaters and across the country during the entire run of the fair, from February to December 1915. Beasley and other race women understood the world's fair as a perfect opportunity to counter the film's message and claim their rights to equal treatment as U.S. citizens. Harnessing the language and symbols of domesticity, respectability, and patriotism, black women took to the streets during the exposition to subvert ideologies that propped up Jim Crow and white supremacy.

The protest of African American women was, in some ways, a response to the fair's promotion of scientific racism. Confirming the state's reputation as a center for eugenics, leaders in the field gave lectures, contributed to educational displays, and organized Race Betterment Week at the PPIE. A wide range of scholars and enthusiasts claimed to show the superiority of European stock and warned of the dangers of miscegenation and the reproduction of the "unfit." The state's belief in the new science of eugenics led to the passage of a eugenic sterilization law in 1909 to assure that only those deemed "fit" would reproduce; it was the third state in the nation to pass such legislation. California would excel in the use of eugenic sterilization, performing the procedure on more women than any other state in the country.[20] Race women insisted on shifting the focus at the PPIE to black accomplishment and citizenship, overturning the fair's message that black bodies were unfit.

By the time Ruby Williams had settled into her new home in California, one of the nation's leading eugenics organizations, the Human Betterment Foundation (HBF), had opened its headquarters in Pasadena. Williams remained in Pasadena despite HBF's commitment to segregation and the science that upheld it. Other members of her family, however, had already found the restrictions in California intolerable. Her uncle, Oscar Overr, arrived in Pasadena nearly three decades before his niece, in 1906, and made a very different choice. Laboring at one of the only jobs available to black men in Pasadena, working as a gardener for the wealthy whites who had settled in and around Orange Grove Avenue, his frustration mounted. After just a few years, Overr joined several hundred other black Californians and retreated to an all-black town in the San Joaquin Valley, where he hoped to escape the stifling restrictions of segregated jobs, housing, and politics.

Chapter 3 examines the community of Allensworth and its promise to provide black people what Pasadena and other California towns could not: open access to schools, no housing restrictions, no color lines. Allensworth had its own polling places, library, post office, churches, barbershop, and justice of the peace. As the westernmost all-black town in the United States, modeled after similar settlements in Oklahoma and Kansas, Allensworth offered a second chance for black Californians to realize their dreams of living west of Jim Crow. Within a decade of the town's founding in 1908, Overr, now a full-fledged farmer and speculator, owned nearly 700 acres in and around Allensworth. "Too much cannot be said concerning his devotion and earnest work for the advancement of Allensworth," Delilah Beasley wrote. Overr had high hopes for the colony, and claimed that it represented "the best proposition ever offered to Negroes in the state."[21] Opting out of Jim Crow by creating a self-sustaining community was a project that appealed to African Americans across the state. Men, and especially women, would, for a time, experience a liberty to create and thrive outside of antiblack sentiment and proscriptions. They would reinvent what it meant to be black Californians.

In spite of Overr's hopes and the industry of the colonists, Allensworth struggled to survive when the railroad service to the colony ended and water sources dried up in the 1920s. Dairy and vegetable farming, the colony's economic foundations, became unsustainable. Many settlers came to believe that they had been cheated by the white developers who sold the original plots to the colonists. By the Great Depression, the colony had become a ghost town and the few families that stayed found it nearly impossible to earn a living. For some, the demise of Allensworth underscored the impossibility of escaping the state's color line and finding—or even building—a place that offered the freedoms they sought.

As Allensworth began its slow decline, California was riveted by a tale from its heartland. Chapter 4 focuses on the 1933 lynching of kidnappers Thomas H. Thurmond and John M. Holmes in San Jose, a crime that sent shock waves across the country. In fact, this hanging received more attention from the press than any other lynching in U.S. history.[22] After a ferocious mob dragged the two white men from jail, they hanged them from oak trees in the city park. Governor James Rolph Jr. made history by praising the lynchers and promising to free any prisoners in San Quentin who had been arrested for the crime of lynching. The murders in California, and the governor's support for lynchers, became a centerpiece of national discussions of mob violence, the power of the state, and the antilynching movement. "It took the governor of California to put the stamp of approval on lynching," reported the *California Eagle*.[23] The events in San Jose inspired a media spectacle, a Hollywood film, and a Pulitzer prize–winning cartoon; few of these depictions of the lynching mentioned African Americans. However, antilynching activists around the country, and black Californians in particular, understood that although the victims in San Jose were white, support for lynching would mean the loss of black lives. Their insistence that this was a crime about black bodies pushed the antilynching movement forward and drew attention to the state. Thomas Fleming and other black journalists refused to let this story languish. As black journalists, activists, and intellectuals argued, the San Jose lynching provided irrefutable evidence that California was not a bystander to the nation's tradition of lynching; it helped to sustain and defend the practice.

Lynching was one of the most common ways of terrorizing African Americans in the age of Jim Crow. But violence in the service of segregation often took other forms in California. For proponents of segregation in twentieth-century California, policing contact between whites and people of color became an urgent affair with the acceleration of the Great Migration. In the two decades after Ruby Williams made her journey, the state underwent a massive demographic transformation that coincided with the onset of World War II. The numbers were staggering: in 1930, 81,048 African Americans made California their home and by 1950 there were 462,172.[24] To be effective, Jim Crow could not be limited to parks, pools, or streetcars—it had to reach streets and neighborhoods. Black Californians, especially property owners, became the target of white supremacists including the Ku Klux Klan.

Chapter 5 examines the Klan's influence and its focus on black migrants. Organized in the 1920s, as part of the second Klan, California's Invisible Empire sought to purge what members saw as un-American elements: immigrants, people of color, feminists, and secular educators, among others. Klan chapters flourished, especially in southern California towns such as Riverside, Inglewood, and Anaheim. By the 1940s, the state's Klan had a more explicit focus on black homeowners; cross-burnings and arson became commonplace and a coalition of activists pushed local and state authority for protection that rarely materialized. The 1945 murder of the family of O'Day Short, a refrigeration engineer employed at Kaiser Steel mill in Fontana, marked the beginning of a terrifying wave of violence specifically aimed at families like the Shorts who had dared to cross the color line.

Chapter 6 centers on the work of Ruby McKnight Williams and other southern Californians who fought racial restrictions. Williams and her allies in the NAACP touched a nerve in the wealthy enclave of Pasadena when they joined forces to integrate the public pool. The backlash against their efforts was swift and lengthy; this civil rights struggle continued for over fifty years. Why were swimming pools and beaches so important to the state's segregationists? Perhaps these amenities had come to represent the good life in California; leisure activities associated with middle-class living that some believed should be reserved for whites. Swimming at the beach or in a pool symbolized the fun-in-the-sun lifestyle that boosters of the state long promoted. Not only did African Americans dare to swim in the public pool, but many had begun to settle in previously white neighborhoods in western Pasadena. By 1909, some of the city's black homes and churches were targets of arson. Some white Californians were outraged that African Americans had moved to Pasadena, to "their" neighborhoods, and had dared to stake a claim to the symbols of middle-class comforts that were on offer. Public swimming facilities, in particular, raised thorny issues that cut to the core of segregationists' fears, including the dangers of interracial physical contact. In the South, anxieties about interracial intimacy dominated the rhetoric about the necessity of separate facilities for black and white, and the West would be no different. While segregating bodies in water was not solely a western project, California had more pools than any other state by the 1920s and pioneered systems of restricting these spaces. Semi-clad bodies mingling across the color line raised questions about hygiene, nudity, and interracial sex. Pools became a focal point for the battle over Jim Crow in the state, just as streetcars had in the previous century. Racial mixing was deemed more likely and more dangerous in these settings by enforcers of Jim Crow.

When Pasadena's municipal pool opened in 1914, on the eve of World War I, the city fathers immediately restricted African Americans patronage to one day a week, creating their Negro Day policy. African Americans working in Pasadena as gardeners and maids, preachers, and small business owners instantly formed the Negro Voters and Taxpayers Association—a name that emphasized their claim to citizenship—to fight the restriction. The city fought off repeated legal challenges launched by the association to maintain Negro Day. By the 1930s, another generation of freedom fighters, including Williams and Dr. Edna Griffin, joined the protest. Again the battle took place inside and outside the courtroom, but this time it was closely monitored by Thurgood Marshall and Charles Hamilton Houston. Indeed, the fight against the city of Pasadena proved to be a valuable lesson as Marshall and the NAACP Legal Defense Fund honed their skills for *Brown v. Board of Education*. The resistance to integration in this western city foretold the trouble that lay ahead in the wake of the *Brown* decision.

Despite a rich scholarship that proves otherwise, the most popular versions about Jim Crow's history still tend to describe segregation as something that was practiced and perfected in the South or the Midwest.[25] This tendency in the national imagination slights the efforts of western freedom fighters and undercuts the expansiveness of the movement. Further, it allows the West to slip out of the narrative of U.S. racism. We have much to gain by restoring Williams and her contemporaries to the story. By foregrounding the West, we begin to appreciate the breadth and depth of segregation's reach. Segregation and its partial undoing came at a tremendous cost to Americans from every region of the country, and they deserve to have their voices heard. The work of Williams and her allies teach us that we have not paid enough attention to the western strands of the long civil rights movement.

Williams's story, and the others told in this book, show that California practiced de jure and de facto segregation with commitment and persistence. The color line surfaced in large cities and small towns in the Golden State. Neighborhoods, schools, restaurants, parks, beaches, and pools were vigorously policed by segregationists. African Americans employed innovative measures to dismantle segregation; some tactics they borrowed from race rebels in the South, and others they improvised.[26] *West of Jim Crow* highlights the western roots of segregation and the equally bold and varied response of black Californians in the years between the Civil War and *Brown v. Board of Education*. In some cases, this book argues, the Golden State set precedent, devising new laws and methods to segregate, using means we might term "modern."[27] Celebrated for its forward-thinking culture, politics, and science, California pioneered new ways to keep citizenship white. The qualities associated with modernism such as scientific discovery, urban development, the consolidation of capital, and the effort to master the environment, all shaped the systems of Jim Crow that Californians created and resisted.

✳ ✳ ✳

Listening to African American voices has been critical to this project. Whenever possible I relied on interviews with black Californians to tell the story of segregation and resistance; these include two collections of oral histories with the settlers of Allensworth that shed light on conflicts over water rights, gender relations, and the politics of an all-black town.[28] In addition, the Pasadena Museum and Archives has preserved interviews with local residents that provide valuable perspectives on segregation in southern California. These sources allow me to foreground stories that have been marginalized in the telling of western history and the history of Jim Crow. I have also mined the recollections published in the state's rich and diverse black press. Peter Anderson, Thomas Fleming, Charlotta Bass,

Delilah Beasley, and other black journalists appear in the chapters that follow, as do journalists working for the national black press. To attend to the differences of class, gender, and generation, I have included the stories of a diverse set of Californians.

This project examines the ways Jim Crow is remembered or forgotten in histories, folklore, monuments, public spaces, and private lives.[29] The record of American Jim Crow is littered with gaps and erasures. Like other states, California exhibits a convenient amnesia—especially in official spaces—in relation to this part of its past. This amnesia occurs alongside a narrative about the state as a bastion of equality. Californians wasted no time claiming the mantle of freedom and proclaiming themselves to be its protectors. In 1856, for example, white abolitionist Eliza Farnham declared that "California is the world's nursery of freedom," even for the sons of "benighted Africa."[30] The histories of black Californians reveal a quite different narrative. Yet this belief *did* shape African Americans' experience in the Golden State, and their belief that the state could be a "nursery of freedom" drew migrants hoping to turn the belief into reality. The juxtaposition of those expectations and the realities of life in the Golden State under Jim Crow reveals the uncertainty of democracy in a state where it was thought to flourish.

West of Jim Crow seeks to compare memories and histories, official and unofficial, in the hopes of changing the stories we tell about U.S. segregation and white supremacy. The memories of Allensworth and Los Angeles and San Francisco reveal contradictory recollections of freedom and inequality. As Ruby McKnight Williams knew, these California cities could be simultaneously both the best and the worst places to live.

CHAPTER 1

Freedom Claims

Reconstructing the Golden State

Getting a glass of whiskey on San Francisco's Barbary Coast had never been difficult. The gold rush meant, among other things, that libations would be plentiful in the towns and camps that sprang up throughout the new state of California.[1] But for African American men, stepping into a bar during the era of Reconstruction meant coming face to face with Jim Crow. By 1872 barrooms and restaurants in the West's most populous city shunned African American patrons. In fact, many African Americans believed, according to one of San Francisco's black newspapers, the *Pacific Appeal*, that "prejudice against color is now as bitter among proprietors of public places" as it was before the passage of the Civil Rights Bill of Act of 1866 and the Fifteenth Amendment. "Colored men are liable to insult, by asking to be served with a meal, in almost any inferior restaurant in the city," quipped the editorial.[2] California, of course, was not special in this regard. African Americans in every state in the nation faced Jim Crow restrictions in hotels, streetcars, bars, and cafés. But the state's reputation as a place free from the harshness of segregation and racialized violence made this treatment in public places noteworthy, and for some, particularly insulting. In Washington, D.C., in the previous summer, a judge had ruled—in a lawsuit black Californians followed closely—that saloon keepers could "make no distinctions on account of color to whom they shall sell liquor."[3] If you could be served a drink in the nation's capital, on the Mason-Dixon Line, reasoned black men in California, surely they should be entitled to the same pleasure.

The problem of men and alcohol surfaced repeatedly in the state's black press during Reconstruction. In 1872, two African American men were scolded publicly for disrupting a Republican meeting in San Francisco while intoxicated. Clearly, the Jim Crowed public facilities had not stopped black men from drinking. But pressure to exhibit the right kind of manhood, as befits new citizens, prompted the anonymous writer of the column about the Drinking Duo to warn that "for the credit of the colored citizens at large, we hope that their friends will persuade them not to make themselves so ridiculous in a Republican meeting again."[4] The fact that these men were torchbearers of one of the city's Republican clubs made the spectacle that much worse. Newly franchised and struggling to stake their claim in the state's Republican Party, some African American men worried that this type of behavior played into the hands of those who argued that black men were not fit to be citizens.

Men's behavior became a central focus of Reconstruction-era black politics, despite the fact that women participated in the campaigns for equal rights in significant and conspicuous ways. The focus on masculinity can be traced to gendered notions of citizenship and the patriarchal assumptions that cast men as voters and agents in the world of politics and women as passive observers or domestic helpmates. These notions assumed the men would be the ones to work out the intricacies of freedom. A number of factors conspired to place men front and center in the politics of freedom. Some of these factors were internal to black communities; churches, Republican meetings, parades, and conventions most often featured male leaders and male speakers. Other forces external to black settlements spotlighted men's role in politics. The white mainstream press and political parties rarely, if ever, envisioned African American women as citizens or constituents. Black men themselves sought to keep the spotlight on manhood rights, not the rights of women. Indeed, some nineteenth-century African American men, including ministers, Republican Party leaders, and newspaper editors, became increasingly concerned with the rights of men precisely because women continued to challenge male prerogatives.[5] The dictates of white supremacy encouraged black men to monitor their behavior and that of black women in order to establish the boundaries of proper political etiquette.

The parameters of citizenship in the new state of California would not be determined solely by men, however. Seven years before the two men disrupted the Republican meeting, in 1865, a group of African American women were also scolded for behavior that was deemed inappropriate for the occasion. In this case, the citizens in question were not drunk; their transgression was voting. At a planning meeting for the fourth black convention hosted in California, three of the seven women in attendance attempted to make their voices heard by voting on a question brought before the committee. For this behavior, they too were ridiculed. This attempt to silence or shame African American women, implying that politics was only for men, did not have the desired effect.

In 1866, black women beat a path to California courtrooms to challenge poor treatment on the increasingly segregated streetcars. As part of their strategy, they placed their bodies on public transportation where they were not wanted, a strategy used later by Sojourner Truth, Ida B. Wells, and Rosa Parks. Black women in the nineteenth century, as Brittany Cooper shows, developed an embodied discourse, including a set of social and political strategies that made legible their role as citizens.[6] In California, as in other states, this process had its roots in slavery and in white fallacies about the accessibility and lascivious nature of women's bodies. African American women in the Golden State challenged Jim Crow and rigid gender proscriptions in ways that centered the body. Their activism and challenges to the racial-gendered order began a soon as California joined the union.[7]

Women claimed freedom by protecting slaves on the Underground Railroad, seeking redress in the courts, boarding streetcars, and opening schools for "colored" students. If the state's goal was to keep black people in their place, women understood that resistance to white supremacy meant physically occupying spaces where they would confront hostile forces. Black women's determination to shape freedom put them in conflict with white men, white women, black men, and others. While little remains in the historical record that documents the political philosophy of black women in nineteenth-century California, their *actions* reveal a political engagement that challenged the very root of Jim Crow's tenets. What their actions tell us is that black women did not shy away from political confrontations over segregation even when the danger was represented as one about bodies. In the battles over schools and streetcars, for example, proponents of segregation argued that unseemly mingling of black and white bodies constituted the core of the danger. These were precisely the places where African American women were most visibly engaged in the battle against Jim Crow.

The black codes that we associate with the Jim Crow South found a comfortable home in California. The state legislature passed statutes that ensured white privilege in most areas of public life. Separate schools for white and nonwhite children originated with statehood. Streetcar drivers routinely ignored or refused to stop for black riders. Antimiscegenation laws criminalized marriage between African Americans and white Californians. And for the first thirteen years of statehood, African Americans could not testify against a white person in court.[8] The presence of Jim Crow in California elicited a forceful response. Black men and women challenged segregation in the courts, the streets, the ballot box, the pulpit, theaters, and in the pages of the black press. These efforts amounted to what has been called "the first civil rights campaign in the West."[9] As in the civil rights movement that would follow in the next century, women and men made meaning out of race and gender, sometimes pushing against rigid definitions, sometimes adopting what we would see as conventional gender roles. Black women often found themselves in precarious positions that shaped their modes of resistance; throughout the nineteenth century their bodies would be the subject of racialized and sexist diatribes and their quest for freedom occurred in response to and challenged such beliefs. Black men, however, also engaged with racist proscriptions that were about gender and sex and that deployed pseudoscientific rhetoric about their impure and dangerous bodies.

This chapter examines African American efforts to wrest freedom from California during the first decades of statehood, revealing the significance of black women and men in the larger project of determining who would be a citizen. Black men and women became integral to the state's efforts to define what citizenship entailed in post-emancipation America. The claims that black Californians made as they articulated their demands for equal rights reveal myriad beliefs about what democracy should look like and who should be entitled to the privileges of citizenship. Sometimes nineteenth-century black Californians understood that their fight required coalitions with other aggrieved groups, especially Chinese; on other occasions, African Americans made their freedom claims separate from and in conflict with Chinese. Black women and men organized a civil rights movement using networks and strategies formed in the abolitionist movement, creating new ways of thinking and being. Whatever the strategy, gender and bodies were always part of the equation.

To undo Jim Crow as it was being created in this western place meant grappling with ever-changing meanings of manhood and womanhood and with diverse ideologies of freedom and equality. Black men and women created multiple routes of resistance in this era, strategies and tactics that laid the foundation for future activism. Their insistence on entering previously white-only spaces drew attention to the hypocrisy of California's status as a free state. Women's insistence on inhabiting white-only and male-only spaces meant that they experienced Jim Crow differently and fashioned their own, sometimes independent strategies. California, or "freedom's nursery," as Eliza Farnham called it, was indeed a nursery of ideas about freedom, though probably not in the ways that Farnham had imagined.[10] That slavery was intact but ambiguous and Jim Crow emerging as California claimed statehood meant that black Californians were in a position to study discrimination and shape freedom. The ways that this unfolded show us that African Americans were central actors in the debates that animated antebellum and Reconstruction politics in California and that the subject of black bodies was deeply imbedded in those politics. This initial era of the state's history reveals Jim Crow under construction in a place where African Americans rarely found the freedom they deserved. This positioned black Californians to shape the contours of democracy in the state and nation.

Slavery's Shadow

Upon entering the Union in 1850 as a free state, California emerged as an innovator of racial restrictions and quasi-freedom.[11] Anglo Californians embraced the rhetoric of freedom and equality as they carefully crafted their limits. Efforts to create, protect, and defend freedom for white men were complicated by the state's multiracial and multiethnic population, and its ever-changing demographics. Creating out of Native American and Mexican territory a republic that privileged free white men required an arsenal of new laws, "sciences" about race and racial categories, and attention to gatekeeping in every area of public and private life. As the meanings of free and unfree labor were refined and adjusted, slavery lingered. Staking a claim to freedom in this environment would be more difficult than most black migrants anticipated.

The process of state making in the territory that became California hinged, in many ways, on the question of slavery and freedom. Believing that the presence of slaves would undermine the freedom of white men, a majority of delegates at the 1849 Constitutional Convention voted to endorse the antislavery constitution. The presence of free blacks worried state makers for much the same reason. Convention delegate O. M. Wozencraft from San Joaquin opined, "I desire to protect the people of California against all monopolies—to encourage labor and protect the laboring class. Can this be done by admitting the negro race? Surely not."[12] Delegates considered a state constitution that would prohibit free black migration as well as slavery, but there was concern that Congress would not approve the constitution. The first state assembly passed an anti-immigration law forbidding free blacks from entering the state only one month after the convention. Although the bill did not gain senate approval, anti-immigration bills were introduced in the California Legislature on three other occasions—in 1851, 1857, and 1858.[13] The message that black people were unwelcome and out of place could hardly be telegraphed more effectively. Try as they might, however, white supremacists could not expunge African Americans from the state.

Freedom was precarious for many in the first years of California's history. Although Mexico had outlawed slavery in the territory in 1829, African American and Native American slaves continued to toil for masters when California entered the Union. Indeed, the trafficking of Native American women and girls became a central feature of Northern California society in the years after the gold rush. As Stacey L. Smith shows, California's contests over slavery were "far more complicated, contentious, and protracted" than historians have realized. Well into the 1850s, slaveholders made every attempt to transplant the culture of southern slavery to free soil. The rights of slaves and slave owners were ambiguous at best, and defining these rights became a central preoccupation of California's antebellum politicians and lawmakers. As Smith notes, "Californians, far from being detached, distant, or unconcerned about slavery, battled over three of the most divisive political and legal issues of the era: the status of slavery in the federal territories, masters' rights to sojourn with their slaves in free states, and free states' obligation to capture fugitive slaves."[14] The specter of slavery dominated state making and pulled slaves, free blacks, and slave owners into the national contest over freedom. Black bodies were a pivot point in state politics.

Most of California's earliest black migrants arrived as part of the mass exodus inspired by the gold rush. Southern slave owners anxious to strike it rich forced African American bondsmen and bondswomen to make the journey west; other slaves escaped to California on the Underground Railroad. The exact number of slaves held in 1850 is difficult to ascertain, but at least two hundred enslaved African Americans were living in the state in its first year of statehood.[15] Smith finds evidence of 178 slaves still being held in captivity two years later.[16] Nevertheless, most free blacks traveled to California to escape the peculiar institution. This group of voluntary migrants were an industrious bunch; many had already distinguished themselves in the Northeast as journalists, educators, and entrepreneurs. A significant number of these free men and women brought histories of abolitionist activism from their former homes in places like New Bedford, Boston, Philadelphia, New York, or Nantucket. These traditions of antislavery organizing and political savvy would be crucial for the state's abolitionist movement. Black Californians formed vigilance committees to rescue fugitive slaves and, with white abolitionists, mounted significant legal challenges to slavery. In 1850 the census recorded a total of 962 black and mulatto men and women residing in the Golden State, most living in the northern counties near gold mining territory. However, due to incomplete census records, these numbers do not account for all of the African Americans living in the state: many counties, including San Francisco, were not included in the calculations.[17] On the eve of the Civil War, the more than four thousand black Californians constituted 1.1 percent of the state population, making California one of three western states or territories with the highest percentage of African Americans.[18] Though to some the black population of California seemed insignificant, their presence alarmed white supremacists.

California statehood coincided with the passage of the Fugitive Slave Law. The admittance of California as a free state and the Fugitive Slave Law were both part of the Compromise of 1850. The new fugitive slave law strengthened the 1793 statute, making it more difficult for escapees to find refuge in free states. Penalties for those who aided fugitives intensified and African Americans in free states faced profound uncertainty. The risks faced by escaped or escaping slaves escalated. Free blacks could be kidnapped and enslaved. In 1852 problems for black Californians compounded when the state passed its own version of the law. Slave masters who had brought their slaves into the state before 1850 had one year to remove them. The courts had initially upheld a slave's right to freedom once the slave landed on California's "free" soil, but the new law ended this practice. The law, in effect, negated the state constitution and reaffirmed the state's support for slaveholders. After California's Fugitive Slave Law expired in 1855, slaveholders were known to keep black men and women as property in California. This did not mean, however, that slaves never escaped. Bondsmen and women who toiled in the Sierra Nevada digging for gold or cooking for miners took every opportunity to run away in the rocky ravines, valleys, towns, and cities of the state. But their efforts to avail themselves of the Underground Railroad were often stymied as a result of the new law. Additionally, slaves who had worked as contract laborers and had purchased their freedom could find themselves re-enslaved.[19]

Freeing themselves from slaveowners was one of the first and most important acts black Californians undertook to force the state to live up to its constitutional promises.[20] This act was undertaken by those who were already imprisoned by the yoke of slavery and those who, although technically free, had been kidnapped and claimed as property. While we associate this act of liberating oneself with the better known routes of the Underground Railroad that moved from southern states to the Northeast and the Midwest, Californians operated a western branch of freedom's highway that spirited fugitives to Mexico or Canada. The conductors of the railroad included women as well as men. As historian Willi Coleman notes, "women were among the rescuers and the rescued, using legal and extralegal means to attain freedom."[21] Scholars rightfully highlight the history of the midwife Biddy Mason, one of the earliest litigants to challenge slavery in the Golden State. Her story shows how African Americans forced the issue of freedom into state politics from its inception. Mason's story also points to women's role in the building of California's free black communities and networks. If the state was Farnham's "nursery of freedom," slaves were among the first to cultivate there.

As the slave of Robert Smith, a Mississippi Mormon, Mason was forced to take the arduous overland journey from Mississippi to Utah in 1848. By 1851 the group, which included Mason's three daughters, had been moved again, this time to San Bernardino, California, a place where, in spite of the law, Mason and at least ten others continued to labor as slaves. In 1855, Smith made plans to return to Texas where he could own slaves without question or difficulty. At this point, free black allies, including horse trader and entrepreneur Robert Owens, alerted officials to the presence of Smith's slaves; Biddy Mason and her family were then placed under the care of a Los Angeles County sheriff.[22] In 1856, Smith's lawyer argued before Judge Benjamin Hayes in the First District Court that Mason and the thirteen other slaves were like members of his family and had left Mississippi voluntarily. The judge, though a southerner and former slaveholder, found this argument unconvincing and granted the petitioners freedom to "become settled" in the state and "work for themselves—in peace and without fear."[23] Mason eventually founded the First African Methodist Episcopal (AME) Church of Los Angeles (which initially met in her house) and became a real estate mogul, making her one of the wealthiest African Americans in nineteenth-century California. By purchasing property in what would become the center of downtown Los Angeles, Mason established a philanthropic legacy that would shape black Los Angeles for decades.[24] While it is tempting to interpret Mason's legal bid for freedom as an indication that black Californians found safety from slavery in the courts, Mason's case was an aberration; Los Angeles County courts usually favored slaveholders in the 1850s.[25] Yet Mason's story alerts us to the wide abolitionist network and to the early political agency of African Americans often thought to be outside traditional abolitionist circles: black westerners, both slave and free.

In Northern California, the infamous Archy Lee case revealed just how feeble freedom could be in this free state. In 1857, two years after the expiration of the state's Fugitive Slave Law, Lee determined to be free of his Mississippi slave master, Charles Stovall. Stovall was the son of Lee's owner, but he claimed Lee as his own slave. Like many slave owners in the state, Stovall counted on the uneven enforcement of the expiration of the Fugitive Slave Law to maintain rights to Lee's labor. After being hired out as a day laborer in Sacramento, Lee ran away and sought refuge in a hotel operated by African Americans. Stovall attempted to regain ownership of Lee through the district court in Sacramento, then again through an appearance before a U.S. Commissioner in charge of federal law enforcement. The California Supreme Court took up Stovall's case in 1858—in the wake of the Dred Scott decision in which the U.S. Supreme Court denied freedom to Scott, a slave living in Missouri who had traveled to free territory. Stovall also benefitted from the federal Fugitive Slave Law, arguing that because Lee had escaped in Mississippi, he was entitled to keep Lee as a slave. Chief Justice David S. Terry, a southerner and known supporter of slaveholders ruled, along with his colleagues, that Lee should be returned to Stovall, who, the justices argued, could be excused because he was "in transit" and not aware of California law.[26] Most observers found this preposterous, and "the press all over the state roared in ridicule."[27] The state's new Republican Party, formed in 1856, expressed outrage over the decision, as did free-soil Democrats, although this outrage failed to prompt any judicial or legislative changes.[28]

Black Californians rallied to Lee's defense. While Stovall prepared to take Lee out of the state and return to Mississippi, a vigilance committee managed to have Lee arrested on the *Orizaba* in San Francisco Bay, and placed in jail for safekeeping. The vigilance committee included African American abolitionists George Washington Dennis, Mary Ellen Pleasant, and David W. Ruggles Sr., who organized a fund-raising campaign to cover Lee's expenses. Finally, Archy Lee gained his freedom in San Francisco

County Court and soon after secured passage to British Columbia. His rescue mobilized the already active cadre of black freedom fighters into what one scholar has called "the first statewide black activist organization" and helped to cement their connections with white Republican allies.[29] Again, the case revealed the ways that slaves and their free black allies shaped local and state politics.[30] The cases of Biddy Mason and Archy Lee made it painfully obvious that the courts would be an essential, if fickle, staging ground for equality. The example of Biddy Mason and the presence of women on the vigilance committee remind us that African American women were among the first Californians to push freedom to its limits.

Gendered Politics

Repealing the anti-testimony law became the focus of much political organizing for the state's African Americans. Black citizens made this a priority in the first three conventions that took place in the state in 1855, 1856, and 1857. Following on the heels of the national black convention movement, these state meetings focused on black codes, disfranchisement, and education. At the first California convention, which convened in Sacramento's AME church, the leaders proposed two goals: to petition the Legislature to remove the anti-testimony law; and to adopt plans for the general improvement of conditions for colored people.[31] Attended by the state's leading black men, the roster of participants included the newspaper editor Mifflin Gibbs, D. W. Ruggles Sr., son of the well-known abolitionist David Ruggles, and educator Jeremiah Sanderson, among others. Forty-nine men representing ten counties attended. Since virtually absent from the official record of these conventions debates were the contributions of women, it has been tempting to read these occasions solely through the language of manhood rights, a prevailing discourse in convention proceedings. Although they were not official delegates, women were in the audience of the conventions and attended the organizing meetings that preceded them; they traveled from across the state to be part of the events, participating in social functions in and around the venue.[32] Women were mentioned in the minutes of all four conventions, and their political influence was noted by the black press.[33]

It is not surprising that black women would be a part of California's convention movement; black women shaped colored conventions across the nation. The participation of women in black political life was not just undeniable—for many it became a topic of debate. As historian Martha Jones shows, black conventions were places where ideas about the woman question would be discussed and refined.[34] Across the country, churches, fraternal orders, mutual aid societies, and conventions all grappled with how, when, and why women would or should participate in politics. Women's active role in California's Underground Railroad had, by the 1850s, created a political culture in the state where women's political work was visible if not commonplace. Mary Ellen Pleasant and Biddy Mason were the most prominent of such women who had established a legacy of female activism. Given this history, it seems clear that politics was already women's business by the first state convention in 1855.

Many of the men in attendance at the California conventions would have been privy to, or participants in, debates about the woman question before they migrated west; chief among these was New England native Jeremiah Sanderson. Sanderson had long argued for the full and equal participation of women in the fight for civil rights and abolition. Influenced by the feminist thinking of Martin Delany and Frederick Douglass, he had also been moved by the female activists he met in New England. "Woman is rising up," he wrote to abolitionist Amy Post, "man cannot be free while woman . . . is enslaved to conventionalisms."[35] Although there is no record that Sanderson expressed such sentiments at the first California convention, it is likely that when women entered public life in his new home state, he was hardly flummoxed.

On the eve of the Civil War, free black women in San Francisco took steps to secure their own interests by forming a mutual aid association. The Ladies Union Beneficial Society was organized in 1860 and incorporated in 1861; Jeremiah Sanderson served on the board of trustees. The society strove to help those who became "disabled by sickness, or other bodily accidents, from following her usual occupation, or otherwise earning a livelihood."[36] All members must be in "good moral character" to receive union benefits. If a member died, the union appropriated forty dollars to defray funeral expenses. Nearly all African American women who worked for wages toiled as domestics; in 1860, a full 97 percent in San Francisco labored as servants in homes or on ships.[37] A predecessor of women's labor unions, the organization spoke volumes about the beliefs women harbored in this expanding black settlement. Providing the support services that Jim Crow states and male-only organizations routinely denied to black women, the union sought to restore dignity to domestic work and health to women whom the city and state often refused to help. Female domestics such as cooks, maids, and nannies were in fact staking a claim to freedom by embracing nineteenth-century rights discourse. Insisting on their personhood and their right to protection from workplace danger, they sought to define the meaning of freedom for working women in ways that secured their bodies and their self-worth.

The Ladies Union Beneficial Society points to a tradition of organizing among nineteenth-century black western women, a demographic rarely associated with this type of activism. Leadership among free, black domestics in the antebellum West was a direct prototype for domestics in later protests, including the laundry strikes in Reconstruction-era Atlanta and the Montgomery Bus Boycott almost a century later.[38] Before their remarkable entrepreneurial careers, Biddy Mason worked as a midwife and Mary Ellen Pleasant as a cook, placing them in this trajectory of domestic workers who became foot soldiers in the struggle for racial justice. Women in Northern and Southern California formed women's associations beginning in the antebellum era. In 1859, women in Placerville organized what one historian calls the first "uplift" organization in the state.[39] Women in Los Angeles, though few in number in 1860, established mutual aid societies and benevolent associations. After acquiring her freedom in the 1850s, Biddy Mason and her extended family founded the city's first AME church, a day care, and an institution to assist orphans and the poor.[40]

Perhaps because African American women in California had already become political actors, some men felt they should limit their participation in politics. For some male leaders, women had no need to become active in the public sphere, since, as they saw it, men would represent their interests. For example, in 1862, when the editors of the *Pacific Appeal* announced the newspaper's raison d'etre, they explained: "We shall Appeal to the hearts and consciences of the people. In the name of every age and sex, we shall appeal for right and justice."[41] This type of sentiment speaks to the communal ethos present in black communities that Elsa Barkley Brown and other historians identify.[42] For black women, however, relying on men to voice their political intentions did not always suffice.

An 1865 incident at a planning committee meeting for the fourth convention indicates that the question of women's participation continued to be a subject of concern and disagreement. The *San Francisco Elevator* reported that during the meeting, which they dubbed the "free speech squashing machine," women had voted about the upcoming convention. Seven women were in attendance, and, according to the *Elevator* "three of them jumped up" to vote, after which "an exclamation arose from the male portion for them to sit down." After the leader of the meeting counted their votes, another "more reliable" counter was found who "omitted the ladies."[43] It is unclear whether the writer for the *Elevator* was sympathetic to the women or indicating that politics was rightfully a male affair. Despite the erasure of women's votes, this account reveals that women continued to assert themselves into convention politics, to the consternation of some of their male contemporaries.

During the war, black activists achieved their goal of revising—if not rescinding—the anti-testimony law. In 1863, after a thirteen-year effort, the state legislature amended the law to allow black Californians to testify in court. Californians who had one half or more Chinese, Native American, or "Mongolian blood" were still prohibited from testifying.[44] Women seized the opportunity to utilize the courts to combat antiblack practices and segregation on public transportation. Charlotte L. Brown, Emma Jane Turner, and Mary Ellen Pleasant spearheaded the effort with lawsuits in the 1860s.[45] Brown filed both civil and criminal suits for being ejected from Omnibus Railroad Company streetcars three times in 1863; she won both suits. Turner and Pleasant then brought suits against the North Beach and Mission Railroad Company in 1866. Pleasant's case, initially decided in the Twelfth District Court in 1867, determined that she had been "willfully and purposefully deprived by the defendant of the exercise of a plain legal right" to ride the streetcar, for which she was awarded five hundred dollars.[46] Pleasant's argument was noteworthy: she claimed that by being denied access to the streetcar she "suffered greatly" in mind and body.[47] When the case was appealed by the railroad company the following year, the California Supreme Court overturned the ruling. Although the court acknowledged that streetcars were not allowed to prohibit African Americans from riding the cars, it was determined that the cost of damages could not be calculated and therefore could not be awarded. Pleasant's case drew significant comment from the California press and was remembered as a symbolic, if not technical, victory. The prominent role of women in these challenges to segregation and antiblack practices demonstrates that sometimes women shaped the direction of the equal rights movement by drawing attention

San Francisco abolitionist and entrepreneur Mary Ellen Pleasant sued the North Beach and Mission Railroad Company in San Francisco in 1866 for discriminatory practices. Her case and the cases of other African American women were some of the first lawsuits to challenge segregation filed by black Californians. (The Bancroft Library, University of California, Berkeley, California Faces: Selections from the Bancroft Library Portrait Collection)

to their emancipated bodies. Gendered politics infused this first western campaign for civil rights, and women's participation would be pivotal in the ongoing struggle for racial justice.

Black women's politics and their role in shaping freedom became increasingly obscured as Jim Crow took shape in California, however. This was partly due to the fact that only black men gained suffrage through the Fifteenth Amendment; indeed, patriarchal language dominated rights discourse in nineteenth-century America. Women's efforts to claim politics for themselves were often ridiculed (as the *Elevator* article demonstrated) or ignored. Scholars of African American women's history show that African American women insisted on defining freedom on their own terms and on shaping politics during Reconstruction and beyond.[48] Southern black women's activism, for example, included church-based organizing, voting in Republican conventions, establishing black-serving institutions, serving as diplomats to white power brokers, and creating centers of learning. California women were no different, though locating their histories can be challenging. We do know that they formed civic organizations, participated in the fund-raising efforts of black institutions including the black press and the churches, attended political rallies and parades, and were instrumental in creating the state's first black schools.[49]

Separate Schools

The limits placed on African American education drew men, women, and children into California politics and rendered visible the state's commitment to separate white and nonwhite. Once again, the presence of black bodies encouraged state officials to craft increasingly restrictive legislation. The state's black population more than quadrupled between 1850 and 1860, from 962 to 4,086 African American and mulatto inhabitants; the number of public school children rose from 1 student in 1850 to 153 in 1860.[50] Segregating these school children became a central focus for California's Democratic lawmakers since contact between white and nonwhite children was thought by segregationists to be one step closer to racial "amalgamation." In this way, California's school policies — and the attending rancor — mimic those that were playing out across the Northeast and in Congress where broader debates about slavery and freedom were taking shape. Black Californians saw themselves as integral members of these debates. In California, the school debates revealed the impossibility of separating bodies completely. Further, policies aimed at separating school children crafted by segregationists were never restricted to African Americans but often named Native American and Chinese children as those needing to be isolated (in addition to black children). Once again, California became the testing ground for who would be considered American.[51]

Women played a central role in the campaign to educate African American youth. Beginning in the 1850s, women in Sacramento, Oakland, and

San Francisco spearheaded efforts to organize church-based Sabbath schools, private schools, and freestanding public schools.[52] In the 1860s and 1870s, as the state refused to desegregate its public schools, "women's efforts to support educational reform became even more crucial," according to historian Susan Bragg.[53] In California, schools became another locus of Jim Crow where women led campaigns to address the increasingly hostile response to African Americans. This makes sense: child rearing was central to women's domestic responsibilities. As Reconstruction progressed, however, male leaders dominated the school debates in the pages of the black press and in the legislature, leading to an erasure of women's centrality to one of Reconstruction's most important staging grounds.

The history of California's segregated schools begins at statehood and reveals a concerted effort by African American citizens to develop multiple pathways in and around black codes. By the end of the 1850s, the climate for Jim Crow education had been solidly established in a number of sites: the state superintendent's office, the state legislature, and local school districts. As early as 1855, the school law dictated that the distribution of school funds would be calculated according to the number of *white* children in each county.[54] The state's nonwhite citizens resisted through political mobilization, through the establishment of private schools, through the cooperation with benevolent or missionary societies, through legislative and judicial means, and through the press.

By 1859, State Superintendent of Public Instruction Andrew Jackson Moulder indicated his contempt for those in the state who had encouraged integrated schools: "if this attempt to force Africans, Chinese, and the Diggers [Native Americans] into our schools is persisted in, it must result in the ruin of our school."[55] A Democrat from Virginia, Moulder had been elected to his post in 1856 and was reelected in 1859; his views on education influenced a generation of educators.[56] Not a single political party supported the education of nonwhites, but the Democratic Party was, as one scholar noted, "particularly hostile even to modest proposals."[57] Moulder's campaign paid off in 1860 when the state legislature passed a law designed to penalize schools that allowed "colored children" to attend—colored children, in this case, meant African Americans and Chinese.[58] That black and Chinese school children would be singled out in the school laws is telling though unsurprising; fears of both groups were conflated and articulated in the state legislature long before the anti-Chinese movement formally organized itself. In 1860 Chinese outnumbered African Americans in the state almost tenfold: the 34,933 Chinese constituted 9 percent of the population of the state, compared to 4,086 black people, who constituted 1.1 percent.[59] The popular press was littered with cartoons depicting the "Negroization of the Chinese," a visual reminder that fears of Chinese were imbued with the language and stereotypes that had originally been applied to African Americans.[60] In the West, Jim Crow restrictions cast a net that took in more than African Americans. The presence of Mexicans, Native Americans, and Chinese heightened anxiety among those charged with upholding white supremacy. The effort to control Chinese immigration, a process that placed California front and center in national debates about race, forced African Americans to grapple with the linkages between race and citizenship in ways that other Americans found easy to ignore.[61]

African Americans discussed the Chinese presence in the pages of the black press, often remarking on their second-class status. William Newby, the California correspondent for *Frederick Douglass' Paper*, reported that "Chinese were the most mistreated group in the state" and that African Americans were the only ones who did not abuse them.[62] Douglass himself repeatedly voiced his concern about the treatment of Chinese immigrants and cautioned African Americans against the dangers of supporting Chinese exclusion. Linking their political fate with Chinese Californians, however, would be another matter—a risk some African Americans were unwilling to take.

During the Civil War, a bloodless battle occurred when Republican John Swett replaced Moulder as superintendent of Public Instruction. Swett's election in 1862, and the policy changes he initiated, would be challenged by those who identified school integration as a first step in a slippery slope toward racial equality.[63] The heated 1862 campaign brought the state's conflict over race and education to a head as the Civil War divided the nation over many of the same questions. "Have Negroes Been Taught and Classed on Terms of Equality in a Public School Under the Charge of Mr. John Swett?" asked an editorial in the San Francisco press. Swett was accused of ignoring the school law when he served as principal of a San Francisco school by allowing black children to attend, even though there was a colored school in the city. The editorialist claimed that Swett was nominated at a convention on July 4, 1862, even though "Mr. Swett's abolition and amalgamating proclivities" were well-known.[64] Swett's adversaries papered the city with illustrated handbills showing a "Yankee schoolmaster" teaching a mixed class of black and white students with a black student "at the head of the class."[65] Swett was elected despite the protests, and California school law was reconstructed during his tenure as superintendent. In 1866, school districts were permitted to allow "colored" children to attend white schools unless the majority of white parents objected in writing. Perhaps Swett and his fellow Republicans felt emboldened by the Civil Rights Act of 1866, which guaranteed that all persons born in the United States (except Native Americans) had the right to "full and equal benefit of all laws and proceedings for the security of person and property." But Swett's reign proved short; he was defeated by a Democrat in 1867 who believed that the citizens of California preferred separate schools for African American children.[66]

The 1867 election was a resounding victory for Democrats, putting Democrats in the governor's seat and giving them an overwhelming majority in the assembly, making the state one of the first to be "redeemed" from Republicans after the war.[67] Two years later, Democrats would control both the assembly and the senate. African American and Chinese citizens did not fit into the Redeemers' plan for the state; indeed, the Democratic Party refused to endorse the Fourteenth and Fifteenth Amendments.[68] Many black Californians believed that the promises of Reconstruction might be realized, however, when the state elected Republican Newton Booth governor in 1870.[69] In his inaugural address, Booth affirmed that all children in the state, regardless of color, should have an education.[70] However, the state's Republican government did not distinguish itself as being particularly strong during Reconstruction, and indeed a weak Republican Party made it difficult for African Americans to secure the right to an education in any state in the Union.[71] Nevertheless, black Californians embraced the party, forming their first Republican clubs in Los Angeles and San Francisco.[72] Black men could, for the first time, threaten to withhold their votes should the party abandon civil rights. Indeed, black male voters helped to deliver Republican victories in San Francisco municipal elections in 1870 and 1872.[73] Unfortunately, their newfound voting rights did not result in improved education for black children.

Despite the increasing number of colored schools—there were twenty-three in 1874—conditions had worsened for many of the state's black youths.[74] "There is no State in the Union," claimed the *Pacific Appeal*, "which has such mean proscription against school privileges of colored children as at present exist in this State."[75] For black parents, the situation in many parts of the state was dire: the choice was a poorly equipped colored school or integrating a white school. The dilemma was complicated by an

John Swett, a Republican, served as California State Superintendent of Instruction from 1862 to 1867. Criticized for allowing black children to attend San Francisco public schools, he was defeated by a Democrat who believed in separate schools for African Americans. (The Bancroft Library, University of California, Berkeley, California Faces: Selections from the Bancroft Library Portrait Collection)

1870 change to the school law allowing districts with fewer than ten students of color to "educate them in separate schools or in any other manner."[76]

Perhaps due to this disastrous state of affairs and the frustration with the state legislature, the state's black leaders changed their approach in the 1870s, developing a uniracial rather than multiracial strategy.[77] Black Californians mounted a twofold objection against including Chinese in their fight for desegregated schools, arguing first that Chinese already had educational opportunities through missionary schools, and second that including them in school bills would result in the bills failing because of anti-Chinese hysteria prevalent in the legislature. "The educational privileges of Mongolians in this State, at present, are superior to those of African descent, who are now fully incorporated in the National and State governments as American citizens," wrote Peter Anderson, publisher of the *Pacific Appeal*, in 1872. He continued: "The Spanish children are admitted. The Chileans children are admitted. And the Chinese have Missionary Schools, supported in part by white American citizens in nearly every church in this city. Notwithstanding which, as a general rule, those termed Mongolians are an educated people in their own language; hence their only desire is to become conversant with the English language."[78] In fact, Chinese children and their parents were not satisfied with educational opportunities in the state; they had opened a Chinese school in 1859 in San Francisco—four years after the first school for blacks had opened—and were struggling to keep it viable.[79] The 1870 school law had removed the word *Mongolian* from the provision that guaranteed nonwhite children an education, albeit segregated. Now the code read: "The education of children of African descent and Indian children shall be provided for in separate schools." San Francisco superintendent James Denman took this opportunity to close the Chinese school; public schools for Chinese in the state were unavailable for the next fourteen years.[80]

Black men's claims to citizenship and its privileges overshadowed more sympathetic responses to Chinese during much of Reconstruction.[81] African Americans assumed that leaving Chinese out of the equation would result in a school bill that allowed black children equal access to public schools. The *Pacific Appeal* explained that "heretofore it has been the policy of our opponents to couple the claims of colored American citizens with the most objectionable classes, such as Mongolians, etc., which would make any just measure obnoxious enough to insure its defeat."[82] What black leaders could not foresee was that many legislators, Republicans included, voted against reforming the school bill even after Chinese were dropped from the proposal. So, the effort to disassociate themselves from Chinese proved fruitless. The struggle to open up schools to African Americans in California occurred in a climate of intense antipathy toward Chinese, a climate that black people could not avoid.

In 1874, African Americans pressured the California State Assembly and the State Senate again to consider a new school bill that would remove the word *white* from the language that determined which children were guaranteed the right to an education. This bill, proposed by legislator J. F. Cowdery, a judge from San Francisco, met with extensive debate due, in part, to the judge's fiery speech making. Cowdery reminded the assembly that California's record in education harked back to the days of slavery: "It was once a favorite expression in the days of slavery that a man was inexpressively mean who would steal the coppers from the eyes of a dead negro baby. If a man would do that he was considered, even by the poor whites, as excessively mean; but in California we have whole communities taking the bread of knowledge from the hungry lips of the black child, and where they do otherwise, applying the microscope to the negro baby's hair to ascertain its moral and intellectual status."[83]

The techniques of scientific racism—including applying microscopes to the hair of African Americans—were already commonly practiced by the time Cowdery addressed the legislature. Before the repeal of the anti-testimony law, it became necessary to "scientifically" determine a person's race since only white persons could testify against other whites. By 1862 the use of pseudoscience on the black body was so prevalent in the state's courtrooms that the *Pacific Appeal* felt compelled to name and dissect the new "science."[84] Under the headline "Mockery of Justice," the editors lambasted the courts for its handling of the murder of the black barber George W. Gordon. "The fact is well known that it was one of the most deliberate and cold-blooded murders that ever disgraced California, even in her rudest and most lawless days," claimed the *Appeal*. A key witness for the prosecution in the trial of Mr. Schell (who killed Gordon) was "subjected to a private examination by two pretended *experts* in the new-fangled science of hairology, (we know no other name by which to designate it) which professes to trace ethnological descent of an individual from an examination of hair and nails." According to the "hairologists" the only witness had "African blood in his veins" and thus proved ineligible to testify.[85] Due to the disqualification of the witness, Schell could only be convicted of second-, not first-degree murder.

California's black leaders repeatedly pointed to the state's dismal record of civil rights: "We would a thousand times rather that the State Legislature would apply the remedy by conforming the School Laws to the Civil Rights bill. It will save the public humiliation of this professed Republican state in the eyes of an intelligent community and an enlightened world. The defeat of both the Senate and the Assembly School bills will reveal the fact that California is more pro-slavery than any of the recent reconstructed states of the South, which now afford school privileges to the Freedmen nearly up to the standard of the school facilities in New England."[86] Shaming the state for its pro-slavery politics would be a common refrain in the early decades of Jim Crow. As Cowdery's bill foundered in the assembly, black leaders proceeded with their test case, that of Mary Frances Ward.

Harriet A. Ward, mother of Mary Frances Ward, who was then eleven years old, took her daughter to Broadway Grammar School in San Francisco, a white school, on July 1, 1872, for the purposes of admitting her.[87] The Wards had been residing in San Francisco for thirteen years but had recently moved to a new residence, and the Broadway School was their neighborhood school. Principal Noah F. Flood promptly refused Mary Frances Ward admittance. Flood claimed in his defense that the school law approved by the legislature in 1870 required separate schools for African and Indian children, and that the existence of two colored schools existed in the city at that time justified his actions. The California Supreme Court ruled in *Ward v. Flood* in January 1874 that since the state maintained separate schools for black children, Mary Ward was not being denied an education, merely an education with whites.[88] The ruling also acknowledged that the Fourteenth Amendment applied to the right to an equal education, so, in places where no separate schools existed, black children could attend white schools. The ambiguity of the decision left black leaders feeling less than celebratory; once again, the *Pacific Appeal* decried the state lawmakers' "colorphobia."[89] Historian D. Michael Bottoms views the ruling as confirming the "deep hostility toward Reconstruction harbored by many white Californians."[90] Only after Reconstruction, in 1880, would the state legislature ban school segregation due to the cost of maintaining separate schools.

Emancipated Black Bodies

As they worked to end the Jim Crow practices of separate and unequal education, black Californians also embraced the new possibilities of freedom. Public spaces played host to a wide range of commemorations where these possibilities were articulated. Parades, socials, picnics, and dances could be sites of celebration and opportunities for speech making and debates about the meaning of a post-emancipation world. For black men, whose voices predominated at such events, these public occasions offered the chance to envision the future but also to analyze the past. Lessons in African and African American history were common.[91] The speeches delivered by male leaders were meant to educate and mobilize the state's black citizens; as such, they reveal the priorities of the first civil rights movement in the West. The prevalence of scientific racism weighed heavily on the minds of state leaders. Educator Jeremiah B. Sanderson, on more than one occasion, warned that African Americans, even in formerly free states, must be ever mindful of the increasing popularity of racial theories that argued black people were unfit for citizenship. The possibilities for citizenship that black Californians demanded were carved out of, and in defiance of, stereotypes and theories rooted in slavery and biology.

African Americans across the country gathered on main streets and thoroughfares to celebrate freedom in the nineteenth century. Californians regularly marked the occasion of the 1834 emancipation of British West Indian slaves with parades and festivals on August 1. Phillip Bell, publisher of the *Elevator*, organized these commemorations along with the West Indian Benevolent Association of San Francisco.[92] As soon as Lincoln issued the Emancipation Proclamation on January 1, 1863, Freedom Day celebrations erupted across the country; commemorations of this momentous occasion were held for decades. Californians took the opportunity to express hope and jubilation about the end of slavery. Speeches, songs, and public displays of military units and bands reinforced the contribution black Americans had made to end that institution. For black southerners, most of whom had been slaves, the celebrations were watershed moments, separating slavery from freedom, the past from the future. In free states such as California, commemorations were no less important. Black Californians, like other African Americans, used Emancipation Day celebrations to note the difference that freedom made; speeches about the proclamation itself, the end of the war, and the Thirteenth and Fourteenth Amendments were standard fare. For this population, however, emancipation did not necessarily change their status: the vast majority of blacks living in California at the time of emancipation were free before 1863. So while they rejoiced for their formerly enslaved brothers and sisters in slave states, Californians also used these commemorations to analyze the shape of white supremacy and mark what had *not* changed.[93]

To mark the fifth anniversary of the signing of the Emancipation Proclamation, Californians turned out in force. The cities of Stockton and San Francisco held major parades and commemorations. Jeremiah B. Sanderson spoke to what was, by all accounts, a large and boisterous San Francisco crowd to address the possibilities and limitations of freedom. Sanderson was well-known to black Californians: after leaving his hometown of New Bedford, Massachusetts, where he was in the company of abolitionists Frederick Douglass and William Lloyd Garrison, he traveled to California in 1853.[94] Initially intending to profit from the gold rush and return east, he instead settled in Sacramento. Drawn to politics in his adopted home, Sanderson served as a delegate of the black conventions in 1855 and 1856. By the time of the 1868 Emancipation Day celebration, Sanderson had waged an impressive campaign to educate African American children in Sacramento, Stockton, and San Francisco. His experience in the abolitionist movement rendered him a powerful speaker with deep knowledge about African American history and the current political climate. Indeed, until his untimely death in 1875, Sanderson remained the favored speaker at such events.[95]

The day began on a festive note "with the usual imposing ceremonies," including a procession of the Brannan Guards, the Pacific Brass Band donning new uniforms, and the Young Men's Union Beneficial Society, an organization founded by Sanderson and "devoted to self education."[96] Children from the public and Sunday schools filled horse-drawn carriages and a long line of buggies followed them at the end of the parade. Adjourning to a hall in the center of town, the program included an opening prayer, the reading of the Emancipation Proclamation, and a performance of "Union and Liberty Forever" by a local choir. Men in uniform, like those in the Brannan Guards, were meant to call up memories of black soldiers and their role in the Union victory. Indeed William H. Carney, a veteran of the Massachusetts Fifty-Fourth Infantry Regiment, was the parade's grand marshal. This demonstration of military prowess was common at Emancipation Day parades and was one of the ways black communities emphasized their loyalty and patriotic service. Women rode on floats and sang in the choir but were not speech makers. How much they shaped this Emancipation Day parade is not apparent from the press coverage.[97] Restricting women to fancy floats or watching from the sidelines was, perhaps, deemed necessary precisely because manhood and masculine privilege seemed so tenuous.

Sanderson's remarks that New Year's Day, at a celebration of the "greatest event in the history of the colored people," did not provide the uplifting message most had expected. Partly due to the fact that black male suffrage hung in the balance, the mood was not altogether joyous. Although he noted the great accomplishments of African Americans, his address made plain that black citizens were facing formidable foes: "Though men sitting in high places of power seek our moral and political annihilation, and essay to make valid as truth the huge lie that we are socially, morally, politically, intellectually and physically inferior to the white man, still with God and the right on our side, we shall win the hard fought day." His argument that white supremacy was being naturalized and lies about African American inferiority made "valid as truth" indicated that bids for citizenship would have to be made over and through these truth claims. The new manhood that freedom promised would never come to fruition if the central beliefs about black men hinged on theories of inferiority that were biologically based. The chief target in Sanderson's speech was the seminal text of what is now known as scientific racism and the men who, in his words "attempted to disprove the inherent equal manhood of the Negro."[98]

Sanderson held responsible Josiah Nott and George R. Gliddon's 1854 classic *Types of Mankind*—the eight-hundred page bestseller that offered "scientific proof" of the inferiority of African Americans—for shaping the political climate and limiting the prospects for freedom. Texts such as Nott and Gliddon's, Sanderson argued, were central to the effort to "degrade the negro [and] separate him from the human race."[99] This was not the first time Sanderson alerted Californians to the dangers of scientific racism; eight years earlier, in 1860, he delivered a lecture on phrenology at a fundraiser for abolitionists.[100] Well aware of the popularity of these theories and their significance to the supporters of slavery, Sanderson reminded his listeners in 1868 that these beliefs continued to hold sway; indeed they undergirded Reconstruction-era arguments that black men were incapable of the duties of citizenship. "A class of politicians find some comfort and aid in these views. President Johnson and Governor Haight have accepted them as the basis of their philosophy of [R]econstruction."[101] Much to Sanderson's dismay, California's governor echoed the enthusiasm for scientific racism that was being touted in the White House.

Indeed, these arguments of scientific racism, as Sanderson noted, provided the central tenets of the annual messages of President Andrew Johnson and California governor Henry Haight, both of whom were elected the previous year. That the governor embraced these beliefs and that his speech mimicked the president's deserved attention:

> One document so closely followed upon the other, and so clear a family resemblance have they, that the inference is natural that the writer of one took his cue from the other. In both, such expressions as "incapacity of the [N]egro," "difference between the negro and the intelligent foreign voter," "domination of a mass of ignorant negroes," etc., are frequently repeated. In reading such portions of these papers, our memory reverts back thirty years. Then the same foolish and prejudiced arguments, the same gross language, were used by men who attempted to disprove the inherent equal manhood of the Negro.[102]

A Democrat, and no friend to African Americans, Haight peppered his inaugural address with words that conveyed anxiety about the threat of African Americans.[103] Fears of black voters and black domination resonated from California to the nation's capital.

In California these fears of blackness collided with anti-Chinese sentiment. The governor's address exemplified such fears: "If the [N]egro requires the ballot to protect himself, as others assert, than [sic] the Asiatic needs it to protect himself. There is, however, no truth in either statement. . . . It is for the good of both these races that the elective franchise should be confined to the whites."[104] Linking Chinese and black Americans became a salient part of the state's anti-suffrage rhetoric, as it had been during the school debates, and was used by members of Congress as a strategy to attempt to defeat black male suffrage.[105] In 1869 the state's Democratic Party published *Shall the Negro and the Chinaman Vote?*, a pamphlet claiming that "three-fourths of the people of the State are opposed to negroes being allowed to vote in California, and . . . four-fifths of the people are opposed to Chinese being allowed to vote."[106] While the California press made sure to keep the association between black male suffrage and the Chinese presence alive during the ratification process, some editors reserved their disgust for black men. The *Sacramento Bee*, for example, asserted that black men were "no more fitted to exercise the elective franchise than . . . so many monkeys."[107] Indeed, in the state legislature during the debates over the Fifteenth Amendment, African Americans were likened to beasts. California soundly refused to ratify the Fifteenth Amendment, in fact not doing so until 1962; black men achieved suffrage in the state only after Congress ratified the amendment in 1870.

Sanderson's Emancipation Day address had highlighted what he thought to be the greatest threat to black manhood: not the presence of Chinese, but the articulation of a "science" that placed both groups in biologically inferior categories. Attacking the intellectual foundations of white supremacy was part and parcel of the African American strategy to undermine the system in the state and across the nation.[108]

Behaving Like Men

In a political climate such as Sanderson described, one that looked to the tenets of scientific racism, black men were relentlessly scrutinized for signs of immorality. By 1872 this scrutiny reached epic proportions, as it was the first year African American men could vote in a national election; it was no accident that the Drinking Duo had been taken to task that year for their behavior at a Republican meeting. Blamed by both Democrats and Republicans for selling their votes cheaply, most black male voters cast their lot with Lincoln's party. But no matter the party affiliation, most white Americans doubted that African American men had the qualifications for the franchise. Horace Greeley, editor of the *New York Daily Tribune*, accused black male voters of wanton irresponsibility, wasting their money on "drink, tobacco, balls, gaming, and other dissipation," instead of saving their cash for land.[109] This characterization of African American voters was one that Californians would be particularly sensitive to, as they were often accused of caring more for gold than for liberty.

As the state's black leaders critiqued racialist science and its influence on the state, they engaged in their own project of defining manhood and equality. This project was fraught with anxieties and often took shape as a contest over the definition of appropriate male behavior, behavior that could either preclude or foster citizenship. In the pages of the state's two black newspapers, lively debates ensued about what constituted proper conduct.[110] The *Elevator*, after praising Sanderson's oration as an "able production, smooth, clear and well written," continued that "owing to the noise and confusion in the hall . . . the delivery was greatly marred."[111]

Chastising drunk Republicans and loud members of Emancipation Day celebrations typified racial uplift ideology. Members of the black elite in the Far West, like those across the country, saw themselves as arbiters of the values of self-control, temperance, and Victorian sexual morality.[112]

In their role as arbiters of proper behavior, the black middle class did not restrict themselves to political meetings or rallies. The black leisure culture that developed at the end of the nineteenth century was a site of contestation as well as a manifestation of a new culture of freedom.[113] One social event of 1876 indicates that the boundary between the newly formed elite of the state and the workers fluctuated as black men struggled to be seen as worthy citizens during the Reconstruction era. On this occasion, workers hosted the Palace Hotel Reception Ball, inviting the elite by printed invitation. San Francisco's extravagant Palace Hotel was billed as the largest hotel in the world when it opened the previous year. With its eight hundred rooms and lavish decor, the hotel signified the wealth and status of a city coming of age and the gold and silver that helped to create it.[114] The city's largest employer of African American labor, the Palace Hotel provided no fewer than two hundred jobs for waiters, bellmen, porters, and maids.[115] The workers organized the ball to thank the black elite for their hospitality. "During the short time we have been in your city, it has been a continued 'go' with us from one place of entertainment to another; and so abundantly have we partaken of the hospitality of your residents that we feel ourselves to be greatly obligated to you for the many social favors," announced E. T. Lewis in his opening remarks. "We, therefore, give this entertainment in order that we may in a spirit of friendship reciprocate." Peter Anderson, editor of the *Pacific Appeal*, and well-known local leader, received the workers' welcome graciously. "The remarks you have uttered on behalf of those whom you represent on this occasion are received on behalf of the colored residents of this city with welcome and with great respect." But Anderson also noted that the employees' *conduct* impressed him and his peers. "Since your advent in this State, you have given us an assurance by your deportment that you are worthy of every respect to mingle in our best associations," he noted.[116]

The ball was a space where black men attempted to secure their own position. "You have come amongst us as an experiment, as it were, to show that the colored employees in a great enterprise can perform every duty of trust with as strict fidelity as any other class of people, when given the same chance or opportunity," Anderson declared. Emphasizing their newcomer status as "easterners," Anderson noted that the conduct of the Palace employ-

When the Palace Hotel opened in San Francisco in 1875, it was the largest hotel west of the Mississippi, employing two hundred African Americans. In 1876, the hotel was the site of a ball given by black workers for the black elite of the city. Discord at the event revealed tensions over definitions of appropriate male behavior. (California Historical Society)

ees would be a litmus test for respectability, not only for white employers, but also for the black elite. In this case, "easterner" could signal not only newcomer but also a physical proximity to the institution of slavery and all that implied. All eyes were fixed on the porters, maids, and bellmen for missing jewelry, coins, and other valuables. Waiters, on the other hand, must impress with their knowledge of the proper etiquette and service as befits the wealthiest class of Americans. On the night of the ball, however, the workers and elite joined in a brotherly embrace. "Hereafter," Anderson heartily cheered, "we shall not look upon you as Eastern friends and strangers, but welcome you in our social circles and institutions as honorable San Franciscans."[117] And for some black men, this proved to be the case. Theosophilus B. Morton, a worker at the Palace, later served as the founder of the state's branch of the Afro-American League and became a leader in efforts to secure employment for African Americans through the Republican Party.[118] It may have been this class mobility—and its possibilities in the West—that worried members of the new elite in the gold rush state.

Unfortunately, the cross-class alliances formed at the Palace Ball ended badly. The behavior of male hotel workers at the ball found its way into the press: "There are as big hoodlums among some of the employees of the Palace Hotel as can be seen anywhere. Only when they are at some place of amusement you discover how one tries to out-hoodlumize the other. With few exceptions the majority are the dregs of our Eastern society who visit California to show their cloven hoofs."[119] Naturally, these remarks raised the ire of the workers and hosts of the ball, who denounced such characterizations. In "Replies to Slander," employees of the Palace responded to the attack. "Sir, were I to recommend you to punishment for the insult you have offered to the employees of this hotel, I would send you to the whipping post and have each of the employees give you nine and thirty lashes upon your bare back."[120]

The rivalry between the city's two black newspapers, the *Elevator* (called the *Degradator* by one letter writer) and the *Pacific Appeal*, allowed for healthy, sometimes rancorous debate among and between African Americans. Editors Philip Bell and Peter Anderson had previously disagreed over a number of critical political questions. During the 1860s, for example, they argued over how to handle the Democratic majority in the state legislature.[121] The newspapers published lengthy debates over the Fifteenth Amendment, with some black leaders supporting universal male suffrage and others in favor of suffrage for a select group of black men.[122] In many ways, the Palace Ball debacle reflected some of these same questions: were all black men entitled to the privileges of citizenship regardless of class, education, or newcomer status? Through articles in their respective papers, Bell and Anderson sparred over appropriate male behavior and, presumably, over who should be the judge of such behavior.

While employees of the Palace voiced their disgust that the *Elevator* would print the original article describing their "cloven hooves" in the first place, the *Pacific Appeal* also complained that the workers should subscribe to the paper and not just the issue that contained their letters. The author of the original letter, according to Palace workers, was down on his luck and had a gambling problem; his letter resulted from his frustrations at being turned away from the Palace after he came begging one too many times. Revealing the class background of the letter writer and therefore destabilizing his critique of the employees was the workers' central defense: "His pants were in a deplorable condition, and, be it known, that this seedy individual has been a frequent visitor in the 'backgate' of the Palace Hotel, and he has been generously permitted to eat offal that otherwise would have [been] consigned to the swill-tub."[123]

What seems to be a case of sour grapes—the offal eater having been told to cut back on his visits to the hotel—also reveals something of the tensions and similarities between men of the elite and the working class. The same author who outed the beggar also responded to the criticism that workers habitually visited places of amusement where they attempted to "out-hoodlumize" each other: "Since the arrival of the employees of the Palace, there has been scarcely three consecutive days that there was not some catch penny entertainment held by those claiming to be the *elite* of colored society in this city: the truth is, they have been so frequent that the greater portion of us have long since looked upon them as little less than a nuisance." According to this worker, the entertainments thrown by the California elite were self-serving compared to those in the East, "for there entertainments are not always given for personal gain, as seem to be the case here."[124]

If the guests of the ball accused the workers of being eastern hoodlums just up from slavery, this comment indicates that some workers viewed the western elites as self-serving gamblers and mercenaries, hardly the civilized men they claimed to be. This certainly provided a forceful counter to the lectures aimed at the workers about their deportment; elite men shared more in common with the newcomers than they might care to admit, including a penchant for gambling. Nevertheless, men who begged for offal had no right to be arbiters of the appropriate male behavior, workers protested. We cannot know if these accusations are accurate; the author of the "cloven hooves" article remained anonymous. But the dialogue does tell us that both sides were expressly concerned with appropriate manly deportment; the employees and the elite accuse each other of uncivilized behavior in their efforts to prove their own worth. And as far as the employees were concerned, their elite hosts stood one step away from begging at the doors of the Palace Hotel.

The Palace Ball incident demonstrates that the conversation about what manhood meant would not be monolithic and was fraught with the kinds of tensions white men exhibited in the same era. To be civilized formed the core of this masculine ethos.[125] But for African American men—who had only recently become citizens in the minds of some—much more was at stake. Social behavior could indicate that certain men were not political party material. Sites of entertainment and a thriving black press made visible the tensions over definitions of manhood. These tensions serve to remind us that black Californians were hyperaware of the scrutiny of the newly enfranchised. Black urban culture in nineteenth-century California was a site where freedom was made and remade in places of work and play. Further, middle-class men did not control discussions about behavior, racial uplift, and class. Workers in this Jim Crow city of San Francisco participated in the process of determining what emancipation would entail and what manhood meant.

A celebration at the city's Horticultural Hall the previous year revealed that while most newly enfranchised black men were Republicans, they were not in agreement about how that should be practiced. On April 20, 1875, a Civil Rights Celebration was held to honor the fifth anniversary of the Fifteenth Amendment and the more recent passage of the federal Civil Rights Bill. The evening began with a reading of the amendment and the civil rights bill by William Sanderson, Jeremiah's grandson. The following musical portion featured three female sopranos and a chorus. But the three male speakers underscored the ambiguity of such a celebration. In his plenary address, William H. Carter admitted to the sizable crowd gathered in the hall that all were not in agreement about the cause for the festivities. "I am aware that there are those among us who are opposed to giving expressions of gratitude to our delivers [sic]," stated Carter, "advancing the doctrine that the dominant race has only given us our natural rights, those they have wrongfully deprived us of, hence, we have no right to celebrate the event." But Carter insisted on honoring those who had supported the amendment and bill, including former Massachusetts senator Charles Sumner and William Lloyd Garrison. Carter's praise of supportive white politicians and black leaders was followed by a speech by Thomas Detter. Detter expressed only guarded optimism about the Republican Party: "The Republican Party is my party, and should be the party of every colored man, until its great mission is completed—until personal and constitutional freedom is ever secure." Peter Anderson, in his remarks, was even less praiseworthy than Detter. The problem stemmed from the watered-down Civil Rights Bill—to some in the hall, hardly a law worth celebrating. The clause related to segregated schools had been removed from the final 1875 bill, which was difficult to accept in California, where blacks had fought for decades for equal educational opportunities. With Sumner's version of the bill abandoned, even by some Republicans, Anderson noted, that African

Americans had "little cause to rejoice over the enactment of the defective Civil Rights bill with the school clause stricken out."[126]

One of those who objected to the celebration was R. A. Hall, who wrote a letter to the *Pacific Appeal* about the "so-called patriotic dancing celebration." Hall had voiced his disapproval at an organizing committee for the affair—a committee that included both Philip Bell and Peter Anderson—and had been summarily removed from the committee. "I was bitterly opposed to celebrating the event and had so declared," he wrote.[127] Hall accused Bell of removing him from the committee and attempting to silence his dissent. Once again, the competition between the two newspapers unveiled a cleavage in African American politics. By printing the letter (that was critical of his rival), Anderson also gave voice to what he found a valid criticism of the Republican Party and their new bill. The fight for equal rights in the Golden State was not peripheral to national debates. Oftentimes, black Californians took center stage.

Jim Crow Entertainments

It is no coincidence that parades, balls, and Republican meetings proliferated in San Francisco; although black Californians had settled throughout the state, in the nineteenth century the state's equal rights movement was headquartered there. San Francisco's African American population constituted the oldest black urban community in the West.[128] It was in this city that the Athenaeum Library and Saloon became a center for learning and socializing. The competing *Pacific Appeal* and *Elevator*, both of which were read across the region, would be published there, and a host of black businesses flourished. San Francisco's black churches, and their ministers, were some of the most influential in the West. Reverend T. M. D. Ward, the first ordained AME minister in the Far West, organized the Bethel AME Church in St. Cyprian Church on Jackson Street in 1854. The Third Baptist Church and an AME Zion church, also founded in the city, exercised considerable religious and secular clout. Black San Franciscans were creating vibrant cultural and political communities that rivaled those of Boston or New York.

Few black San Franciscans could have failed to notice, however, that an increasing number of white men with blackened faces dominated the theaters of the U.S. West's largest city. Blackface minstrelsy had moved west with the forty-niners and helped make national the antebellum entertainment of white men in burnt cork singing so-called Ethiopian melodies. Minstrelsy arrived as statehood and segregation were under construction. As historian Michael Rogin observed, "The Forty-niners who sang as slaves . . . had no interest in emancipating blacks; they wanted to preserve California for free white men."[129] The fact that California's history of minstrelsy begins with the gold rush and statehood underscores the centrality of this tradition to the development of western culture and entertainment, but also its centrality to the politics of the Golden State. As Alexander Saxton, David Roediger, and others show, minstrelsy was and is always about politics as much as it is about entertainment.[130]

Within a few short years after the discovery of gold, San Francisco had gone "minstrel-crazy."[131] A Works Progress Administration study conducted in the 1930s describes minstrelsy's trajectory: "During its initial epoch, minstrelsy was restricted to the populous Eastern cities where the theatre has always flourished. New York had its resident companies, as did Brooklyn, Philadelphia and Chicago. Nearly every season one or several of these took to the road, but their circuits were confined to relatively small areas until 1849, when discovery of gold in California occasioned a vast exodus to the West. *Then San Francisco became a minstrel town*" (original emphasis).[132] Originally confined to smoky dive bars and saloons, minstrel shows catered to the largely white male mass of gold miners, shopkeepers, and entrepreneurs. By the mid-1850s, however, minstrel shows played in the city's more respectable theaters where, unlike the saloons, women and children were in attendance.[133]

As African Americans met in conventions to hammer out possibilities for citizenship and freedom, pressed for equal treatment in schools and on public transportation, hundreds of San Franciscans paid to watch white men smeared in blackface impersonate "Negro dandies." In the 1850s alone, over sixty-six minstrel productions appeared on city stages.[134] The white "delineators" devoted the first part of their shows to mocking the "northern" black man, wearing elegant dress, diamond stickpins, and gold watches.[135] It is difficult to believe that no one noticed that free black men who had overstepped their place in society were the subject of this mockery.

Minstrelsy in the Golden State achieved its greatest popularity with the help of theater owner and impresario Thomas Maguire. Maguire had been a New York saloon keeper, Tammany politician, and member of the volunteer fire department before he heard news of the gold rush and left the East Coast for San Francisco.[136] If Maguire did, as one theater historian claims, put San Francisco "on the theatrical map of the world," he did so with minstrelsy as his vehicle. In 1859, after opening a string of theaters (many of which burned down in the city's catastrophic fires), he opened the Eureka Minstrel Hall to capitalize on the city's new theatrical obsession.[137] His timing could not have been better, since "minstrels were pushing out Shakespearean actors to become the city's biggest stage attraction."[138]

By most accounts, Maguire was at the top of his game after the Civil War. He reaped untold profits from minstrel entertainments. However, the year of the centennial, 1876, did not start out well for the showman. On January 4, U.S. marshals arrested Maguire for denying a black patron, Charles Green, a seat at Maguire's New Theater. Green and another black patron, George M. Tyler, had been refused entry at the door. Maguire's arrest would precipitate a landmark challenge in civil rights law. Tyler's suit would become one of five that together formed the *Civil Rights Cases*, 109 U.S. 3 (1883). Defendants in those cases insisted on the right of African Americans to access places of commerce, including theaters, as established by the Civil Rights Act of 1875.[139] The significance of the 1875 act (called the Supplementary Civil Rights Act) had not been lost on westerners. In a city rife with theaters, black San Franciscans were well-positioned to insist on and test this new right to pleasure-seeking. As Amy Dru Stanley notes, "By no means was the Civil Rights Act of 1875 an ascetic article of freedom. It was intended as a culminating decree of slave emancipation, and newly defined pleasurable liberties as affirmative rights." The law transformed human rights, affirming the humanity of ex-slaves and free blacks by insisting on their "public right to play."[140] Claiming freedom included the right to take your seat in a theater.

On the night in question, Green and Tyler paid a dollar each for tickets to see a show of the Tennessee Jubilee Singers, whom Maguire billed as the "most superb colored company in America."[141] When Green attempted to take his seat, the doorman, Michael Ryan, as instructed by Maguire, stopped him. "The refusal was solely on account of the fact that Green is a colored man," reported the *Pacific Appeal*. According to some, the problem was that Green had tickets for the dress circle of the theater. The *San Francisco Call* reported that Green had been refused a seat in the dress circle because it would be insulting to white patrons. "The reasonable portion of our colored fellow citizens have the good sense and the magnanimity, on the facts being made plain, to accept the situation," said the *Call*. The "situation" to which the *Call* referred was Jim Crow. Black San Franciscans took great offense, forthwith organizing a committee to support Green. Meeting at the

Young Men's Union Benevolent Hall, the organization that had marched in the Emancipation Day parade eight years earlier, supporters raised funds for Green's case and drafted a resolution that the *San Francisco Chronicle* printed the following day: "Whereas, we are American citizens, the American flag is our flag, we hold it with pride; it floats over us . . . it assures to us the plenary rights of free men and women . . . be it resolved . . . That Thomas Maguire, in this act, has violated the laws of the land, infringed the just rights of American citizens, and insulted the honor and patriotism of the colored people of the city and coast, and of the United States."[142]

Despite an impressive legal team, the support of a committee led by Peter Anderson, and of the city's leading newspaper, the *San Francisco Chronicle*, Green's case against Maguire, under the Civil Rights Act of 1875, was lost in federal court.[143] Black spectators filled the courtroom to hear Judge Lorenzo Sawyer rule that the jury must acquit Maguire. Despite testimony from African American theatergoers confirming that Maguire regularly gave orders to turn away black patrons, the judge found the evidence insufficient. The community of supporters rallied to pursue a new strategy, filing a case against Michael Ryan, the doorkeeper, on behalf of George Tyler. Again their efforts failed. Judge Sawyer and Judge Ogden Hoffman ruled on February 12, 1876, in *U.S. vs. Ryan* that the Civil Rights Act of 1875, "so far as it is claimed to apply to the theaters and other places which are conducted by private individuals[, is] unconstitutional."[144] This decision met with little surprise but with sharp words: "We thank God that the Judge has delivered himself of the pro-slavery burden before the 4th of July, saving himself the embarrassment of proclaiming such hypocrisy in juxtaposition to the Fourteenth and Fifteenth Amendments and the Civil Rights Bills," wrote the *Pacific Appeal*.[145] Tyler and his attorneys appealed the case to the U.S. Supreme Court, but seven years passed before it appeared before the nation's highest court, bundled with four others and defeated, using the same argument that Sawyer had made earlier.

Minstrel-like entertainments continued to be a staple of California culture throughout the latter nineteenth century. Eager to capitalize on the popularity of the minstrel stage, the *San Francisco Examiner* began running a special Sunday supplement with "coon songs" in the 1890s. Sheet music of songs such as "I'll Carve Dat Nigger When We Meet" were printed in the *Examiner*'s special feature. The popularity of such musical fare at the end of the century testifies to the staying power of these representations of blackness in the state. Minstrel tunes served as the centerpiece entertainment—the pièce de résistance—at the most prestigious affairs for lofty white audiences. In 1899, at a banquet for the new president of the University of California, minstrel songs rang out through the Palace Hotel after the president made his inaugural remarks.[146] Never an exclusive sport, humor at the expense of African Americans occurred in less haughty venues as well. One of the most popular amusement parks in the state, San Francisco's Woodward Gardens, featured a game where, as the magazine the *Wasp* described, participants hurled leather balls at "a complaisant darky, sitting with a roofless silk hat, partially concealed behind a wooden frame."[147] In short, nineteenth-century Californians created and partook of all manner of Jim Crow entertainments, organizing them with much enthusiasm.

By the end of the nineteenth century, a state that had once seemed to present unlimited possibilities seemed to be hemming in its small black population more than most black men and women had expected. As Jim Crow ascended, African Americans found less to brag about in the Golden State. In spite of two victories against segregation—the 1890 *Wysinger v. Crukshank* case that marked the technical end of separate schools for black children in the state, and the passage of an 1893 law that prohibited discrimination in public accommodations—black Californians often felt unwanted, if not under siege. Severely limited work opportunities for most African Americans meant they faced the same choices in 1899 as they had in 1860.[148] Although black Californians organized new political associations at the end of the century, the state of affairs raised questions about just how much had changed since the war. Neither the Republican nor the Democratic Parties had the will to incorporate African Americans into the political leadership or to make claims for black citizenship a priority. San Francisco, still the dominant city of the state, supported a culture and politics that not only excluded African Americans from places of entertainment but used these spaces to mock campaigns for equality.[149] The 1896 *Plessy v. Ferguson* decision confirmed what black Californians already knew: their state and their nation embraced Jim Crow.

* * *

Resistance to the state's color line took place at parades, in court, in schools, on streetcars, and on stage, all places African Americans were discouraged or prohibited from occupying. African American men and women could readily name the foes of equality: former Confederates disguised as Democrats, western entrepreneurs (like Thomas Maguire), and damning representations of blackness on the minstrel stage and in the press. Jeremiah Sanderson's speeches at Emancipation Day parades point to the significance of scientific racism and its role in justifying and sustaining California's color lines. The court cases initiated by Biddy Mason, Archy Lee, Charlotte Brown, Emma Jane Turner, Mary Ellen Pleasant, Charles Green, and George M. Tyler all signaled a concerted effort on the part of black Californians to force the issues of emancipation and post-emancipation rights into the state's legal and political culture. These efforts to shape freedom in the Golden State secured California's place as the epicenter of the nineteenth-century western civil rights movement.

Debates on the convention floor, at the Palace Hotel Reception Ball, and in the Horticultural Hall reveal that the fight for citizenship was imbued with contestations over the meanings of manhood and womanhood. As they argued over civil rights bills and educational reforms, black Californians necessarily attended to the tricky business of what freedom looked like and how issues of race, class, and gender intersected. Should drunk Republicans be allowed at meetings? Should gamblers be allowed at the Palace Ball? What was the proper role for women at colored conventions? Working out the parameters of post-emancipation rights in a state and nation where they were shrinking meant that black Californians felt under siege and under surveillance. This did not deter their activism, but it pushed them into decisions that could be restrictive. If joining with Chinese activists for school reform hindered legislative reform, some black leaders advocated black-only politics. Elite men, often first-generation black Californians, criticized the presence, style, and politics of new black migrants who did not exhibit what they considered the right kind of manhood. And African American men ridiculed women who took an active part in convention politics. Practicing democracy in Reconstruction California meant determining who belonged and who did not. This occurred on both micro and macro scales; black citizens came closer to modeling actual democracy than the state legislature, but that does not mean it was simple or without contention.

African American men in California struggled to control the representations of and possibilities for black manhood in the nineteenth century. Their relative freedom to exercise the franchise gave them opportunities to shape state politics; it did not, however, translate into control of the Republican Party or the ability to stop the spread of Jim Crow. By 1900, the state's black women organized one of the earliest and most active club movements in the country and worked to counter the rhetoric about their inadequate mental and physical capacities. The relative safety of segregated California made it possible for men and women to forge an equal rights movement to challenge antiblack codes, laws, and customs. As they faced the twentieth century, they would draw on the strategies established in the previous century to resist Jim Crow and agitate for change. Black citizens would confront a culture and politics that clung to Jim Crow practices and an increasingly "scientific" understanding of race—all of which would be on display at the Panama Pacific International Exposition in San Francisco in 1915.

CHAPTER 2

"This Is Our Fair and Our State"

Race Women, Race Men, and the
Panama Pacific International Exposition

June 10, 1915, was a beautiful spring day in San Francisco when Delilah Beasley made the journey across the bay to the Panama Pacific International Exposition (PPIE) from her home in Berkeley. Beasley, writing simultaneously for northern California's mainstream daily and largest newspaper, the *Oakland Tribune*, and for one of the city's black newspapers, the *Oakland Sunshine*, had visited the world's fair before. But this time, she went with a different purpose: to witness the Bay Area's African American citizens as they marched in a parade at the state's most spectacular event of the year. Beasley and other African Americans believed that the PPIE would be an ideal setting to assert their presence as citizens. Black readers in California and around the country looked to Beasley, one of the state's most influential black reporters, to convey news about cultural events and the pressing political concerns of a population living through the age of Jim Crow.

Beasley had moved to California in 1910, already a newspaperwoman. Originally from Cincinnati, Ohio, she began her journalism career in her home state, writing first for the black newspaper, the *Cleveland Gazette* (when she was only fifteen), and later for the white paper, the *Cincinnati Enquirer*.[1] She also studied to be a professional masseuse and an expert in alternative medicines such as hydrotherapy. These therapeutic skills took her west to Berkeley to work for a former client. Beasley's journalism expertise and her commitment to the progress of African Americans landed her the opportunity to write for the leading white and black newspapers of the largest city in the East Bay and one of the largest in the West. A race woman and member of the black women's club movement, Beasley informed readers of

The journalist and historian Delilah L. Beasley wrote for the
Oakland Sunshine and the *Oakland Tribune*. She was a leader
of the state's antilynching movement and the black women's
club movement. Her *Negro Trail Blazers of California*, which
she self-published in 1919, celebrated black achievement and
ingenuity, as did her newspaper columns. (California State
Archives)

the wonders of the world's fair, the second to have occurred in California.
The PPIE brought to the fore issues that were central to black women's
struggle against Jim Crow including the scientific justifications for oppression, and the limits imposed on citizenship. Delilah Beasley and her community of race women understood the fair as a space to make public their
concerns. The parade that Beasley attended that June day was a spectacle
of citizenship and patriotism with black women at the center. To some

observers, African American women seemed out of place in the exposition parade—and that was precisely the point. The PPIE, however briefly, became a place for African Americans to claim the state and the nation.

The year of the fair—1915—marked a pivotal moment in the history of black Americans, including Californians. In that year, African Americans and their allies formed the Northern California branch of the National Association for the Advancement of Colored People (NAACP) and organized a massive outcry against Thomas Dixon's new play, *The Clansman*, and the subsequent film version by D. W. Griffith, *The Birth of a Nation*. The Great War, not six months old, occupied the minds of all Americans and would have a particular resonance for those, like black men and women, who constantly struggled to reinvent democracy within the borders of the United States. Beasley interpreted these events for a large readership. Her viewpoint as a journalist and her role as a historian of the black presence make her a compelling figure through which to examine the convergence of these events in state and national history. Her commitment to the women's club movement and the rights of black citizens provides a provocative lens through which to rethink the fair and the politics of race and gender. Overshadowed by the male leaders of the national civil rights organizations, women like Beasley struggled to redefine womanhood, manhood, patriotism, and citizenship at this pivotal moment in black history.[2] Between Reconstruction and the age of the New Negro, this period brought epic challenges for black America including the systematic erasure of the civil rights gains of Reconstruction, the constant threat of lynching, and the celebration of white supremacy in *The Birth of a Nation*. When a new technology called motion pictures made its world's fair debut at the PPIE, media-savvy Beasley anticipated its revolutionary potential to change hearts and minds. Like other clubwomen, Beasley understood that moving pictures could be an effective vehicle for racial uplift; churchwomen and clubwomen had already embraced the power of film in black exhibition spaces across the South and West before Griffith's notorious film.[3] This familiarity with the potential of cinema made the appearance of *The Birth of a Nation* all the more infuriating. In 1915, Beasley sensed the time was right to agitate for change amid the intersection of two contested and highly visible events: a world's fair and a motion picture, both attended by millions, and both launched in her new home state of California.

Though women had been granted full suffrage by California's male voters four years earlier, they were not yet considered equal participants in matters of state. Yet black women refused to stand on the sidelines of state politics. The efforts to secure African Americans the rights of citizenship changed dramatically during World War I, and for black women this translated into an opportunity to enter politics in unprecedented ways, even before they secured the right to vote in federal elections. Beasley and other African American women used the fair to carve out real and figurative spaces in which to articulate their political agendas and challenge Jim Crow. By harnessing the language and symbols of patriotism so prevalent at the fair, black Californians—men *and* women—claimed the nation as their own at the precise moment that the social and political messages of Griffith's images attempted to discredit their history as citizens. Claiming citizenship was a gendered affair, however, and the language and symbols available to women differed from those accessible to men. To counter negative stereotypes of African Americans like those present in *The Birth of a Nation*, Beasley and other clubwomen sought to convey a message of respectable black womanhood. With imagery that often invoked domesticity, race women challenged definitions of state, nation, and femininity. In their efforts to redefine citizenship, they used every venue at their disposal: the press, the church, women's clubs, public parades, and exhibitions.

African American participation in the PPIE underscored the ways in which all black citizens and especially women found themselves on the margins of state and national politics. Yet world's fairs, the "most important international mass events of the modern era," also presented opportunities for African American men and women to reshape the state's rigid notions of womanhood, manhood, and blackness.[4] While the PPIE wove, as Robert Rydall claims, "elaborate racial fantasies about California's history," these fantasies did not go uncontested.[5] Reading the PPIE with an eye to black participation reveals the successes of Jim Crow in California, but it also underscores the interventions African Americans made in the state's practice of segregation. By charting the possibilities and challenges of the PPIE, this chapter shows how black women refuted the racial discourse of the era, refashioned the language and meanings of patriotism, and articulated their own politics on the world stage.

Jim Crow Fair, Jim Crow State

California already had a well-developed women's club movement when Beasley arrived in 1910. The Woman's Afro-American League and the

National Association of Colored Women (NACW) were organizing new branches at a feverish pace. Reporting in the NAACP's journal, the *Crisis*, Addie W. Hunton claimed that, by 1912, "no state had more strongly and clearly demonstrated the blessing of a united womanhood than California."[6] Embracing the NACW mission and motto, "Lifting as We Climb," groups such as the Mother's Club and the Arts and Industry Club of Oakland were the backbone of this movement. Clubwomen's efforts to fight Jim Crow would prove critical in this era and provide a counterpoint to male leaders. In the years in and around World War I, black women in California methodically attacked discriminatory practices, utilizing judicial, nonviolent, and performative strategies decades before the official beginning of the civil rights movement. The PPIE would prove to be the setting of their most public intervention yet.

In the early twentieth century, an ever-increasing number of African Americans immigrated to California hoping to find a more hospitable racial climate and opportunities for education and employment. In fact, when W. E. B. Du Bois, patriarch of the NAACP and editor of the *Crisis*, visited the state in July 1913, he found much to celebrate. He praised the palm tree–lined streets of Los Angeles and the stately single-family homes of the black elite, offering a litany of the good works race men and women in the state were conducting.[7] He visited the state in large part to drum up enthusiasm and, more importantly, dues-paying members of the fledgling NAACP, a goal that would soon reach fruition. The journey, and especially its coverage in the *Crisis*, stimulated tourism (including to the PPIE) and migration to the state. Du Bois was not alone in his praise. National black newspapers such as the *Colored American* also heaped accolades on the Golden State and encouraged readers to move there. Just four years before the fair opened, Jefferson L. Edmonds, the editor of the *Liberator*, a Los Angeles black newspaper, claimed that California was "the greatest state for the Negro."[8]

But the very attributes that Du Bois, Edmonds, and others complimented, such as the availability of single-family homes and jobs, were often scarce and segregated. Where some African Americans saw opportunity, many more experienced discrimination; for them, race relations in the Golden State were nothing to celebrate. Between 1900 and 1930, African Americans had few opportunities for skilled or semiskilled jobs in the Bay Area, which had no large-scale manufacturing. Black women found even fewer opportunities for work and across the state were generally restricted to domestic labor.[9] Southern California held more opportunities for manual labor, though these were reserved for men—and white men always received the better-paying jobs. The occasion of the PPIE itself inspired the *Oakland Sunshine* to warn of the dismal employment situation. "We hope members of our race will not come here expecting to find employment, as the conditions are not favorable," the editors announced.[10] Depending on where in the state one lived, the housing situation could be equally bleak; many black Californians with sufficient income to purchase property encountered restrictive housing covenants. For renters, the situation could be worse. Black men and women in the Bay Area, where the majority of the state's African American population lived until World War II, found that "real estate agents do not care to rent to Negroes."[11] Restrictive covenants inserted into property titles as early as the 1890s became commonplace in the 1910s, effectively turning neighborhoods across the state white-only.[12]

In 1915, partly as a result of Du Bois's much-publicized visit and Griffith's film, black Californians founded the NAACP's Northern California branch, headquartered in Oakland. In its first year, the branch counted 150 members, making it among the largest in the nation; two years later membership figures soared to over a thousand.[13] The fledgling branch took on an immediate challenge: the opening earlier that year of *The Clansman*—the stage adaptation of Thomas Dixon's 1905 novel of the same name—that claimed to depict the history of Reconstruction. D. W. Griffith's film version, *The Birth of a Nation*, followed almost immediately. African Americans were appalled by the depiction and straightforward message: black men and women were unfit for citizenship, but white supremacy could be reinstated with the aid of the Ku Klux Klan. In one of the most telling scenes, a black man played by a white actor in blackface chased a white woman to the edge of a cliff, where she jumped off rather than, presumably, be raped. Black members of Congress were depicted as lazy and worthless buffoons.

The film was first shown in Riverside, California, on January 1, 1915. On February 8, twelve days before the PPIE welcomed its first visitors, 2,500 filmgoers flocked to Clune's Auditorium in Los Angeles to the official premiere of Griffith's much-hyped motion picture.[14] Black leaders and the black press called for a boycott. The Los Angeles branch of the NAACP organized the first local protest, securing a court injunction to ban the screening, but the injunction was ignored.[15] The Northern California branch pressured the mayors of San Francisco and Oakland to prohibit the showing of the film, a strategy adopted by other branches across the country. Indeed,

California's NAACP branches set a precedent for the national protest. But despite several meetings between the president of the Northern California branch, John Drake, and the city fathers of Oakland and San Francisco, the film played in the Bay Area the rest of the year and throughout the entire PPIE.[16] Angered by the film's stereotypes and their implications, Beasley made it her mission to educate readers about its detrimental messages and historic untruths, juxtaposing the film and the fair to highlight the fallacies of black inferiority. Her efforts did not go unnoticed. According to the black newspaper the *Oakland Independent*, "*The Birth of a Nation* was making people of all races very unhappy and promoting unfriendly feeling toward the Negro by playing in San Francisco during the entire period of the exposition. In an effort to counteract the effect of the [film,] Miss Beasley began writing for *The Oakland Daily Tribune* featuring the Negro exhibits in the Panama Pacific International Exposition."[17] This was no small feat. Through her columns in the *Tribune*, one of the state's largest daily newspapers, and the *Oakland Sunshine*, Beasley reached a wide and interracial audience.

Convincing her readership that race pride and racial uplift could be exercised at the PPIE would not be easy, however. For the nearly 19 million people who attended the fair between opening day on February 20 and December 4—wandering through eleven major exhibit halls, twenty-one national pavilions, over twenty-five buildings devoted to states or regions—representations of race would be hard to ignore. From the midway, or Joy Zone, to the ethnological exhibits and even the Palace of Food Products, visitors witnessed a range of racialized subjects, stereotypes, and caricatures of African Americans. What most visitors gleaned about people of color they most likely learned in places like Dixieland or the so-called native villages. Beasley would have to muster all of her journalistic prowess to encourage African American visitors to look past these representations to find the few black exhibits that spoke to race pride.

Elites organized fairs in order to present particular visions of a well-ordered hierarchical society that, not incidentally, married the ideas of progress and white supremacy. For those who crafted the vision of the PPIE, the key to national progress—and civilization—was something euphemistically called "racial progress" or "race betterment." Coming as it did on the heels of the opening of the Panama Canal and at the onset of the Great War, the PPIE occurred at an auspicious time to celebrate national progress and scientific triumph.[18]

With the input of a wide array of scientists—including anthropologists, horticulturalists, biologists, geneticists, and psychologists—exhibits and lectures conveyed theories about race and breeding. This world's fair was the first to host a panoply of eugenics-related displays and conferences.[19] Thousands of visitors were drawn to the wildly popular six Race Betterment booths in the Palace of Education. Recently founded in Michigan by cereal magnate John H. Kellogg, the Race Betterment Foundation enjoyed a receptive audience in California. David Starr Jordan, founding president of Stanford University and its chancellor in 1915, attended the Second National Conference on Race Betterment held at the fair and soon became one of California's leading eugenicists.[20] The PPIE also attracted up-and-coming proponents of better breeding, including Paul Popenoe, who would be instrumental in California's eugenics movement and one of the leading architects of the state's sterilization program. Popenoe designed an eye-catching photo display for the Race Betterment booth and delivered a lecture at the fair, "Natural Selection in Man."[21] As the secretary pro tem of the American Genetic Association's Eugenics Section and editor of the *Journal of Heredity*, he was positioned to influence countless other scientists. After his stint at the fair, Popenoe would patrol the U.S.-Mexican border for the U.S. Army Sanitary Corps and then become a founding member of Pasadena's Human Betterment Foundation, as would Jordan.

Eugenics pervaded California culture and government, and the PPIE provided a crucial public platform for these ideas. Members of the Ninth International Congress of the World's Purity Federation convened at the fair throughout July and August, and the lectures delivered at a meeting of the Education Congress also addressed race betterment.[22] The fair's official chronicler, Frank Morton Todd, described the Race Betterment booth as "one of the exhibits that caught the eye of every visitor."[23] There, among sculptures of classical Greek figures, visitors could read charts warning against interracial marriage or mixed-race breeding, as it was then called. Messages about so-called better breeding were not restricted to one display; another popular booth belonging to the Department of Labor warned about the weakening of America's racial purity due to recent immigration trends.[24] As historian Alexandra Stern explains, "the nucleus of California's eugenics movement converged at PPIE."[25] Fair organizers thrilled to the concentration of eugenicists at the fair, and breathlessly wrote to the leaders of the Race Betterment Foundation: "you represent the very spirit, the very ideal

The Panama Pacific International Exposition was a meeting place for the nation's eugenicists. Sponsored by the Race Betterment Foundation, this booth was one of many exposing fairgoers to ideas about race, eugenics, and black inferiority. (San Francisco History Center, San Francisco Public Library)

of this great Exposition that we have created here."[26] As a reporter, Beasley would be well aware of the eugenics themes of the fair; the Race Betterment conference received more press than any other attraction, more than a million lines of coverage by the Associated Press and the United Press.[27] According to the eugenicist discourse presented at the fair, African Americans threatened racial purity, and their presence in the state could only be a hindrance.

California had proven itself receptive to messages about black inferiority and white supremacy long before the fair opened. Fears of race mixing led Californians to enact one of the earliest miscegenation laws in the nation. An 1850 state law forbade marriage between whites and "negroes" or "mulattos," and in 1878 the statute was revised to include "Mongolians" to the list of proscribed races.[28] The state doggedly attempted—often through city clerks—to prevent interracial marriage even though, as Peggy Pascoe has shown, enforcement proved uneven. The NAACP kept a watchful eye on the state and monitored similar laws across the country. Intermarriage, and its criminalization, received its own column in the pages of the *Crisis*. "Believing these laws to be unjust and degrade the colored race and especially the colored women, the branches have taken an active part against such legislation," wrote W. E. B. Du Bois in the June 1913 issue.[29] Over half of the states had passed such laws by 1900. The fear of racial degeneracy and even of "race suicide" intensified among middle-class white Californians. Indeed, the state embraced this fear and its popular solution, female sterilization, passing its first eugenic sterilization law in 1909, only the third such law in the nation. Eventually the state would perform twenty thousand operations, one-third of the nation's total number of sterilizations.[30] California was fast becoming a center of eugenicist thought and practice, a place where racial purity was championed and race mixing despised. As one scholar of eugenics puts it, "California offered a model that eugenicists in the Deep South and elsewhere sought to emulate."[31] It is no coincidence, then, that a film celebrating white supremacy and a fair promoting eugenic ideologies found such enthusiastic audiences in the Golden State.

Black women knew only too well that policies aimed to control unfit mothers and encourage the scrutiny of women considered to be on the margins of respectability could have serious implications for their own choices, reproductive and otherwise. Beasley chose to ignore the eugenicists, at least in print, and she would have had many reasons for doing so. Stereotypes about black sexual appetites may have discouraged some race women from participating in discussions about sexual mores. Cast since slavery as oversexed jezebels, black women of this era, especially those engaged in racial uplift, had to be careful about openly discussing sexuality or reproduction, as the risks were great. Race women had to navigate this terrain carefully, but they did not avoid topics of sex and gender altogether.[32] By drawing attention to themselves as mothers, they reclaimed their bodies and shifted the discussion of black female sexuality. The era between 1890 and 1930 brought issues of black reproduction into the public: infant mortality rates for African Americans were alarming, and the birth rate was in decline. In the South, state health departments blamed black midwives. In the West, black women doubled their efforts to "prove" their worthiness as mothers.[33] Many reform-minded women argued that race progress depended upon "increasing the number of 'well-born' children."[34] California clubwomen emphasized their own respectability, their role as mothers, and their excellent domestic skills. Forming mother's clubs and focusing on reproduction became a central way that black women countered a discourse—and scientific theory—that cast them as unfit.

Some middle-class African Americans embraced arguments that could be deemed eugenicist as they engaged in race politics. As Michele Mitchell shows, race men and women "could actually subvert racism within eugenic thought through the guise of racial uplift." W. E. B. Du Bois promoted healthy baby contests in the pages of the *Crisis*, in conjunction with racial uplift rhetoric detailing who should reproduce and who should not. Racial fitness and the future of the race were on the minds of many middle-class African Americans who expressed their views in various venues from lecture halls to print media to fiction. Race women, hemmed in by the dictates of respectable womanhood, worked within these boundaries to advance racial uplift agendas including educating the race about black health, parenthood, and sexuality.[35] The potential for audience and education at the PPIE prompted black men and women to work tirelessly to secure a place for themselves in the fairgrounds, but gender expectations dictated that these places would be very different.

In the months prior to the fair's opening day, newspapers carried innumerable stories of the preparations and the fair's potential; African Americans knew that the PPIE would bring thousands of jobs to the state. Black men had their hopes set on jobs as guards, ticket takers, waiters, entertainers, and groundskeepers. For black women, whose employment opportunities across the country were largely limited to domestic jobs, employment aspirations would have seemed far-fetched. Securing a space for women at this venue would mean finding a different way to break the color line. In a series of letters to the fair organizers, African American men used the occasion of the world's fair to chip away at segregated hiring practices. In January 1915, a month before the fair opened its gates, the Colored Non-Partisan Leagues, an organization that helped educate and organize black voters in the state, charged that hiring practices at the fair had been discriminatory. In a letter to the president of the fair's board of directors, Charles C. Moore, S. L. Mash, the organization's president, wrote that he had confirmed with the superintendent of the service building, a Mr. Flynn, that "the [color] line had been drawn to the extent that no Colored Man [*sic*] would be allowed to be employed as Guards and other various positions at the Fair Grounds, and that it would be a waste of time for any Colored Man to make any such application."[36] In his letter, Mash, a black attorney, also reminded Moore, president of the local Chamber of Commerce, that the Leagues had lobbied to have the fair in California because of the state's antidiscriminatory legislation.[37] Further, he noted that black voters were "a great factor" in securing the fair for the state, as was the black press. "There is no question, but that all the Colored Newspapers of the United States, as well as the Colored Press Association of which I am a member . . . assisted greatly in this matter, to the success of San Francisco." Mash closed his letter with a warning: should the discrimination continue, "the same influence that was used favorably to San Francisco, might be the means of causing a great injustice to the fair minded good citizens of the State of California."[38] Moore never replied to this accusation of discrimination. Unbeknownst to the Colored Non-Partisan Leagues, Moore's attorney sent a memo to Moore assuring him that "a few tactful words will quiet these 'wards of the nation.'" Two weeks after Mash's letter, PPIE secretary R. J. Taussig sent those tactful words to Mash, declaring that, "speaking officially, the Exposition has not at any time drawn a color line." As for the complaint about employees, Taussig had conducted a personal investigation and found "quite a number of colored men employed in the buildings and on the grounds. . . . So you must admit," he wrote, "that there is no discrimination based on race." When it came time to address the absence of black guards at the Fair, Taussig's excuse amounted to the fact that only "veterans of the Spanish war" had been hired in this capacity; and while the fair might entertain hiring a segregated unit of black men "just as it is done in the U.S. Army," it "was out of the question at the present moment."[39]

As confident as the secretary sounded, Mash was not fooled. In his letter responding to Taussig's assertion of a Jim Crow–free fair, he offered to print Taussig's assurance in the black press: "A copy of your letter will be sent to our Eastern correspondents . . . and our people may be made to feel welcome by the Officials of the Great Panama Pacific International Exposition." But Mash did not leave it at that. He happily took up the secretary's point about veterans serving as guards, reminding the secretary of the valiant service of the Ninth and Tenth Cavalries and the Twenty-Fourth and Twenty-Fifth Infantries—commonly known as the buffalo soldiers—in the Spanish American and Philippine American wars. The Buffalo Soldiers inspired tremendous race pride and their appearance at the fair would be an ideal representation of black manhood, Mash believed. He continued: "and in the hope that all mark of discrimination may be removed, both in fact and in appearance . . . we most readily meet your suggestion, that a Colored Company of Guards be formed."[40] Unfortunately, there is no record of Taussig's response to this letter, and despite Mash's offer to organize that unit of veterans himself, it seems unlikely that anyone took him up on his proposal. Raising the record of black troops and their historic service to the nation while the war raged in Europe would become a key strategy for race men and women fighting for racial justice at home.[41]

In the end, Mash would win a partial victory. The PPIE invited black soldiers to participate in Lincoln Day, during which a thousand black troops paraded through the fairgrounds. Getting black soldiers to the fair would not be difficult. In the summer and fall of 1915 the Twenty-Fourth Infantry was stationed in San Francisco at the Presidio, nearly adjacent to the fairground. Their presence in the city meant a great deal to black Californians, including Beasley, who was so proud she wrote to the *Crisis* that "the conduct of the Infantry was so very good that the Exposition officials decided to honor the Negro soldiers with a special day."[42] "The exercises were opened by a Military Parade," she reported, "which was led by the entire Twenty-fourth Infantry . . . headed by a Negro band and bandmaster. . . . The Negro led the day." Beasley's pride about this parade seemed a bit overblown. But her sentiment is in keeping with her goal to emphasize race pride and African American patriotism. She also reminded readers of the *Crisis* that three days before the military parade, black troops had escorted the Liberty Bell out of the PPIE on its way to Philadelphia.[43] However, the fleeting appearance of black soldiers was a far cry from the demands of attorney Mash.

The exchange of letters between Mash and PPIE officials is a strong indication that black Californians, before and during the fair, voiced their concerns about segregation and racial discrimination quite pointedly. Whether the complaints from the Colored Non-Partisan Leagues made a difference in hiring practices is unclear. But the records tell us that the PPIE, the city of San Francisco, and the state of California, came under intense scrutiny. Jim Crow practices did not go unnoticed—indeed, they were advertised nationwide. By March, San Francisco mayor James Rolph Jr. had a letter on his desk from James C. Waters Jr., an alumnus of Howard University Law School, training ground of the nation's top civil rights attorneys. Waters stated his requests quite simply: "What the colored folks want is equal treatment in all the purely public and quasi-public places such as are commonly open to all comers in the city of San Francisco. For instance, if they find themselves in need of food or drink, or both, they want to be able to enter the first restaurant they come to, and not have to trudge, mile after mile until they come to some 'Jim Crow snack house' or 'chit'lin den' . . . before they can get a mouthful to eat or a glass of milk."[44] Waters, attorney of the Washington, D.C., firm Wilson & Waters, pulled no punches as he described the myth of racial equality in San Francisco: "colored persons who propose to visit the Panama Pacific World's Exposition in San Francisco during the current year, believing they will be accorded the same civil treatment accorded decent, responsible members of other races, will find they are entertaining a wild notion."[45] Waters requested an honest assessment of the situation from the mayor.

Rolph chose not to respond personally to this matter and instead referred it to Secretary Taussig. Waters, like Mash, seemed singularly unimpressed with Taussig's handling of the situation: a "32 word letter" that he "so generously sent" on March 15. Though no record exists of Taussig's letter, it is clear from Waters's response that the secretary resorted to the same policy he initiated when addressing the concerns expressed by the Colored Non-Partisan Leagues: deny the presence of segregation at the fair.[46] There is no indication that any further action was taken. Rolph's unwillingness to address the issues of African American employment or segregation did not surprise most. When a black man did get hired at the PPIE, the *Crisis* found it newsworthy, reporting that Billy Hooper became one of the few African American employees.[47] Hooper secured this position only after he worked without pay and traveled to Oregon — at his own expense — to drum up visitors to the fair. Blowing his six-foot-long trumpet festooned with a banner advertising the fair, he made such a commotion on the streets of Portland that the chief of police put a stop to it. This stunt, according to the *Crisis*, landed Hooper a full-time job as the official herald of the fair, a "self-invented job" that, according to one scholar, "guaranteed his invitation to most of the great parties before and after the PPIE."[48]

Entertaining audiences was a safe way for black men, in particular, to seek employment at the fair and across the country. Other than Hooper, one of the few men to be seen regularly at the PPIE was the bandleader Captain Walter H. Loving. Loving served in the Philippines in the U.S. Army before joining the Philippine Constabulary, a civil police force. Beginning in 1902, Loving conducted the Philippine Constabulary Band, which enjoyed a successful tour at the fair. The ninety-member unit played daily on the bandstand at the Court of the Universe. Beasley wrote that the presence of this band helped prove there was a "spirit of an equal chance at the PPIE."[49] Perhaps she believed that the presence of Captain Loving countered the mythology that black men were inherently uncivilized. Beasley had her reasons for heralding representations of strong black manhood at the fair. As far as she was concerned, to rescue black manhood was to rescue the race from the most heinous characterizations—the type that were regularly on offer in *The Birth of a Nation*. In so doing, Beasley joined the ranks of other African Americans, including Frederick Douglass, Booker T. Washington, Ida B. Wells, and W. E. B. Du Bois, who understood fairs and expositions as essential locations to challenge racial hegemony during the era of Jim Crow. Beasley's sometimes stilted efforts to embrace the fair speak to her insistence that she could exploit this world stage for the purpose of racial uplift. Not unlike the conflict that developed between Ida B. Wells and Frederick Douglass at the 1893 Columbian Exposition in Chicago, Beasley stood at the center of a much wider debate about how to push back against segregation and race hatred.

Racial Uplift and Fairs Past

African Americans have a long and complex history with U.S. world fairs. As spectators, exhibitors, workers, performers, and activists, they shaped the outcome of fairs and often countered the messages of elite white planners. In the nineteenth century, fairs were places where black Americans staged protests and attempted to wrest control of their histories and representations from the stereotypic insults on offer. Most leading race men and women of the day grappled with the import of world's fairs and their potential as vehicles for political thought, leadership, and education. But these were contested sites and black Americans argued about how best to counter the rampant segregation at the fairs. The period from 1877 to 1915, the heyday of world's fairs, coincided with Jim Crow's most vicious years and some of the most offensive representations of black Americans in history, fiction, and film. Some African Americans felt that fairs, like other segregated institutions of the era (schools, theaters, streetcars), should be boycotted altogether. Others perceived only opportunities; fairs were "a momentous opportunity and obligation to set the great white world straight about black people," as one scholar puts it.[50] Building on the antebellum tradition of black abolitionists such as William Wells Brown, who traveled the world with his diorama of slavery, postbellum black Americans understood the power of display. Abolitionists made use of fantastic imagery and theatrics to educate mostly white audiences about the peculiar institution; only a couple of generations later, race men and women followed this example at the new expositions. Fairs presented an extraordinary opportunity to counter the onslaught of damaging beliefs about the benefits of slavery and the impossibility of African American citizenship.

The best-known example of African American participation—and lack thereof—in a world's fair occurred in 1893 in Chicago at the World's Columbian Exposition, which was designed to commemorate the four-hundredth anniversary of Christopher Columbus's "discovery" of America. There, antilynching activist and journalist Ida B. Wells and orator and statesman Frederick Douglass publicly questioned the role of black Americans at the fair and, in particular, their participation in so-called Colored American Day. The debates surrounding the representation and participation of African Americans at the Columbian Exposition revealed significant differences in what black people thought fairs could be and do. Members of the elite class of black Chicagoans, including clubwoman Fannie Barrier Williams, the only African American to hold an administrative position in the fair, believed that the exposition could showcase the achievements of the nation's black population and was a tremendous opportunity that should not be missed.[51] Others found the very notion of a single day devoted to black achievement patronizing and offensive.

The 1890s marked a period in post-Reconstruction America characterized by the worst offenses of Jim Crow: lynching, violence, and the erosion of rights that African Americans had achieved during Reconstruction. Not surprisingly, black men and women did not always agree on how best to stand up for their rights at the fair or otherwise. Colored American Day became the flashpoint for voicing some of these disagreements. The publication and distribution of a pamphlet cowritten by Ida B. Wells, *The Reason Why the Colored American Is Not in the World's Columbian Exposition: The Afro-American's Contribution to Columbian Literature*, helped to galvanize African Americans. Wells raised the $500 needed to print the pamphlet by speaking in Chicago's black churches at events organized by clubwomen. She published the pamphlet herself and had the preface, which she wrote, translated into French and German.[52] Already in the forefront of an international crusade against lynching, Wells and her coauthors Ferdinand Barnett, Frederick Douglass, and journalist I. Garland Penn exposed the history of racism that had disfranchised African Americans. The authors encouraged a boycott of Colored American Day. Wells posited that an exhibit of African American progress, just twenty-five years after slavery, "would have been the greatest tribute to the greatness and progressiveness of American institutions which could have been shown the world." Instead, Colored American Day proceeded on August 25th and free watermelons were on offer. In her article "On Tole with Watermelons," Wells condemned "Colored Folks Day," as an eleventh hour attempt to boost attendance (which had been poor) and a "scheme to put thousands of dollars in the pockets of the railroad corporations and the world's fair folks who thought no Negro good enough for an official position." She also alluded to the class tensions simmering at the fair by referring to "the class of our people" found at Colored Folks Day "roaming around the grounds munching watermelons" and lowering the race "in the estimation of the world."[53]

The response to the pamphlet was mixed and Wells received harsh criticism from men and women who felt she had overstepped her bounds. Some clubwomen felt the publication would turn back the gains they had made with sympathetic whites. The most damning criticism, however, came from black newspapermen, thus ensuring that a wide swath of black America heard the scolding. The *Indianapolis Freeman* accused Douglass and Wells of airing dirty laundry, showing the fissures among the black elite, and drumming up trouble for black folks where there was none.[54] C. H. J. Taylor, in the pages of the *Kansas City American Citizen* wrote "someone should put a muzzle on that animal from Memphis [Wells]."[55] The response to Wells reflected the general anxiety that some black men felt about women's dominance in the debates about the fair. Since the early planning stages in 1892, black clubwomen condemned the lily-white fair commissioners' Jim Crow policies. When it was determined that all women's exhibits would be handled by the Board of Lady Managers with not one African American woman on the board, clubwomen rallied and sent a representative to protest at the first meeting.[56] These efforts met with little success, but they had made headlines in the black press. Black women knew much was at stake: the signature representation of an African American woman at the exposition was the inaugural portrayal of Aunt Jemima by Nancy Green at the R. T. Davis Milling Company booth, a performance that won the employer a gold medal.[57]

In the end, Wells and Douglass disagreed about attending Colored American Day; Douglass had come to see the benefits of the impressive exposition and its position on the world stage. Due to his official role as the former ambassador to Haiti, Douglass addressed an exuberant crowd of over 2,500 people on August 25, 1893, in the Haitian Pavilion. He used the day to deliver a blistering criticism of slavery and the treatment of African Americans in the United States. Other representations of black Americans were few. There were individual black exhibitors, such as the sculptor Edmonia Lewis, but there was never a collective exhibit of black artists, educators, or inventors.[58] Wells eventually came to regret her decision to boycott the fair, but her intervention made a lasting impression. Clubwomen made their voices heard and were roundly criticized. The Chicago fair served as a lesson in gender politics and inspired women's political agency. Indeed, the National Association of Colored Women formed soon after the fair, in part as a result of the networks Wells and her supporters had organized during the Chicago exposition.[59]

Beasley no doubt remembered Wells and the Columbian Exposition when she penned her own thoughts on racial uplift in her newspaper columns. In fact, Wells visited Oakland the year of the PPIE, and it is likely that the two women met. The California clubwomen invited Wells to speak about her antilynching work, and the *Oakland Sunshine* devoted considerable press to her visit; Beasley probably covered this event for the *Sunshine* since she was the only clubwoman on staff. As black newspaperwomen and clubwomen, Beasley and Wells had much in common. Beasley devoted much of her life to the fight against lynching and coauthored an antilynching bill in California. Wells's career and her international profile garnered significant attention from her contemporaries and later from historians. Her strident and forthright manner, for which she was ostracized from the NAACP, came to be much appreciated in the historiography of black women, while Beasley's legacy has been largely overlooked.[60] Yet both women attacked Jim Crow practices and claimed a place for black women on the page and in public fora. The interventions of Wells and Beasley at this critical juncture in black politics shifted conversations about racial uplift, often in ways that made men uncomfortable. Although ultimately Wells was a more strident—and visible—critic of American race politics than Beasley, they both intervened in the largely male domains of black politics and world's fairs.

Perhaps no fair better illustrates the significance of expositions as platforms for black political thought, including debates about segregation, than the Atlanta Cotton States and International Exposition of 1895. Held only two years after Chicago's World's Columbian Exposition, it inspired a rift among African Americans that became one of the central events in the history of racial uplift ideology. This time it was not Douglass who delivered the signature oration but Booker T. Washington. In what came to be known as the Atlanta compromise, Washington laid out his vision for a new and unified South, which many African Americans, most notably W. E. B. Du Bois and the other founders of the NAACP, found accommodationist at best. While Washington's address has been the focus of extensive commentary, it was not the only controversy about race and Jim Crow at the exposition. Atlanta's exposition would be the first world's fair in which African Americans had their own dedicated hall for showcasing black progress and accomplishments. As Mabel O. Wilson shows, the debates surrounding the Negro Building would reprise many of the issues raised by Chicago's Colored American Day. Many black southerners worried that a separate pavilion would send the wrong message: a willingness to accept segregation. Given the extent of racial apartheid in Atlanta and across the New South, this concern was not unwarranted. In spite of the fact that the Negro Building's director, Irvine Garland Penn, had been a vocal critique of segregation at Chicago's fair, the exhibits in the pavilion focused on the success of industrial education programs, a very Washingtonian message.[61] As Wilson explains, the Negro Building "reinforced the notion that the appropriate home for the Negro was the farm, away from urban life, and with no intellectual aspirations whatsoever."[62] In this way, the exposition, including Washington's infamous address and the Negro Building, delivered a clear and welcome pronouncement to the white elite of the New South.

Before he delivered his biting criticism of Washington's Atlanta Exposition speech in his 1903 *Souls of Black Folk*, Du Bois, with input from Washington, curated a showcase of black progress: the Negro Exhibit at the Paris Exposition of 1900. Convinced that an impressive display of black churches, clubs, schools, farms, and homes would dispel the myths about African Americans, Thomas Calloway, state commissioner for the 1895 Cotton States and International Exposition in Atlanta, lobbied the black elite and the U.S. Congress to support the special exhibit. He enlisted Du Bois, his former classmate from Fisk University, to assist. In defense of his idea of a Negro pavilion at the fair, Calloway wrote to colleagues, "everyone who knows about public opinion will tell you that the Europeans think of us as a mass of rapists ready to attack every white woman exposed . . . how will we answer these slanders?"[63] From the $15,000 he secured from Congress, Calloway advanced Du Bois $2,500 to prepare the bulk of the visual display for the exhibit. Du Bois thought it best to counter the slanders with a small but fastidious display of photographs of African Americans and charts and graphs of data about black life prepared with the help of his Atlanta University sociology students. Whether this approach altered racialized notions is not clear, but the exhibit earned Du Bois a gold medal for his role as "Collaborator and Compiler of the Georgia Negro Exhibit" that did not go unnoticed by the black press in the United States. There are no photographs of lynching or poverty and there is a decided preference for photographs of light-skinned African Americans. However, as Wilson points out, Du Bois's photographs also countered prevailing racial science by refuting the idea of a natural Negro type.[64] Though exhibits like those in Paris were intended to counter racial caricatures, the stereotype of the black male rapist had not yet reached its zenith; that would occur five years later in *The Birth of a Nation*, as millions of viewers watched a white female jump to her death while fleeing the black male pursuing her.

Du Bois, who by 1915 was mobilizing members of the NAACP against *The Birth of a Nation*, also had hopes for a Negro department at the PPIE. The previous year he wrote to music director George W. Stewart about "staging an impressive pageant and celebration about black culture and history."[65] Although nothing came of his efforts, Du Bois, like Beasley, thought Negro exhibits at PPIE might be an effective way to "answer the slanders."

By the time of the PPIE, Du Bois and Washington had come to represent distinct schools of black intellectual and activist thought. Du Bois embodied the civil rights and protest wing of black America, Washington the self-help school of thought. Though scholars consider this binary framework for black Americans' responses to Jim Crow—resistance and accommodation—a drastic oversimplification, it has often shaped the ways we interpret African American history. This false dichotomy obscures the complexities of club-women such as Beasley, who objected to antiblack representations, embraced civil rights, and championed African American achievements while seeking ways to position the black American experience at public venues. Like other clubwomen of the era, Beasley cannot easily be placed in either the Washington or Du Bois camps; although she worked for a decidedly Washingtonian newspaper, the *Oakland Sunshine*, she also championed the NAACP. Beasley's story—and those of women like her—illustrates the problems with oversimplifying African American resistance to Jim Crow.

Race Pride and Parades in "Jewel City"

The PPIE, like the fairs preceding it, elicited mixed reactions from black men and women. The discussion in the black press reveals that not everyone embraced the possibilities of the exposition. In addition to the discriminatory hiring practices, stereotypical displays of Africans and African Americans would be difficult for fairgoers to ignore, none more powerful than the attraction called the African Dip. Nestled between a concession stand selling orange blossom candles and a fruit pavilion, the African Dip, an enormous booth in the Joy Zone, recalled popular images of savage Africans. To experience the African Dip, fairgoers approached the enormous body of a pierced African of indeterminate gender; inside the booth, they tried to toss a ball at a parade of "dummy figures." If patrons knocked a hat off a figure, they won a cigar. The figures represented racial and ethnic caricatures of Irish, German, and Chinese; it is not clear if African American men were in the lineup.[66] Demeaning caricatures of African Americans at the fair were not restricted to the African Dip; at the Sperry Flour booth, women dressed as the stereotypic mammy figure made pancakes for the hungry crowds. As with Aunt Jemima in Chicago, pancake-flipping black women were the sole representation of African American womanhood at PPIE.

On March 27, in response to a proposed "special day" devoted to black Americans, the leaders of the Afro-American League, in the pages of their paper, the *Oakland Sunshine*, asked its readers: "Do We Want a Negro Day at the Exposition?" The editors seemed skeptical about the merits of such a day and its feasibility: "Is it too late for the Negroes to begin planning for a Negro Day at the Exposition, when the whole grounds will be turned over to the Colored People of the United States. . . . But do we really want a Negro Day and would it be a Jim Crow Day?" Readers of the paper were encouraged to mail in their "25 word answer" to this question by the next issue.[67]

Negro Day promised to be a grand affair, a display of sports, singing, reciting, and all sorts of talents. According to the *Sunshine*, fifty "ministers, business and professional men" were appointed to a committee by the fair's president and directors to make arrangements. Attempts were under way to organize a choir of a thousand schoolchildren to perform in a singing contest. Races of all kinds were planned, including a "fat men's and short men's race." And perhaps most significantly, the mouthpiece of racial uplift, Booker T. Washington, was invited to be the orator of the day. Members of the black elite took the fair, and the committee, quite seriously: "Let every race-loving, patriotic citizen join the committee in their endeavors to show the world that we have brainy, talented and skillful artists, poets, and musicians, both men and women in our race. To the thirty men in and around San Francisco and Oakland to whom this day's program has

Millions of visitors attended the exhibits in the Joy Zone, an amusement thoroughfare with more than a hundred concessions, including the popular African Dip. Delilah Beasley endeavored to counter such representations of black people with her journalism about the achievements of African Americans. (San Francisco History Center, San Francisco Public Library)

been entrusted (in the main), do your full duty. This is a service you owe the race," the *Sunshine* reported.[68]

But Negro Day did not occur. The *Sunshine*, which had posed the query in the first place, never published any readers' responses to its question about holding a Negro Day. Maybe they received too few to discuss in the pages of the paper. Most likely, it was too late to organize the event, as the Afro-American League posited. Special days happened with much fanfare, but, as the *Sunshine* warned, they required "elaborate preparation and expense." Black leaders had difficulty mustering the funds and the enthusiasm that Negro Day demanded, and they faced considerable objections to the idea.[69] The editors of the *Western Outlook* were against it from the outset: "We can enjoy any day, county, State, or national, but let us taboo Negro Day. We don't want it, don't need it, and should not allow ourselves to be used like a set of 'dummies.'"[70] As Abigail Markwyn shows, a range of organizations across the state, including the Northern California Branch of the NAACP and the Interdenominational Ministerial Union of Los Angeles, voted in opposition to the idea.[71] Among PPIE planners, Negro Day was never a priority. African Americans had little influence with fair officials, and, unlike other groups (including Chinese and Irish), they were unable to attract attention from organizers, sponsors, or politicians for their efforts to claim the fair as their own.

By May, plans for Negro Day had been abandoned and a new avenue for black participation emerged. This time, it was not a race-specific day but a matter of civic pride. African Americans decided that Alameda County Day's centerpiece "industrial parade" was a more appropriate venue for demonstrating their contributions to the county and state. Since Oakland was Alameda's county seat and the home of a large African American population, support for the idea came largely from the city's many black organizations. Black women took the lead, immediately organizing a forum to discuss the new event, which was planned for June 10. Myra V. Simmons, the president of the Civic Center, a black women's club, called a meeting at Oakland's Cooper Zion Church on Campbell Street to decide the matter. The Afro-American League supported the idea of participating in Alameda County Day: "Now, to our mind we could, with a degree of pride go right into this day's festivities with all our might as loyal citizens of Alameda County, not as Negroes or any other race, but as citizens, march together, ride together, sing if necessary together, and still be citizens of the county." Some believed that attending Alameda County Day might impress on fairgoers that African Americans considered themselves citizens, even though they might not be treated as such by others. Indeed, participation would demonstrate the rightful place of black people in the state. "So we are quite in favor of just as many of our colored citizens turning out on Alameda Day," announced the *Sunshine*, "and show to our visitors that this is our Fair and our State."[72]

Black women enthusiastically embraced the Afro-American League's plan to claim the fair and the state; in fact they had initiated it. Despite a forceful call to action in the black press and the forum, the only organizations that participated in Alameda County Day were black women's clubs, including the Colored Civic Center, which commissioned a decorated car that could hold fifty women. The other organizations that pledged to enter the parade were the Fannie Jackson Coppin Club and the Household of Ruth, both of which, like the Civic Center, were black women's clubs. Planning proceeded at a frenzied pace: a committee formed, choirs rehearsed, children decorated floats, and all fraternal organizations and political clubs were encouraged to march or ride in the parade. Indeed, members of the organizing committee framed participation as a responsibility that African Americans should embrace as a matter of race pride. James Hackett, chair of the general committee, said that he considered it "the duty of every colored resident to rally at this time." Clearly, women in the Civic Center and the other clubs saw participation in the parade as an extension of their activism on behalf of the race. Prior to the fair, the Civic Center had taken center stage in a protest against the dismal conditions faced by African American prisoners at San Quentin; the club also led the way in the fight against *The Clansman*.[73]

The "industrial parade" on Alameda County Day began at 10 a.m. sharp on June 10 at the San Francisco Ferry Building; it then proceeded along Market Street through the center of the city to Van Ness Avenue, which led to the eastern gates of the fair at the Joy Zone. Marching down Market Street, a favorite large boulevard for city parades, meant parading before thousands of spectators; it also meant spectators could watch for free without paying admission to the PPIE. Once inside the fairgrounds, the parade moved through the Joy Zone, past the African Dip, and down the Avenue of Progress, eventually finishing at the band concourse.[74] The event drew hordes of spectators, and if the *Sunshine* accurately assessed the extent of African American participation, it was sizable. "Everybody shut up shop and [got] themselves across the channel to the big Exposition grounds."[75] Indeed, the *San Francisco Chronicle* claimed that the parade was "a revelation," one of the best parades of the fair since its opening in February. The official PPIE band led the parade, and white women of the Grand Army of the Republic marched behind it. Lavishly decorated floats dominated the day. Everyone praised the entries from San Leandro, which were covered in cherry blossoms and "ripe cherries the size of plums."[76] Black women's clubs had their own plan to impress the crowd. Two floats sponsored by the Colored Women's Clubs, including one overflowing with seventy-five uniformed schoolchildren waving U.S. flags and California Bear flags, carried African Americans across the city and through the fairgrounds. The Fannie J. Coppin Club and the Household of Ruth Club contributed to the Civic Center's children's fund so that youngsters could participate and parents would not have to pay for any decorations or expenses for the car, "as the parents will have other expenses in connection with the children," such as flags and patriotic outfits.[77] The other float was a decorated car carrying fifty clubwomen who held Japanese parasols.

Parades have, historically, marked critical moments in the struggle for African American freedom. In the nineteenth century, they became an important form of cultural and political expression. The significance of the shift from antebellum festivals like Election Day and Pinkster—places for African Americans, free and slave, to socialize among themselves—to public parades in northern and western cities had important implications for women.[78] One scholar argues that "the transformation from festival to parade narrowed the public role of African American women" in the nineteenth century.[79] Clearly, the twentieth century saw a reversal of this trend. Bay Area clubwomen who marched at the PPIE joined the ranks of other black women who, in the first decades of the new century, participated in parades and claimed the streets for themselves. African American women drew from their experiences in the women's suffrage movement, where they also occupied public spaces, organized petitions and parades, and raised questions of citizenship.[80] Taking up space at the PPIE, black women challenged the very authorities who had denied them jobs, exhibit space, and representation on the governing boards.[81]

Black women who organized the Alameda County Day parade had a surprise on their float of schoolchildren, about which most white spectators knew nothing. Earlier that year, PPIE officials and the *San Francisco Call* newspaper had announced a contest to name the fair. Unbeknownst to them, of the thirteen thousand entries, an African American schoolgirl, Virginia Stephens, had won the contest with her submission, Jewel City. The committee, made up of dignitaries and Mayor James Rolph Jr., learned that Stephens was African American hours after they made the selection. They chose not to advertise the fact. The *Crisis* reported the incident this way: "when it was discovered that Miss Stephens had colored blood, there was a sudden silence on the part of the press and the only recognition ever given her was a season ticket to the grounds."[82] The Civic Center and other black women's clubs decided there could be no better way to enforce the message of black equality than to celebrate the winner by presenting her on the float of schoolchildren. Stephens stood proudly under a showy banner that declared her an American. Members of the Afro-American League put it thusly: "As very few of our white friends knew that Miss Stephens was colored, the clubs took this means to inform the public by a large banner of her presence in the float of her nationality. . . . It was indeed a great day for our county and especially our people."[83] The Oakland Bournemouth Circle Club held a Jewel City Ball, where Virginia Stephens received a gold necklace and a bouquet of roses. One scholar calls Virginia Stephens "the child who had the most profound effect on the Exposition." Stephen's influence in the state did not end with the fair; she went on to attend Boalt Law School at the University of California, Berkeley, and became the first African American woman to be admitted to the California bar.[84]

African American women seized on the fair and its very public—and newsworthy—opportunities to draw conspicuous attention to patriotic black citizenry. Doing so through the spectacle of children is unsurprising given that gender constructions of the time associated women with domesticity and mothering in particular. By featuring children on the float along with Virginia Stephens riding in state, black women merged the politics of family and respectability with the tropes of nationalism and patriotism. The day's gender norms dictated that their patriotism be expressed in ways compatible with home and family. Pressure from male contemporaries could also have influenced the ways black women expressed their politics. For while the male editors of the *Sunshine* and other black men praised the clubwomen's entries in the parade, many still clung tightly to prescribed roles for women. A few months after the parade, an editorial about women in business claimed that while women may have been helpful in years past (washing and ironing in the days after the Civil War), black men in business were currently receiving little to no help from their wives and mothers. "Our girls are not now prepared to go into business. They do not understand the conditions of the game."[85] Coming as it did in the wake of the women's intervention in the parade, this remark indicates how intensely men monitored the boundaries between public and private as women worked to blur those boundaries.

Delilah Beasley understood, as all clubwomen did, that notions of black womanhood framed all of their social and political work; after all, the NACW had formed in response to a white editor's claim that black women "were devoid of virtue." As historian Michele Mitchell notes, the "turn towards domesticity" in this era was "a surrogate for electoral politics in [the] quest for self determination."[86] The presence of scores of children atop flowery floats signaled a refutation of eugenicists' claims that African Americans were incapable of "healthy" reproduction and bred deficient racial stock. Du Bois attempted to counter these claims himself by publishing an annual

"Children's Issue" of the *Crisis* filled with photographs of healthy black children. In addition, the most popular fund-raiser in the NAACP's early years was the baby contest.[87] While the fact that Virginia Stephens won the contest to name the fairgrounds could not have been planned, the fact that clubwomen filled their floats with children indicates political strategy and intentionality.

Though a record number of spectators witnessed Alameda County Day, the *San Francisco Chronicle*'s extensive coverage of the parade included not one mention of African American participation.[88] Instead, the paper ran a front-page photo of a float from the California Cotton Mill Company, whose enormous banner read "Cotton Is King." For black men and women only a generation or two removed from slavery, a reference to King Cotton would not conjure up happy memories. It would be up to Delilah Beasley to emphasize black involvement in the parade and at the fair and to interpret its significance. She would point to a different history and memory—that of black citizenship, domesticity, and patriotism.

Delilah Beasley's Campaign

Hired by the *Oakland Sunshine* as a special feature writer in June 1915, Delilah Beasley championed African American participation in Alameda County Day. She reminded readers that black people's presence in previous civic parades had rattled more than a few members of the Bay Area's elite.[89] "There was a time," she wrote, "when the mere mention of the colored people to even want to participate in a Fourth of July celebration with the white people called forth some very harsh criticism from one of the largest papers in San Francisco."[90] Referring to the *Chronicle* and its legendary disdain for African Americans, Beasley set out to counter this hostility. For her, the Alameda County Day parade signified nothing short of an intervention in white people's inclination to lay exclusive claim not just to the county, but to the state, the nation, and patriotism. In her columns, Beasley not only reminded readers of the fair's patriotic possibilities but provided the history of the long and devoted service of African Americans to the nation and the state.[91] While she was not the first African American to utilize fairs as opportunities to interpret the role of black America in the nation at large, Beasley interpreted race and nation in a different and quite specific context: this fair occurred during a world war, after thousands of black women in California and other western states had earned the right to vote, on the eve of national women's suffrage, and shortly after the opening of *The Clansman* and *The Birth of a Nation*. For many black women, the convergence of these events marked the onset of a new role in American public life. As the war years pushed the black elite to confront what democracy meant at home and abroad, women found a new language to critique the nation's horrific treatment of black Americans. The juxtaposition of the *Birth of a Nation* and the PPIE became Beasley's vehicle to address her lifelong passions of civil rights and history.

Beasley's first special feature about the fair, published on June 26, was titled simply "Colored Race at the Exposition." It began by directing readers to an earlier concern and campaign: the staging of *The Birth of a Nation* in California theaters. Beasley had written repeatedly, as had her Los Angeles counterpart, Charlotta Bass, editor of the *California Eagle*, to encourage black Californians to protest and, if possible, ban the performances of both the play and the film. She reported that while the film was enjoying a "return engagement" in San Francisco, "we as a people will have to grit our teeth and ignore [it]." But she did not feel that protests against the film by black Californians had been in vain; in fact, she believed "and not without a reason" that the invitations to African Americans to participate in Alameda County Day was as a direct result of their protests. According to Beasley, black resistance to the demeaning stereotypes of *The Birth of a Nation* had paid off; the state's elite, as represented by the fair's organizers, had taken heed of black Californians and their numbers if not their political presence. As far as Beasley was concerned, "the mere fact that colored children marched through the streets of San Francisco, carrying the Stars and Stripes, showed a decided advance and change of feeling toward the colored race in these parts."[92] What may have looked like a cavalcade of cherry blossoms to some people, to Beasley signaled a reinscribing of the rights of citizenship. This may have been wishful thinking on her part. Black participation in the parade could also be interpreted as an appeasement strategy: the city continued to show *The Birth of a Nation* and gave African Americans a float or two in the parade to appease them. Beasley's desire to encourage African American activism on all fronts, and her belief in the efficacy of that activism, could lead her to overestimate the positive outcomes of black protest.

But Beasley's initial report of the fair—and her account of the parade—ended on a less than positive note: the acknowledgment that in its appropriations for the PPIE, the U.S. Congress "adjourned without voting an appropriation for a colored exhibit and building." In spite of the fact that

Congress had appropriated money earlier for the Negro exhibit at the 1900 Paris exposition, money was not forthcoming for one at this fair. Putting a positive spin on this negation of African American contributions to arts and industry proved difficult for the journalist. "We often say we have no building, no exhibits," she wrote. Arguing that this fact should pose no impediment to black participation, she continued: "I often make the remark that Old Glory is good enough for me." According to Beasley, attending the fair under the patriotic symbol of the flag should suffice. Stating that the Stars and Stripes flew at the fair and that they would "protect negro exhibits," Beasley tried, rather awkwardly, to encourage black Californians to claim patriotism at the fairgrounds as their own.[93]

The headline of Beasley's next article and that paper's lead editorial, "Negro Under The American Flag At the PPIE," helped to drive her point home. This piece details some of the cultural and industrial exhibits highlighting African American contributions. In the Palace of Education and Social Economy, a display of black colleges and universities impressed visitors, she reported. Similar to the photos of like institutions compiled by Du Bois for the Paris exposition, these images brimmed with "proof" of black achievement. This type of presentation likely was nonthreatening to the mostly white audience of the fair, since black men and women were safely contained in the segregated spaces of "colored colleges," of which there were none in California. The same building housed an exhibit that "showed the progress of the race from the cotton fields to a clinic of negro doctors and nurses in a colored hospital." Beasley found these exhibits "splendid" probably because they proved to be the places where the history and contributions of African Americans were made visible. The article included lengthy descriptions of the art of expatriate Henry O. Tanner, a favorite in France and a world-renowned painter whose *Christ in the House of Lazarus* was exhibited at the PPIE's Palace of Fine Arts, winning a gold medal. But Beasley's glowing account of Tanner's work was not without a blunt observation of U.S. racism; even after graduating from Harvard, she wrote, "because of the one drop of negro blood in his veins," Tanner never received the recognition he deserved in the United States, whereas in France, "the great artists of the world readily recognized his ability."[94] Still, the fact that his painting was displayed in the Palace of Fine Arts proved a source of great pride to many black fairgoers.

Beasley also commented on what might be described as the domestic arts at the fair. Her elaborate description of Margaret Hatton's Persian cats, for which Hatton received first prize and a "handsome silver cup," seemed designed not only to inspire race pride but also to draw attention to a most domestic pursuit: breeding domestic pets. Her report about the "two colored people living in Oakland" who invented a fruit juicer—which was displayed in the Palace of Food Products and which supplied all the fruit juice consumed at the fair—conjures images not only of California's abundant produce but also the domestic and normative scene of a happy heterosexual couple.[95] The celebration of the domestic was part of Beasley's goal to showcase the civilized heights achieved by African Americans.

Following these glowing reviews, Beasley returned to her other pressing concern: protests of *The Birth of a Nation*. Indeed, as her reports make clear, she saw these campaigns as one and the same and used her coverage of black accomplishments to counter the degrading portrayals of African Americans on the stage and screen. In her September 4 column, she reviewed at length an August 26 benefit concert, held at Hamilton Auditorium in Oakland, in protest of the play and film. "The object of the concert was to change public opinion from the damaging effect of *The Clansman*." Beasley reported that a choir of the finest singers from around the Bay Area sang a series of hymns, folk songs, and spirituals. The chorus closed with a song that had become the theme song of the exposition, "I Love You, California." Written just two years before the PPIE, the song was played aboard the SS *Ancon*, the first merchant ship to pass through the Panama Canal (whose opening was the occasion for the exposition); it is still the California state song. Beasley noted the opportunity to demonstrate patriotism at the benefit concert with a song: "It required a genius to be able to write such a clever little verse just at the right time."[96] This remark praising a love song to the state seems at odds with the treatment black people were receiving in California. Beasley's insistence on claiming the symbols of state and nation in spite of the pervasive antiblack sentiment and unjust policies could be read as naive. Beasley's embrace of the state, no doubt, was informed by her keen awareness of the conditions across the South, where black Americans faced dangerous reprisals for such protests. Whether naive or not, this embrace of state and nation was consistent; it marked the strategy she used to counter eugenicist claims of the unfit nature of African Americans.

When the lights went out on the Jewel City and the fair closed, what had black Californians gained in 1915? Dixon's play and Griffith's film had continued to show during the exposition. In fact, D. W. Griffith proceeded with his plans to distribute the film nationwide, where it enjoyed tremendous success. Had black people benefited from the fair in any tangible ways? Many called attention to the fair's few measurable benefits and its numerous detrimental effects. At least one scholar has pointed to the PPIE as a marker for job cuts for Bay Area African Americans.[97] Even the *Sunshine*, the standard bearer of the Afro-American League, expressed bitter disappointment: "The great Panama-Pacific fair is over. The radiant lights are out. The sparkling and rippling fountains have ceased to pour forth. . . . The Negro had not one day of his own and no building, etc, and derived but very little benefit outside of a few minor jobs as maids and helpers. The management did not solicit very largely of Negro product. The Hampton Quartet sang a few weeks, but our local promoters were not given any financial aid to put on a single production."[98] Perhaps part of this disappointment stemmed from the vanquished hope that a Negro building would have made a difference or that a greater presence at the fair would have signaled greater respect for black Californians. In the fair's closing months, in a column headed "What The Sunshine Would Like To See," the paper's editor included in a wish list the following: "Booker T. Washington visit the Fair this year."[99] It was not to be.

Although African Americans in California played marginal roles at the PPIE, black men and women did much to make the fair a messier place to "read race." They raised the ugly specter of Jim Crow in public discussions of Negro Day, commandeered considerable public and civic space during Alameda County Day, buttonholed fair organizers, and, upended notions of racial progress and race betterment during the naming contest. Never as simple as the charts in the Race Betterment booths, the meanings of race and segregation were contested daily in California's press and shaped in streets, universities, and parades. Thousands of African Americans living in California saw the PPIE as a chance to reinscribe racial hierarchies and challenge the tenets of Jim Crow at the same time as their rights were mocked in the theater and on film. Staging race happens on and off the stage, as Beasley understood so well.

The fair provided its millions of visitors, including African Americans, a world of information—and disinformation—about the country's black citizens. Though some of the sites, lectures, and exhibits reflected a deep commitment to racial hierarchies and white supremacy—especially the native villages, the African Dip, and the Race Betterment booths in the education building—other messages about race and black people were on offer at the PPIE. Visitors could learn about black colleges and universities, sample the musical expertise of a number of ensembles, and witness the power and tenacity of black women's clubs as they paraded through the fairgrounds. The presence of African Americans at the fair, as visitors and presenters, as Mabel Wilson explains, ruptured "the nation's narrative of freedom, liberty, and equality."[100] Delilah Beasley hoped the parade and exhibits of African American accomplishments would convince nonblack fairgoers that African Americans deserved the same respect due all the nation's citizens.

As memories of the fair faded—and with it an opportunity to alter notions about African Americans—Beasley turned her attention and considerable skills as a reporter and researcher to a much broader project, one that would have a lasting legacy: a history of black Californians. Four years after the fair's lights were extinguished, she self-published her most ambitious work, *The Negro Trail Blazers of California*. A former history student at the University of California, Beasley conducted oral histories with African American pioneers, combed the archives of the university's Bancroft Library, and queried scores of archivists in her quest to document the story of black Californians. The book could explore in greater depth than newspaper articles could the accomplishments of black men and women; Beasley included copious material about antiblack sentiment, Jim Crow laws, and white supremacy in the state. She paid particular attention to the way black Californians were subject to unjust laws, including the Fugitive Slave Law of 1852 and the anti-testimony law; and the establishment of the state's NAACP branches received serious treatment in the text. Indeed, Beasley records verbatim the most momentous court decisions in the state's black history up to that point. Beasley utilized folklore and oral sources to record the history of black westerners, interviewing farmers, teachers, soldiers, and former slaves, practicing new modes of social and public history before the history profession welcomed such efforts.[101]

The Negro Trail Blazers of California was the first published study to chronicle the lives of black Californians. Beasley informs readers in her preface to the book that it took her "eight years and six months to the very day" to complete the three-hundred-page narrative.[102] The results garnered both praise and skepticism, partly due to the combination of hard data—facts and figures about African Americans—with folklore and memory. Reviewing the book for the *Grizzley Bear*, the University of California–Berkeley historian Charles E. Chapman admits that "if one were looking for flaws, they could find them in this volume. But the present reviewer prefers to pass over these occasional slips and lay most emphasis on the solid merit of the book." The reviewer made much of the fact that Beasley performed a valuable service not only to black people in California but also to African Americans across the country: "She has given them a tradition that few realized they had the right to possess." Chapman encouraged every library in the state and any private collector who "makes any pretense of all round adequacy" to purchase the volume.[103]

Carter G. Woodson, the patriarch of African American history at the time, was not as kind a reviewer as Chapman, who had helped Beasley locate sources on Spanish California. In his review in the *Journal of Negro History*, Woodson took no notice of Beasley's remarkable detective work tracking down archival material and locating black settlers to interview.[104] Clearly disappointed with her suitability as a representative of the race, Woodson felt that as the standard-bearer of black history, he was duty-bound to be a gatekeeper. In a judgmental tone, he criticized her methodology, the organization of the book, its style, and her poor grammar. "[I] must regret that the author did not write the work under the direction of someone grounded in English composition," he quipped. He only grudgingly admitted that the work was extensive: "there is something about almost everything." Like other historians working on the margins of the new "scientific" methods, Beasley had found a voice—a more popular style—that she felt, perhaps, would be more readable, much like her columns. Woodson's most damning criticism was for that new voice: "Judged from the point of view of the scientific investigator, the work is neither a popular nor a documented account."[105]

Beasley's career trajectory as a journalist and historian brought physical and financial challenges. Despite the exposure her book received in the black press, marketing the volume in the 1920s proved arduous. To publish it, she had relied on the help of white friends and benefactors including Francis B. and Elizabeth Loomis.[106] Francis B. Loomis, the general manager of the *Oakland Tribune*, had been responsible for securing Beasley her job at the paper, and they remained friends throughout her life. When Beasley traveled throughout the state on a book tour, she wrote to the Loomises to keep them abreast of her successes and disappointments. "Just a line to tell you that I finally completed my tour of the San Joaquin Valley. It was very hot at times. I had splendid success wherever I went and everybody readily subscribed [ordered a book]," she cheerfully reported. But the book tour also took its toll on her health: Beasley had chronic heart trouble and problems with her hearing, and in the middle of this particular tour she had foot surgery, staying for six weeks in the home of the doctor, a personal friend, to recover. She rarely stopped her promotional campaign, however, traveling to over a dozen cities, among them Fresno, Riverside, Bakersfield, San Bernardino, Paso Robles, Santa Cruz, and Salinas. Sales were slow but steady, "Last week I sold 10 copies to the Los Angeles County Library for use [in] the branches," she wrote. Living in Berkeley at the time, Beasley was determined to stay on the road and make enough sales to pay back the Loomises: "decided to stay 2 or 3 weeks longer and perhaps then I can come up in my indebtedness," she wrote.[107] The hardship of touring affected her work and her health and, as Elsa Barkely Brown notes, it tells us a great deal about the lack of support for black female historians.[108]

Beasley's efforts to shape race relations, racial uplift, women's rights, and the nascent civil rights movement spilled across the printed page on a regular basis, beginning in 1923, when she began writing an "Activities Among Negroes" column for the *Oakland Tribune*. In doing so, as Shirley Ann Wilson Moore notes, Beasley became the only African American journalist to have a regular column in a white-owned newspaper.[109] The column was published every Sunday until Beasley's death in 1934. These articles afforded her the opportunity to address a wide range of concerns, and seemed a logical extension of her 1915 PPIE and *Clansman* columns in that same newspaper. In a tradition that would be taken up by Harlem Renaissance novelist Dorothy West in the pages of the *Vineyard Gazette*, Beasley described black life in her community and the nation at large, providing personal and political commentary. While she included news of weddings, births, and funerals in her columns, Beasley also took on difficult issues and conflict. She challenged lawmakers, other newspapers, and often criticized contemporary gender roles. Her role as a reporter gave her access to a wide range of venues—and she made the most of it. In 1925, for example, she covered the meeting of the National League of Women Voters in Richmond, Virginia, and the International Council of Women convention in Washington, D.C.[110] One of the major interventions she made as a journalist took place at the latter, when Beasley attempted to stop white reporters from using the derogatory terms for African Americans that they regularly employed: "darkey," "nigger," and "pickaninny."[111] A supporter of women's expanding role in politics, Beasley reminded readers of women's role in all worldly matters: "The writer does not hesitate to say that the women's work has become a great factor in the world, not only in the efforts for universal peace, but for everything else in the advancement of civilization."[112]

In 1927, the California Conference of Social Workers took place in Oakland. Beasley noted in her column that not one black person spoke at any of the sessions except when the Probation Officer's Association invited a local clubwoman, Mrs. O. M. Ruffin, to a roundtable discussion. Further, Beasley reported that the session, titled "Shall the Married Woman Continue in her Job," answered that question in the negative. This, she noted, did not square with reality for African Americans—black women would find it nearly impossible to quit working when they married, since black men could barely earn a sufficient income to "maintain and rear a family."[113] Beasley continued to use her columns to agitate for racial justice. In the year before she died, she worked to pass a state antilynching bill in 1933, on the eve of the state's most infamous lynching.[114] This effort proved successful and seemed a fitting culmination of a lifelong battle for racial justice.

Sometimes characterized as an accommodationist and ridiculed as an amateur historian, Beasley nevertheless made a significant intervention in the history of black Californians. A firm believer in the doctrines of racial uplift, Beasley tried to rewrite the record of black America, presenting civilized men and respectable women. While her coverage of the PPIE fits squarely in the tradition of those like Booker T. Washington and W. E. B. Du Bois, who championed the accomplishments of African Americans and promoted racial uplift, it also adhered to her broader strategy: countering white supremacy and antiblack sentiment by chronicling the histories of African Americans living and working in the state. Her efforts fit squarely within the tradition of race women who manipulated the dictates of gender conventions to become professionals and then used that position to work toward uplift. *How* Beasley (and her clubwomen) sought to undermine contemporary racial beliefs reveals the limits of uplift ideology—including uplift eugenics—and early twentieth-century ideas of womanhood and race. Beasley was hemmed in by the eugenicist society she lived in; the respectability politics embraced by Beasley and other clubwomen skated dangerously close to eugenicist beliefs about proper breeding and the role of women. As white eugenicists infused the fair with celebrations of empire and dire warnings about the dangers of immigration and interracial marriage, Beasley and other black leaders countered with messages about the collective health, fitness, talents, and bravery of black Americans. The fair's refusal to provide equal employment and representation relegated African

Americans to the sidelines. In the rare moment that black Californians led the parade, they did so in a way that embraced women's domestic, reproductive roles. Was this subversive? Perhaps so. African American women appeared to gain little benefit from the intervention, but seen as a whole, black clubwomen's efforts during the fair and across the state significantly improved the social health and welfare of men, women, and children who called California home.

The fact that black Oaklanders invented the first juicer or that a black schoolgirl won the contest to name the fair may not strike the contemporary reader as transformative, but for some black men and women of the day, the naming of these achievements made a dent in the fair's politics. With a series of columns about a world's fair and a new film, Delilah Beasley encouraged black readers to claim the state as their own and to push back against white supremacy and dangerous representations of black Americans. She criticized state practices when she found the outlook bleak for African Americans. In addition to her columns about the PPIE and *The Clansman*, Beasley would write repeatedly about the all-black colony of Allensworth in the San Joaquin Valley. Her embrace of this town—one that promised a respite from Jim Crow violence and discrimination—signals her awareness of the state's hostility toward African Americans. Along with hundreds of other black Californians, Beasley recommended leaving the towns and cities where black Californians were subjected to the vagaries of racial injustice. Although she never moved to Allensworth, her belief in this all-black town speaks volumes about the success of Jim Crow in her beloved state.

CHAPTER 3

"The Best Proposition Ever Offered to Negroes in the State"

Building an All-Black Town

Joshua Singleton knew a thing or two about living and working in an all-black town. His father, Benjamin "Pap" Singleton, urged thousands of African Americans to leave the South in the 1870s and establish all-black towns in Kansas. Migration to Kansas, according to Benjamin Singleton, would reward African American settlers with land free of the violence and oppression that characterized southern Reconstruction; it would deliver a virtual promised land. Benjamin Singleton's efforts inspired the founding of Nicodemus, the best-known black town in the state, and resulted in another Kansas colony that bore his name. While he did not act alone in these emigration projects, Singleton claimed credit for the Kansas Fever Exodus and the Exodusters: "I am the whole cause of the Kansas immigration"[1] His migration movement sought to "see Black people safe and secure" and encourage African Americans to invest in their own farms, goals that were identical to those his son harbored for California's black town, Allensworth. Benjamin's son Joshua moved from Winfield, Kansas, to Allensworth with his wife, Henrietta, and their three children in 1910 when the colony was just two years old; he became a central figure in the politics and social life of the westernmost all-black town.[2]

In California, Joshua Singleton adapted to his new surroundings the lessons he learned from his father about black political and economic autonomy. He was considered a "New Negro," that is, a child born to former slaves. An avid supporter of W. E. B. Du Bois and the newly formed NAACP, Joshua hoped to avoid in Allensworth the color line problems that haunted African Americans who had migrated west to Kansas. For a time, Allensworth offered the safety and protection the colonists craved. Singleton started a general store (known later as the Allensworth Cash Store) and served as postmaster, justice of the peace, and president of the Progressive Society in the small community. The Singleton store sold colonists "everything from soup to nuts," according to Joshua's son Henry; "as a matter of fact I think my father sold groceries, clothing, shoes, even suits."[3] Joshua ran the store until the Great Depression.[4] The town used his building (which housed the post office and the store) as a central meeting place to discuss farming, politics, and local news. Along with a handful of other pioneers, he helped create a town that modeled black self-sufficiency: the African American inhabitants opened churches, a library, and a school.

Henrietta Vera Singleton worked as the town's midwife and nurse, delivering babies and tending to the sick. "She knew a thousand different remedies" and regularly sent away for herbs like goldenseal, asafetida, and licorice root to heal the townspeople, according to her son.[5] This dual role of midwife and nurse, so common in black communities in the South, earned Henrietta the respect of other colonists, if not a significant income. Like other women in Allensworth, she helped sustain the community in meaningful and tangible ways. Women established and maintained many of the central institutions of the town including the school and the library and provided vital social services such as health care, many of which were segregated or simply unavailable to black Californians.

The draw of a black town in California was powerful for the Singletons. For three generations, from Reconstruction to the Great Depression, the family cherished the idea of a self-sustaining all-black community. "I'll tell you one thing," said Henry in the 1970s, "that my experience in Allensworth has meant a whole lot to me all my life because there was a great, great unity among us people. And they had a purpose"[6] Henry's grandfather Benjamin had also believed in racial unity, the founding principal of his short-lived organization, the United Colored Links.[7] Racial betterment through racial pride formed a core principal of the Singleton family and many of Allensworth's initial settlers.

Not all of Henry's memories celebrate the colony, however. "It's a shame that actually there was some little exploitation going on there . . . that land at Allensworth was, to tell you the truth, alkaline packed," he remembered. Like his father and grandfather, Henry knew that Jim Crow haunted black towns; it was a part of their reason for being, and it clung to the histories and the outskirts of each community. His family told stories about the ways black men and women had been cheated out of resources and out of the right to earn a living. Indeed, the initial settlers had been swindled: as we see in this chapter, land that had been advertised as some of the richest farmland in America was in fact not arable without plenty of water to irrigate, and the water that was advertised in initial promotions would dry up and become contaminated with alkaline. Allensworth became a sanctuary for black Californians, but only briefly. What was meant to be a place of belonging was, for some, a mirage.

The dreams that African Americans brought to California from points east, north, and south evaporated for many as soon as they settled in Pasadena or Oakland or San Diego in the early twentieth century. Job opportunities were few, and segregation informed most areas of life in the Golden State. Some areas of the state did offer more possibilities for housing, education, and employment than towns in Mississippi or Louisiana. But many black migrants to California compared their expectations of the state with what they found on arrival and were profoundly disappointed. Allensworth offered many migrants a second chance, a final migration to a town that promised to live up to the dream. Having already been thwarted in other parts of the state, the black men and women who founded Allensworth strove to make the community self-sufficient and independent. The experiences of individual residents were shaped by age, class, gender, political persuasion, and the hopes and disappointments they carried into the town.

In the southwest corner of Tulare County in the San Joaquin Valley between Fresno and Bakersfield, Allensworth was incorporated in 1908. It was the best known of several black towns in California and the only self-governing one.[8] The initial settlers established their community on land adjacent to some of the most valuable real estate in the United States, in the middle of the nation's fruit bowl. Modeled on the Oklahoma all-black town of Boley, the site was the brainchild of Lt. Col. Allen Allensworth, an ex-slave from Kentucky who became a chaplain of the Twenty-Fourth Infantry of the U.S. Army. The community supported upward of three hundred families during its heyday in the decades before the Great Depression; its rise and fall follows the state's economy, the rise of agribusiness, and the politics of land and water that came to dominate the state. Allensworth is the only black town in the country to be preserved as a state park. After the colony ceased to be self-sustaining, black Californians refused to let it fade from the public imagination; it is through their efforts that the history and memory of the state's most successful all-black town has survived.

The stories told about Allensworth range from triumphant to apocryphal. Sometimes it is a hopeful history about a thriving experiment in black nationalism, an example of one way for hundreds of African Americans to opt out of Jim Crow. The story, as told by former residents, is also one about the raw deal black people were dealt in a state that promised a better life. It is a particularly western narrative involving Buffalo Soldiers, railroads, water sources, and land speculation; it is a narrative rooted in black history and linked to the South. Like the Exodusters, these settlers fled southern-style segregation, although many came from Los Angeles. Like other migrants, colonists in Allensworth eventually found that leaving segregation behind proved impossible. Racial segregation and discrimination played a part in every era of the town's history from its founding to its slow decline. Most black towns disappeared because they could not survive the disappearance of the railroad or the disappearance of water sources; Allensworth suffered both losses.[9] While access to water and railroads could be interpreted as issues that have little to do with race, there is no doubt that access to these was determined by the fact that the colony was founded by and for African Americans. Joshua Singleton maintained that the original settlers of Allensworth were the victims of a racist scam; they were sold land that would never have enough water.[10]

Gender determined much about how the town was promoted and how it functioned. Advertised initially as a home for retired Buffalo Soldiers, Allensworth (both the town and the founder) celebrated masculine ingenuity and initiative. In the daily life of the colony, however, gender proved to be more flexible. Freed from the constraints of traditional gender roles of long established black communities, men and women were able to reenvision the tasks assigned by gender: women taught but also farmed, served as postmasters, and played central roles in the most important institutions and businesses of the town, including churches, boardinghouses, and the library. Black towns were sites where ideas about what black people and black bodies could be and do could be reimagined and reconfigured. This had particular significance for women. As one female resident made plain, even the idea of beauty would be rethought in Allensworth: "it is here that we are not overshadowed by the presence of beautiful white women and handsome white men, in such overwhelming numbers that we see no beauty in ourselves."[11] The possibility of being independent in mind and body—to see the beauty in themselves—inspired black women to build a community in Tulare County. What they created shows us that race women, not just race men, had a vision for what freedom should look like; it was a vision that entailed economic self-sufficiency, education, philanthropy, and gender parity.

Exodusters in the Golden State

Where water flows in California's Central Valley—which encompasses nineteen counties and stretches over 400 miles long north to south—it is an agricultural Eden supplying over half of the nation's nuts, fruits, and vegetables. Today, however, Allensworth is a dry and dusty place. The colony is miles from any sizable town, and while there are still dairy farms nearby, the area remains sparsely populated compared to the rest of the state. What would bring African Americans to such a desolate place? To understand its attraction and appeal for black settlers, one needs to imagine the limits California had presented to the founders of the colony in the early twentieth century. The difficulty of finding work, education, and political autonomy in the rest of the nation made the creation of an all-black community an imperative. The founders of Allensworth hoped and believed they would leave the dangers and restrictions of Jim Crow behind and that their salvation lay in separation from the white population. Unlike Benjamin Singleton's followers and the Exodusters, the founding families of Allensworth migrated from elsewhere in the West, having left southern violence, segregation, and disfranchisement decades earlier. None of the original group of settlers came from the South. In essence, Allensworth's settlers constituted a second wave of Exodusters and a second generation of migrants.[12]

The connections between the Kansas migrants and the founders of Allensworth did not begin and end with the Singletons. Oscar Overr's grandparents "had come out of the South with a group that migrated to Kansas" and, like many Exodusters, felt dissatisfied with the new home that had been sold as a haven from southern oppression.[13] Overr's grandfather left Kansas in search of a better life, working as a cook on a wagon train headed to California. Oscar Overr's mother, Ruby William's grandmother, followed through on her promise in 1906 and moved part of her family to the southern California town of Pasadena, where orange trees covered the hills and valleys. Along with its beauty, Pasadena harbored its own forms of Jim Crow and would soon be engulfed in a fifty-year dispute over segregation at the public pool. Employment opportunities for Oscar and his siblings proved limited at best. Before his niece Ruby arrived in 1930 and likened the town

The uncle of Ruby McKnight Williams, Overr conducted the survey of land that became the colony of Allensworth, which he cofounded. In 1914 he became the first African American in California to be elected as justice of the peace. He described the colony as "the best proposition offered to Negroes in the state." (Courtesy of California State Parks, 2019)

to Mississippi, Uncle Oscar took one of the only jobs available for African Americans in this wealthy enclave: gardening for the rich people.[14]

Oscar Overr surveyed the site that would become Allensworth to determine whether it would be an appropriate place for a Jim-Crow-free city of black men and women. Overr parlayed his knowledge of landscape into successful investments in the new town of Allensworth. His disappointment with southern California and its restrictions was one of the reasons Overr envisioned the black colony as a salvation. According to historian and journalist Delilah Beasley, he purchased 12 acres as soon as he surveyed the land and made "a handsome margin" when he sold them. Less than a decade after the town's founding in 1908, Overr had realized his dream of independence. He owned 24 acres in the colony and another 640 acres just east of the town. Even more impressive, Overr had irrigation water, four wells, and a pumping station, making it possible to thrive in the San Joaquin Valley. Beasley bragged of his accomplishments in her 1919 *Negro Trail Blazers of California*. Overr's property included "a modern home located on a plat of land consisting of twenty acres" and a bevy of livestock including chickens, turkeys, ducks, and cattle. Beasley made use of Overr to sing the praises of the decade-old town, "He is quite enthusiastic concerning Allensworth, and, when asked for an opinion, replied: 'It has passed the experimental and pioneering period, and, while it is still in its infancy, for many reasons, it is the best proposition offered to Negroes in the State.'"[15] From what Overr had seen in California, in terms of opportunities for African Americans, nothing compared to Allensworth.

Southern California, and Pasadena in particular, served as a recruiting center for the fledging black colony. In the early twentieth century this fast-growing city near Los Angeles drew migrants from across the country seeking better weather, land, and employment. William A. Payne, another key figure in Allensworth history, had settled there in the early part of the century, joining his parents, who had retired in Pasadena.[16] Born in West Virginia, Payne had attended Doane Academy, the preparatory school associated with Denison University in Granville, Ohio. He graduated from Denison in 1906, earning a teaching credential. His wife, Zenobia Jones, studied music at the university. William Payne felt certain he could get a teaching job in Pasadena. But as fellow schoolteacher Ruby Williams found out later, Pasadena did not hire black teachers, forcing Payne to accept a position as a janitor at a bank.[17] Like Overr, Payne left Pasadena for the all-black colony. In Allensworth Payne could pursue his vocation. Payne served as head teacher of the colony's school for ten years, becoming one of the state's most important black educators.

Black towns were not new in 1908.[18] Establishing self-sufficient towns that did not depend on the beneficence of white men and women had been a dream of African Americans since the emigration movement of the nineteenth century.[19] The endemic oppression that characterized post-emancipation life for black men and women inspired a new wave of town building, much of it motivated by the Exodusters. Poll taxes, grandfather clauses, Ku Klux Klan attacks, and Jim Crow laws of every description wrecked freedom's potential all over the country but especially in the South. African Americans with the means to leave such conditions did so, establishing settlements in the Southwest, the Midwest, and West. The exact number of all-black towns is difficult to pin down, but roughly a hundred were established between the early 1800s and the mid-1900s.[20] By 1900, Oklahoma had over thirty such towns, more than any other state.[21] Texas, Iowa, New Mexico, and Michigan also had all-black settlements. Some African Americans, including Benjamin Singleton, established self-sufficient black communities in the former slave states of Alabama, Mississippi, Kentucky, and Tennessee.[22]

The high hopes that migrants brought to the West explain, in part, the founding of Allensworth. For the families of men like Payne and Overr, the Golden State represented the antithesis of southern-style racism. Oscar Overr's grandfather found it magical; William Payne's parents envisioned that same paradise when they moved to California from West Virginia in their retirement. But Overr and Payne — and Allen Allensworth — were less enamored with the Golden State. Their plan to find a Jim Crow–free space started with a dream shattered: California would not be that free place. When this became obvious, these men adopted a particularly western plan: to speculate and plat "unsettled" land. Once Native Americans were removed and Mexican land was seized, new western towns arose through real estate speculation, and Allensworth was no exception.

Up from Slavery

Allen Allensworth's history, much like that of Booker T. Washington's, is the perfect parable of racial uplift.[23] Born a slave in Louisville, Kentucky, in 1842, he was named for the founder of the AME Church, Richard Allen. After several attempts to run away, Allensworth was sold and, like thousands of slaves, sent down river to the infamous slave market in New Orleans, where he was purchased by another Kentuckian. This sale proved fortuitous not only because it returned Allensworth to his home state and familiar territory near Louisville, but it also brought him back to a border state at the onset of the Civil War. This allowed Allensworth the opportunity to have contact with Union troops and communicate his "desire to be free" to an officer. In 1862 he served in the Forty-Fourth Illinois Infantry as a nurse but soon joined the U.S. Navy, working on riverboats for the duration of the war. After the war, he, like Washington, focused on education: he taught at a Freedman's Bureau school and then attended Roger Williams University in Nashville, Tennessee, eventually becoming ordained as a Baptist minister in 1871.[24]

Never averse to self-improvement, the young minister took elocution classes at the National School of Elocution and Oratory in Philadelphia,

This 1898 portrait was taken when Allensworth was a
chaplain in the Twenty-Fourth Infantry Regiment of the
U.S. Army. After his retirement in 1905, Lt. Col. Allensworth
planned a colony modeled after the all-black towns of
Oklahoma. (Courtesy of California State Parks, 2019)

which resulted in a successful lecture tour managed by the William Lecture
Bureau in Boston.[25] Allensworth created a set of five lectures that he delivered across the country.[26] Lecture titles included "Masters of the Situation;
or, the Five Manly Virtues Exemplified," "The Battle of Life and How to
Fight it," and "America."[27] These lectures are infused with Allensworth's
thoughts on racial uplift and serve as a primer on the beliefs of race men

at the end of the nineteenth century. His notions of the responsibilities of manhood resonated well with the rhetoric of contemporary figures like Washington and Theodore Roosevelt.[28]

Active in party politics, Allensworth served as a delegate at large at the 1880 Republican National Convention and in 1884 he represented the Third Congressional District of Kentucky at the convention.[29] Having been selected twice for that role indicates Allensworth's prominence in the world of black politics and in the state as a whole. He was therefore well-positioned for his commission in the U.S. Army as chaplain, which he secured in 1886 after a two-year self-promotion campaign in which he lobbied friends, army personnel, and the president of the United States, Grover Cleveland. In a letter to Cleveland he wrote that his appointment "will give me an opportunity to show, in behalf of the race, that a Negro can be an officer and a gentleman . . . I know, from past association with both Northern and Southern white men, that I can perform the duties . . . without socially embarrassing the officers of the Regiment and the Army."[30] His campaign successful, Allensworth became the chaplain of the Twenty-Fourth Infantry and one of the first black regulars.[31]

Allensworth and the men of the Twenty-Fourth Infantry formed one of the all-black regiments called Buffalo Soldiers. The Twenty-Fourth were sent to Fort Bayard in New Mexico, Fort Harrison in Montana, Fort Douglas in Utah, and Cuba during the Spanish-American War, for which the men of the "fighting Twenty-Fourth" received much praise. During his eighteen years in this infantry, Allensworth covered thousands of miles across the West, working with or displacing Native Americans, Filipinos, Mexicans, and Mormons. Allensworth witnessed the fear of blackness that was exhibited toward members of his regiment. In Salt Lake City, the local paper admitted there was much apprehension about their arrival but that the soldiers had "been on their very good behavior every day."[32] The chaplain took his educational duties seriously and garnered praise for the classes he taught to infantrymen.[33]

Allensworth's military service impressed some members of the African American elite, whereas others were more critical. In 1890, the *Cleveland Gazette* printed the following: "Chaplain Allensworth says the army is the place for intelligent young Afro-Americans. Well, he may be right, but we doubt it. If any reliance at all can be placed in the statements of those already in the army, we would advise both old and young Afro-Americans; especially the intelligent ones, to give the army a wide berth. It is no place for you."[34]

It may have been strategic for Allensworth to champion the military, but as the *Gazette* noted, not all African Americans found it a safe or encouraging environment.[35]

In 1905, Allensworth retired from the U.S. Army as the highest-ranking African American.[36] Retired Lieutenant Colonel Allensworth and his wife, Josephine, whom he had met in Nashville, moved to Los Angeles. The couple must surely have had friends and associates in the western city; by the summer of 1906, the *Los Angeles Herald* described Allensworth as "one of the best known negroes of southern California."[37] The Allensworths led high-profile lives, and the black press never tired of reporting on their whereabouts.[38] Nothing did more to promote Allen Allensworth in print as a charismatic, heroic figure, however, than the publication of Charles Alexander's 1914 biography, *Battles and Victories of Allen Allensworth*. Like Booker T. Washington's *Up from Slavery*, published in 1901, Alexander's book told the story of how a slave overcame adversity and rose to become a leading race man. The author aggressively promoted his book, taking out quarter-page ads in the *California Eagle* and arranging to sell copies through the offices of the paper.[39] Alexander also advertised the book in the *Cleveland Gazette* and the *Indianapolis Freeman*. The four-hundred-page treatise served as a lesson in heroism and, at least according to the author, was a must-have text for young race men: "Colonel Allen Allensworth is one of the heroes of our generation—a strong link in the chain which binds the strenuous present to a fast fading past. While reaching forward to his seventy-third birthday, he is still possessed of a buoyant, youthful spirit, and is ever active in good works for the elevation of his race."[40] Appearing in print only six years after the settlement's founding, the book became central to the town's promotion of itself as a black town.

"Make the Negro Popular": Allensworth's Plan

Building a model town required aggressive recruitment. Colonel Allensworth devoted considerable energy to advertising the colony, traveling the nation to promote the idea of an all-black enclave. His efforts to drum up support for colonization began on the eve of his retirement in the early years of the century.[41] Allensworth had acquired valuable knowledge of the West as a Buffalo Soldier and had made numerous contacts through Baptist organizations and Republican politics. He exploited these networks to reach a vast audience of potential colonists. The slogan for his proposed town, "Make the Negro Popular," captured Allensworth's aspirations for his planned community and suited Washingtonian politics.[42]

Allensworth believed colonization would prove black self-sufficiency and fitness for citizenship. In a 1907 public address, he expressed concern about "the race problem in the Southern States" and proposed a national convention to discuss "the desirability . . . of establishing a purely Negro colony in some part of the United States." The editors at the *Indianapolis Freeman* (who had printed the address) did not find this a particularly original plan or one that would necessarily meet with success: "The community idea is not a new thing, nor is it new to the colored people. It has proven in many instances more theoretical than practical because [they are] founded on too fantastical ideas—sentiment approaching the poetical—which is disillusioned so often by the hard facts of life." The colony was not for everyone, and the *Freeman* editors warned that it may appeal to "those that prefer a society of their own kind."[43] Like many critics of emigration in the nineteenth century, they worried that colonization could lead to enforced segregation and the ultimate expression of Jim Crow. In the antebellum era, black leaders debated the merits of emigration to Canada and the dangers of removing African American citizens from U.S. political life. But settlements within the United States also faced the same risks; isolating African Americans from the systems that kept Jim Crow in place may not be the best way to challenge its foundations.

Criticism of Allensworth's project arose soon after his announcement. From the black newspaper the *Washington Bee* came the most direct response: "Lieutenant Colonel Allensworth, U.S.A., colored, has a movement on foot for the establishment of a Negro Commonwealth in the United States. (It would be one of the worst mistakes that the race could make.)"[44] It is unclear why the editors described the proposed settlement as "the worst mistake," but perhaps they were worried that the colony promoted segregation. The *Indianapolis Freeman*, long a supporter of the colonel's work, seemed fatigued by overexposure to the plan: "Colonel Allensworth should get busy with his colony scheme. Such projects do not need fuss and feathers. It looks like a good thing; somebody will follow. Much advertising in some instances works ruin."[45]

The next year, the colonel got busy: he and Payne recruited other Angelenos to support their cause and in June 1908 they formed the California Colony and Home Promoting Association, setting up office in the San Fernando building on Main Street in Los Angeles.[46] The other partners of the all-black association included Willie H. Peck, an AME minister; J. W. Palmer, a miner formerly from Nevada; and Harvey Mitchell, a real estate developer.[47] The four acquired land in Tulare County on the Santa Fe Railroad line in the southern part of the San Joaquin Valley. The land was about 40 miles north of Bakersfield, 200 miles from Los Angeles, and about 250 miles from San Francisco and Oakland. William O'Bryan's Pacific Farming Company owned the majority of the acreage in this section of the Tule Swamp Region, including the town of Solito, which would become Allensworth. The strategy of developers like O'Bryan involved acquiring land and establishing a simple water system, then enlisting an intermediary group of promoters to handle the actual selling of the plots; along with their land the buyers would purchase a share in the mutual water company.[48] The California Colony and Home Promoting Association was the intermediary. On August 3, 1908, the new association filed the site plan with Tulare County and began to sell plots.

Allensworth sought approval from the national spokesman for racial uplift to advance the plan. In June 1908 he wrote to Booker T. Washington: "I take great pleasure in informing you that I have just completed an organization to be known as the California Home Promoting Association. The object of the Association is to unite with you in creating favorable sentiment for the race."[49] Attempting to align himself with the best-known African American leader was certainly a wise strategy. Washington had visited Los Angeles in 1903, and his support for all-black towns no doubt encouraged the colonel.[50] Allensworth worked to convince Washington that they were united in their goal to gain liberty, if not equality. His final plea read as follows: "We intend to demonstrate to the world that we can *be* and *do*, thus meeting the expectation of our friends, and to encourage our people to develop the best there is in them under the most favorable conditions of mind and body. This we have in California, as you are aware."[51] He assured Washington that African American settlers would "commence with ownership of the public utilities," pointing to the strategy that would prove so elusive. Allensworth had a final request: Could he name the park in the soon-to-be town after the leader of Tuskegee?

The association publicized the plots in venues across the country, including the black press, which had already done a great deal to promote the fledging community. The positive publicity could easily have been the work of Washington, who, by this time, controlled the *New York Age* and influenced countless other black newspapers. The ads, fliers, and handbills created by the Association boasted of the bounty that could be coaxed from the land. "An inexhaustible water supply" would ensure that new settlers could raise the best oranges, grapes, and beets, in the state.[52] In 1910, home building began in earnest, and by year's end thirty families had moved to the colony.[53]

The next year, the *Cleveland Gazette* published an ad for the colony titled "Attention Race Lovers" that read as follows: "This is not a dream but a sober, serious reality: that the sun-kissed fertile valleys of California call to you to come and partake of bounteous offerings. . . . The requirements are so small that it would be criminal on your part to ignore them; the benefits that are derived are beyond your wildest expectations."[54] These early promises contained hints of the town's—and the promoters'—eventual problem. For the colony to flourish, water sources must be constant, if not "inexhaustible." Yet by 1910, only two years after the town's founding, the artesian wells that supplied Allensworth's water had already dried up.

In the early settlement years, however, the promotional efforts paid off and praise for the colony poured in. One of the local papers, the *Daily Tulare Register*, printed the retired colonel's promotional announcement, including its message of racial uplift: "the town . . . is to enable colored people to live in equity with whites and encourages industry and thrift in the race."[55] The plan to "make the Negro popular" charged forward, and Allen Allensworth held up the colony as a model of interracial cooperation. In a letter he wrote to the *New York Age*, he claimed that the town showed "that there are great white friends who are willing to cooperate with us in helping the great masses of our people."[56] The town's black settlers had little choice but to cooperate with white developers, farmers, and shopkeepers. In a few years this "cooperation" went terribly awry and protection from Jim Crow seemed flimsy at best. However, Allensworth's initial dream to "make the Negro popular" continued to attract scores of black settlers eager to escape Jim Crow California.[57]

Living the Dream

Former residents of Allensworth tell conflicting stories of the town's past. For some, California's all-black town brought up memories of a hardscrabble life, of Jim Crow, of disappointment, and of loss. Others remembered the place as one of hope and renewal. Certainly the colony provided some African Americans with a respite from the discrimination and humiliation they experienced elsewhere; for example, Professor Payne could not get work as a teacher in Pasadena, but he flourished in Allensworth. Residents reminisced about the community life, the shared culture of work and play; everyone pitched in and helped one another with little interference from the outside world. As one resident put it, "we never felt deprived.[58] Understanding the town as a place where residents felt betrayed *and* a place where no one felt deprived seems untenable. From the vantage point of the recessions of the 1970s, however, when many former settlers were interviewed, an all-black community between Watts and Oakland that sustained itself for several generations must have seemed idyllic. The catastrophes faded in significance, for some, while others never forgot Pacific Farming's underhanded tactics with the artesian wells or the Santa Fe Railroad's departure in 1914. The conflicting memories remind us that, throughout the twentieth century, black Californians had ample reasons to seek and protect the history and memory of a place that was free of Jim Crow, even if that freedom was short-lived. Whether it was possible for colonists to escape from segregation and racism and thrive in the colony depended on when they migrated to Allensworth, if they farmed or sought other work, how long they stayed, and many other factors. Yet it is not difficult to imagine the attraction of a dynamic, self-sustaining town built and maintained by African Americans at the height of Jim Crow.

Early colonists created a thriving town from the ground up. By 1914 at least 900 acres of land had been "deeded to Negroes with an aggregate value of $12,500." The colony supported a school, library, hotel, barbershop, general store, and post office, and a Baptist church was under construction. Residents grew an abundance of fruits, vegetables, and grains; many made their livelihoods from the dairy business. The *Eagle* took great pride in the community, assuring its readers that there was not "a single white person having anything to do with the affairs of the colony at all."[59] This, of course, was never the case. From the initial dealings with the Pacific Farming Company, most business transactions (except the ones in the local stores, barbershop, and the hotel) involved white people, usually men. The dairy farmers sold their milk to distributors who were white; many colonists like Armilda Archer Smith and Norvell Powell worked in white-owned canneries or as domestic laborers for white people. The dream of living in an "all-black" town never completely materialized because the settlers relied on the national, state, and regional economies that controlled, among other things, the water, the railroad, and local markets.[60]

Yet, in Allensworth's first decade, agricultural successes were many. Rainfall in the Tulare Lake basin was above average between 1906 and 1914.[61] Alfalfa grew like weeds. Charles Alexander, the author of Allen Allensworth's biography, reported that he visited "every farm under cultivation" in spring of 1912 and found every farmer to be "industrious, enterprising, and thrifty." Men and women not only made a living at farming, they excelled at it.[62] Fields filled with wheat, barley, and oats grew chin high, causing Alexander to wax poetic: "The Allensworth people are a cheerful, happy people, and they are on the road to great prosperity."[63] The biographer joined Beasley as one of the greatest promoters of the colony, and other members of the black press chimed in. The *Indianapolis Freeman* even compared the colonel to the brave Puritans: "imbued with the spirit that caused those frail crafts, the *Mayflower* and the *Speedwell*, to tempt that vast expanse, fleeing persecution, this man and his followers thought to erect an asylum where the Negroes might come and enjoy all of the possibilities and responsibilities of citizens."[64]

The dream of owning land was a powerful draw for potential colonists. As former sharecroppers—or the children of former sharecroppers—many African Americans migrated to California with a determination to own property. In spite of the fact that agriculture was becoming the state's most significant economic activity, African Americans made little headway as either farmworkers or farm owners.[65] In the early twentieth century, most black Californians lived in towns and cities, with few settled in rural areas. For the colony to be successful, the promoters had to convince farmers or would-be farmers that the land would yield a living.

In addition to creating a community of farmers, the founders hoped to attract retired Buffalo Soldiers. The town's broadsheet, the *Sentiment Maker*, announced plans to build a Home for Soldier's Families once two hundred soldiers bought lots at a cost of $150 each.[66] A few members of the military did invest in plots, though a retirement home never materialized. Settler Joe Durel remembered Allensworth as a place of Buffalo Soldiers: "everyone who retired from the 24th, 25th Infantry, 9th and 10th Calvary, was over there."[67] Soldiers not only represented potential investors, but they could provide protection should the town require it. According to Henry Singleton, racial tensions in the area prompted the retired colonel to encourage former soldiers to buy plots: "In 1910, when we came to Allensworth, there was a great deal of prejudice against Negroes . . . there was a lot of fear in those days. This particular group of pioneers didn't know how the people in these little white towns were going to react toward them. Allensworth, being an Army man, was interested in having soldiers settle in Allensworth. There were eight or ten sergeants there." Singleton remembered: "Since so many ex-soldiers were here, they formed protective groups. They even went so far as to drill, they had signals so if something happened in the town and we had to get together for protection, they had signals they'd give, and people a mile and a half away would get together. They trained and got real good, but they never once said anything about the little [nearby white] towns—but they were ready." In spite of the military protection—or perhaps because of it—Singleton waxed romantic about the colony: "But the most interesting thing that makes it lovely is that every one of these little towns became extraordinarily friendly to Allensworth. There was never one difficulty, racially."[68] While others remembered the Jim Crow signs posted in nearby towns, Singleton remembers racial harmony. What accounts for the stark differences in such recollections? Henry Singleton might have had a privileged position in the town because his father, Joshua, operated a store; Henry also left when he was a boy and attended high school in Sonoma.[69] It is also the case that, compared to blacks in large towns and cities, black residents of Allensworth *were* better protected from racially motivated harassment and violence. Singleton's adulthood in the Bay Area during the black freedom struggle may have caused him to reflect fondly on the colony. Again, compared to inner-city Oakland in the 1970s (when this interview took place), Allensworth looked idyllic.

After Reconstruction, the options for black men and women to exercise political sovereignty dwindled. Within a few short years after settlement, however, Allensworth residents had elected an African American postmaster, members of the water board, and a justice of the peace, proving that black people could create a self-governing community.[70] The *California Eagle* reported that in June 1914 "the supervisors of the county, recognizing the intellectual abilities of the citizens of the Allensworth colony, created a judicial district, and defined the boundaries thereof, the same as the Allensworth voting precinct and the Allensworth school district." Perhaps the author of this article overstated the case, however, by claiming that the new district demonstrated that Allensworth was "the only community in which Negroes live where Negroes have made any advancement along the material lines."[71] Yet, unlike Los Angeles or San Francisco, Allensworth could be touted as a place where black residents governed, educated, and protected themselves.[72]

Not surprisingly, political sovereignty led to political struggle. In Allens-worth, where African Americans could voice political opinions without fear of dangerous repercussion, debates about the nature of freedom, civil rights, and citizenship formed part of the town's everyday life. Discussions about race politics occurred in the barbershop, over the counter of Singleton's store and post office, and in town meetings held at the schoolhouse. Some residents were disciples of W. E. B. Du Bois and the newly established NAACP, others would become followers of Marcus Garvey, and still oth-ers espoused political philosophies that resisted simple classification. In that sense, the town was a microcosm of black political thought in this era. While retired Colonel Allensworth had solidly aligned himself with Booker T. Washington, pinning down his politics can be tricky. By 1910, the former chaplain was attending a "Back to Africa" meeting in Los Angeles at the Reverend John D. Gordon's Tabernacle Baptist Church.[73] Gordon became a leading member of Garvey's Universal Negro Improvement Association when it organized in 1914. His church in Los Angeles became an important meeting place for local black nationalists.[74] Allen Allenworth's embrace of black nationalism is hardly surprising given his predilection for colonization. Whereas the tendency has been to exaggerate the distance between figures like Washington, Du Bois, and Garvey, a figure like Allensworth borrowed from the philosophies of all three.

Black nationalist ideologies often collided with the material questions of land and water. Joshua Singleton, an avid Du Bois supporter, had heated arguments with Oscar Overr, who was seen as "a company man" of Pacific Farming Company.[75] Even after the debacle with Pacific Farming, Overr worked with that company to set up agricultural demonstrations showing residents what crops could be grown in the town, and he acquired the wood to build Allensworth School from them. This alliance created major dis-agreements within the colony. The conflict between Overr and Singleton represented a central question for all-black colonies: How much or how little should African American colonists associate with white powerbrokers? This question had particular and immediate ramifications for Allensworth pioneers. For men like Overr, the colony's survival depended on coopera-tion with the large landholders who also controlled the water. Singleton felt that this kind of dependency threatened the very foundation of Allensworth and its ability to live free of Jim Crow.

Singleton was just one of the NAACP members in the colony. James Hackett was elected treasurer of the Northern California NAACP branch in 1914, having moved to Allensworth in 1910. "My father was very race conscious," remembered his daughter Sadie, "and that was why, after all his long residence in Alameda, he decided he wanted to go and be a part of [Allensworth]."[76] Hackett's story suggests that the colonists maintained ties to the vibrant political debates and organizations that flourished in black America. Local affiliates of the NAACP and the UNIA made up a significant part of the town's civic culture and these, in turn, connected the colony to wider debates in the world of black politics. The women of Allensworth had their own ideas about democracy, national politics, and how best to achieve racial justice. Before the establishment of the NAACP, the black women's club movement had a strong presence in California and clubwomen brought their organizing expertise to Allensworth. In fact, the NAACP owed much of its structure and philosophy to the National Association of Colored Women.[77] Unfortunately, the record of women's political beliefs—and how they expressed them in the colony—is scant. Alice Royal, author and former colonist, observed that "the political views of the women of Allensworth have not been recorded."[78] To understand the ways women shaped the politics of the community, we have to look to their deeds as well as their words.

What women *did* tells us quite a bit about how they imagined an ideal community and how they understood racial uplift. As Brittany C. Cooper notes, we must pay attention to where and how black women "take up and transform intellectual and physical space" if we are to appreciate the work of race women.[79] Lifting the status of the race in Allensworth meant women labored in all areas of town building, from construction to farming to cloth production to food preservation. Women established community institutions and businesses to provide education, recreation, and economic and physical well-being. They healed the sick and housed people struggling to make ends meet. Several of the most successful businesses in the colony, including the hotel and the boardinghouses, were owned and operated by women and provided food and shelter. It was also important to women to have a voice in how the colony handled the critical questions about governance, water, and land rights. Women attended meetings of the town's governing body, the Allensworth Progressive Association; they organized a Women's Improvement Association; and participated in the decision making that shaped the colony's maintenance and survival.[80]

While a story of great race men dominates official accounts of Allensworth's founding, oral histories tell a different story of the colony's early years.

Women's labor enabled this experiment in black self-sufficiency to flourish. Historian Lonnie Bunch described the gender dynamics this way: "Men worked at pioneering and the women made pioneering work."[81] Women sustained the colony by canning fruit, churning butter, growing vegetables, making clothes, teaching school, and operating businesses. After problems emerged with the soil and water, women often had to find other kinds of work in addition to farming. Sadie Calbert explained that her mother ran a hotel and had a vegetable garden, but "she didn't have too many things there because it was too much alkali there."[82] Given the town's isolation, feeding the townspeople proved more of a challenge than the promotional materials had indicated. Alice Hackett sold produce, canned goods, and bread from her "unofficial grocery store." Alice's daughter Josephine recalled that her mother "became known in the community as a thrifty woman and a good provider. Those less foresighted in their shopping looked to her to supply their needs from time to time." Josephine remembered that "women in the community relied on Mama to supply the needs of their larders."[83] In addition to sustaining the colony through food production and distribution, women provided health care. Like Henry Singleton's mother, Henrietta, Josephine Cowes worked as a midwife. Black midwives frequently attended to the general health of their communities. Medical care of any kind was difficult to obtain because of segregated clinics and hospitals.[84] Most doctors in nearby towns refused to take black patients unless the patient was employed by a white rancher.[85]

The disjuncture between the way the town was represented, one founded and settled by men, and what it was, a town where women had a central if not equal role in the politics and economy, is telling. This is a place where women had autonomy to model racial uplift. All-black towns were places that could demonstrate the suitability of African Americans for economic, social, and political success. A town where women participated in decision making, however, amounted to a community that promoted transgressive gender roles, which could trouble the reputation of the town and its promotion. For this reason, perhaps, we hear little about the necessity of women's labor and their ideas; they were noted by Beasley, herself a club woman, but ignored by many of her contemporaries.

The ostensible founder of the colony, Allen Allensworth, pontificated about women's roles. His sermons prescribed roles for women in keeping with the politics of respectability: women were to be pious, virtuous, obedient, and subservient to men. In San Francisco in 1899 he warned women to "maintain pure and virtuous characters, without which the standard of the race could not be maintained with a degree of dignity which it ought to have as a race."[86] Women of Allensworth, like other race women, worked around these proscriptions as best they could and perhaps had a bit more flexibility to circumvent the restrictions that rigid gender norms imposed. Many married women in the town, including the colonel's wife, Josephine, conducted colony business without their husbands. One of the central leaders of the town, Josephine Allensworth donated her own land for the library and the school. She often spent summers in the settlement with her daughters while her husband worked in Southern California. The colony was also home to many widows and single women. While much has been written about the ways family patterns shaped black migration, the case of Allensworth shows that women made choices to live in the colony based on work, politics, and economics as well as reasons related to kinship.[87]

A variety of formal and informal groups initiated by women shaped the political life and culture of the community. Women organized ice cream socials, chocolate hours, quilting bees, musical entertainments, community celebrations and associations. Pioneers recalled the glee club with particular pride, as it toured the state, bringing the community to the attention of outsiders.[88] During the town's formative years, settlers from a variety of religious affiliations worshipped in the colony. The First Baptist Church began services in March 1916 and served approximately twenty to forty members for the next thirty years, though it never had a resident pastor.[89] The women of Allensworth constituted the leadership of the church, supervising the Sunday school and overseeing daily operations. The Methodists met in the schoolhouse and Seventh Day Adventists gathered at the home of Joshua Singleton.[90] Most weddings, funerals, and graduations took place in the Baptist church, which by all accounts was a beautiful building that served secular as well as sacred purposes.

The school and the library, however, formed the core of social and political culture. Women supplied the land and the labor to establish and maintain these institutions.[91] Josephine Allensworth spearheaded the effort to establish a library, purchasing the building materials with help from Pacific Farming, donating the land, and dedicating the library to her mother's memory.[92] The structure had a wood-burning stove and oil lamps for its patrons and had the capacity to hold 627 books. When it opened in July 1913, the Mary Dickerson Memorial Library held only the colonel's book collection, but soon donations poured in from all over the state. Beasley

Built on land donated by Josephine Allensworth, the Mary Dickerson Memorial Library opened in 1913 and was part of the Tulare County Library system. Books about black history and literature filled the shelves. The library provided rare job opportunities for black female librarians. (Courtesy of California State Parks, 2019)

cataloged these gifts in *Negro Trail Blazers*: "Others of the race have followed [Allensworth's] example, namely a Mrs. S.M. Ballard, of Fresno, giving a set of encyclopedias . . . a Mrs. Green, of North Dakota, a set of books on agriculture; Mr. Jerry Williams, San Francisco, two volumes of [Paul] Dunbar's works."[93] That the library was a branch of the county library system allowed patrons to borrow books from other branches. In her dedication speech, Josephine Allensworth emphasized the significance of women's work: "I appear before you in a dual capacity, that of a daughter to honor the memory of her mother; and that of a citizen to serve the community in which she lives. David prayed that our *daughters* be as *corner stones*, polished after the similitude of a palace. These were the sentiments of my mother and she prayed that I would be a useful woman to the community in which I lived" (original emphasis).[94] In addition to uplifting the race, it is clear that Josephine Allensworth worked for women's concerns;

she actively participated in the black women's club movement and was elected chair of the executive committee of the state's federation of colored women's clubs in 1907.[95] She made her hopes for the library quite clear: "I also desire to make it possible for a worthy young woman to have employment."[96] Beginning with Ethel Hall, black women served as librarians until the library closed in 1943.

Allensworth School opened in 1910 in the former home of the Hackett family, saving children from the humiliation of segregated schools. Here, William Payne strove to give black children the best education they could get in the state. At a cost of $5,000, the colony erected a modern schoolhouse in 1912, sporting a beautiful bell tower; it would be the largest building in the settlement and, by most standards, the most important. Eva Whiting and Margaret Prince, both of Pasadena, became the first teachers in the new building. The town had formed its own school district, with a three-member school board, responsible for hiring personnel, raising funds, and working with the state. Josephine Allensworth, an original member of the school board, had donated a sizable piece of land for the new schoolhouse. Despite the donation, the town of Allensworth outspent their neighboring school districts in every area of education: building, personnel, and equipment.[97] The philanthropy and labor of race women sustained a community of students, thinkers, and teachers for at least two generations.

Twenty-five years after the new school opened, Cornelius Pope, who would become the leader of the movement to preserve the town, attended school there. Pope's parents had moved to the town of Allensworth from another all-black town, Boley, Oklahoma. They arrived during the Great Depression and worked as migrant farmers, initially moving into the original schoolhouse and later into the colonel's house.

Pope's memories underscore the significance of the school for African American children:

> When I came to Allensworth, everyone was Black. It was the first happy school experience I ever had. It made everything altogether different. I even had playmates for the first time in my life. Allensworth was paradise to me. Miss Alwortha Hall welcomed me to the Allensworth School and with open arms and asked, "Learn something for me today." History in school didn't focus on black history. We got enough of it; we had the picture of Colonel Allensworth and Booker T. Washington right up on the wall. There wasn't a day that we didn't pay honor and tribute to the Colonel and Booker T. Washington. The teacher would make reference

The Allensworth School, like the library, was a center of community life. Cornelius "Ed" Pope, who led the campaign to create Colonel Allensworth State Park, attended the school and remembered how his teacher, Alwortha Hall, instilled a sense of black pride in her pupils. (Courtesy of California State Parks, 2019)

to them and sometimes we would look at their pictures, and the teacher would say nice things about them. It was really the first time I'd ever heard nice things said about black people from a historical perspective. And the teacher and the people running the town, the leading people, the business people, were Black, the pictures on the wall of black heroes—it was a black paradise; we couldn't miss it.[98]

Pope's education in Allensworth School instilled a sense of black pride and provided an education he would have been denied outside of the colony. The lessons learned in the two-classroom schoolhouse sustained him. "Once I got into high school and went to an integrated school with white kids and was able to compare what I knew with what they knew, it didn't take me long to find out that I was equal to the very best. I was just as powerful, could think just as good, there was nothing inferior about me. I was pretty hard to stop from there on in."[99]

Decades before Pope attended Allensworth School, the colony attracted statewide attention when residents lobbied to establish a polytechnic school based on the Booker T. Washington model of education. The colonists hoped to acquire state funding for the school but the issue quickly became a referendum on segregation. The plan to start a "Tuskegee of the West" brought forth a hailstorm of protest, becoming a flashpoint in the black press and the Los Angeles chapter of the NAACP. Local supporter and county librarian Bessie Herman Twaddle lobbied state senators and members of the State Board of Education in favor of the school. Speaking for "her colored people," Twaddle assured the politicians that residents of the colony "feel that their young people ought to have vocational training rather than classical education."[100]

The Allensworth School Bill was introduced in the state legislature in January 1915. The new school would not be a place where black men and women trained to fill the nation's professional ranks; the polytechnic institute promised to "fit the students for the non-professional walks of life." Pandering to Washingtonian proponents of manual labor, the bill assured legislators that the school would "at all times contribute to the industrial welfare of the state of California."[101] Some believed that a separate school played right into the hands of segregationists. For over half a century, black Californians and their allies had fought and defeated segregation in the schools. This proposition seemed a backward step in this battle. "[W]e will soon have jim crow schools" worried many members of the Los Angeles Forum, an early civil rights organization in the state.[102] The creation of the school might "make it difficult for Negroes to attend other schools," claimed an editorial in the *Oakland Sunshine*. Although supportive of Booker T. Washington, the *Sunshine* refused to endorse this Washingtonian project. The state's history of Jim Crow, they argued, did not bode well for an all-black school: "Forty years ago Negro children were not allowed to attend any public school with the whites, we hardly see the necessity of borrowing this trouble, as we are sure the whites will construe it to mean separation asked by us. So in view of our peculiar situation here we must oppose all forms of separation."[103] Oakland was not alone in objecting. According to the *Eagle*, 90 percent of African Americans in Pasadena opposed the creation of the polytechnic school.[104] With the *Plessy v. Ferguson* decision not twenty years old, a separate school struck many African Americans as the epitome of consent to the creed that separate was equal.

"Just ask Oklahoma what separate schools will do for you," quipped columnist S. B. Carr in the *Eagle*.[105] That state spent $192 million annually to educate white children and only $16 million on black children; a vote for Allensworth School is a vote for segregated schools and southern-style segregation, he argued. Not to put too fine a point on the issue, Carr also declared that "every one but two" of the lynchings of the previous year (1914) took place in segregated southern states. Building a segregated school was a slippery slope to the worst kind of conditions for black Americans. "We have no such thing as colored schools in California, and if we can only keep the carpet baggers out it will be a long time before we have any," Carr told his readers.[106] The plan to build a Tuskegee of the West had stipulated that the state would provide $50,000 for the land and the construction of the school. In May 1915 the state legislature defeated the bill.

As townspeople and their allies organized support for the Tuskegee of the West, news reached the colony that the retired colonel had been in an "accident" in Monrovia, California, where he worked occasionally as a minister.[107] On September 14, 1914, Allen Allensworth had been crossing the main street in the community near Pasadena when he was struck by two men riding a motorcycle. Rushed to the local hospital, he died the next day from complications related to his fractured skull and broken bones. Neither of the two white men on the motorcycle was arrested, but Josephine Allensworth ordered an investigation into her husband's death. The jury returned an open verdict, meaning no one was charged but the "death was not ruled an accident."[108] The retired colonel was buried in Los Angeles at the Rosedale cemetery; his grandson emphasized that even in death, his grandfather experienced Jim Crow: "well, he was entitled to be buried with military honors in a military plot in Rosedale, but colored couldn't enter into it at the time."[109]

Despite the setbacks presented by the death of Colonel Allensworth, the failed school bill, and the diminishing water supply, promotion of the town continued after World War I. Delilah Beasley devoted herself to the cause in her 1919 *Negro Trail Blazers of California*. The story of an all-black town in her own state showed Beasley's readers that California's African Americans were most enterprising, the overall theme of her book. "While hundreds of race men all over the State are anxious about employment," she wrote, "Allensworth citizens are given all they have to do. Were there a larger population they could secure many contracts." This is followed by biographical sketches of over twenty members of the community, emphasizing upward mobility and entrepreneurial "pioneering" spirit. Mr. Zebedee H. Hinsman, for example, "conducts a general merchandising store. . . . was appointed the notary public of Tulare County . . . [and] places the value of his stock in the general merchandise store at $7,000." Beasley emphasized ambition and racial uplift with every stroke of her pen. She wrote, "When asked for a statement as to his success with so small a beginning, [William H. Wells] replied, 'I am trying to prove to the white man beyond a shadow of a doubt that the negro is capable of self-respect and self-control.'"[110]

But even by 1919, town promoters like Beasley had to overlook some problems to paint the town in a positive light. *Negro Trail Blazers* goes to great lengths to explain how black residents had solved the water problem, although Beasley also addressed rumors to the contrary. "Much has been said about water in Allensworth," Beasley began, then informed her readership that her source of information on the issue was Professor Payne, "a gentleman who has been connected as secretary of the colony from its formation and who ought to know the condition better than any one else." Payne is quoted at length, assuring readers that "the main irrigation system is under the Allensworth Rural Water Company, a State corporation, owned and controlled by negroes, with a capital stock of $45,000 all paid in." Residents of the town, Payne explained, had ample sources of water and storage for "immense quantities of water" in three reservoirs plus a storm and drain system.[111] It could not be better.

"Water Was Worth More than Food"

Water rights became a deep and protracted crisis for the settlers of Allensworth. The three artesian wells Pacific Farming had originally installed not only proved to be inadequate but also only a temporary water supply. When these wells ceased to be viable, the town's inhabitants elected a committee to represent them and threatened legal action. By September 1913, five years after the town's incorporation and after six months of struggling with Pacific Farming, the settlers had acquired the stock of the Allensworth Rural Water Company and the right to develop and control the water supply. Unfortunately, this acquisition was hardly worth fighting for, as Pacific Farming was in the process of defaulting on its taxes. The colonists inherited an antiquated, undercapitalized, and legally shaky water system. The new board of the Allensworth Rural Water Company, forced to raise funds to maintain the water supply, sent a notice to the town's property owners, who were also the stockholders of the water company: "Are you aware of the fact that water is really of more importance in California than land? That land with water rights but little or no water, is almost worthless?" began the plea.[112] In the end, a new property tax was necessary to fund the electricity needed to pump water out of the ground.

Early settlers' oral histories relate the story of the battle for water. Henry Singleton recalled that his father, Joshua, was outraged—but unsurprised—that the town had been cheated: "The venture was a skin game, plain and simple—White men cheating Black men. Pacific Farming did not intend to honor the contract, and the Race could not command the political support to make them do so." Another settler, Anna Hall, thought similarly: "Colonel Allensworth was deceived by some white people who had money enough to start the Colony. After they saw colored people didn't have the necessary money, they abandoned the project."[113] Marjory Towns Patterson, whose whole family "put money into [Allensworth]," recalled that "it was just impossible to make a living" due to the water shortage. Patterson believed that the founders had been swindled by Pacific Farming: "Mother was always saying they were crooked."[114] When interviewed in the 1970s, Josephine Hackett explained: "One issue that was always guaranteed to produce a good fight was the question, 'Who will get the water first?' Because Allensworth developed a water shortage, which persists to this day, the farmers had to take turns irrigating their fields one at a time. Papa usually got his turn at night. . . . Once tempers flared so high that one farmer attacked a neighbor with a pitchfork, thinking the neighbor had robbed him of his turn at the water."[115] Sadie Calbert remembered that "the water situation became increasingly worse and I think that was what proved the death knell of Allensworth, because people who had been raising cotton and raising alfalfa, and you know a lot of people had cows and everything, well, after so many things had dried up well you know there wasn't sufficient, well a cow does have to have plenty of water and green stuff to provide milk."[116] As the water crisis became apparent to residents, their hopes of finding a haven from Jim Crow faded; for some it was a rude awakening.

Conflicts over water came to define the town. Marjory Patterson Towns recalled a number of family feuds over water and claimed that "water was worth more than food." Recalling that neighbors refused to speak to one another, she mused, "I always thought that a place like Allensworth where everybody lost, how long could you hold the hate?" The strain took a toll on the community. For instance, Professor William Payne's neighbors thought that the professor stood to profit from the formation of a water company owned by the town, causing discord. According to Payne's daughter, Elizabeth Payne McGhee, "Allensworth began dying, because people moved away, and people would put in crops and they would go so far, but they need water, and they didn't have it, and sometimes there were terrible quarrels about water rights." These quarrels shaped the memories of Allensworth residents who witnessed these altercations as children. Elizabeth Payne McGhee recalls "one gentleman hitting another in the head with a shovel because it was his turn to have the water, and this other man decided he wanted the irrigation privileges, so they fought. And these things were quite distressing to those of us who were little kids."[117] Looking back fifty or sixty years, many of these interviewees found little to celebrate about the place where they spent their childhoods.

After the failure of the wells, coaxing an agricultural living from the dry, dusty soil in Allensworth became nearly impossible. One colonist, Armilda Archer Smith, remembered that "life for us in Allensworth was hard. There simply was not a developed water system. Productive farming demanded ample irrigation water and we just did not have it. As a result, Dad for the most part worked as a farm laborer, assisted by Mother and all of us children." Despite the difficulties, most residents continued to try to grow some produce. Smith recounted with pride her father's efforts to "cultivate a cash crop," including watermelons, sugar beets, and alfalfa. But farming alone could not sustain the family economy; in addition to farming, Smith's father managed a nearby dairy farm and sold lamps and farm equipment; and her mother picked grapes, had a job in a cannery, and worked as a midwife and domestic. "Well, you know you had to get out to get some money because there was no money in Allensworth."[118] If you were female, getting jobs elsewhere often meant domestic work, as it did for Smith's mother.[119]

Regardless of where they lived in California, African American women had precious few choices for employment in the early twentieth century. Training for a career in education, women like Margaret Prince, who grew up in Pasadena, faced near impossible odds to be hired in the school systems of California. Even with her family connections to the black elite, Prince held out little hope for a teaching job. Interviewed when she was eighty-two years old, she still expressed dismay at the lack of options:

> Occupational choice! No, for me there have never been any options. I was, in fact, privileged to have received even the few job offers presented me. Regrettably the opportunities have always involved separation from my family. The thought even today, brings me sorrow. To many, it might appear to be aimless wandering; however, it was certainly not meandering,

Members of the Towns family in their wagon. Marjory Towns (Patterson) and other settlers who were interviewed in the 1970s remembered the conflicts over water shortages that plagued Allensworth. (Courtesy of California State Parks, 2019)

but rather an effort to secure employment in a society where I could not exercise a choice, even though I was formally educated and well prepared to teach. My occupational pattern, characterized by a number of moves, is like so many other people I met in Allensworth.[120]

Recruited by William Payne in 1914 to teach in Allensworth School, Margaret Prince thought herself lucky to have her first teaching job, despite the low pay—$50 a month after room and board. As she reminded her interviewer, "I, too, had to supplement my income, for some of the same reasons that prompted many other pioneers to find wage labor outside the Colony." Giving piano lessons helped Prince pay for clothes and incidentals, including train tickets home to Pasadena. Perhaps she took some comfort in the fact that her boss and principal, Mr. Payne, also had to supplement his salary and work: "seasonally, he spent his summers in Delano working as a laborer repairing dikes."[121]

The interviews with Armilda Archer Smith and Margaret Prince hint at the fact that while there were at least two classes of settlers, professional and working class, all colonists, even William Payne, "had to get out [of Allensworth] to get money."[122]

For those working in the surrounding towns, Jim Crow met them at every turn. Cannery and domestic work, all segregated labor in Tulare County, provided no respite from oppression or persecution. For those who could remain in the colony, agriculture and animal husbandry offered one route to survival. Dairy farming proved a profitable venture for some, but only for a time. Henry Singleton said that "the milking industry was the only thing that was holding Allensworth [up], and the reason that happened was that we had a sort of communal grazing area. There were no strict regulations in those days . . . the cattle would go together and they'd graze." Having a milk cow helped many families make it through tough times. Josephine Hackett remembered her mother milking the family cow and selling milk to Mexican farm workers and cream to a nearby dairy. The town's location on the Santa Fe Railroad made dairy farming pay, at least in the early years. Colonel Allensworth's grandson, Allensworth J. Blodgett, remembered that "the train used to stop and pick up the milk in cans every morning for processing in Bakersfield. That was the principal industry of the township."[123]

Most residents raised some livestock and grew produce for their own consumption; many attempted to grow cash crops such as beets or grapes for the market. Mrs. Mattie Johnson, for example, operated her own bakery and short-order lunch business, raised chickens, ducks, and turkeys, and grew alfalfa on her 12 acres.[124] In addition to animal husbandry, some colonists made do by catching local wild animals for food. The town was awash in wild rabbits and at least one family, the Hacketts, hunted them and ground the meat for hamburgers.[125] Rarely could a colonist make ends meet from one crop or one enterprise. Although he had trained as a chemist, Norvin Powell recalled that "postmaster, farm laborer and farmer were all jobs that I had to do, however reluctantly, to make a living."[126] Finding no work when he first arrived in Allensworth in 1912, he looked in the surrounding communities of Alpaugh, Earlimart, Corcoran, and elsewhere. He described memories "still graphic and humiliating" of the ubiquitous signs in shop and restaurant windows: "no Negroes, no Filipinos, no Mexicans, no Dogs." Eventually, friends from his fraternal order, Knights of Pythias, helped Powell find work in Bakersfield as a janitor. Nor was moving up the occupational ladder possible: "slowly, I learned there were a lot of things a Black man was not permitted to do even in California." After his father's death in 1914, Powell returned to Allensworth and began piecing together a living. "That winter I worked on a neighboring ranch as a steady field hand plowing, scraping and leveling," he remembered. His day's wages in the fields amounted to about $1.40; Powell had no intention of farming, however, "it was just not what I considered my life style."[127] Agricultural labor helped his family scrape by but it was not what he had envisioned when he made the move to Allensworth. A stint as postmaster, after Joshua Singleton resigned, brought relief from farmwork, but dreams of being a chemist never materialized.

When farmers had a rough year, other businesses in the colony suffered. Henry Singleton recalled the colonists' strife when crops failed. His father, Joshua, who operated a general store when he was not serving as postmaster, experienced economic disaster: "These people at Allensworth depended on agriculture. If they had a bad year, my dad had a bad year. There was little cash money. Everybody bought on credit. My old man was a poor man when he came there. He and Zebedee Hinsman [the other store owner] both were simply trying to carry that colony, to some extent, on their shoulders. You can't do that. Many people couldn't make it. They couldn't get work. They'd move out owing a bill. Finally my dad couldn't pay his wholesale bill and they closed in on him and . . . he went bankrupt."[128] Joshua Singleton closed the store in 1915 and returned the following year to reopen with a cash-only policy. Oral histories like Henry Singleton's make plain the connection and dependence between the residents of Allensworth. As with Armilda Archer Smith's, Singleton's story reveals that financial troubles were a staple of this "Jim Crow–free society."[129]

The entrepreneurial, promotional, and agricultural skills of Overr, Allensworth, Payne, and the other settlers were no match for the state's agri-business interests. Even the praise and journalistic skills of Delilah Beasley could do little for the town as the Great Depression loomed. The heyday of Allensworth was over. As jobs, already scarce, became rare, young people left the town for the bigger cities of Oakland and Los Angeles. Twentieth-century wars created industrial jobs that black Californians finally had access to and this, as well as the military, drew men and women out of the colony. Beginning in the 1920s, the unquenchable thirst of corporate farms literally drained water from the landscape.[130] When Colonel Allensworth envisioned his utopia in the early part of the century, the Central Valley still contained family farms, but these were fast disappearing during the first decade of the town's history. The state's agribusiness interests consolidated in the postwar years, putting the squeeze on communities like Allensworth. Profits of over $1 billion poured into agribusiness annually by the 1960s; small-town farmers were no match against the corporate giants.[131]

After World War II, Allensworth became a sparse and dusty town in the Tulare County basin where a few folks struggled to make a living. It was no longer an all-black colony. Mexican American and European American families lived and worked alongside their black neighbors, and the school struggled to stay open with only a handful of students. In 1958, three white families in Allensworth petitioned the county board of education to allow them to send their children to the elementary school in Delano. Their request was denied. Allensworth School principal George A. Finley said, "This is a race problem. They aren't afraid the children won't get an education. The point is they don't want to go to a Negro school."[132] Four years after the momentous *Brown v. Board of Education* Supreme Court decision, white parents of the formerly all-black colony were still seeking ways to avoid integration. The three white families told the school board and the press that they wanted their children to go to school in Delano because the educational opportunities were better; some mentioned the fact that only one teacher taught all the grades in Allensworth School, where only fourteen students were enrolled.[133] Typical of cities across the nation, tiny Allensworth faced its own crisis over integrated schools in the wake of *Brown*. The irony of how far the town had come from its origins as a haven from segregation was quite lost on the white inhabitants.

In some ways, however, the town had come full circle. Indeed, repeating the past became dangerous for the postwar residents as the small community faced yet another water crisis. In 1967 the inhabitants were informed by health department inspectors that their drinking water was unsafe due to unusually high levels of arsenic. As the *Visalia Times Daily* put it, "no disappointment . . . has proved more difficult to overcome than the trick nature played against it in depositing arsenic in its water supply."[134] This discovery came after some townspeople became ill. Grassroots efforts, including a church rummage sale, raised the funds necessary to purchase a water purification system for the thirty-four families living in the town. Some praised the county for its cooperative spirit. "During the week when Martin Luther King Jr. was murdered as an example of the hate in our nation it is gratifying to know that there was so much brotherly love here in Tulare County," said local attorney George Thurlow.[135] This crisis did not resolve itself with a church rummage sale, however. Residents spent two years importing potable water from other towns before construction could begin on the new system in 1968. At that point, none of the buildings in the town except the school had indoor plumbing.[136]

Allensworth residents did not remain silent about their lack of water, but few in the county or state capitol showed much concern. One of the few communities that *did* pay attention was that of the United Farm Workers (UFW), headquartered a few miles down the road in Delano. The farm workers newspaper, *Malcriado*, covered the story in detail, and with good reason: the water in Delano also had dangerous levels of arsenic. The UFW Organizing Committee visited Allensworth in 1967 and interviewed the school teacher, Juanita Bruce, who told the committee: "The people have been trying to get water piped into their homes, but the Farm Office in Visalia says that they will have to pay for the piping. And now they are trying to find out if the government will lend them the money but even if they did, it would put people into debt for 10 years or more, because the piping and water is so expensive, and the government will not pay for it." The UFW investigation pointed to the obvious connection: agribusiness wielded tremendous force in the state—as farm workers well knew—and their water needs trumped Mexican American farm workers and residents of a mostly black and Mexican town. "Why is . . . Governor Re[a]gan's biggest scheme to spend billions of tax payers dollars on new irrigation systems for the growers?," asked the Organizing Committee. "And why has the government allowed the growers around Delano to get water free from the irrigation canals EVEN THOUGH IT IS AGAINST THE LAW FOR ANY GROWER WHO OWNS OVER 160 ACRES TO USE THIS WATER WITHOUT PAYING FOR IT? Why won't the government pay to have water for the families in Allensworth?"[137]

For some, the lack of water spelled the end of their dream; they sought other employment or they left the colony altogether. For others, the disaster that most worried them was the rerouting of the railroad. In 1914 the Santa Fe railroad built a spur off the main line (which originally went through Allensworth), diverting freight trains to nearby Alpaugh. Farmers and families like the Singletons that relied on the railroad to buy and sell grain, merchandise, dairy products, and the like lost a crucial link to California markets. The spur eliminated Allensworth's role as a transfer point for freight trains, transforming the colony to a place where trains stopped for passengers but little money changed hands. All shipping and agricultural production shifted from Allensworth to Alpaugh.[138] This was a devastating loss for the colony: between $4,000 and $5,000 worth of "shipping money" had been collected at the Allensworth station by 1914, whereas in 1929 only about $13 passed hands there in a month. With the onset of the Great Depression, the train stopped coming to Allensworth.[139]

Saving the Town: A State Park

By the 1960s, a visitor to California would find no evidence of black residents in any of the state's landmarks, monuments, and historic sites. San Francisco created a city park on the site of abolitionist and entrepreneur Mary Ellen Pleasant's mansion in the 1980s, though this only occurred after black women chained themselves to the eucalyptus trees on the site when the city threatened to knock them down.[140] The house had burned down in the 1920s, and the trees were the only tangible legacy that remained of the impressive empire Pleasant constructed from profits in mining and real estate in gold rush California. Historic sites that addressed the African American past were a rarity across the nation in the 1960s, but most states had one or two. California had none. To lobby for the creation of an Allensworth state park meant asking the state to preserve this past through extensive funding—taxpayer money—and acknowledge its significance in state history. Drawing attention to this omission of black history in the 1960s became the rallying cry for those who spearheaded the movement to establish Colonel Allensworth State Park; timing was everything.

By all accounts, Cornelius "Ed" Pope initiated a movement to restore the colony and create a state park.[141] In the aftermath of the assassination of Martin Luther King Jr., Pope sought ways to channel anger into action. He was working as a draftsmen and planner for the California Department of Parks and Recreation (DPR) in 1968 and described the moment this way: "A bunch of us were angry, and we wanted to do something violent after that, because of Martin. . . . But my wife said I shouldn't get involved in anything like that. I had to do something, though. And I remembered Colonel Allensworth and the town he founded." Pope submitted a proposal to the California State Parks system to explore the possibility of creating an historic park.[142] In its response, the DPR admitted that the park system had "been delinquent in its historical preservation and interpretation program in not having given attention to the contributions of its black citizens."[143] The Allensworth Advisory Committee was formed in 1969, and with help from DPR staff, groups of activists, educators, and Allensworth residents, they organized a campaign to educate the public. Through formal and informal networks including those of the NAACP and the Negro Historical Societies, programs about the colony emphasized its significance and that of the state's African American history.[144] The fact that black history had been rendered invisible in the state's telling of its own past seemed undeniable. In 1971, 112 state-owned historic sites made up the "historical resources" supported by the people of California and they provided "for the general public knowledge of the historical and cultural contributions of the Indian, Spanish, Chinese, English, Russian, Mexican, and White American," stated the DPR feasibility report. The report concluded: "Neglect of the Black American has been total." As the students of University of California, Berkeley, and San Francisco State University organized for ethnic studies departments and courses that reflected the diversity of the nation's population, a quieter, though not unrelated, revolution over the representation of state history simmered. Park advocates consciously linked their struggle to that of the students when they prepared the feasibility study: "California needs to educate its youth in the history and culture of the Black American so that adults of tomorrow will have healthy attitudes towards persons of different backgrounds and cultures. The recent establishment of ethnic studies programs in schools, corporations, the military and a host of other institutions points out the demand for this type of project."[145] The argument that black history could address and even ameliorate racial tensions — only six years after the uprising in Watts shook the state to the core — proved powerful for citizens across the political spectrum.

After a lengthy campaign, Governor Ronald Reagan authorized the DPR to establish Colonel Allensworth Historic State Park in 1974. Plans for the park stalled, however. Ironically, it was *President* Reagan's trickle-down economics of the 1980s that stripped the park of the very dollars he had promised as governor of California in the 1970s. By 1990, only seven of the thirty buildings planned for restoration had been finished; even today a trailer still houses the visitor center.[146] The park, in a state of neglect, caused State Assemblywoman Gwen Moore of Los Angeles to lodge a complaint in 1993. "It is a state park. It should be treated as a state park equally."[147] The treatment of the park seemed reminiscent of the treatment of the town's residents. Finally, at the end of the decade, Governor Jerry Brown and the state legislature pledged $4 million to restore additional structures and maintain existing ones.[148]

By 2006 at least a dozen structures, all carefully researched and designed to look as they did in the first decade of the colony's history, were open to visitors.[149] The Singletons' store and post office, the hotel, the library, the school, and the barbershop all gave visitors a sense of the town in the early twentieth century. In 2006, eight thousand people visited the state park.[150] The Friends of Allensworth, a group that organized to support and sustain the town's legacy, holds annual programs, including a rededication ceremony every October, the Old Time Jubilee in May, a black history month program in February, and a Juneteenth celebration.

For former residents like Alice C. Royal, who chaired the advisory committee from 1985 to 1989 and had worked so hard to save the town, it must have seemed like a cruel twist of fate when dairy farming threatened the park's survival again in 2006. In that year, the Tulare County Supervisors voted to approve plans for a 12,000-cow dairy farm to be built next to the park. Allensworth supporters worried that the stench from the dairy farm, the runoff, and the clouds of flies would deter visitors and drastically reduce the park's tourist appeal.[151] Tulare County was producing more milk than any other county in the United States, giving its dairy farmers significantly more clout than the state park could muster. The controversy led state Attorney General Jerry Brown and the Natural Resources Defense Council to file lawsuits to stop construction of the dairy farm.[152]

Central to the debate over the park's fate was the significance of black history. Ed Pope gave multiple interviews reminding Americans of the lessons he learned in the colony and those that the park could teach visitors. Interviewed for the *New York Times*, Pope described his teacher Alwortha Hall: "She taught me how to read and write. . . . It was the first true happiness I'd known." The mayor of the nearby community of Allensworth, not the park, told the paper "You can relocate cattle. You can't relocate history." This time academics weighed in on the significance of the town, including David J. Organ, an historian at Clark Atlanta University, who told the *Times*, "Preservation is the last frontier of the civil rights movement. Especially post-Katrina, we have to reconstruct the memories of these communities before we can physically reconstruct them with hammer and nails. That's the legacy of Allensworth."[153] That legacy, under threat since the founding of the colony, seems finally to be secure. The California Assembly passed bill 1077 in June 2011 to ban development within two and a half miles of the park. Allensworth remains the only all-black town in the United States that has been preserved as a state park.[154]

Strolling through the 240 acres of state park today forces visitors to confront questions easily avoided everywhere else in the state: What inspired African Americans to start a town here? How and why was California segregated? What would it be like to live in an all-black, or mostly black town? How did the colonists survive in a place so far removed from other black communities and institutions? The park does its best to answer these questions, and children on field trips flock to the park to see the old-fashioned schoolhouse, sit in the barbershop, and hear stories about the colony. If the Friends of Allensworth have their way, no one will ever be allowed to forget the lessons of California's only self-governed black colony.[155]

* * *

Segregation across California inspired African Americans to flee to the San Joaquin Valley, where they could create a town that belonged only to black men and women. For a brief time, the town that segregation built flourished. Children could learn freely and study black history for the first time in their lives. Women and men practiced skills and professions closed to them outside the colony; they became politicians, teachers, librarians, judges, institution builders, and leaders. But as the water dried up, so did the possibilities to carve out a living. The Great Depression and wars of the twentieth century pulled colonists back to cities for jobs and into the armed forces. What began as an experiment to escape from Jim Crow, by the middle of the twentieth century, resembled a ghost town.

Oral histories with colonists make it possible to tell the history of the town from their perspective. This is rare. Most of the accounts of black towns are told through the histories and memories of black men who founded the colonies, many of whom never lived in the all-black towns they established. Female colonists in Allensworth, however, made a community that for some came close to a utopian society. The voices of Allensworth citizens reveal an alternate world, a town that encouraged African Americans to imagine and create a life that was not plagued by antiblack laws, sentiments, politics, or culture. In many ways, Allensworth presaged the black main streets and black neighborhoods like Harlem in New York and Central Avenue in Los Angeles. Like these spaces, the colony protected African Americans from the vagaries of Jim Crow, promoting black self-worth, black beauty, and black pride. In the classroom of Allensworth School, Ed Pope learned, a generation before the freedom schools in Mississippi taught the same lesson, that "black is beautiful." Allensworth stands as an example of a black nationalist community that predated the black freedom movement and the Black Panther Party. Its history, and the memories of its pioneers, show how black Californians created a freedom sanctuary in the age of Jim Crow and how difficult that was to sustain. The "best proposition ever offered to Negroes" in California was a sweet, if fleeting, memory.

As the Great Depression reverberated across California, it touched small towns like Allensworth, big cities, and the large swathe of farming communities that dotted the fields and valleys. These communities of central California would play host, in the 1930s, to some of the most volatile agricultural strikes in U.S. history. Vigilantes, often sent by law enforcement, were responsible for the death of scores of strikers, including cannery workers and cotton pickers. In the midst of this violence, the highest elected official in the state, Governor James Rolph Jr., offered his support to vigilantes and lynchers. Black Californians found the praise chilling and the state's support of lynching abhorrent. They watched as their state became the center of two movements: one to pardon lynchers and one to end the practice of lynching altogether.

A Lesson in Lynching

African American journalist and founding editor of the *San Francisco Sun-Reporter* Thomas Fleming felt relatively safe growing up in the small town of Chico in the Sacramento Valley, even though there was never a very large black population. He attended college—when he could afford it—at Chico State University in the 1930s, making friends with "white liberals" on campus. One incident, however, shook him to the core and forced students at the college to rethink race relations in their town and state. On November 26, 1933, two white men were lynched in San Jose in what proved to be a watershed event in U.S. history. The lynching changed Fleming's opinion of California, and he wrote about the incident sixty years later:

> As I walked to school that morning, I read the big bold black headline of the Chico morning paper that a mob had stormed the jail in San Jose. The story quoted a senseless statement made by Governor "Sunny Jim" Rolph, in which he failed to condemn the mob for lynching a kidnapping suspect. I was well aware that this type of mob rule was common in some Southern states, and the victim was always a black person. By the time I reached the campus, I was very angry, and my anger centered on the lawless white world of the South that used mob violence to uphold white supremacy.[1]

On campus, students gathered around Fleming as he condemned the lynching in San Jose. When white male students began shouting at him, one of the professors took him into a classroom before he "got himself into trouble." Fleming asked his professor if he "was proud to be a white man."

"Of course he understood what I meant, and shook his head in disbelief that such a thing as a lynching had taken place in a downtown city." News of Fleming's angry outburst traveled fast in the small black community and he was told to be careful because "some whites had been talking about [his] verbal outrage." A local janitor delivered the warning, "[adding] that he did not want any trouble, and of course I answered that I did not either, but that I was a firm believer in justice for all, and I was not going to change my opinion for him or anyone else."[2]

Fleming's vivid recollection of the events in San Jose tell us that he found the event chilling and deeply disturbing. Lynching news, as Fleming reminds us, usually came from the South. That the California victims were white did not stop Fleming, the black press, or civil rights organizations from linking the event to the murder of thousands of black men and women. However, the outrage in San Jose and the state's response infuriated not just black Californians; Fleming remembered that "liberals from all over California" met near Monterey, days after the event, "to protest the governor and the mob."[3] Fleming wrote a column in the *Sun Reporter* for over sixty years, beginning in 1944, in which he exposed the Jim Crow policies and practices of the state, covered civil rights demonstrations, and reported on national events.[4] But he never forgot the time a California lynching was front-page news.

✻ ✻ ✻

In 1933, when the news media erupted with reports of a lynching, no one expected the dateline to be California. The lynching of the two white men in San Jose sent shock waves across the country; it would receive more attention from the press than any other lynching in U.S. history.[5] The whiteness of the victims changed everything: from the way the crime was depicted in the press to the strategic rhetoric adapted by the antilynching movement. The white bodies also allowed California to avoid questions about its treatment of African Americans, Latina/os, Asians, and Native Americans, who had been targets of violence since statehood. But antilynching activists across the country insisted on connecting California's crime to the lynching of black men, as well as to the pending trials of the Scottsboro Boys. Their insistence that crimes against black bodies must figure in the discussion of and response to this event took considerable mobilization. But their efforts bore fruit. The murders in San Jose became central to the national—and international—debates about mob violence, the power of the state, and the antilynching movement. The event exposed the crime as never before and galvanized Americans who had heretofore stood on the sidelines of the antilynching movement. Although it was not the first time white men had been lynched in the United States, the timing—and the governor's response—made *this* lynching different. All eyes were on California. The ways in which the state and the nation responded changed the U.S. lynching landscape.

The San Jose lynching—and its repercussions—provides irrefutable evidence that California was not a bystander to the nation's history of lynching; it helped to sustain, defend, and strangely, end the practice. Some of these repercussions were calculated, some unintentional. Just as the Golden State segregated housing and neighborhoods in ways that claimed national attention, it set precedents in the history of lynching. This chapter examines the role California played in shaping the national understanding of lynching and the antilynching movement, and the ways in which this history has been obscured. In spite of the interventions of the black press, the antilynching movement, and U.S. popular culture, memories of the San Jose lynching, and the robust protest movement that followed, have disappeared. But this erasure is no anomaly: The desire to keep lynching a secret is a national pastime, and the impetus to forget is overwhelming.[6] Thomas Fleming fought against this type of amnesia when, in the 1990s, he insisted on remembering and retelling his story about a Depression-era California lynching in the pages of the *Sun Reporter*. As he well knew, lynching was a national crime, but so was forgetting it.

Violence Obscured

Lynching has been understood as a crime committed by southern white men against southern black men. This understanding is not without merit, since most victims of the crime were African Americans from the South. As a tool of southern racism and Jim Crow, lynching—and the threat of lynching—worked to establish and maintain white supremacy. Although the practice occurred in every region of the United States and victims could be men or women of any race or ethnicity, that is not the way it has figured in the public imagination. What did it mean, then, when the victims were western white men? In order to appreciate the significance of California's most infamous lynch victims, we first have to examine the state's lynching history and the confusing legacy this history has created. On the one hand, the Golden State, like other states in the West, has been seen as a place where extralegal violence, part of "frontier justice," occurred regularly in the nineteenth century. On the other hand, there has also been an assumption that, unlike southern states, California did not practice lynching as a tool of white supremacy. Two factors have been at the root of this obfuscation: the history and historiography of vigilantism, and a reliance on twentieth-century lynching statistics as a measure of racial violence. Making certain kinds of violence, including the lynching of people of color, invisible, has helped to support a fiction that the state did not practice Jim Crow or violence toward African Americans and other people of color.

California's reputation as a place where frontier justice originated and triumphed has had a significant impact on efforts to understand the state's violent past. The notion that vigilantism is natural in the Wild West meant that observers and historians of the West expected to find lawless activity and murder. This naturalization of western violence is partially responsible for the erasure of the details of that history. In the first decades of statehood, California gained a well-deserved reputation for vigilantism, including extralegal executions by hanging. In Los Angeles County, in the first five years of statehood, the murder rate was fifty times greater than that of New York City.[7] The lynching of criminals became a common method of "justice" in the gold mines as well. Hangtown, now known as Placerville, in the foothills of the Sierra Nevada mountains, proudly displayed the effigy of a lynch victim on the site where lynchings regularly occurred.[8] Because the crime became associated with the infamous vigilance committees of the 1850s, it seemed to draw few comparisons to similar crimes across the country. Lynching was part of the Wild West, and criminals like the Sydney Ducks who terrorized San Francisco could not and did not deserve a fair trial. California's best-known historian and archivist of the nineteenth century, Hubert Howe Bancroft, played an essential role in crafting this narrative. In his efforts to establish a western (what he called Pacific States) exceptionalism, he glorified the state's history of vigilantism, securing the reputation of vigilantes as "distinct from lynch mobs of the South."[9] Setting up this distinction between "good" frontier lynching and "bad" southern lynching, Bancroft blazed a trail that would be well-worn by the time of the San Jose murders. This logic, crystallized by a revered historian, reached its apogee in 1933.

While western lynching was excused in the press and historiography, twentieth-century civil rights organizations saw the crime as anything but excusable; lynching represented the epitome of racial terror during the era of Jim Crow. Naming, studying, and counting the number of lynchings, became a central preoccupation of the nation's civil rights organizations and a way to come to grips with the extralegal violence African Americans experienced in the United States. Antilynching crusaders Ida B. Wells and Jesse Daniel Ames relied on statistics and the truths they showed and concealed to mount their campaigns.[10] The NAACP kept meticulous records of lynching as part of their own war on terror, aimed particularly but not exclusively at southern practitioners of the act. As many scholars have noted, the imprecise nature of the term and the difficulty of quantifying the data of the victims have not stopped anyone from relying on the numbers as a yardstick for the severity of Jim Crow.[11] Although lynching statistics alone will never be an adequate indicator of the kind and intensity of violence experienced by African Americans in any state, it has served that purpose in years past.

California's statistics seem unremarkable: according to NAACP records of lynchings that occurred between 1889 and 1918, for example, the western state ranked in the middle of all states in terms of the number of lynch victims.[12] This data, first published in 1919, became critical to the antilynching movement. Because of the timing of their publication—at the height of the lynching epidemic and the efforts to pass antilynching legislation—these numbers were some of the most important ones available in the fight against Jim Crow. A dispute over the accuracy of the numbers and what they represented, however, has existed since the counting began. The debate resulted in part from the confusion over what, exactly, constitutes the definition of a lynching. The NAACP believed that the difference between a murder and a lynching lay in the public or community support for the act and encouraged other civil rights organizations to adopt its definition.[13] Tuskegee Institute, another clearinghouse of lynching statistics in this era, developed a more precise definition of what constituted a lynching. According to Tuskegee, a lynching had to fit these criteria: "There must be legal evidence that a person was killed. That person must have met death illegally. A group of three or more persons must have participated in the killings. The group must have acted under the pretext of service to justice, race or tradition."[14] A murder had to fulfill all of these criteria for it to be counted by Tuskegee statisticians, which explains why the data collected by Tuskegee and the NAACP varies. Complicating matters was the NAACP's Walter White 1929 study, *Rope and Faggot: A Biography of Judge Lynch*, which provided another set of numbers.

Because these early twentieth-century sources consider different eras and utilized different definitions of lynching, they necessarily report different findings vis-à-vis numerical data. The NAACP, Tuskegee, and White's study disagree substantially on the total number of lynchings in the United States and the number of California cases. All three of the sources, however, reported two African American victims in California.[15] The NAACP documented twenty-five lynchings in California between 1889 and 1918 out of a national total of 3,324.[16] Tuskegee records counted lynchings that occurred between 1883 and 1968, and they found evidence of 4,743 cases, of which thirty occurred in California.[17] Walter White's study claimed 4,951 U.S. lynchings occurred between 1882 and 1927; fifty people were lynched in California according to his records.[18] Regardless of which numbers one cited, California's record led most observers to assume that the state simply did not deploy this crime in the ways southern states did.

Ken Gonzales-Day, a twenty-first-century authority on California lynching, believes that these numbers underrepresent the history and significance of lynching in the state. One of the central problems in these statistics, he points out, is that they erase the lynching of Native Americans, Mexicans, and Chinese. By omitting the years between statehood and 1880 in their surveys, some of California's bloodiest, the earlier data loses value and meaning. Gonzales-Day found evidence of 352 lynchings that occurred between 1850 and 1935, a sevenfold increase over previous estimates. Shifting his timeline back to 1850 and researching victims' identities allowed him to show that California lynched Native Americans, Chinese, and Latinos (of Mexican or Latin American descent) with impunity. The new evidence reveals that eight—not two—African American men had been lynched between 1850 and 1935.[19]

Of the eight African American victims in the state, the majority, (five) of them were lynched in the 1850s, the so-called vigilante era, and all were men.[20] Two of the eight victims were accused of murder, one of robbery, and one of larceny. One, an unnamed man of Yreka, died in 1855 as part of the Scott's Bar Massacre, and two men were lynched for reasons unknown. The final victim, lynched in Mojave in Kern County in 1904, was accused of raping a boy. Of note is the case of Henry Planz, whose alleged crime is unknown; he met his death in 1892 in San Jose. Planz is never mentioned in the extensive press coverage of the 1933 lynchings in San Jose. Like the other seven African American men, Planz disappeared in the historical record.

In the first half of the twentieth century, the general assumption was that African Americans in California were safe from racially inspired violence — including lynching. Many if not most Americans, including members of the NAACP, did not see California as a place where violence against African Americans occurred, at least not in a way that warranted serious attention. Black Californians repeatedly sounded the alarm regarding violence in their state but often felt ignored or dismissed. Two years before the San Jose crime, Delilah Beasley, reporter and stalwart antilynching advocate, wrote to William Pickens, NAACP field secretary, about a near-lynching in San Francisco. On January 21, twenty-eight-year-old Hillyard Denton was chased down by a group of teamsters, who then kicked and beat him until he was bloody. The teamsters said Denton had stolen a box of cheese from the sidewalk in front of the Kraft Cheese Company, on Battery Street near the docks. By the time the police arrived, he had been hit with a two-by-four and had an eighteen-foot rope dangling from his neck. As the men dragged him to a telephone pole to lynch him, a riot squad and an ambulance arrived and dispersed the "milling mob." Denton appeared before a municipal judge the next day, accused of petty theft, and told the judge that he stole the cheese because he was hungry; he received a sixty-day suspended sentence and was released. Denton was reluctant to leave the judge's chambers, for fear "those boys may be waiting outside with the rope again."[21] Given that an antilynching bill that Beasley helped draft would soon appear before the state legislature, she felt that the local branches of the NAACP were not taking the matter seriously. But in January 1931, Beasley's concern about this near-lynching barely merited a response from NAACP headquarters. Pickens passed her letter on to the publicity office and there is no record of further action. For Beasley, the attack and near-lynching of Hillyard Denton confirmed the necessity of state and federal antilynching legislation. For others, violence against black Californians was comparatively benign and, therefore, a nonstarter in the war on lynching.[22]

Throughout the twentieth century, the assumption that California's black lynch victims were numerically insignificant gave the state permission to congratulate itself on its record. Lynching had no place in histories of the state; its victims illegible. Written records and historiography that did acknowledge lynching in the state's history rendered it irrelevant or benign. This erasure of racial violence did not end with lynching. Other forms of racial violence could and would be written off as aberrations, pranks, or well-deserved. This was exemplified in the gruesome 1945 murder of O'Day

Short and his family and the subsequent cover-up (see chapter 5). Most of the violence aimed at African Americans in the state would technically fall outside of the legal definition of lynching: they were shot with guns, sometimes by law enforcement, they were beaten, or they died in prison. This is true for African Americans across the nation during the era of Jim Crow; they were much more likely to be murdered, assaulted, or raped than to be lynched.[23] Ironically, the lynching of white men, and the state's response, laid bare the nation's support for lawlessness and white supremacy.

California's Lesson

On November 9, 1933, in San Jose, California, Thomas H. Thurmond and John M. Holmes, both European American men, kidnapped twenty-two-year-old Brooke L. Hart, the son of Alexander J. Hart, a wealthy San Jose businessman.[24] Brooke Hart had been seen driving his Studebaker near the family's department store that evening but didn't show up as expected to retrieve his father and sister from the store. On the night Hart disappeared, the kidnappers placed two calls to the Hart family to demand $40,000 in ransom, enabling authorities to trace the calls to San Francisco. The San Jose police chief John Black alerted U.S. Department of Justice agent Reed Vetterli in San Francisco, who wired his boss J. Edgar Hoover, and thus began what one journalist called "one of the largest manhunts in California history."[25] In consultation with the police, A. J. Hart issued a public appeal to the kidnappers—published on the front page of the city's paper of record, the *San Jose Mercury Herald*, and every newspaper on the West Coast—promising to "play absolutely fair" and "do whatever is necessary, with no questions asked, to secure Brooke's return." The press reported that guards were removed from the family home so as to permit contact with the kidnappers.[26] In fact, this was a ruse; federal agents hid upstairs in the Hart home for the duration of the search. In the next few days a series of crank calls, bad leads, mysterious letters, and false arrests turned the manhunt into a national cause célèbre.

After only a week of searching for the kidnappers, Santa Clara County Sheriff William J. Emig arrested Thurmond, aged twenty-eight, and Holmes, aged twenty-nine, in San Jose on November 16. The men admitted to abducting and killing Hart. Gruesome details of the murder followed: Thurmond and Holmes had abducted Hart in downtown San Jose, driven him to the countryside, smashed Hart's skull with a "concrete brick," and "bound his body with bailing wire," before tossing his body off the San Mateo bridge into the San Francisco Bay. The brick and the wire, discovered in the San Francisco Bay, were displayed on the front page of the Sunday newspaper as the search for the body continued. Next, Hart's hat floated to the surface of the water, near the bridge, and one week later, on November 26, the body of Brooke Hart was discovered by two duck hunters in the mud flats of the bay.[27]

Long before the body of Brooke Hart was found, San Joseans raged over the kidnapping. The Harts inspired widespread sympathy partly due to their status as an elite, white family, but it was the nature of the crime that ultimately galvanized supporters. At no other time in U.S. history had kidnapping been so fixed in the news; many referred to an epidemic of kidnapping in the 1930s.[28] Charles Lindbergh's baby was kidnapped and found dead the previous year, and by 1933 no one had been prosecuted for the crime.[29] True crime fiction whetted the appetite of the reading public, and newspapers repackaged kidnapping stories to satisfy what seemed an insatiable desire for details. On the day after the arrest, the *San Jose Mercury Herald* printed five front-page stories about the Hart kidnapping with headlines that included "Here's Full Confession of Hart's Kidnappers."[30] Little embellishment was needed to garner attention; Hart's kidnapping had all the elements necessary to attract a record-setting audience. And Holmes and Thurmond appeared eager subjects for media celebrity.

Thomas Thurmond (or Harold, as he was sometimes called) told Sherriff Emig shortly after his arrest that the kidnapping was not the first crime that the two men had attempted. In October 1932 they had held up two clerks in San Francisco who worked for Shell and Union oil companies, stealing over $1,000. Descriptions of the holdups were leaked to a public curious about the profiles of the suspected criminals. While in custody, each man submitted his confession. Thurmond described the kidnapping in greater detail, including the kind of pillowcase they threw over Hart's head when abducting him, and Thurmond fingered his accomplice as the mastermind behind all their criminal activities.[31] Holmes, in his confession, claimed that he had known Thurmond for about a year and that, spotting Hart as they came out of the movies one day, Thurmond suggested the kidnapping.[32] The men's histories received intense scrutiny as officials and journalists looked for clues that would explain the horrific crime. Baffled by the pair, one editor claimed that these were not Depression-era hooligans or unemployed drifters, but upstanding men who "earned their living by honest employment" and "sustained good reputations" despite evidence to the contrary. Yet the same newspaper reported that unemployment plagued "Jack" Holmes.[33] Holmes and Thurmond had started hanging out at gambling and bootlegging spots, turning into "full-fledged gangsters," reported the *San Jose Mercury*.[34] Much was made of the fact that Holmes was married with two young children, though he and his wife were recently estranged. Interviews with the estranged wife, Evelyn Holmes, had all the pathos of a cinematic melodrama. "Oh, I know John never could have done this thing," she told a reporter from the *San Francisco Chronicle*. "Do they think that just because he is out of work he would become a kidnapper?"[35]

Jack Holmes was the son of Maurice Holmes, a tailor who had emigrated from Denmark, and Hulda Peterson, who was born in Sweden and raised in Iowa. The couple lived first in Los Angeles, where Jack was born in 1904; they moved to San Jose sometime before 1915, when Maurice opened a shop downtown. An only child, Jack attended San Jose public schools while his parents became involved in local benevolent societies. After Jack married Evelyn Fleming in 1924, he took a job as a salesman for Standard Oil Company. When Jack switched jobs to work for Union Oil Company he met Harold Thurmond, who was working downtown at a service station. They were very different personalities: while Holmes was described as "All-American" and aggressive, Thurmond was described as "delicate" and "hesitant." Holmes had been expelled from San Jose High School for insubordinate behavior; Thurmond dropped out of high school and worked in a lumberyard before his father got him the job at the gas station. Thurmond's mother, Lillie, and his six siblings attended the local Baptist church, and for a time so did Harold. Most accounts of the two men portrayed Holmes as the leader and Thurmond as his gullible accomplice.

As soon as Thurmond and Holmes were arrested and in custody at the San Jose county jail, word of a possible lynching spread. The crowd outside the jail increased exponentially, and Maurice Holmes voiced concern that his son could be the victim of a lynch mob.[36] Most of the press agreed that the men should be hanged, "legally but promptly."[37] The *San Jose News* editorial titled "Human Devils" left little to the imagination: "If mob violence could ever be justified it would be in a case like this."[38] Sheriff Emig, hearing threats of lynching, sneaked the prisoners out of the county jail and transported them to the Potrero police station in San Francisco. After a power struggle between the federal officials and local authorities in San Jose, Thurmond and Holmes were shuttled back to San Jose to await trial;

Governor James Rolph Jr.'s statement about the lynching of Holmes and Thurmond, "This is the best lesson California has ever given the country," caused an uproar and galvanized the antilynching movement. (Courtesy of the California Historical Society)

Sheriff Emig wanted Thurmond and Holmes to stand trial in his county.[39] Ten days between the arrest of the men and the discovery of Hart's body gave the crowd outside the jail ample time to organize a mob. On November 24, sixty to seventy San Joseans formed "an old-time vigilance committee" and claimed they were prepared to "see justice done," reprising a Wild West theme that would become a popular trope in the weeks to come.[40]

California governor James Rolph Jr. had until now stayed on the periphery of the unfolding public drama, but his name soon became irrevocably linked to the ordeal. Rolph built his political reputation in San Francisco, spending nineteen years as mayor, five consecutive terms beginning in 1911, repairing the damage of the 1906 earthquake and fire and restoring the city to its former glory. His nickname, "Sunny Jim," spoke to his outsize personality, his sense of humor, and his popularity with the voters and the press. Elected governor in 1930, Rolph reputedly received three-fifths of the vote, and the election was declared a landslide. But his handling of the San Jose kidnapping would prove his undoing.[41]

A mob of thousands began gathering outside the San Jose jail on Sunday, November 26, as soon as Hart's body was discovered. Informed of the possibility of a lynching, Rolph declined to call out troops to protect the prisoners. The mob stormed the county building, using a heavy steel pipe from a nearby construction site to bash in the jailhouse door. In what was described as a "three-hour assault," the mob dodged tear gas, city police, and sheriffs, including Emig, to wrest the prisoners from their cells. Holmes and Thurmond were beaten up and then dragged across the street to St. James Park. The lynching occurred at 11:25 p.m. in front of a crowd of thousands, including members of the press and dozens of law enforcement. Holmes was stripped of his clothes and Thurmond's pants were removed; each man was hung from an oak tree in the park. Thurmond was already unconscious by the time he was lynched, and Holmes had been beaten so severely that his face was a bloody pulp.[42] In the process of trying to fend off the lynchers, Sheriff Emig was pelted in the head with a rock and taken to the nearest hospital. Crowds tore at the lynched bodies, claiming pieces of rope and the victims' clothing as souvenirs.

This murder had all of the characteristics typical of the crime of lynching, not least of which was the size of the mob.[43] Estimates of the crowd ranged from five thousand to fifteen thousand.[44] Indeed the press coverage sounded eerily familiar: "A howling mob beat the prisoners as they were dragged to the park. Every inch of space in the square within a block of the principal business corner of San Jose was filled with pushing humanity. . . . Girls, women and college youths joined in the burst of cheers." The sheriff's statement also emphasized the madness of the crowd: "That mob seemed to be insane. The tear gas never fazed them. They came through it with eyes streaming and smarting but determined to get those men and lynch them—and that was all that mob cared about."[45] Readers of the national press could not fail to notice the similarities between this western mob and those from the South: frenzied men, women, and children, all hoping to bear witness and, in some cases, find a souvenir. Even after the police took

In November 1933, John or "Jack" Holmes and Harold Thurmond were lynched for the kidnapping and murder of Brooke Hart, son of a wealthy San Jose business man. Photographs of Holmes and Thurmond were splashed across the pages of the white and black press. (Courtesy of the California Historical Society)

down the bodies of Thurmond and Holmes, crowds stayed in St. James Park all night, hacking away pieces of the trees and the rope as mementos.[46]

Governor Rolph's response to the lynchings shocked even the most cynical observer. As soon as the mob had hung and burned the bodies, Rolph proudly announced "This is the best lesson California has ever given the country."[47] With those eleven words, California provided lynchers across the nation with unprecedented support from a governor's office. Rolph did not stop there, however; in the first few days after the lynching he boasted that he would pardon "all persons who participated in the Holmes/Thurmond lynching should legal proceedings be taken against them."[48] The governor seized the opportunity for national attention and provided the press with a veritable gold mine of proclamations. "They'll learn they can't kidnap in this state," he promised, "If anyone is arrested for the good job [of lynching] I'll pardon them all." Next he announced that he would review the cases of all prisoners in the San Quentin and Folsom Penitentiaries who were serving time for kidnapping, and release them into the hands of "those fine, patriotic San Jose citizens who know how to handle such a situation."[49] Rolph delivered the ultimate justification of the nation's most heinous form of racial terror: lynching was patriotic. It mattered little that his incantation was meant to be a threat to kidnappers; Rolph's words were a gift to those seeking validation for the crime of lynching.

Many accused the governor of not just praising the murders of Thurmond and Holmes but of inciting them. In a maneuver that foreshadowed events of the civil rights movement, the governor refused to call out the California National Guard to, as he said "protect those two guys."[50] Rolph did not make a secret of his intentions; he delayed his visit to a conference of western governors in Idaho in order to make sure that troops were not called to the jail.[51] As The Nation noted, Rolph announced his support of the lynchers not once but "again and again in response to the shocked protests of his fellow-citizens." Claude Hudson, president of the Los Angeles branch of the NAACP, blamed Rolph explicitly: "In my opinion, he was an accessory before the fact, a part of the mob itself, and a disgrace to the high office he holds."[52]

The dangerous repercussions of the San Jose crime were not lost on members of the black press corps. Kelly Miller, in the pages of the widely read black newspaper, the Pittsburgh Courier, noted "Every right-minded Negro in America will condemn the California outrage with as great severity of denunciation as if the victim had belonged to his own race and blood."[53]

In the wake of California's news, two other lynching stories shocked the nation. Americans watched in horror as a nineteen-year-old African American man was lynched in Missouri on the heels of Rolph's proclamations. In Maryland, just days after the event in San Jose, a mob secured the release of four men who had been jailed for a lynching. Stories about lynching filled the headlines.[54] The concurrence of lynchings in California, Maryland, and Missouri was seen as a clear indication that the recent decline in the number of lynchings had been an aberration. Governor Rolph's endorsement of the San Jose lynchings—labeled Rolphism—was blamed for the new upsurge of violence. "It took the governor of California to put the stamp of approval on lynching and it seemed that this was just what the bloodthirsty mobs of Missouri and Maryland wanted," reported the *California Eagle*. The NAACP agreed and placed the blame squarely on Rolph for the Missouri lynching.[55] After a mob dragged Lloyd Warner, who was accused of rape, from his cell in St. Joseph, Missouri, they attacked the forty state troopers sent in to control the crowd, captured their tank, and lynched Warner only two days after Rolph's endorsement. The *Chicago Defender*, one of the most widely read black newspapers at the time, ran the headline, "Missouri Mob Agrees with Rolph."[56] A few days later, in Maryland, a mob tried to free the suspected lynchers of an African American man, George Armwood; Governor Albert Ritchie sent Maryland National Guards to the armory in Salisbury, where the four suspects were being held. The battle between the guardsmen and the mob escalated and rioters were captured on film by cameramen.[57] "Governor Ritchie stands for law and order. Judging from the words he has spoken, Governor Rolph favors lynching," wrote one California editor. Perhaps the most damning evidence of the role Rolph played in supporting lynchers came from a telegram the California governor received: "when you run for President you will have one hundred per cent support from the Eastern Shore of Maryland."[58]

Support for the San Jose lynching poured in from across the state and across the nation. The Hearst papers were especially lavish in their praise for Governor Rolph. A *Washington Herald* editorial complained about the "revolting" crime of kidnapping and commended the state of California for teaching a lesson: "The crime of kidnapping will not brook. It must stop even if the people are forced to take the law into their own hands." Kidnapping was a challenge to manhood, the paper claimed, reprising one of the most common defenses of lynching.[59] Sounding another familiar theme, the paper claimed that the San Jose lynchings "flung California back to the days of '49." Californians, some keen to defend their governor, lynching, or both, rallied to support the killing of Thurmond and Holmes. From towns around the state, including Ventura, Burbank, Salinas, and Orange, accolades arrived in the governor's office in the form of telegrams or newspaper editorials. In the aftermath of his remarks, Rolph received hundreds of telegrams and claimed that 267 were positive and only 57 negative.[60] In Santa Paula, a town in central California, the local paper claimed to have polled fifty of their readers, "and every one of them expressed approval of the summary justice."[61]

Not surprisingly, many in the state pointed to the history of vigilantism to explain the lynching. "The West has spoken" wrote one Pasadena columnist. "Thanks to citizens of San Jose, the spirit of the early vigilantes has been dragged forth from the moth balls, cutting stuffed-shirt legality and red tape. It'll do very nicely until Mr. Roosevelt fixes up some new rules. In the meantime it looks as though our ancestors won't have to be ashamed of us, after all."[62] Once again, the lines between lynching and vigilance committees blurred, and for many this became a "good" lynching. Interpreting the lynching as another case of vigilantism naturalized the events of San Jose, making them part of the typical western landscape and thus, for some, legible and acceptable.

In the aftermath of the lynching, the accusation that California had "gone southern" became a popular refrain. Initial *New York Times* coverage of the California crime claimed that southerners everywhere could be heard to say "California's my address from now on." "Those Westerners are learning how the South handles 'em." "That California man oughter be President."[63] California had gone farther, even, than the South. "The Governors of Southern states have not only never praised lynchers but have usually attempted to prevent lynching," claimed the *Times*. This accusation of "southernness," was meant to show the backwardness of California. But more to the point, California exceeded the South in its support for lynching, and this could prove devastating for the millions of African Americans living in the United States who were most often the victim of lynch mobs and for whom any defense of lynching at the state level had deadly implications.

The NAACP and the Antilynching Movement

Across the nation, the forces against lynching condemned the California atrocity, seeking to transform the widespread outrage into support for their movement. In addition to energizing the NAACP, now the leading organization of the antilynching movement, the murders mobilized a wide range of groups and coalitions, including the Association of Southern Women for the Prevention of Lynching (ASWPL), the American Civil Liberties Union (ACLU), and the Federal Council of the Churches of Christ. The fact that the California victims were not African American had the potential to strengthen their cause. The lynching occurred just as many organizations, most notably the ASWPL, emphasized the significant danger the crime posed to whites and society as a whole. The NAACP had also been moving away from an emphasis on black victims to stress the savagery of the white mobs that committed and witnessed the crime.[64] Walter White, who had become executive secretary of the NAACP the previous year, was quite explicit about the ways California could help the cause: "the wave of lynchings . . . spurred on by Governor Rolph's open endorsement of lynch law has simply given new strength to the movement."[65] Portraying the uncivilized and un-American nature of lynching had been a goal of the organization after World War I.[66] The fact that this lynching occurred in the West allowed the movement to underscore that lynching was a national — not a southern — problem. Historically, the West had the fewest number of lynchings. In the NAACP study, the West had, by far, the lowest numbers of the three regions it counted: the South, the North, and the West. Between 1909 and 1913, for example, there were 343 victims in the south, 15 in the North, and 4 in the West.[67]

Members of the antilynching movement had worked diligently to bring the crime to an end and had reason to believe their campaign was succeeding. The number of victims had reached epidemic proportions in the 1890s, peaking in 1892, when 235 people had been lynched. Since then, the intrepid journalist Ida B. Wells had been a powerful leading figure in the movement, initiating the antilynching movement in the United States. Wells focused her campaign on African American victims in the South and the "threadbare lies" that white southerners used to justify the crime. Wells' influential A Red Record, published in 1895, served as a primer for later activists such as James Weldon Johnson and Walter White of the NAACP, as well as the thousands of women in clubs and church groups who formed the movement's grassroots.[68] Johnson and White began collecting data at the end of the nineteenth century, as did Monroe Work at Tuskegee, and soon focused their efforts on a federal antilynching bill. Jesse Daniel Ames and the ASWPL, like Wells, exposed the mythologies behind lynching logic, especially the argument that lynchers were protecting white southern womanhood.[69] The numbers of lynchings steadily declined from the early 1920s; sixteen people were lynched in 1924, all African American, setting an historic low.[70] But numbers started to spike again in the 1930s, culminating in 1933, when twenty-eight people were lynched. Nothing in the antilynching campaign up to this point, however, prepared them for the shocking news that erupted from the California governor's office. The San Jose lynching of 1933 provided the movement with an example of the heinous crime like no other.

The NAACP's response to the lynchings was decisive and immediate. The executive officers understood the ways in which this particular lynching episode—more than any in the recent past—could be simultaneously disastrous and fortuitous for their antilynching campaign. The organization believed that the San Jose lynching must be addressed with all of the resources at their disposal, chief among them legal intelligence and the ability to garner publicity. The first response of Walter White, by then one of the nation's leaders in the fight against lynching, was to telegram Governor Rolph. The day after the lynching White sent an official message to the governor: "Your reference to yesterday's double lynching as best lesson California has ever given country is shameful official encouragement to mobs to defy authorities. No citizen and no government is safe with anarchy sanctioned from governors [sic] chair. California has given country a lesson in most brazen approval of lynching by highest officials country has ever seen." White made clear in the telegram that the NAACP demanded "prompt inquiry, arrest, and punishment of lynchers."[71] If there was any doubt that the organization's leadership stood firmly against the lynching of European Americans, White meant to squelch it and, simultaneously, use this lynching to push the antilynching project forward. White sent memos to every NAACP branch in the country with strict instructions on how to respond to the crisis. First, all branches should issue statements to the press denouncing the lynchings in San Jose, then they should follow with a request for the impeachment of Rolph.[72] Ever conscious of strategy, White also included the full text of his memo to Governor Rolph, so that all branches were informed about the campaign from the outset.

The NAACP lawyers had their own message to send to California's governor. Four days after the lynching, Charles Hamilton Houston, Leon A. Ransom, and James G. Tyson sent the following telegram to Governor Rolph:

We call upon you to close all state courts, dismiss all the state judges, expel all the lawyers, and abandon all the law schools in the State of California. We further demand that you pay the members of the lynching mob reasonable compensation from the state treasury for loss of time from their private business in the performance of what you denominate a public service. Do not hesitate to take the next step which inexorably ensues from your official endorsement of lynching as an agency for the administration of public justice. Then those of us who disagree with your stand can at least respect you as benighted but sincere, vicious but honest, an open enemy of orderly government who has the courage of his convictions.[73]

Twenty years before *Brown v. Board of Education*, but well on his way to laying the legal groundwork, Houston kept his eye on the case as it sent shock waves through the nation. He recognized it as a major setback for his brain trust of lawyers at Howard University Law School who were whittling away at segregation. However, as a legal strategist, he understood the ways in which it made a mockery of justice and could be used to his advantage. The black press, including the *Chicago Defender*, the *Norfolk Journal and Guide*, and the *Washington Tribune* reported the entire content of the lawyers' telegram and used it to garner publicity for the NAACP and Houston's fight against racial injustice.[74]

Black Californians responded to their governor with indignation. African American Angelenos spearheaded a campaign for Rolph's impeachment. One of the local political clubs, the Thomas Jefferson Democratic League, and its president, Theodora Jones, circulated a petition for impeachment in early December. Jones wired the governor that "we denounce you as physically and mentally unfit to serve as chief executive of this sovereign state." A flurry of telegrams from other individuals and organizations followed, including one from Dr. Claude Hudson, president of the Los Angeles branch of the NAACP, and one from the Los Angeles Forum, the powerful black caucus of southern California.[75] Black newspapers across the country called for Rolph's impeachment and warned voters—not just in California—to monitor this dangerous turn of events.[76] An editorial in the *Kansas City Plaindealer* cautioned: "Negro voters in California and in any other state should see to it that men like Governor Rolph never hold political office. This is our salvation and we must not consider this issue a mere trivial matter."[77]

The antilynching movement took every opportunity to shame those who voiced approval for Governor Rolph. When Dr. Henry Darlington, the influential New York City minister of the fashionable Church of the Heavenly Rest on Fifth Avenue, praised Governor Rolph for taking a stand against criminals, he faced a hailstorm of protest from the NAACP, the black press, and other religious leaders.[78] Walter White fired off a telegram to Episcopal Bishop William T. Manning, calling for a repudiation of Darlington's endorsement of the crime. "It is difficult to see how a man professing to be a disciple of Jesus Christ who was himself turned over to a mob by a governor can applaud a modern governors [sic] unashamed approval of a lynching and still be allowed to wear the cloth of the church." Several days later, on December 3, a forum held at City College in New York drew 1,500 people, half of whom were African American, for an interfaith mass meeting. Bishop Manning addressed the huge crowd, followed by representatives from the American Jewish Congress and the Roman Catholic Church. Finally the well-known religious and community leader Rev. Adam Clayton Powell of the Abyssinian Baptist Church in Harlem took the podium.[79] Powell lambasted Rolph in a sermon-like address. Referring to the lynchings in California and Maryland, the minister and politician found both examples chilling: "during the last ten days we have witnessed the deplorable spectacle of a Governor endorsing lynching and a judge and district attorney refusing to try lynchers." Lynching white criminals amounted to the first link in a chain of unchecked violence, next "they will lynch governors and state officials who attempt to enforce the law," he warned. Mob rule in New York City was only a matter of time. Powell warned his audience that "the Negro cannot go down beneath the on-rushing feet of the mob without carrying the white man down with him."[80] The evidence lay in the white bodies of Thurmond and Holmes. At the end of the meeting, a series of resolutions passed, including resolutions calling for a federal antilynching law, the removal of Governor Rolph, and a fair trial for the defendants in the Scottsboro case.

Raising the specter of Scottsboro was both unavoidable and risky. In 1933, the nine black men and boys known as the Scottsboro Boys languished in prison in Decatur, Alabama, after being falsely accused of raping two white women in 1931. Although the U.S. Supreme Court had overturned the convictions of the first trial, a second trial in April of 1933 had, again, resulted in a guilty verdict. In December, when Powell delivered his oratory, it was not at all clear whether the defendants would escape execution. The travesty of justice that the Scottsboro case represented—all-white juries convicting black men for rape on the basis of faulty evidence—helped the antilynching movement make its case about the necessity of immediate action to stop lynch law. Making Scottsboro the centerpiece of the fight against lynching, however, brought the nation's attention to the South and to the question of black men raping white women; it was a risk some in the antilynching movement were not willing to take. In addition, the NAACP had been engaged in a struggle with the International Labor Defense (ILD), the legal arm of the Communist Party USA, over questions of who should defend the men. The NAACP did not want its antilynching efforts sullied by accusations of communist sympathies. Yet the NAACP joined the cause when Walter White visited the Scottsboro Boys in prison in 1931.[81] In 1933, the NAACP assiduously avoided the connection between Scottsboro and San Jose. Many Californians, however, pointed to the national culture that would let lynchers go free in California and falsely accuse black men of rape and let them hang or be lynched in Alabama. Under a banner headline "Who Is Guilty?," the *Eagle* asked if the governor of California, the state, the nation, or the metropolitan newspapers were to blame for the resurgence of lynching. Only days before the San Jose lynching, FDR had refused to call out the national guard to protect the Scottsboro Boys, the paper reminded readers.[82] Charlotta Bass, then editor of the *Eagle* and member of the Communist Party, scolded the NAACP: "The NAACP and all organizations . . . against lynching in the nation should join hands with the ILD and not stop until the nation is rid of the lynch evil."[83]

Shifting the focus of the antilynching movement to California forced the nation to confront the danger lynching posed to whites, or so Walter White and members of the NAACP hoped. An essential NAACP strategy in this era was to develop discursive frames about violence that could win the support of white citizens.[84] One of these discursive frames was the notion that lynching was no longer just a danger to black people. To get white citizens to care about the antilynching movement, the focus had to be pushed to safer ground: away from Scottsboro, and away from rape.[85] Better still, the NAACP tried to shift the discussion about lynching to European Americans—and Europe.

Connecting the California lynching with the international discourse on race, violence, and fascism became especially salient after Adolf Hitler came to power in 1932. Antilynching activists insisted that this U.S. crime exposed the nation to dangerous criticism from abroad and revealed democracy to be a sham. With the advent of Nazism, lynching became a subject of particular interest to the German press. The contrast between the treatment of African Americans at home and the U.S. government's condemnation of white supremacy abroad made lynching an international sensation. The San Jose example provided ample fodder for such publicity. In a story about the California lynchings, the New Republic quipped, "Hitler and his cohorts . . . must have read the recent dispatches with wry smiles." Walter White worked this angle as best he could, telling the press that "if I were a Communist, a Nazi, or a Fascist, and wanted to destroy or weaken American Democracy, I would work unceasingly to prevent passage of anti-lynching legislation." W. E. B. Du Bois was more direct in the pages of the Crisis: "Hitler himself could learn a beautiful technique by visiting us."[86]

As the NAACP tried to steer clear of communism in its ranks and locate it strictly in Europe, many saw communism, real or imagined, at the heart of the San Jose lynching. In no place in America was the Red Scare as blatant as it was in San Jose in 1933, where state-sanctioned violence was directed at workers in California's agricultural heartland. The city's location—in the center of the agricultural empire—meant growers wielded significant power over local politics and policing. The surrounding area also served as a center for agricultural workers and their unions, including the Cannery and Agricultural Workers' Industrial Union (CAWIU). Many of the leaders in this union were Communist Party members; Red-baiting became common practice for police, farmers, and the press. The San Jose press, in particular, fanned the flames of anticommunism, claiming that "a red invasion of Santa Clara County" was planned for the 1933 fruit-growing season.[87] That year was, in fact, a turning point for the state's agricultural workers: thirty-three major agricultural strikes happened in California, and twenty-four of them were organized by the CAWIU.[88] Their most impressive strike was that of the San Joaquin Valley cotton pickers, which drew over ten thousand workers to the picket lines and, according to state historian Kevin Starr, was "the largest agricultural strike in the history of the nation." Three workers were killed by growers during the strike.[89]

Some of the worst violence that summer took place in San Jose during a cherry-pickers strike. According to the New Republic, it was there in June that "police first used their clubs and pickaxe handles on a large scale," initiating a campaign of what farmers and police called "pickaxe handle justice." Calling the growers "California's Little Hitlers," the New Republic informed readers that Police Chief Black and Sherriff Emig (who lead the search for the Hart kidnappers) had been stockpiling weapons to attack "communist trouble makers." Farm workers were imprisoned, beaten, and harassed, and Ku Klux Klan members terrorized Filipino and Mexican workers.[90] The *New Republic* article noted that authorities promised that "no harm would come to any American citizen who attacked a worker. Just as Governor Rolph promises no harm to lynchers who lynch kidnappers." This was not the only report that connected the Red Scare to the lynching, however. "A wave of brutal official oppression has swept the State," *The Nation* reported. "Strikers have been put down ruthlessly, striking workers have been killed, the law has been invoked with a gun."[91]

The culture of violence that swept through the valley, the intensity of the Red Scare, and the alarming power of agribusiness and the police made for a dangerous combination, especially for workers. This was a society that had little sympathy for the Depression-era worker and increasingly painted the elite of the county, represented by growers, as the beleaguered class. In the Hart kidnapping case, the lines were clearly drawn: the son of the Hart family represented the ruling class, his kidnappers represented what working-class men could become if not heavily policed and controlled.

The controversial aspects of the California lynching did not, however, deter the NAACP from pressing its case. Walter White, in his autobiography, claimed that Rolph's comments served to rouse organizations and individuals "which had hitherto been indifferent" to lynching. For White and the NAACP, the most important of these previously indifferent individuals was President Franklin D. Roosevelt, who had been in office less than a year. The organization's leaders had waited in vain for the president to make a statement deploring the crime at his first press conferences.[92] But the San Jose lynching and the governor's blatant disregard for the law became impossible for the president to ignore. On December 6, a week after he refused to defend the Scottsboro Boys, FDR addressed the Federal Council of the Churches of Christ in a live radio broadcast. The president took the opportunity to reference the California lynching of the previous week, stating that "this new generation, for example, is not content with preaching against the vile form of collective murder, lynch law, which has broken out in our midst anew. . . . We do not excuse those in high places or in low who condone lynch law." This thinly veiled scolding of Governor Rolph was much appreciated by the antilynching forces, but nothing came of it. Again, W. E. B. Du Bois, as editor of the *Crisis*, did not mince words: "it only took 157 years for a president to denounce lynching," he wrote in the first issue published after FDR's speech.[93]

The NAACP was not the only organization to investigate the California crime. The ACLU made California's lynching central to their efforts to defend civil liberties, often working in tandem with the NAACP. The focus of ACLU work on the case became the recall of Governor Rolph and the prosecution of the lynch mob. Rolph's threat that he would pardon all lynchers caused the organization to offer $1,000 in reward for the capture of the lynchers.[94] Prosecuting the criminals who lynched Holmes and Thurmond became their chief priority, and, it was timely. In May 1933, Rolph had signed into law a bill providing a twenty-year prison sentence for anyone convicted of lynching.[95] It was clear to most observers, however, that the sheriff and the district attorney preferred to avoid this plan of action. Roger Baldwin, founder and national director of the ACLU, sent Los Angeles lawyers A. L. Wirrin and Ellis O. Jones to San Jose to investigate as soon as the lynching occurred. Wirrin, who would head the LA branch during World War II, began searching for witnesses in order to expedite an arrest. In less than two weeks after the crime, on December 7, Wirrin announced to the Associated Press that he had secured two witnesses and planned to present them to District Attorney Fred Thomas on December 12.[96] Efforts to secure the witnesses—two teenage boys assumed to be braggarts and a host of unnamed men—came to nothing. Although at the time there was no statute of limitation on murder cases in the state, no one was ever convicted of the lynchings, and a veil of secrecy kept the identity of the mob unknown.[97] The ACLU continued their efforts in the state, convening a series of mass meetings across California and across the country to pressure Congress for federal antilynching legislation. By keeping the lynching and the perpetrators in the headlines, the ACLU widened the coalition of the movement against lynching. Although Baldwin's actual involvement in the case was minimal, his high-profile relationship with the nation's elite, and legal counsel, helped draw attention to San Jose.

In the flurry of activity after the lynching—calls for impeachment, telegrams to the governor, and a frenzy of news coverage—the movement did not abandon one of its chief goals: the passage of federal legislation. The lynching in San Jose forced the matter, and Edward Costigan, senator from Colorado, wired Walter White days after the event to make the news official: "you may announce anti-lynching bill will be introduced by me in the Senate on opening day of Congress." The NAACP and the ACLU called a joint meeting in New York for December 7 to rally support for the Costigan-Wagner bill. The bill promised to retain the "good features" of the Dyer bill, which had died in the Senate in 1922, but additional clauses "[gave] it teeth."[98] The new clauses spoke directly to the San Jose lynching and the governor's refusal to take action. As members of the movement knew, the only way to pass federal legislation was to argue that the states were unwilling or unable to prevent the crimes from occurring. James Rolph once again delivered the goods. Under the bill, state and local officials who "failed to protect citizens or to arrest or prosecute violators of the law" could be jailed up to five years, fined up to $5,000, or both.[99] To draw attention to the fiasco in California, Los Angeles representative Thomas F. Ford introduced the bill on the Senate floor. Despite widespread support, the bill was filibustered in 1934 and again in 1935; like the Dyer bill, Costigan-Wagner was successfully stalled and never passed into law. Whatever momentum was gained by the antilynching movement from the spectacular news of the San Jose lynching and the deafening response of the governor did not translate into federal legislation. Secrecy and shame coalesced to protect the perpetrators and bury the news of the murderous mob and a state that supported them. In the future, it would be left to filmmakers, journalists, and artists to reclaim this history and its lessons.

San Jose Memories

Dramatic visual representations kept the San Jose lynching in the public imagination for years after the event, a development that was applauded and aided by the antilynching movement. Photographs would prove to be the most pervasive representation, but certainly not the only one to achieve wide circulation. In addition to the photographs, a Pulitzer Prize–winning cartoon of the lynching, and a 1936 film based on the event, turned a western spectacle into a cause for national shame. These visual narratives reached an international audience of millions. Historical memory of the murders shifted over time and space; different publics had different levels of exposure. Yet knowledge of the San Jose lynching entered the public imagination in a way unlike previous lynchings, partly due to the strategic use of the race of the victims by the black press and the NAACP. The specter of Holmes and Thurmond hanging from an oak tree made good copy for journalists, but photographs and a Hollywood film about the lynching achieved something mere words could not: they delivered the California tragedy to the hearts and minds of spectators in ways more direct and more affecting than traditional news sources. This infiltration of lynching imagery into the public sphere turned San Jose into a more powerful tool for the antilynching movement than Thomas Fleming or Delilah Beasley could have imagined. The visual record was one of the strongest weapons the black press, the NAACP, and antilynching agitators could deploy to keep the memory of the San Jose murders alive.

Because pictures of lynched black bodies raised the specter of white supremacy, rape accusations, and other uncomfortable truths, the mainstream white press generally did not print images of lynching victims. White-owned newspapers feared inciting, as Amy Wood argues, "volatile and unmanageable emotional responses, including white guilt and shame."[100] In the case of San Jose, however, erasure from the public sphere seemed unnecessary; lynched white bodies, no matter how gruesome, did not raise the issue of racial domination, or so many in the media believed. Partly due to this belief, this lynching became seen and "known" to viewers like no other. The way the images were received, of course, varied. For Thomas Fleming, it did not take much to imagine black bodies in place of the bodies of Holmes and Thurmond. For the antilynching movement to make best use of this event, however, Americans did not have to think of black bodies at all; they could and should focus on the fact that white bodies were lynched and that white people perpetrated and enjoyed the spectacle. The presence of white victims, white lynchers, and white spectators would all become essential to the visual narratives spun after the crime.

First and foremost, the memory—and the understanding—of the event was filtered through the medium of photography. More than any single representation, including newspaper stories, the lynching photos reproduced in the press and on postcards became the essential markers of the crime and its significance. Photographs had already been used to great effect by the antilynching movement, although their use had inspired controversy. Since the 1890s, activists feared that lynching images only inspired further acts of terror. Ida B. Wells shunned the use of photographs in her 1892 study *Southern Horrors*, but she included photographs in her most influential work, *A Red Record*, published in 1895.[101] Black activists of the twentieth century struggled to determine the effectiveness of photography in their campaigns. In the 1920s, for example, James Weldon Johnson, then executive secretary of the NAACP, questioned the effectiveness of photographs in the promotional materials for the Dyer antilynching bill.[102] Walter White, who succeeded Johnson in 1931, championed the use of photographs.[103] Indeed, the NAACP had been printing lynching photos in their pamphlets since the organization began, but the debate regarding their effectiveness and efficacy still simmered when the California news broke. With the 1933 lynching of Holmes and Thurmond, however, "all the rules regarding what could and could not be represented in the press changed."[104] For the first time, many mainstream daily newspapers printed a lynching photograph on the front page.[105] The technology of photography changed in the 1930s, making the reproduction of half-tone photographs more economical and thus a possibility for most newspapers. The race of the victims also made it possible—indeed preferable—to print images of the bodies. Whiteness, in this case, allowed the national press to avoid discussion of black criminals and violated white women.

Due in part to the outsized publicity of the Hart kidnapping, there was a camera crew at the ready in St. James Park when Holmes and Thurmond were dragged from the jail. Reporters from the San Jose and Bay Area newspapers had clearly received advance warning. Indeed, a local radio station had announced that there might be a lynching.[106] At least four photographs from the jail raid circulated in the press: one depicted the crowd slamming into the jailhouse door with the steel beam, one of Holmes's lynched body, one of Thurmond's lynched body, and one of spectators at the lynching. Since Thurmond was naked below the waist and Holmes had been stripped of all of his clothes by the lynch mob, their genitalia were clearly visible in the photographs. Not all newspapers and magazines chose to print the graphic photographs. San Francisco banned photos of the lynching; but the Hearst paper, the *Oakland Post-Enquirer*, published a special edition emblazoned with the photographs.[107] That such potent images exist at all tells us much about the preparation or preparedness of the press for this crime; it was understood that the lynching would be filmed and that the images would be widely circulated.

The image that most newspapers, including the San Jose newspapers, printed was of the crowd wielding the metal pipe to break down the door of the jail.[108] That photograph, taken by an unnamed photographer, conveyed the mob's frenzied violence and avoided the difficult editorial decision of whether to expose the readership to nude lynch victims. San Jose police Chief Black banned the printing of the other lynching photos and confiscated as many copies of the *Oakland Post-Enquirer* as he could find. Local officials and editors feared that the images damaged the reputation of the city and might incriminate locals who would be recognized in the mob. One local paper, the *San Jose News*, tried to justify its censorship of the photos in question by calling attention to their female readership. Under the headline "Weren't Scooped," the paper editorialized that although their cameramen shot pictures of the men hanging by their necks in St. James Park, the News was delivered to the homes of "children and sensitive women" and therefore it could not publish the "gruesome and horrible pictures." It clearly hurt circulation, but "there are some standards of good taste which the News would not violate." Coming as it did from a paper that all but condoned the lynching in their editorial, it appears, as reporter Harry Ferrell noted, that for this paper "lynching was acceptable; pictures of it were not."[109]

Newspapers were not the only site of photographic images of the lynching, and by no means were they the most graphic. Postcards produced by amateur photographers and news agencies hit the streets in the days following the murder. Sold to Californians and tourists alike, the postcards looked not unlike those sold after southern lynchings and were among the only souvenirs available to those not present during the crime. The title of one postcard, "The Kidnapper's Fate," spoke volumes about the sentiments that fueled the lynch mob and the spirit that Governor Rolph helped unleash. A small scrapbook of the lynching was also bought and sold across the state.[110] The booklet consisted of six photos: Thurmond's face, Holmes's face, the mob battering down the jail door, Holmes's lynching, Thurmond's lynching, and the mob crowded in front of the jail. In addition to the imagery, the booklet contained Rolph's infamous quotation about California's lesson.

Cartoons allowed the observer more distance from the event than did photographs or postcards, but they were no less damning. For decades, white cartoonists had avoided portraying the bodies of lynched black men, instead depicting white officials or inanimate objects that interpreted lynching without addressing blackness, the gruesome carnival atmosphere, or white supremacy. Since their white bodies were thought to be race neutral, Thurmond and Holmes again provided the perfect antidote to the sticky problem of how to depict a lynching and not draw attention to race. Rolph had not only delivered the perfect copy for journalists with his outrageous statements to the press, he also became the ideal subject for cartoonists across the country. Already an easily caricatured figure with his round belly, cowboy boots, and cowboy hat, Rolph made the work of ridicule simple. Edmund Duffy's drawing of the lynching in the Baltimore Sun earned him a Pulitzer Prize. Duffy's cartoon, printed on November 28, two days after the murder, depicts Rolph pointing above his head to the lynched bodies of Thurmond and Holmes. The only words in the cartoon were "Gov. Rolph"

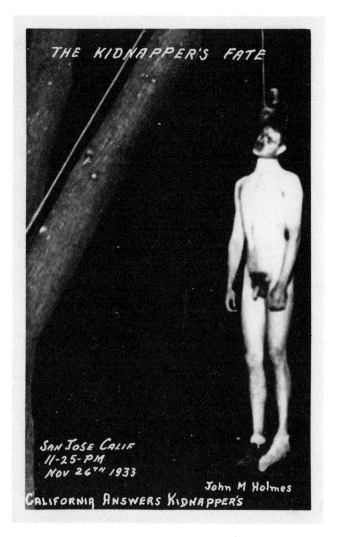

Souvenirs from the San Jose lynching included pieces of the tree in St. James Park, postcards, and pamphlets. (Courtesy of the California Historical Society)

printed on his vest. The readers of the *Sun* knew all they needed to know from Rolph's understated smile and self-satisfied look. The lynched figures are not abstract but not grotesquely graphic like photographs of lynched bodies. And, more importantly, they are fully clothed. The most disturbing element of the cartoon was the bent fingers and crooked hand of the figure on the left, a small but frightening detail, signaling the onset of rigor mortis.

This hand would look familiar to anyone who had seen the photograph of African American lynching victim George Hughes in Sherman, Texas, three years earlier. The image of Hughes's charred body, his protruding hand, and bent fingers produced one of the most horrendous lynching photographs ever distributed, and the black press saw it for the weapon it was, reprinting it in the *Chicago Defender* and the *New York Afro-American*.[111] In a full page in *The Nation*, William Steig drew an equally damning representation of the event. In his cartoon, Rolph is called "Gov. Lynch of California," and he urges on a character called "The Mob" who is stringing up a body on a tree limb, telling them "Go right ahead." A liquor bottle is visible in the mob's back pocket, referring to the widespread but erroneous belief that a drunken crowd lynched Thurmond and Holmes.[112] This cartoon, combined with *The Nation*'s lengthy reportage, made for some of the most scathing criticism in the country.

The visual culture of lynching shifted with California's crime, as did antilynching rhetoric. Among the many changes wrought by the murders in San Jose, the focus on white bodies and white citizens is undoubtedly one of the most significant. The victims' whiteness gave license to artists in the mainstream white press to depict bodies in ways that had previously been the domain of the black press and antilynching organizations. This shift coincided with the NAACP's focus on the psychic damage that lynching caused to whites, in particular the danger of the uncivilized white mob and the disturbingly carnival atmosphere of lynchings. This focus did not begin with San Jose but the events in California accelerated the strategy and crystallized the message. One of the new tactics utilized by the NAACP was to highlight the presence of white children as spectators. Again, the San Jose lynching provided fodder for the movement. In the crowd photo, which was published by *Time* magazine, children crowd up against the barricade to watch the lynching, and a man holds up a little girl, who looks straight into the camera.[113] This image no doubt inspired antilynching activists, and as Amy Wood argues, it influenced Fritz Lang when he directed the film based on events in San Jose.[114] In 1935, the NAACP used the focus on children in its final efforts to pass federal antilynching legislation; one pamphlet pictured the shocking photograph of the lynching of Rubin Stacey in Fort Lauderdale, Florida, with the text: "Do Not Look at the Negro. His earthly problems are ended. Instead look at the seven WHITE children who gaze at this gruesome spectacle. What kind of America will they help to make after being familiarized with such an inhuman, law-destroying practice?"[115]

"Go Right Ahead!"

William Steig's cartoon appeared in the December 13, 1933, issue of *The Nation*.

The lynching of Holmes and Thurmond became fodder for Hollywood as it did for journalists, photographers, and cartoonists. Just as the victims' whiteness altered traditions in print journalism, it opened up possibilities in the film industry for new ways to address the topic of lynching. Getting films past the state and local censors became increasingly difficult after 1934, when codes were formalized by the Production Code Administration.[116] Depicting lynched black bodies was expressly forbidden, as were direct references to white supremacy. Thus, filmmakers who wished to address the topic did so largely in symbolic ways. Rarely, if ever, did a film reference a particular lynching. Again, this changed after the lynching of Holmes and Thurmond. In 1936, three years after the lynching, Metro-Goldwyn-Mayer released *Fury*, the first U.S. film of Austrian director Fritz Lang. There was no question that the film was based on the events in San Jose, and it garnered significant attention in the United States and Europe. Walter White was so taken with the film that he wrote to Eleanor Roosevelt asking her to arrange a screening at the White House.[117] Starring Spencer Tracy and Silvia Sydney, the film received rave reviews, many praising it for its stark realism, and earned an Academy Award nomination for screenwriting. But White's interest in the film stemmed from what he saw as its usefulness to the antilynching movement. Writing to MGM, he praised the film for its ability to "bring home to America what mob violence really means."[118] The timing of the film was critical to the NAACP: the Costigan-Wagner bill still lacked congressional approval, and White hoped the film could act as a catalyst to push the measure into law.

The plot centers on a working-class Chicagoan, "Joe," played by Tracy, who finds himself falsely accused of kidnapping and jailed for the offense. Unbeknownst to the mob, Joe escapes from the jail before they burn it down. While in hiding, Joe becomes obsessed with convicting the mob for a murder they did not commit. Producer Joe Mankiewicz, screenwriter Norman Krasna, and Fritz Lang, studied the kidnapping case that became the Holmes-Thurmond lynching, and there are many visual and narrative references to the case in the film.[119] There is a Rolph-like governor who does nothing to stop the lynching and other details that most viewers of the day would recognize as references to the California case. The scene of the burning jailhouse is clearly a reference to the photograph of the mob attacking the San Jose jail. Amy Wood notes that Lang based another one of his shots on the infamous photo of the child spectators; the scene features an adult holding up a young child to watch the burning of the jail. For many, however, Joe's transformation delivers the most significant condemnation of lynching. Joe becomes tainted by his desire for revenge and represents what can happen when a law-abiding citizen turns into a vigilante. Eventually Joe repents and, in a moving courtroom scene, comes clean and exonerates the mob. *Fury* required viewers to think about the damage lynching posed to whites and the rule of law. Wood argues that the film "impelled white audiences to recognize their own culpability and responsibility, just as Joe recognizes his."[120] It's no wonder that White had high hopes for the film, as it took up some of the very strategies the NAACP had been concentrating on in its campaign.

Reviews of the film were mixed. Some critics find this one of Lang's darkest and best films. Others felt the love story and corny ending (insisted on by the studio) diluted the film's message about lynching.[121] But the antilynching message was not lost on audiences, and black and white critics alike offered high praise for the film's message.[122] Not only was the plot an indictment of mob violence, but the film did not shy away from addressing the prevalence of lynching in the United States. During the courtroom scene, for example, the district attorney tells the judge that "mobs have lynched 6,010 human beings by hanging, burning, cutting in this proud land of ours, a lynching about every three days." Publicity for the film included statistics on the numbers prosecuted—only 675 in the last fifty years.[123] White encouraged all members of the NAACP to see the film, and black newspapers across the country promoted it.

Although *Fury* opened in mainstream theaters in Hollywood and New York in June 1936, it did not play in the black neighborhoods of Los Angeles until that fall, when it opened at the Tivoli and Rosebud theaters on Central Avenue. The *Los Angeles Sentinel* ran an ad for the film under a broad headline "Mob Storms Jail." Californians could hardly mistake the reference. Underneath the screenshot of the mob pushing into the jail with the iron pipe, the text read "The mob was wild. He was innocent. Just a kidnap suspect, but the mob was ready and wanted to lynch him." The Los Angeles NAACP promoted the film and, along with the Florence Mills theater, even sponsored a contest for the best essay on mob violence. The attorney Thomas Griffith, president of the local branch, clubwoman Mabel Gray, and actor Clarence Muse acted as judges of the contest and presented the winners with cash prizes. Muse, who had a column in the *California Eagle*, called *Fury* "the best argument to date against lynching," and encouraged all local schoolchildren and their parents to enter the contest.[124]

While leaders such as Walter White may have been temporarily buoyed by the success of *Fury*, it was difficult to measure the impact of the film on the public understanding of lynching. In 1936, the year *Fury* was released, eight of the Scottsboro Boys awaited trial after one of the men, Haywood Patterson, had been found guilty; the Costigan-Wagner Bill stalled in Congress. Opponents of Jim Crow and racial violence had little to celebrate in the middle of the Great Depression. Even Delilah Beasley, ever an optimist, found it difficult to recover from California's lesson on lynching, in spite of the fact that 1933 started out as a banner year for the state's antilynching activists. Beasley had fought for years to secure an antilynching bill in her home state, succeeding in May 1933. Using her *Oakland Tribune* column, "Activities Among Negroes" as a platform, she wrote repeatedly about the state and national movements to stop the crime. She also convinced the *Tribune* to print an antilynching editorial and wrote to ask the NAACP to send a letter of support to the newspaper.[125] On learning of the November murders and the governor's response, she refused to believe it. "His words last week in regard to lynching were spoken without first stopping to consider the effect of the same coming from him as governor. He did not mean what he said he simply did not stop to consider what he was saying." A hailstorm of protest followed, and in Beasley's column the following week she explained herself; she honestly believed that Rolph had made an innocent mistake and would recant his words. Instead, as she discovered, "he made other statements that proved that he had given the matter careful thought before the occurrence." Lulled by his signature of a bill she considered one of her greatest victories in the fight against Jim Crow, Beasley was unprepared for his embrace of lynchers. "This writer, as a loyal citizen of the great state of California, is very sorry that the Governor made these additional statements."[126] Beasley ended her column by asking every California citizen to write to their members of Congress to support the NAACP's federal antilynching bill, the Costigan-Wagner bill. All month the journalist kept her readers apprised of the campaign to denounce and impeach Rolph. On December 24 she congratulated the Alameda County League of Colored Women Voters for publicly condemning Rolph in the *Oakland Tribune*.

Beasley remained steadfastly optimistic that California would prove to be a better place than the South. She may have felt that her optimism was rewarded when her editor at the *Tribune*, William Knowland, and California's first black legislator, Frederick Roberts, introduced the state's first antilynching bill and the governor signed it. Beasley, as she did in her columns about the PPIE, tried valiantly to maintain her optimism about her home state. But the governor delivered a crushing blow with his strident support of the San Jose lynching.

James Rolph's death in January 1934 presented another occasion for the nation to relive the horrendous events of the past November. Columnist Ralph Matthews of the *Baltimore Afro-American* found the criticisms of Rolph a bit naive: "Very few of the criticisms aimed at Dr. [*sic*] Rolph are sincere. There are few who do not actually believe that lynching was too good for the reprobates who kidnapped a youth, killed him in cold blood, and then attempted to collect the ransom. Colored folk, least of all, had any reason to complain. Instead of raising a howl we ought to rejoice that the color line had been removed from the lynch industry." Matthews believed, like many proponents of antilynching, that a federal antilynching law would only be passed if white folks also felt threatened. As he put it, "the only hope for the passage of an anti-lynching bill in America is that more white necks are cracked with the same dispatch with which brethren of color are sent to eternity at the end of a hemp rope." Like Robert Abbott of the *Chicago Defender*, Matthews found the lynching of white men not just newsworthy; it might mean the beginning of the end of lynching. "There would be no law against murder in America if only black folk got bumped off," Matthews wrote, "but since the carcasses of blue bloods are just as perishable when loaded with hot lead as a transplanted African, slaying is outlawed."[127]

Remembering San Jose and James Rolph was essential for antilynching activists and those working to end racial violence. Matthews reminded his readers: "The late Jimmy Rolph put his stamp of approval on necktie parties without any restrictions as to race, creed, or color. This was a magnificent contribution to society and will live long after his bones are returned to dust." At least Rolph was honest, Matthews pointed out, unlike all the southern governors who feigned horror at lynch mobs. Matthews was right that California did teach the nation a lesson, but not the kidnapping lesson Rolph intended. The San Jose lynching gave President Roosevelt pause. It presented unprecedented opportunities for the black press and mainstream cartoonists and filmmakers to address lynching and shame the nation. Certainly, the international press was damning. Thus the 1933 California crime ultimately helped end the epidemic of lynching in the United States. After the lynching of Holmes and Thurmond, and with Hitler's pronouncements of white supremacy, the practice would lose most of its defenders.[128]

The lynching of two white men in California permanently changed the way Americans understood lynching. As black critics like Ralph Matthews noted, shifting the focus away from black men helped end the practice and this saved black lives. It also, however, decoupled the connection of lynching and Jim Crow. This decoupling did little to improve the lives of black Americans. Thomas Fleming understood these contradictions when he condemned the 1933 lynching. Already a keen observer of California's antipathy toward African Americans, he knew too well that praise for lynchers could not improve the lives of any U.S. citizens, least of all black ones. What Matthews and Fleming could not know at the time is that the landscape for black Californians was about to be radically transformed by the second phase of the Great Migration. White supremacists, including members of the Ku Klux Klan, would target black migrants who they deemed "out of place," and the racialized violence of 1940s California would stun even seasoned black journalists.

CHAPTER 5

Burning Down the House

California's Ku Klux Klan

By 1945 the African American refrigeration engineer O'Day Short had lived and worked in Los Angeles for nearly twenty-five years. Like many black Angelenos, however, he was frustrated by the housing shortages precipitated by the war and the massive influx of migrants to the Golden State. The father of young children, Short felt prices had become prohibitive; his options for housing deteriorated as restrictive covenants squeezed black families out of desirable neighborhoods. East of the city, the San Bernardino County town of Fontana promoted itself as a place free of the Jim Crow restrictions that increasingly hemmed in and humiliated black citizens.[1] This promise, and the jobs at Kaiser Steel mill, drew the Shorts to Fontana. The small town, in spite of the promises, restricted black workers to a segregated area north of the town center. O'Day Short, however, would not be hemmed in by the dictates of segregation. Short, his wife, Helen, and their two young children moved into a previously all-white neighborhood in central Fontana in early December 1945, on 5 acres of land on the corner of Randall and Pepper streets, where they had their home built.[2] Two weeks after they moved in, Short and his family were the victims of a house fire that killed Helen and both children. O'Day Short was rushed to Kaiser Steel mill hospital where he survived five more weeks before dying January 21, 1946. African American friends, family members, the NAACP, labor leaders, and the black press believed that the arson had been the work of the Ku Klux Klan. Short had received a warning from a vigilante group earlier that month. The fiery blast was suspicious enough to warrant an FBI investigation, but only after

Short himself informed the agency. What followed was a cover-up of enormous proportions. The murders and the subsequent silence surrounding the crime speaks volumes about the power of the California Klan and their connections to law enforcement throughout the state. The murders of Short and his family epitomized just how threatening white Californians found the black presence and black homeownership in particular. "Southland residential racism reached its gruesome climax with the Fontana *auto da fe*," wrote Mike Davis.[3]

By the time the Short family died, California had become a hot spot in the national movement against restrictive covenants—and Los Angeles "ground zero."[4] No one understood this more than the people of color under siege. In the years before the U.S. Supreme Court determined that racial property restrictions were unenforceable in *Shelley v. Kraemer* (1948), a coalition of California citizens led the war over segregation, which was waged block by block in the region's most populous state. However, the assault on the state's black homeowners helped transform the state into a civil rights frontier.[5] Western black homeowners posed a threat not only because they integrated neighborhoods but also because in so doing they integrated schools, parks, pools, and beaches. Black Californians could and did buy property in respectable middle-class neighborhoods, send their children to the schools in those neighborhoods, and visit parks, pools, and playgrounds all over the state. They also took jobs in wartime industries that became progressively scarce as the war drew to a close. By World War II, black homeowners in California were increasingly at the center of the national controversy over segregation. This controversy, like those over southern integration, drew blood.

Violence directed at African American homeowners in California peaked in the 1940s. This dramatic episode in California's history of Jim Crow can be attributed to a convergence of several factors, not least of which was race mixing in intimate spaces. As Charlotta Bass, editor and publisher of the *California Eagle*, pointed out, many believed that white hysteria over housing restrictions and the increase in Klan activity was prompted by a controversy over integrated swimming in Pasadena's public pool (see ch. 6). California segregationists faced an onslaught of threats in the war years: the exponential increase in the black population; the successful lawsuits brought forward by Loren Miller and the NAACP over restricted housing; and the equally successful attacks on miscegenation laws and segregated schools, pools, and labor unions. Just as the Short family was moving into their new home, NAACP lawyers were writing their brief for *Perez v. Sharp*, a case that would declare a miscegenation law unconstitutional; the Pasadena pool case was in its final phases of litigation; black Boilermakers Union workers won their landmark victory against segregated unions in 1944; and the *Mendez v. Westminster* case, which would challenge school segregation, was winding its way through the California courts. It was a perfect storm.

White vigilantes, such as those in the Ku Klux Klan, made it their business to attack those on the front lines of these battles over the color line. Organized in the 1920s as part of the second iteration of the Ku Klux Klan, the California Klan's initial chapters formed in Los Angeles. A 1922 raid of the Klan headquarters by the district attorney revealed a powerful organization whose members infiltrated all levels of city and state government. New Klan members moved to the state during World War II just as black homeowners renewed their offensive against restricted housing. The fears that motivated segregationists and white supremacists found new outlets once black, Mexican, and Japanese veterans returned from the war and moved to their neighborhoods. In their persistent and expansive attack on black homeowners, Klan members mustered an assault on African American citizens in ways eerily similar to activities of the first Klan formed during Reconstruction. The violence of the 1940s became one of the most dramatic reminders of the state's commitment to the color line. This chapter focuses on the California Klan and their attack on black home-owning Californians, a history that demonstrates that Jim Crow in the Golden State could be modern, insidious, and violent simultaneously.

Following the trajectory of the Klan in the Golden State underscores the centrality of black migrants—and the racial animosity they inspired—to the politics of twentieth-century California. In the 1950s, an effective coalition of Californians opposed to the civil rights movement embraced many of the same issues that had motivated the Klan, including opposition to black homeownership and school integration. The successes and failures of California's Invisible Empire help to explain the right-wing mobilization that gave rise to Presidents Richard Nixon and Ronald Reagan. In many ways, the Klan offered a lesson for the state's "moral majority," which would redirect its tactics to appeal more broadly to California voters. Voters' election of Reagan as governor in 1966 was in part a rejection of Governor Edmund G. "Pat" Brown's embrace of a civil rights agenda; Reagan was opposed to school desegregation.[6] The deep commitment to keeping neighborhoods, schools, and public spaces white-only that was embraced by white supremacist organizations such as the Klan found new expression in Reagan's America.[7] This turn to the right in U.S. politics began much earlier than the 1960s, however. By honing in on 1940s California, we can locate the antipathy and racialized violence that integration inspired. This focus also underscores the centrality of gender, sexuality, and interracial mixing in particular, to the twentieth-century backlash against black freedom.

The California Klan retained an intense focus on black men and women—a trait associated with the first KKK and with the southern Klan—as it infiltrated the ranks of state and local government and law enforcement. The unusually high rates of homeownership by African Americans in California became a potent symbol of the ability of African American men to claim the rights of manhood, just as voting had been that symbol in the nineteenth century. The threat of black masculinity has been understood as a central concern of the first Klan. The rights of black men, and their insistence on claiming those rights, motivated members of the second Klan to commit violence during and immediately following World War II. Whereas most histories of the second Klan stop in the 1930s, pushing the chronology forward to examine the 1940s reveals how the presence of African American homeowners and workers elicited some of the strongest and most violent reactions of California's white supremacists. Placing the activities of the Klan into the story of the fight against restrictive covenants underscores the risks taken by black Californians and the multiple threats they posed to segregationists. Framing the struggle against segregated housing in California as one that was fought solely in the courts obscures the significant role of the Klan and other white supremacists and the violence directed at the state's freedom fighters.

In order to understand the story of O'Day Short and his family, we have to take seriously the *resistance* embodied in the Shorts' history. The Klan faced formidable pushback in the Golden State. Charlotta Bass, Carey McWilliams, and other progressive, activist Californians made the state an uneasy home for white supremacists and hate groups. By calling attention to the Klan's actions and naming them in the press, at rallies, in the governor's office, and in the offices of the NAACP and the ACLU, activists helped to suppress the Klan by the 1950s. African Americans like O'Day Short and his family pushed up against the color line and were murdered for doing so.

A California "Club"

The second Ku Klux Klan, founded in Georgia in 1915 by William Joseph Simmons, represents, as historian Nancy MacLean states, "the most powerful movement of the far right that America has yet produced." It recruited more members than any of the Klan's iterations before or since. At its peak, by the mid-1920s, the organization counted upward of 4 million members nationwide, with four thousand chapters spread across the length and breadth of the country.[8] This Klan had a wider geographic reach than the original southern Klan, with strongholds in places like Indiana, Ohio, and Oregon. By all accounts, Simmons's inspiration for the revival of the Klan sprang from D. W. Griffith's new film *The Birth of Nation*, which was made in Los Angeles and based on Thomas Dixon's novel, *The Clansman*. This film, as discussed in chapter 2, played to packed theaters up and down the state despite a well-organized and vocal protest led by journalists Delilah Beasley and Charlotta Bass, among others. The first showing of the film took place fewer than twenty miles from Fontana, in Riverside, California. The filmic celebration of the Reconstruction-era Klan, the first KKK, provided Simmons with the motivation to organize a new, and in many ways, more expansive Klan. While the Klan of Reconstruction targeted African Americans, the second Klan added Catholics, Jews, and immigrants to its list of offenders. Showings of *The Birth of a Nation* provided perfect opportunities for recruiting new members across the country, demonstrating the importance of new technologies for this modern Klan. Indeed, less than a decade after the film premiered, the community of Riverside hosted a massive Klan initiation ceremony and parade. The Golden State proved especially hospitable to this new organization, founded the same year eugenicists met in San Francisco at the Panama Pacific International Exposition (see ch. 2). The enthusiasm in the state for eugenics and *The Birth of a Nation* made for a welcoming climate for a resurgent Klan.[9]

In the 1920s, Simmons seized on the West as prime territory for recruiting new Klansmen and women. While Klan members in western states, as a whole, never amounted to more than 7 percent of the organization's national membership, California and Oregon proved especially fruitful sites for initiating new members.[10] In 1921, Simmons sent Grand Goblin William S. Coburn to Los Angeles to organize chapters. Coburn promptly opened "a three-man office" downtown in the Haas building and set up a dozen klaverns or meeting halls in nearby communities.[11] By 1922, Oakland, Fresno, Riverside, Sacramento, San Francisco, Anaheim, and San Jose all had chapters. Recruiting proceeded "at a furious pace up and down the Pacific Coast."[12] Coburn was particularly successful in southern California; Los Angeles had three branches and would become the epicenter of Klan strength in the state. The California Klan had a wide reach; its initial successes becoming a model for other Klan chapters in the West. The organization's national magazine, the *Imperial Night-Hawk*, shows that California ranked eleventh out of all forty-eight states in terms of the number of Klan events held between March 1923 and November 1924.[13] Hosting eighty-nine events in that twenty-month period, California outranked the old slave states of Mississippi, Louisiana, West Virginia, North Carolina, and Tennessee. In fact, the Golden State had nearly twice as many Klan-sponsored events as Oregon, a state often described as the most Klan-infested western state.[14] The strength of Oregon's Klan can, in part, be traced to California. The first Klan chapter to organize in Oregon arrived from California in 1921.[15] Other kleagles or recruiters from California followed. Unlike California's Klan, however, Oregon's chapters did not embrace violence as a central tactic.[16]

The participants in the second Klan were originally depicted in popular and scholarly literature as rural, uneducated backward southerners or as small-town, narrow-minded midwesterners, men who objected to the changes wrought by the emerging consumer culture of the jazz age.[17] According to this view, sometimes called the traditional school, the Klan represented the antithesis of modernity. This portrait of the second Klan helped to obscure the success of the organization in mainstream U.S. life. By envisioning Klan members only as white-robed extremists, we have "sidelined [them] to the margins of American history despite [their] large membership and cultural influence," according to Kelly J. Baker.[18] Some have argued that rather than a fringe terrorist organization, the Klan was made up of middle-class, educated Protestants who, in socioeconomic terms, differed little from their neighbors. Armed with messages about American patriotism, the Klan, in this interpretation, looks less like an aberration and more resonant with what we might call mainstream U.S. politics and culture. Kenneth Jackson, one of the first to articulate this argument, charted the strength of the second Klan in U.S. cities and debunked the myth of a small-town rural Klan. This approach helps us understand the group's popularity in the Golden State and the ways their fears, if not their behavior, looked similar to those of many other white Californians who resented the presence of nonwhites.

The Populist-Civic School of thought has dominated the study of the second Klan in the U.S. West. Klansmen, as these studies show, were reform-minded Protestants, middle-class white men looking to influence local and state governments. They relied on fraternal lodges and Protestant churches for support, and often struggled against elites for civic control. The studies in Shawn Lay's 1992 edited volume, *The Invisible Empire in the West: Toward a New Historical Appraisal of the Ku Klux Klan of the 1920s*, are emblematic of this approach. Lay argues that the authors in the anthology sought to evaluate the second Klan in "as objective and sensitive manner as possible," never forgetting that "beneath the threatening white robes and hoods walked millions of otherwise respectable Americans."[19] Christopher Coltcochos, for example, shows that members of the Anaheim Klan in Orange County came from the same socioeconomic background as Anaheim's non-Klan or anti-Klan citizens, and included a high proportion of property owners. In fact, with access to a comprehensive members list, he could determine that the jobs Klansmen held were "a bit more prestigious" than those held by their non-Klan counterparts. By 1923 the Anaheim Klan had almost nine hundred members and was poised to insert themselves into city elections and city planning, both of which had been dominated by the German American first families of the city. These Klansmen registered to vote (in higher percentages than non-Klansmen) and joined civic organizations like the Chamber of Commerce and the Rotary Club. By the spring of 1924, the Anaheim city council was dominated by Klansmen who initiated a program to replace non-Klan city employees with their own members. Their plan succeeded: ten new policemen (of a total of fifteen) were members of the Invisible Empire. Coltcochos admits that the period of Klan-dominated civic life was brief, but it "demonstrated the order's desire for a more moral, law-abiding, and formally bound community."[20] There can be no doubt that the California Klan exerted significant pressure in the 1920s: winning seats on city councils, gaining control of the press and airwaves in some towns, and pressuring public officials. Yet, descriptions of a "moral" and "law-abiding" Klan do little to explain what happened to O'Day Short and his family.

Linking the California Klan's belief in law and order to the racial ide-ologies of a growing class of white homeowners makes the intensity of the Golden State's Invisible Empire, and their eventual use of violence, more legible. Chris Rhomberg found that Oakland Klansmen of the 1920s were concerned with the "rights and privileges associated with white racial identity." Chief among these concerns were homeownership and city services. The Klan capitalized on Oakland's growing white middle-class and their antipathy toward the ethnic political machine. New homeowners in the rapidly expanding city embraced restrictive covenants that kept neighborhoods white, and they worked to wrest city government from the machine and the business elite. Rhomberg finds that the Klan's actions do not fit neatly in the Populist-Civic School because they are as concerned with race, ethnicity, and power as they are with law and order. During their brief stint in Oakland politics, Klansmen proved more corrupt than the members of the machine, operating bootlegging and gambling operations they publicly claimed to abhor. "The ease with which Klan leaders were able to cross over into the political mainstream underscores the extent to which local civic issues and participation were already framed in ethnic and racial terms," Rhomberg argues.[21]

So far no studies examine the California Klan after their 1920s heyday. This is likely due to the fact that the historiography holds that the second iteration of the KKK fizzled out in the 1930s. The traditional chronology sees a third Klan emerging in 1954 in response to the *Brown* decision, while the period from 1930 to 1954 has often been viewed as a Klan-free era. Glenn Feldman, in his study of the Alabama Klan, argues that as tempting as it is to abide by this timeline, "a small core of determined right-wing Klan members" remained active in this period and their significance has been ignored by historians. One of Feldman's key points is that this Klan, which he calls a "bridge Klan," suffered a series of humiliations and setbacks in the 1920s, not least of which was the struggling national leadership and bad publicity brought on by scandals. "These Knights," he argues, "stripped of substantial political influence, waged a rearguard action that was more extreme and less representative of white society than that mounted by the 1920s order had been."[22] This profile fits the Golden State to a T. The Great Migration, and the unusually high rate of African American homeownership in California, ushered in a new wave of Klan activity in the late 1930s and 1940s, inspiring an epidemic of violence. Yet this aspect of the California Klan has been virtually ignored. Only one study of the KKK draws attention to the violence in California; David Chalmer's 1965 text *Hooded Americanism* argues that Klan violence in the Golden State was "as brutal as anywhere in the South."[23] Often, but not always, this violence occurred in the parts of the state that had the highest numbers of African American homeowners such as Los Angeles or the Bay Area. By the 1940s, however, the threat of the Great Migration united fearful whites in towns and cities even where there were very few black families, like Fontana. The case of the Short family reminds us that the Klan often operated in areas where the black population was relatively meager and their vigilance to enforce the color line was as important to them as influencing local elections and school curricula.

The California Klan could be both extremist and reformist. Separating these characteristics of the Klan—creating a false dichotomy—ignores the ways racial and gendered ideologies served to motivate their actions, whether these were civic-minded or more violent in nature. California Klansmen and Klanswomen harbored a host of concerns about what they perceived as the tumultuous state of affairs in their communities including the composition of their neighborhoods, the state of civic institutions, the presence of social-ists and communists, interracial intimacy, and the role of women. While issues such as urban improvements and school curriculum motivated Klan members up and down the state, the issues of race and gender undergirded these agenda items. The story of O'Day Short and the violent attacks of the 1940s realign the history of the Klan, making it impossible to understand the Invisible Empire in California as a nonviolent, law-abiding organization divorced from racial ideologies that fizzled out by the Great Depression.

Raiding Los Angeles

Los Angeles provided the perfect breeding ground for Klan sympathies in the 1920s. The populace included an increasing number of African Americans, Mexicans, and Asian immigrants as well as a burgeoning white population from the South. Having recently surpassed San Francisco as the West's largest city, the rapid growth of Los Angeles surprised even the locals who were long accustomed to real-estate booms. The population jumped from 305,307 to 576,673 between 1910 and 1920, with Los Angeles fast becoming one of the most diverse cities in the nation.[24] The black population doubled in that same decade from 7,599 to 15,579; and the Asian population more than doubled.[25] By 1920, the Fourteenth Census recorded 21,598 Angelenos who had been born in Mexico, with probably many more who were un-reported.[26] Maintaining segregation in the city was becoming increasingly difficult. Due to zoning regulations, restrictive covenants, and unchecked industrial development, whole sections of Central and East Los Angeles were becoming heterogeneous, mostly ethnic populations.[27] Boyle Heights, Watts, and other neighborhoods were home to a diverse mix of Angelenos, and, much to the chagrin of Jim Crow's enforcers, these groups did not or could not always self-segregate. Interethnic mixing and marriage occurred across Southern California, raising anxiety among lawmakers, politicians, and demagogues. The multiracial character of the central districts meant that when Anglos traveled to the areas in and around downtown to work or play, which was nearly unavoidable, they encountered this increasingly diverse population. The unregulated growth of the city combined with the surge in ethnic and racialized populations caused elite Anglos palpable distress. Much of this anxiety focused on districts populated by the poor, immigrants, and African Americans. The city, already known to be antilabor and proudly open shop, also developed a reputation for being virulently anticommunist. The Red Scare played well in the western metropolis and this, combined with anti-immigrant and antiblack sentiments, helped create a nurturing environment for segregationists including the Klan.

At the same time, the Los Angeles branch of the NAACP was fast becoming a force to be reckoned with. It doubled its membership between 1919 and 1920, after a very successful visit from James Weldon Johnson, the national field secretary, and was on its way to becoming one of the largest branches in the nation. Also in 1919, local attorney Burton Ceruti had been elected to the national board of directors, the first westerner to hold that position.[28] Already a seasoned civil rights attorney, Ceruti read an unnerving news story in the spring of 1921. On May 23, the *Los Angeles Examiner* announced the arrival of the Klan in the city, and Ceruti immediately wrote to the national NAACP office for information about statutes designed to suppress the KKK.[29] Walter White, then assistant secretary of the organization, sent Ceruti two articles about fighting the Klan and praised his work: "I am glad to see that the California branches are actively on the job in stamping out this movement of organized lynching at its inception."[30] In addition to Ceruti, another local NAACP member, Charlotta Bass, made sure black Angelenos learned about this organization as soon as it arrived in town. Managing editor of the *California Eagle* since 1912, Bass used her newspaper to monitor the activities of LA's rising extremism including its red baiting and antilabor practices. As soon as the Klan started organizing in Los Angeles, Bass pointedly published news articles about their activities. Bass and her paper became a leading force in California's anti-Klan

Charlotta Bass, publisher of the *California Eagle*, sounded the alarm when the Ku Klux Klan arrived in the state. The *Eagle* was a leading voice against Jim Crow in the West. (Courtesy of the Southern California Library)

movement. In the fall of 1921, the *California Eagle's* front-page headline asked two questions: "Shall We Entertain the Klan?" and "What Are We Going to Do about It?"[31]

Bass frequently attributed the surge in Klan activity and white supremacy in Los Angeles to the "southernness" of some white Angelenos.[32] For many in LA, including Bass, one southerner in particular deserved the credit for promoting the KKK in their city. As a minister at Trinity Methodist church in downtown Los Angeles, Robert Shuler preached a pro-Klan message to a wide audience from his pulpit; with his own radio show and magazine, however, he reached thousands more. Bass called him "the Klan's Moses."[33] He had worked in Texas before moving to California in 1920. Keen about the Klan's plan to place Bibles in all California schoolrooms, Shuler hosted Klan meetings at his church and advertised Klan-friendly merchants in his magazine, although he claimed that he never officially joined the organization.[34] But he was just one Angeleno organizing and promoting Klan activities. Deputy Sheriff of Los Angeles Nathan Baker regularly recruited members and was thought to be a member of the Klan himself. As a result of vigorous recruiting efforts by high-profile men, Klan activity flourished in the beach communities and the suburbs in and around Los Angeles with chapters in Santa Monica, Huntington Park, Redondo Beach, Hermosa Beach, Long Beach, and Glendale.[35] The proliferation of chapters helped the organization spread across the state. In the spring of 1922, a Klan action called the Inglewood Raid confirmed the successful infiltration of California by the Invisible Empire.

On April 22, thirty-seven Klan members participated in a nighttime raid in Inglewood, a community about ten miles southwest of the city center. The Klan's target was a Spanish couple, Fidel and Angela Elduayen, who were operating a ranch. Accused of bootlegging by the Klan, the Elduayens had, according to most press reports, obtained a federal license to operate legally during Prohibition. Bootlegging was something the Klan associated with the vice and corruption spreading across the nation, considering it the first step toward societal moral decay. The Elduayens had at least three strikes against them according to the precepts of the second Klan: they were Catholic, they were not white, and they were supposed bootleggers. The family was abducted by a mob that may have included as many as two hundred Klansmen.[36] Angela Elduayen and her teenage daughters, Mary and Bernarda, were made to dress in front of the mob, and several press reports emphasized that the women were forced "to stand nude before them."[37]

The raid did not go as planned: after terrorizing the Spanish family at their home, chaos ensued. Incredibly, the Klansmen released the Elduayens after failing to find a sympathetic jailer to take them into custody. Meanwhile, back at the ranch, a western-style shoot-out ensued between Inglewood police and the Klansmen occupying the property. A constable of Inglewood, Marion Mosher, was killed, and two other men were wounded at the scene. A coroner's jury revealed that Mosher died from gunshot wounds incurred while he was acting as "a member of an illegal, masked and armed mob" instigated and directed by members of the Ku Klux Klan.[38] The coroner's announcement confirmed Klan participation and made a further recommendation: that the district attorney investigate Klan activity in the county to determine who was responsible for the crime and prosecute them.[39] The Los Angeles County District Attorney Thomas Woolwine would lead the grand jury investigation.

The Inglewood raid confirmed what black Californians, and especially those in southern California, already knew from experience: the Ku Klux Klan and the police had, in many cases, merged forces. A second raid that took place a few days later—this one of Klan headquarters instigated by the district attorney—revealed the extent of the merger. Hoping to determine the contours of the Klan in Los Angeles, Woolwine got more than he bargained for. With a search warrant in hand, "an automobile load" of deputy sheriffs raided the downtown Los Angeles office of the Klan on the night of April 26.[40] The scene unfolded as if out of a Hollywood script. After Grand Goblin Coburn was surprised in his office, the Klansman denied having any records: "What you want is not here. I have taken it away. I will never surrender it, not even to the court." Then Coburn stuffed some documents in an envelope and ran into the hall to drop them in the mail chute.[41] Chief Deputy District Attorney William Doran, who was in charge of the raid, arrived as officers were ransacking Coburn's desk and safe. Despite Coburn's claim that he removed all valuable documents, the raid proved devastating to the Invisible Empire. Inside the safe were applications for membership as well as the names of thousands of Klan members from across the West. As the headquarters for the Pacific states, the office held information about Klansmen not just in the Golden State but also in Idaho, Oregon, Arizona, and Washington. When the names on the membership lists were revealed to the public, even the most cynical were astounded at the Klan's strength in California. "Look at the list and study it over and over," wrote the editors of A. Philip Randolph's *Messenger*. "No sane, courageous thinker would contend that Negroes can afford to rely on the police and the authorities when the evidence reveals the police and authorities are members of the Ku Klux Klan."[42]

The membership lists included three thousand Klan members in Los Angeles County, over a thousand members in the city limits, and three members on District Attorney Woolwine's own staff.[43] Two names on the list spoke volumes: Los Angeles Chief of Police Louis D. Oaks and Los Angeles County Sheriff William I. Traeger. Both men insisted that they were unclear about the organization's purpose when they joined and had resigned their memberships shortly after.[44] Law enforcement from nearly every city in California appeared on the list of Klansmen, including twenty-five San Francisco policemen. District attorneys from across the state rushed to Woolwine's office to obtain the names of members in their counties. The central California city of Fresno removed seven policemen from the force after their names were revealed.[45] In May, a Bakersfield newspaper printed the names of the Klan members of the town, including the chief of police, the justice of the peace, three deputy sheriffs, the superintendent of the courthouse, and four firemen.

The membership lists provided California politicians with an opportunity to take a stand against the Klan, although this often turned out to be disingenuous. Los Angeles Police Chief Oaks and Sheriff Traeger, for example, threatened to fire any officers under their command whose names appeared on the list, only to be exposed as Klansmen themselves.[46] The governor of the state, William Stephens, ordered state employees to quit the Klan or be dismissed, a sentiment that may have inspired more confidence coming in the wake of Stephens's recent stand against lynching.[47] Fraternal orders, including the American Legion and the Elks lodges, also denounced the Klan. In Ventura a massive resignation of 130 members of the Klan—the whole of the city's membership—revealed just how worried California Klansmen had become.[48] Mayors and police chiefs across the state scurried to make public statements and prove their anti-Klan credentials. The mayors of Venice and Long Beach denounced the organization and warned any members employed in their cities to quit the KKK immediately.[49] Kern County, just east of Los Angeles County, had enough Klan activity to warrant their own grand jury investigation, and membership lists confiscated from the LA office were copied and sent to the district attorney in Bakersfield.[50] Over a hundred cases of Klan violence, including tarring and feathering, had occurred in Kern County in 1922, amounting to a veritable reign of terror.[51]

It was abundantly clear to black Angelenos that distinguishing between members of the Klan and members of the Los Angeles Police Department was a losing proposition. By the 1920s, as Kelly Lytle Hernández has shown, the LAPD was "a den of corruption" that practiced retaliatory policing in the city's black neighborhoods. "In speaking to the police, you are frequently talking to the Klan," warned the *Eagle*.[52] Unlike the mainstream media, the black press gave African Americans practical advice about the Klan's resurgence and warned them about the Klan's increasing presence in southern California. In May 1922, Chandler Owen, coeditor of New York's *Messenger*, who had been visiting Los Angeles, wrote a series of articles for the *Eagle*: "The KKK and Negro Life," "Protecting Your Life," and "Keep Cool."[53] Owen, like Bass, was a socialist, and formulated his recommendations accordingly, "As an economist and a socialist, I understand that this nation is dominated by property; that in the eyes of its rulers property rights stand above personal or human rights." Readers of the *Eagle* were advised to use caution in their homes lest Klansmen and/or police attempt to surprise them and remove the residents from the property. "Refuse to be arrested at your home late at night or at any unseemly hour," the paper warned. While the *Eagle* was loathe to promote violence, Owen advised "business, professional, and chief property holding men" to obtain guns and prepare for the worst. "They are the objects of vandalism and attack by the Ku Klux because their success excites the envy or jealousy of white competitors," wrote Owen.[54] Owen's warnings about Klan and police violence held true for over two decades.[55]

Following the membership list fiasco, members of the Inglewood raiding party were put on trial. The Los Angeles Grand Jury indicted thirty-seven Klansmen on five felony counts, including kidnapping, assault with intent to commit murder, and false imprisonment. Among the accused were William S. Coburn, Grand Goblin of the Pacific Domain; G. W. Prince, King Kleagle (or organizer) of the state; and Deputy Sherriff Nathan A. Baker, Kleagle for Los Angeles County. Bail was set for $1,000, except for Baker, whose bail was $10,000 because he confessed to leading the raid. Baker was soon admitted to the county hospital's psychiatric ward, due to what the press described as a nervous breakdown.[56] Coburn and Price fled to national Klan headquarters in Atlanta, only to be summoned back for the trial. By mid-May 150 men had been subpoenaed from the towns of Inglewood and nearby beach communities.[57] After the biggest roundup of Klansmen in the history of the Invisible Empire, the state was prepared to be the first to expose and convict the nation's preeminent secret society.[58] For those opposed to the Klan, this trial signaled a long-awaited comeuppance; the previous October, a congressional committee had questioned members of the Invisible Empire but failed to take action against them. Most agreed that Imperial Wizard William Simmons came out of the congressional investigation unscathed.

The sensational trial began on August 7, 1922. On the eve of the proceedings, officials from the Department of Justice praised California's handling of the Inglewood raid, claiming there was "more than enough evidence" to convict most if not all of the defendants. In their vigilant pursuit of the Klan, the state authorities served as a model not only for California but for the nation as a whole, said the federal officials. However, what appeared to be a fairly straightforward case soon turned into an embarrassment for the state's prosecuting attorneys. Less than a week into the trial, Nathan Baker fainted in the courtroom, apparently suffering from another nervous collapse, and he was removed on a stretcher; his case was declared a mistrial. A few days later, it was revealed that a significant report was stolen from District Attorney Doran's office, and Doran accused the Klan of operating a "gigantic spy system" to promote their organization and obstruct justice. On April 25, after fewer than four hours of deliberation, all of the defendants were acquitted. The defendant's attorneys argued that the men who raided the Elduayen ranch were enforcing the law and were responding to a request for backup from Constable Mosher. Indeed, the judge's instructions to the jury stated that whether the men were members of the Klan or any other organization should have no bearing on their decision.[59] Though it was never determined to be the case, the defense spent a significant amount of time during the trial painting the Elduayen family as bootleggers in violation of the Volstead Act.

Several months later, Beatrice S. Thompson, the secretary of the Los Angeles branch of the NAACP, wrote to the national office about the Klan: "The trial of their Inglewood raid was a farce and they have been working openly ever since." The organization was "growing alarmingly strong" she reported.[60] Indeed, the Klan staged a huge initiation ceremony in the fall of 1922 in Los Angeles's Walker Auditorium, just a few miles from the new Klan headquarters.[61] Also in the fall of that year, Democrat Thomas Lee Woolwine lost his bid for governor of the state, suggesting that his fight against the Klan was a political liability.[62] The Klan backed the winning candidate, Republican Friend Richardson. Some believed Richardson was, himself, a Klan member, and he never denied the fact.[63] Regardless of the raids and the damning exposure of Klan infiltration of local and state government, a Klan-friendly politician moved into the governor's mansion and, as Thompson put it, the Klan worked in the open with friends in high places. Richardson supported segregation after he became governor, and anti-Klan forces in the state regrouped. Some took solace in the fact that in spite of Richardson's election, black Republican Frederick Roberts managed to push an anti-mask bill through the California legislature with legal aid from Burton Ceruti.[64] Stopping Klan members from wearing masks did not stop them from organizing events, terrorizing Californians, or recruiting new members, however. Between March 1923 and April 1924, nine Klan events were held in the city of Los Angeles. In 1929, the Klan and Robert Schuler helped elect the mayor of Los Angeles, John Porter.[65] The Inglewood trial and the acquittal buoyed Klan members who proceeded with their agenda in ways public and often spectacular. In fact, the exposure of the Los Angeles raids would inspire Klan members, and those sympathetic to the Klan's agenda, to redouble their efforts.[66]

Inland Empires

At the end of the nineteenth century, the Inland Empire, consisting of Riverside and San Bernardino Counties, established itself as a leader in agriculture, dairy, citrus, and oil. These counties, east of Los Angeles, also became known for their receptivity to the Ku Klux Klan. Just fifteen miles from Fontana, where the Shorts would build their home in the 1940s, the city of Riverside, the "birthplace of the citrus industry," fostered one of the most active chapters of the Ku Klux Klan in the state. The priority of the Invisible Empire in Riverside—policing the boundaries of race and gender—highlights the ways California Klansmen felt threatened by integration as the Great Migration crept eastward from Los Angeles. Understanding the Klan in the Inland Empire helps elucidate how the murders of the Shorts could occur long after the Klan was thought to have disappeared from the U.S. landscape.

The Riverside Klan of the 1920s, like chapters in Anaheim, Oakland, and Los Angeles, took to the civic stage with a dramatic flair. The indictments in Los Angeles, rather than having a chilling effect on the Klan in the Inland Empire, instead served as a motivation for a stronger Klan. In 1924, two years after the trial, an initiation ceremony in the stadium of Riverside's Polytechnic High School could easily vie for the most flamboyant and well-attended Klan event in California history. Estimates of attendees range wildly from 3,500 to 15,000, with eyewitnesses reporting the spectacle in majestic terms. At least a thousand Klansmen and Klanswomen from across the state stood in the center of the stadium as 217 new members were inducted into the Invisible Empire.[67] A fiery cross was pulled across the sky by a small airplane just as dusk settled over the high school. "It was almost as though the great crowd were seeing a vision. Or it might have been a visitant from heaven, bearing with him some of the glory of the Celestial world," wrote one reporter at the scene. "Again and again the glowing, gleaming cross sped over the field," the observer described.[68] Another cross, lit by seventy-two automobile batteries, burned inside the arena. Showmanship and pageantry, a hallmark of the second Klan, aided in the recruitment of new members across the country, and California chapters were no exception.

Many in Riverside, indeed, across the state, saw the Klan as just another civic organization. This view, promoted by one of the local newspapers, reflected the fact that large numbers of this branch had been drawn from the ranks of the local American Legion.[69] The "greatest crowd ever seen in Riverside" witnessed speeches and rituals that summer night, which, according to the reporter for the *Riverside Enterprise*, were typical to those found in "any lodge hall on the initiation of a class of candidates." The Klan embraced American values, and there "was much emphasis on love of and loyalty to the country." The organization could be a "power for good," boasted the local press.[70] The keynote address was delivered by Klan celebrity Dr. Horace Lackey, who, while full of praise for the Klan's good works, also expressed concern about the Klan's reception in the state's largest city, Los Angeles. "First the Klan was exposed," he said, referring to the raid of headquarters and subsequent revelations, "and now there is a conspiracy of silence, intended to keep the order from obtaining publicity" and, presumably, more members. The Riverside Klan must not be silenced, said Lackey.[71] But Klansmen in Riverside had little to fear; the Inglewood raid and trial provided inspiration for recruitment, as it had in Los Angeles. Scandal, in this case, emboldened Klansmen and women of the Inland Empire to come out into the open.

Shifting gender roles were of paramount concern to members of the second Klan. Feminist organizing and suffrage campaigns had brought women's issues to the fore in the 1910s and 1920s. Women entered the workforce and universities in ever-increasing numbers, and all of these shifts disturbed the national Klan leadership in Atlanta. Men seemed to be losing authority as husbands and fathers, and the proliferation of vice — in the form of flappers, automobiles, and speakeasies — made Klansmen anxious about the slippage in traditional gender roles. Local chapters of the Klan were instructed to "clean up their towns" and conduct campaigns of moral purity. Efforts to rectify moral standards were aimed at controlling, among other things, women's behavior, especially challenges they might pose to the authority of their husbands; these campaigns were at the center of recruitment drives across the country.[72] Riverside members embraced the moral purity campaign and harbored their own concerns regarding women's roles and gender conformity. The same year of the initiation ceremony, local Methodist minister Reverend J. E. Fisher praised the Klan for their belief in "every principle of the Christion religion," and "pure woman-hood," encouraging his congregation at the Arlington Methodist Church to support their mission.[73]

Messages about the appropriate behavior for men and women were dis-seminated from the pulpit, the meeting halls, and Klan spectacles such as parades, which additionally brought the message to bystanders—potential recruits. In 1925, six months after the initiation ceremony, the Riverside Klan held an extravagant parade down Main Street to celebrate the visit of "Imperial leaders" from national headquarters in Atlanta. The parade promised to be "the most spectacular ever conducted in the Citrus Belt district."[74] After the Inglewood raid and trial, the Klan had to regroup and appoint new officers to manage western branches, especially in California. The parade and other Riverside events could help to revive California's reputation as a Klan stronghold. To drum up support for the celebration, the klavern paid for a front page ad in the *Riverside Daily Press*, touting Klan music by a Klan band, floats, Klavaliers, Klanswomen, and Junior Knights in full regalia.[75] The Junior Knights, part of the national Junior Order of the Klan organized in 1924, had come from San Bernardino and represented the Klan's effort to create schools of manhood for boys between the ages of twelve and eighteen.[76] Of the dozens of floats in the parade, the one belonging to the Junior Order attracted the most comment in the press.[77] The presence of the boys also helped to convey the Klan's focus on masculinity, which was central to their recruiting efforts. An advertisement for the parade claimed that the members of the Riverside Klan were "of the highest standing. . . . ministers, doctors, lawyers, bankers, merchants, former service men—in fact REAL MEN from every walk of life."[78] What mattered more than the economic class of the Klansmen, the ad promised, was that the men in the Riverside Klan shared a commitment to a particu-lar kind of "real" manhood that enforced traditional gender roles as they understood them, which included "protecting" white women from contact with nonwhite men.

The parade and stadium spectacle coincided with the push for purity campaigns that emanated from the national Klan headquarters in Atlanta. Riverside Klan members, and their allies in law enforcement, supported this goal. Sheriff of Riverside County from 1924 to 1930, Clem Sweeters remembered that protecting white womanhood was central to the Klan's concerns. Sweeters attended meetings in the nearby town of Banning and recalled: "The obligation was a good one as I saw it at first, but they weren't living up to it. It was a good obligation—to protect womenfolk—but they got too radical."[79] What worried Sweeters was, in part, the violent methods that the Klan employed to "protect womanhood." Riverside Klan members were emboldened to use extralegal methods in the name of protecting white women. "They wanted to take out and hang anybody who was molesting women or practicing bigamy. Some of these fellows wanted to take the law into their own hands," Sweeters explained. This vigilante practice mimicked the actions of Klan members in Inglewood, actions that were acquitted by judge and jury just before Sheriff Sweeters took office. While Sweeters approved of the agenda of the Klan but objected to giving them the power to enforce the law, the man who followed him in office, Carl Rayburn, had only positive things to say about the county's Klan. "There were a lot of damned good men belonged to it," remembered Rayburn. "They were sincere in their beliefs and they had a right to belong to it."[80] In the 1930s, the sheriff recalled seeing the letters "KIGY," meaning "Klan I Greet You," painted on streets and sidewalks throughout the county.

One of the dangers to womanhood that most disturbed the Riverside Klan members was the potential contact between black and white bodies at the public swimming pool. African Americans had been unofficially allowed to swim in the Fairmont Plunge one day a week since it opened in 1912. The subject of a protracted lawsuit brought by the Riverside NAACP, the pool, like Pasadena's Brookside Plunge, inspired one of the most serious battles over racial mixing in the town's history. In 1922, the city of Riverside settled out of court with the NAACP and, at least on paper, African Americans were technically welcome at the pool seven days a week. To the Klan, that meant that white women might see or even meet seminude black male bodies at the pool, an unacceptable consequence of the settlement as far as the Klan and other white supremacists were concerned. The backlash to the NAACP settlement was swift and severe as defenders of segregation retaliated against African American swimmers. When they dared to use the facility, black swimmers were met with humiliation and violence. Frances Allen, a black resident of Riverside, remembered white resentment over the integration of the pool as one of the central preoccupations of the Riverside Klan.[81]

The Riverside Klan prioritized policing interracial contact—or its potential occurrence—which meant monitoring the actions of black citizens, other people of color, and sympathetic whites. On one occasion, fifteen Klansmen marched into a black church in full regalia. "It was an evening meeting," recalled Ray Wolfe, reporter for the *Riverside Press-Enterprise*, "and they walked in during the service, marched down the aisle to the front of the church, then filed out. I've forgotten what the heck they were demonstrating about, but they scared the heck out of the Negroes." Wolfe was stunned when a Klansmen ambushed him at the newspaper office just after the threatening incident at the church, "He told me not to print any story about this church deal or he'd bomb the office." The *Enterprise* printed the story and the office was never bombed, but Wolfe was accosted again and told to "join the Klan, or else." "They . . . scared the heck out of me," Wolfe remembered.[82]

The Riverside Klan's recruitment drives of the 1920s paid off; the Invisible Empire claimed to have over two thousand members in the city. If that figure is accurate, the Riverside Klan had twice as many members as the better known Anaheim Klan.[83] Even if the number of Riverside members was inflated, it seems safe to say that the Riverside Klan was as influential and prominent as the branch in Anaheim, influencing local politics and law enforcement with notable success. In 1927 the Klan helped to elect Riverside's mayor and brought widespread attention to the Invisible Empire. One candidate, local grocer Edward M. Deighton, admitted to support from the Klan and claimed to be proud of it.[84] His opponent, former pastor Horace Porter, had been mayor between 1918 and 1922, and had the support of the businessmen and local civic groups; Porter seemed the obvious candidate to many. Deighton ran on a platform to clean up the mayor's office and strengthen law enforcement. One of his more colorful, if fantastic, concerns was candy that contained "dope evil" and was being peddled in Riverside schools.[85] Despite having no experience in politics, Deighton won the election with a third of the votes and 70 percent voter turnout.[86] After the election, the Riverside Klan made a few appearances in the 1930s and continued to burn crosses on Box Springs hill.[87] The Riverside Klan's strength of the 1920s was a high point, however. The Great Depression resulted in a significant decrease in dues-paying members across the country in the 1930s. Recruitment drives waned, and the organization's leadership floundered. The turmoil at national headquarters when Simmons was deposed in 1922 had long-lasting effects, and although his successor, Dallas dentist Hiram

Wesley Evans, remained in control for seventeen years, a series of scandals continued to plague the Imperial Palace.[88]

By 1939, when Indiana veterinarian Jimmy Colescott took charge of the Klan in Atlanta, klaverns were closing and many states had lost most of their members. When Colescott received a bill from the Internal Revenue Service for over $685,000 in 1944, his reign was over and the second Klan pronounced dead.[89] The death sentence of Klandom was in fact a ruse to avoid paying the tax bill. The new leader, Dr. Samuel Green of Atlanta, worked to maintain the organization and support the struggling chapters, though without much success. California, however, was the one state in the West that could still claim to be "an active realm."[90] The Klansmen and Klanswomen in California did not seem to be much affected by the tax fiasco, and the state remained a stronghold for the Klan throughout the 1940s. Why California continued to be among the handful of states that supported a new, post-Colescott Klan has everything to do with the dramatic upheavals brought on by World War II, the fear of an encroaching black population, and the cooperation between the police, the state, and the Klan.

The Story of O'Day Short

Defense contracts changed forever the state's economic, political, social, and physical landscapes. Northern and Southern California ports, valleys, deserts, and bogs turned into homes for shipyards, airport hangers, and steel mills. The investment in the state proved staggering: over half of the nation's $70 billion defense budget went to California during the war. In the competition to attract federal dollars, however, Southern California won the lion's share. Los Angeles County alone acquired 5 percent of all federal contract funds during the war, while the city of Los Angeles could boast of one of the most dramatic increases in employment in the nation.[91] The aircraft industry became central to the economy of Southern California with Lockheed alone employing more than ninety thousand workers.[92] During the war, unemployment dropped to 1.4 percent in the city and the number of Angelenos employed in manufacturing jobs jumped from 94,000 in 1935 to 540,000 in 1944.[93] After President Roosevelt began calling for a stronger merchant marine in 1940 and 1941, shipbuilding yards put Californians to work up and down the state. Calship, one of the largest shipbuilding facilities in the country, opened in Los Angeles and dominated the industry until Henry Kaiser opened four shipyards in the Northern California city of Richmond.

Pulled to the Golden State for defense jobs, black migrants were anxious to leave the dangerous and desperate conditions of the post-Depression South. The dismal constraints of sharecropping, lack of adequate education, anti-black violence, and a series of legal and extralegal measures that criminalized African Americans provided more than enough incentive to leave the South. Migrants from the South and Southwest transformed western cities, and none more than those of California. The Golden State became the destination for thousands of black families traveling west. In 1930, there were 81,048 African Americans who made California their home and by 1950 there were 462,172.[94] These numbers tell part of the story, but the extent of the migration proves difficult to comprehend. Los Angeles, Richmond, Oakland, and San Diego all experienced unprecedented population booms and dramatic demographic shifts. Perhaps the most telling statistic is the fact that over a quarter million African Americans moved to the state during wartime, making California the state with the largest increase in its black population nationwide. The massive influx of war workers precipitated a staggering housing shortage in California's cities. It is no coincidence that the Golden State would become ground zero for the challenge to racially restricted housing.

The presence of black migrants inspired the formation of a new and revised California Klan. In December 1939, the Klan marched through downtown Los Angeles burning crosses in "full view of many thousands." The hooded order handed out fliers at the march, proclaiming that communists and members of the German-American Bund should be driven out of the country. As they did in the 1920s, the black press monitored the Klan's presence and warned readers of the danger. The *Los Angeles Sentinel* reported that "its professed desire to make war on Bundsmen and Communists is only window dressing for its real purpose . . . to persecute negroes and members of other minority groups." Carrying out a renewed campaign to influence California politics, this 1930s Klan organized in "a quiet yet effective manner," according to the *Sentinel*. While the new KKK appeared to adapt to the shifting global politics, the reporter noted that "it still ma[de] the basic appeal on the old anti-Negro, anti-Catholic, and anti-Jewish program that was so successful" after World War I. A central strategy of this Klan would be to stop black residents like the Shorts from integrating neighborhoods. The writer for the *Sentinel* harbored no illusions about the Klan's goals: "one of its objectives in Los Angeles and the outlying communities will be to curtail the growth of the Negro communities and to force the Negroes to live in segregated districts."[95]

California's Klan revival made national news, at least in the black press. The *Plaindealer* (published in Topeka, Kansas) noted in 1943 that "a drive is underway in California to revive the Klan after it had been virtually nonexistent there for several years. California has had huge migrations from the south to work in aircraft and shipbuilding, and these southerners dislike the comparative freedom enjoyed by Negroes on the west coast." California's African American wartime workers, as the black press noted, had a remarkably high standard of living compared to black workers in the South. The "comparative freedoms" they enjoyed motivated white supremacists to organize against black workers and homeowners. This revived Klan had two clear focuses: keep neighborhoods, schools, pools, and parks across the state all-white, and monitor people of color who transgressed racial boundaries. Homeownership by people of color, and especially African Americans, became for many white Californians the heart of the problem. As historian Jacquelyn Dowd Hall observed, "homeowner politics" were the politics of the long backlash to civil rights gains across the country.[96] Interracial neighborhoods were, for many segregationists, the first step toward integration, which could lead to miscegenation and, in the minds of some, the end of the white race. White homeowners associations became the most ubiquitous manifestation of the movement to stop people of color from buying property in majority-white neighborhoods; arson and physical attacks on homeowners, however, became the preferred method of the World War II–era Klan.

When O'Day Short purchased his five-acre lot within the city limits of Fontana in September 1945, he violated the Klan's plan. African Americans who had flocked to Fontana for jobs at Kaiser's new steel manufacture plant had been restricted to the "citrus ghetto," the segregated neighborhood built on a rocky floodplain just north of the Fontana city limits. The Shorts were the first black family to move within the city limits. O'Day Short, described in the black press as "a progressive young man," began building his house in early December; he and his wife, Helen, seven-year-old Carol Ann, and nine-year-old Barry took occupancy just as the construction was coming to a close.[97] A relatively good job at the mill and the dream of owning their own home had brought the Shorts to Fontana; they believed the Inland Empire would be more hospitable than Los Angeles. Owning a home for O'Day Short was one way he could assert his status as a citizen and strike a blow against the color line. The significance of the connection between homeownership and interracial contact only intensified during World War

II. Enforcers of segregation in Los Angeles had reason to be concerned. In 1910, over 36 percent of African Americans in Los Angeles lived in owner-occupied homes. In New York City, by comparison, only 2.4 percent of black men and women owned their homes.[98]

Jobs at Henry J. Kaiser's shipyards, and then his steel mill, were a boon for the African American migrants to California. Kaiser revolutionized ship production, creating assembly lines and mass-production techniques that allowed for large-scale employment of workers with little or no experience in shipbuilding, including black men and women who had been kept out of these wartime jobs. Employment at Kaiser's operations in Northern and then Southern California was highly prized, earning workers a relatively good wage. This would have been reason enough for Short to move his family to Fontana. Perhaps Kaiser's reputation as an employer who supported the AFL-affiliated unions and ran a closed shop drew Short to the job. However, the dominant union for shipbuilders, the Boilermakers' Union, was famously segregated and hostile to black workers. African American members, many of them Kaiser employees, were forced into auxiliary locals and prevented from voting. When Short was promised a job in Fontana, black members of the Boilermakers' were embroiled in a discrimination suit that would eventually require the AFL to award the workers full membership in the union.[99] It is likely that Short knew about the lawsuit, which had been covered extensively by the black press, and that he knew that Kaiser hired black employees at all his operations. O'Day Short would not be the only black worker in the mill or in the town. In 1942 Kaiser began actively recruiting black workers and announced his policies for equal opportunity for all workers, as well as medical care and decent housing.[100] Kaiser's shipyards in Richmond employed nearly eight thousand black workers by 1943.[101] Some believed Kaiser to be a pioneer in nondiscriminatory hiring.[102] For a black worker living in Los Angeles at the height of Jim Crow, a chance to work for Kaiser—and find adequate housing—was a lucky break.

Kaiser Steel's Fontana plant, called the Fontana Works, was the first West Coast facility to turn ore into steel products on one site; its opening turned Fontana into "a mighty forge for war."[103] When the plant opened on December 30, 1942, Henry Kaiser hosted a huge celebration, spotlighting the newest addition to his industrial empire. Kaiser had complained that as long as the West imported most of its steel from the East Coast, the region could never realize its potential. With the completion of the Fontana Works, a new day had dawned for Kaiser and for the West. Kaiser believed that the Fontana plant struck a blow for the end of western colonialism in the steel industry.[104] Initially these dreams were realized. In its first decade of operation, Fontana was responsible for one-third of the total steel production in the U.S. West.[105] Despite heightened competition and resentment from East Coast steel companies, Kaiser had achieved unprecedented success in Fontana, and the facilities became "an international benchmark of advanced steelmaking."[106] Five thousand workers and their families moved to Fontana in the 1940s. As an engineer, Short garnered better wages than most black workers who worked in the coke ovens and blast furnaces in lower-paying and lower-status jobs. Black workers like O'Day Short also may have shared some of Kaiser's optimism about this new western enterprise, but the *California Eagle* would soon describe Fontana as a place of "hate-mongering and religious cults."[107]

As soon as the Short family moved into their home south of Baseline Street, a place no black family had ever lived, they received threats from vigilantes. Deputy Sheriffs Cornelius "Tex" Carson and Joe Glines warned the Shorts to leave the white-only neighborhood. Short was "out of bounds," according to the sheriffs, and to avoid "disagreeableness" he should move his family to the segregated black neighborhood on "the other side of the Baseline." J. Sutherland, the real estate agent who sold the lot to O'Day Short, visited the family on December 3 and delivered a warning: "Short, the vigilante committee had a meeting on your case last night. They are a tough bunch to deal with. If I were you, I'd get my family off this property at once."[108] Short asked Sutherland about the repercussions if he failed do so, and Sutherland replied that physical violence would be the result.[109] O'Day Short, prepared for trouble, did two things after the real estate agent delivered the threat: he called his attorney, Ivan J. Johnson of Los Angeles, a prominent lawyer of the NAACP and associate of civil rights attorney Loren Miller, and, upon Johnson's recommendation, he then contacted the FBI. In order to broadcast the threat to black Californians and rally support, he also told the members of the black press about the incident. In her article, "A Fire in Fontana," journalist Hisaye Yamamoto remembered Short "making the rounds of the three Negro newspapers" to ensure that his story was told.[110] On December 6 the *Los Angeles Sentinel* published an exclusive, front-page interview with Short. Under a banner headline, the *Sentinel* recounted Short's encounter with the vigilantes and his dangerous predicament. Ten days after the *Sentinel* headline, between 5:30 and 5:45 p.m. on Sunday, December 16, the Shorts' home burst into flames.

The fire that engulfed the property began with an explosion. Neighbors rushed to the scene. The flames and the explosion knocked the walls on their sides, and the cries of Helen and the two children were heard by bystanders. The family managed to escape the house, but not before they were all severely burned. One neighbor, Mrs. Penner, described a horrific scene of seeing Helen Short, whose hair had been burned off, "her face a mass of raw flesh," trying to beat out the flames engulfing her children.[111] This same neighbor also revealed that because the Shorts were light-skinned, she was not aware that they were African Americans, and that she and her husband rushed to the aid of the family. She told the reporter that someone in the neighborhood drove the family to the hospital in their automobile. The little girl, Carol Ann, had suffered the worst burns and died fifteen minutes after she was admitted to Southern Permanente Hospital around 6 p.m. Barry died at 2:10 on Monday morning, and their mother, Helen, died at 9:40 a.m. the same day.[112]

But as soon as the flames subsided, conflicting reports circulated about the cause of the blast. The white neighbors all seemed to agree that the responsibility for the fire lay with the Shorts, some claiming that an oil stove, lamp, or lantern, exploded when Mrs. Short was lighting it. That version was repeated by the sheriff's office, a nurse at the hospital, and "gained wide circulation among the whites," according to the *California Eagle*.[113] The sheriff's report stated that Mr. Short had been using gasoline or a coal stove to cook on and it had exploded.[114] The writer for the *Eagle*, Cyril Briggs, sensed foul play. He was not alone. In a series of interviews with local black residents, Briggs found little support for the accident theory. E. P. Smalley, local leader of the Negro Chamber of Commerce, found the accident theory ludicrous. Even if the lantern had exploded, Smalley reasoned, the Shorts' fuel supply must have been tampered with by hostile neighbors. White business interests in Fontana had been pressuring African Americans to live only on the north side of Baseline and "the Fontana Chamber of Commerce offered to reimburse the Shorts if they would get out," Smalley recalled. A blast of that magnitude, blowing out the walls of the house, did not result from a self-combusting lamp or lantern. The coroner's jury determined that Helen, Carol Ann, and Barry died from "shock from extensive burns" sustained from "a fire of unknown origin."[115] The words "unknown origin" meant that the cause of the fire could still be classified as arson, giving hope to those who knew it to be a racially motivated crime. Others found the coroner's inquest a sham that deliberately obscured the actual events surrounding the fire.[116] The single most disturbing fact about the process, according to the *Sentinel*, was that the coroner refused to admit as evidence testimony about the threats made to Short two weeks before the blaze.

San Bernardino County District Attorney Jerome R. Kavanaugh orchestrated an elaborate cover-up of the murders. In order to have the fire declared an accident, he utilized methods of evidence collection that would be inadmissible in most courts. Kavanaugh's evidence for the accident theory came from Mr. Short himself, whom he claimed to have interviewed in the hospital, though many would argue this was conducted under intimidation. His proof, which he placed in evidence at the coroner's jury, was a transcript of an interrogation in which Short said the fire could have been an accident. The district attorney elicited Short's statement using what Briggs of the *Eagle* called "the technique of auto-suggest," meaning Kavanaugh put words in his mouth. According to the *Eagle*, Short told Kavanaugh from his hospital bed, "I cannot speak competently for myself. Not at this time."[117] When Kavanaugh told Short that the papers reported that an explosion from a coal lamp caused the fire, Short replied, "I do not believe I am compelled to make any statement one way or the other. I am not competent to give any reply—until I can be given the proper legal advice and not before, I am here on my sick bed, my hair burned off my head, my legs twisted under me. You have no respect for my position. All you want to do is get the information you are looking for."[118] During this exchange Kavanaugh told Short that his wife and children had died, a fact that hospital staff and his family and friends had worked to keep from him until he recovered because they feared the news would kill him.

After constant pressure from activists, the black press, and the labor movement, a San Bernardino grand jury convened in January to investigate the deaths. Members of the NAACP, the black press corps, and expert witnesses provided damning evidence at the hearing. The NAACP hired a special investigator to determine whether the fire was arson or an accident caused by a kerosene lantern. Paul T. Wolfe, former chief arson investigator for the Los Angeles Fire Department, found the fire to have been "incendiary in origin."[119] "Some highly inflammable or explosive substance other than kerosene was present," Wolfe explained. In all of his twenty-five years of investigating fires, he had "never heard of kerosene causing such an explosion as that which occurred at the Short home," he told a reporter from the *Sentinel*.[120] Science simply did not support the accident theory. In addition, J. Robert Smith, editor of the newspaper *Tri-County News*, produced the oil

Violence Threat Against Short Must Not Go Unchallenged: AN EDITORIAL
Los Angeles Sentinel (1934-2005); Jan 3, 1946; ProQuest Historical Newspapers: Los Angeles Sentinel
pg. 1

Violence Threat Against Short Must Not Go Unchallenged

(AN EDITORIAL)

Three people, Mrs. Helen Short and her two small children, Carol Ann and Barry, lost their lives as the result of a fire of unknown origin in their Fontana home December 16. The husband, O'Day H. Short, is still in hospital suffering from third degree burns.

A coroner's inquest, held on Thursday of last week, confined itself to an attempt to determine the immediate causes of the fire, and refused to admit testimony dealing with threats of physical violence reported by Short two weeks before the tragedy.

The Sentinel has no desire to make unsubstantiated charges of malicious arson or premeditated murder against any individual or group.

At the same time, in view of the fact that Short reported to a number of people, including a representative of the Los Angeles Sentinel that he had been threatened with violence shortly before the tragedy, a full investigation into the threats themselves is mandatory.

Responsibility for such an investigation rests in the first instance on District Attorney Jerome B. Cavanaugh of San Bernardino county. In the event that Cavanaugh takes no action, then California's Attorney General Robert W. Kenny has an obligation to the people of this state to make a thorough-going probe not only into the immediate causes of the explosion, but also into the actions and activities of all those who were in any way involved in the threats.

Two deputy sheriffs, Joe Gilnes and "Tex" Cornellson, reportedly visited Short prior to the fire, told him he was "out of bounds," and warned him that "neighbors" had complained of his presence on his own property.

As law enforcement officers, these deputies should have explained to such complaining neighbors that the Shorts had every right to live on their property and that right would be protected. Instead it appears that these officers attempted to bring pressure to bear against the Shorts to deprive them of their constitutional rights.

It is to be hoped that the self-styled "vigilante" committee" had no hand in starting the fire that has cost three lives. But vigilante threats are serious in themselves, whether or not there is any direct connection between these particular threats and this specific fire.

If threats of this kind go unchallenged, and those who made the threats are not even questioned, then law and order no longer exists, and vigilante violence becomes the rule.

The danger is one that extends far beyond the limits of Fontana itself or even of San Bernardino county.

Full light must be thrown on this incident, or colored citizens and members of other minorities will be safe nowhere in California.

When O'Day Short was threatened by so-called vigilantes in Fontana, he informed the black press and the FBI. The *Los Angeles Sentinel* provided extensive coverage of the murders and the cover-up. (ProQuest Historical Newspapers) lantern that had supposedly started the fire and had been left at the scene of the crime. It was intact, the metal in place, not destroyed as it would have been had it caused the explosion.[121] The lantern and Wolfe's testimony seemed to provide the evidence necessary to push the case forward. In a letter to Thomas L. Griffith Jr., president of the Los Angeles chapter of the NAACP (and attorney for the Pasadena pool case), District Attorney Kavanaugh explained that he had presented the jury with Wolfe's report.[122] In the midst of the grand jury's investigation, on January 21, O'Day Short died of complications from his first-degree burns. Short's lawyer, Ivan Johnson, told the *Sentinel* that once District Attorney Kavanaugh told Short that his wife and children had died, Short "stopped fighting. The news had killed his spirit. I think he wanted to die."[123] A few days later, the jury adjourned and failed to recommend any further action.

Short's death sparked outrage and organized protest on the part of civil rights workers and the labor movement. Less than a week after his death, the Los Angeles and San Bernardino County labor unions mobilized their members. The unions of the Congress of Industrial Organizations (CIO) had followed Short's condition when he was in the hospital, organizing blood drives and pushing for a grand jury investigation.[124] On hearing the news of his death, the International Longshoreman and Warehouseman's Union and the United Automobile Workers called for a mass meeting. At the Shrine Auditorium in Los Angeles over six thousand people attended a meeting days after Short's death to drum up support; they unanimously agreed to sign a "strongly worded resolution" demanding that law enforcement properly investigate the fire, including the vigilante threats.[125] The resolution also called on union members and other Californians to fight against racially restricted housing, the cause of the problem and "a hateful practice which has no place in a free and decent America."[126] The CIO had recently filed a brief in the ongoing legal battle against restrictive covenants; a battle that in 1948 would result in the landmark Supreme Court decision of *Shelley v. Kraemer*. The murders of O'Day Short and his family became a lynchpin of the movement to stop the Klan and to stop residential segregation across the state.

The interracial coalition of Californians insisting for justice in the murder investigation included members of the NAACP, the CIO, local communists, socialists, and myriad civil rights activists. Among the coalition of groups that doggedly pushed for action in the Short case, the Socialist Workers Party (SWP) was one of the most vocal. Myra Tanner Weiss, a Los Angeles leader of the SWP, wrote a pamphlet about the Shorts and traveled across the West to build support for further investigation. Speaking in San Bernardino, Seattle, Portland, Eugene, Santa Cruz, San Diego, Eureka, and small towns up and down the coast, Weiss garnered significant coverage in the black press.[127] The pamphlet, *Vigilante Terror in Fontana: The Tragic Story of O'Day H. Short and His Family*, detailed the events of the case and the cover-up. The goal of her tour, Weiss explained, was "to break the conspiracy of silence of the daily press on the vigilante threats preceding the mysterious fire."[128] The publication contained a foreword by Helen Short's sister, Carrie Morrison, that drew attention to the vigilantes and her brother-in-law's courage: "He didn't want them hushed up and he didn't intend to submit quietly to them. He went to the newspapers with the story and he refused to give up his right to live in his home, the fight against race discrimination." "Now an entire Negro family in Fontana has been burned to death," wrote Weiss, "Let us tell the full story, for as yet the capitalists newspapers, those organs of 'public enlightenment' have kept silent."[129]

In early February, 250 people gathered at the San Bernardino YWCA for a meeting organized by a host of civil rights organizations, including the San Bernardino chapter of the NAACP. Myra Tanner Weiss, Pettis Perry, state committee member of the Communist Party and chairman of its minorities commission, and Dan Marshall, cofounder of Catholic Interracial Council of Los Angeles, all spoke at the meeting. Marshall called the lack of an investigation a travesty and compared the apathetic treatment of these murders with "what would happen were a family of four to be burned out in Beverly Hills after vigilante threats." "Imagine with what zeal the district attorney would investigate such an event, run down the criminals," Marshall noted.[130] No stranger to civil rights work, Marshall would soon be leading one of the most significant challenges to miscegenation law, the *Perez v. Sharp* case.[131] Ruth Moody, chairman of the Council for Human Rights, reminded the audience of perhaps the most damning evidence of foul play. As soon as O'Day Short was threatened at his home, Moody said, her organization wired San Bernardino County Sherriff Emmett Shay to request that he ask his deputies to stop threatening the Short family. Law enforcement had been informed of the threats and had obviously been complicit in the murders. Moody and others formed a delegation at the rally to pressure State Attorney General Robert W. Kenny.[132] The next week, Kenny's office sent word that a thorough and independent investigation into the fire would be conducted.[133]

Vigilante Terror in Fontana

THE TRAGIC STORY OF
O'DAY H. SHORT AND HIS FAMILY

By
MYRA TANNER WEISS
Organizer, Los Angeles Local
Socialist Workers Party

Price 10 cents

Myra Tanner Weiss wrote this pamphlet after the murder of the Short family. The pamphlet contained a foreword by Helen Short's sister. Weiss was a leader of the Socialist movement in California and fought to keep the Shorts' murders in the public eye. (Bancroft Library, University of California, Berkeley, California)

After the grand jury investigation adjourned without issuing a report, the case seemed hopeless. According to Weiss, "the only aid Short was given if we can call it that, was the advice by the FBI to report any further developments." Clearly, the FBI abdicated its responsibilities by refusing to protect Short. When Charlotta Bass summed up the case in her memoir, *Forty Years*, she described it in a chapter titled "A Community Outrage." "Most of all," she explained, "it pointed to a resurgence in the Los Angeles area of the Ku Klux Klan."[134] An editorial of the *Los Angeles Sentinel* agreed and placed the blame squarely on racial segregation and white supremacy: "what any person can know with entire certainty if he wants to is that the Shorts were victims of Jim Crow." The story was a simple one: "Jim Crow had kept Short from finding a home in Los Angeles; Jim Crow had cast him in the role of a violator of Community traditions if he built a house on the lot he purchased; Jim Crow had warped the sense of duty of deputy sheriffs to the extent that they themselves had joined in a plan to deprive an American citizen of his constitutional rights. . . . All the Shorts are dead. Only Jim Crow is alive."[135]

The Fire Spreads

Following the explosion at the Shorts in December 1945, black homeowners in Southern California were increasingly under attack. These incidents, attributed to the Klan by civil rights organizations, were deemed "childish pranks" by law enforcement officials and the mayor of Los Angeles, Fletcher Bowron. White resistance to black neighbors could take many forms. Sometimes homeowners watched a fiery cross burn on their front lawn, in other cases African Americans were verbally or physically threatened and warned to vacate the neighborhood, in others the home was incinerated. The Short murders were but an extreme version of an all-out war on African American homeowners, especially those living in predominantly white neighborhoods. This surge of Klan violence—which peaked in 1946—became the focus of most of the state's civil rights organizations, including the NAACP, the American Council for Race Relations, and the Council for Civic Unity. The Los Angeles branch of the NAACP spent most of their energy that year in an intensive campaign against the Klan, whose presence in southern California had reached unprecedented levels. Nothing in the city's history matched the record of cross burnings and terror experienced by black citizens in 1946. Veterans who had acquired mortgages through the GI Bill became popular

Attorney and journalist Loren Miller won significant victories in the fight against restricted housing in the 1940s and 1950s. His law partner, Ivan J. Johnson, was O'Day Short's attorney. (Huntington Library)

targets, as did African Americans who challenged restrictive covenants. For black homeowners, moving to a previously all-white neighborhood meant preparing for struggle and putting themselves and their families in danger.

Black activists and their allies understood housing discrimination as a lynchpin of white supremacy in the state. Fighting racism in the housing market became a hallmark of Charlotta Bass's career, and the *California Eagle* began sounding the alarm about restrictive covenants as early as 1914.[136] Loren Miller, a black lawyer who moved to Los Angeles in 1929 and wrote for both the *California Eagle* (which he eventually bought) and the *Los Angeles Sentinel*, would be instrumental in the movement to end restrictive covenants. Miller's insight about California's use of restrictive covenants led him to become the national expert on this area of law for the NAACP. Alongside Thurgood Marshall, Miller would prepare briefs and oral arguments that led to the Supreme Court's ruling in *Shelley v. Kraemer*, but his earliest experience in housing discrimination litigation occurred in

Los Angeles. With the help of Miller, the NAACP, and other civil rights organizations, African Americans brought an avalanche of complaints about housing restrictions to the courts. Between 1919 and 1933, at least fifteen cases were brought before the bench by black Californians challenging restrictive covenants.[137] As World War II began, the movement to keep housing in Southern California white only escalated. Bass believed the escalation stemmed, in part, from segregation protests in Pasadena. "Real estate dealers of the San Gabriel Valley were said to have been instigators of the scheme," she wrote. They "attempted to arouse white people by pointing to protests of Negroes being barred from the Brookside Park Plunge."[138] Bass knew that segregationists would take action at the specter of mingling in pools and neighborhoods. White homeowners, realtors, and developers in Los Angeles and the surrounding beach and valley communities had tied up as much as 80 percent of the housing stock in the city as white only.[139] Bass believed African Americans were being "confined to a ghetto area comprising only FIVE PERCENT of the residential area in the city."[140]

The war ushered in a new chapter of resistance, in part due to the extreme conditions of the housing market and the presence of more black homeowners with the means to litigate. The desire to leave substandard housing pushed African Americans into new neighborhoods; some African Americans, like the Shorts, did so as a deliberate effort to strike against Jim Crow. O'Day Short and Charlotta Bass were not new to the state, but some of the leaders and activists that pushed against restricted housing were recent migrants who brought traditions of resistance from places like New Orleans and Houston. The lessons learned about Jim Crow in the South would be invaluable for the newest Angelenos as they confronted western discrimination and violence. As Josh Sides shows, many of the migrants who settled in Los Angeles had been city dwellers rather than sharecroppers from the rural South, as popularly believed.[141] Some had been central players in the fight to establish southern chapters of the NAACP and brought to Los Angeles histories of confronting white supremacists, including the Klan.

The Klan's resurgence in the Inland Empire and Southern California, as the war ended, can be linked to the gains made by black workers, homeowners, and the state's civil rights activists. In the same month that the Shorts were murdered, Loren Miller won a decisive victory in California Supreme Court, called the Sugar Hill case, when he defended wealthy black homeowners who had moved to the exclusive West Adams neighborhood in Los Angeles.[142] The suit attracted significant press in part because

Academy Award–winning actress Hattie McDaniel (who had appeared in *Gone with the Wind*) was one of the residents. Klan members and other segregationists saw Miller's victory as an indication that they were rapidly losing ground. No doubt most Californians also knew about the shrinking job market. The money and jobs that flowed into the state during the war began disappearing even before war's end. Eighteen billion dollars in war contracts had already been canceled by October 1944.[143]

Black leaders in Los Angeles, including Miller and Charlotta Bass, would lead the resistance to housing discrimination. In 1945, Bass formed the Home Protective Association to help people of color defend their properties and their persons; the group met every Friday night near the *Eagle* office.[144] Well aware that housing restrictions targeted most people of color in the state, the group issued an invitation to Chinese, Mexican, and all minority groups being discriminated against in the housing market. Bass chaired the organization. The role of the *Eagle* in this fight was well-known to the Klan; Bass found the letters "KKK" painted on the sidewalk in front of the newspaper's office and was threatened by the group on more than one occasion.[145] That same year, according to the Workers Party in Los Angeles, more African Americans filed lawsuits challenging restrictive covenants in the city than in the rest of the country combined.[146]

As the investigation of the Short murders stalled and the cover-up persisted, the Klan's resurgence became headline news—again. Not coincidentally, the stronghold of this revitalized Klan was the Inland Empire. The arson and murders of the Shorts occurred just a few short months before the Klan staged a comeback in San Bernardino County's Big Bear Valley; indeed the murders signaled their return. Again, the threat posed by nonwhite homeowners surfaced as the central concern of Klan meetings. The new Big Bear Klan announced it would proceed with restrictive covenants and violence to achieve a "'One Hundred Per Cent Gentile Community' on all available land." A local minister, Wesley Swift, told a crowd at the American Legion that "the Klan is here in Bear Valley to stay. We intend to form restrictive covenants here and elsewhere to hold the line on Americanism." Four cross burnings in the valley in February and March caused State Attorney General Robert W. Kenny to issue a statement: "The worst thing that could happen in Southern California with unemployment prospects and racial tensions would be the revival of the Klan. We intend to smash the organization before it gets started."[147] Kenny sent his own agents to Big Bear to investigate the secret order, though this appears to have had little

Hired in 1932 by the City of Pasadena as its first black professional worker, Williams also campaigned for better jobs for the city's black men and women. The discriminatory hiring practices in Pasadena and by the city itself were already legendary. As early as 1924, the *California Eagle* made note of the dire situation for black workers: "The condition of affairs surrounding racial issues in Pasadena is nothing less than nauseating." Indeed, Williams's hire by the city seemed largely symbolic, and she made little headway either with private companies operating in Pasadena or with the city itself; by 1936 she had taken a job in Los Angeles. By 1940, little had changed: "the City of Pasadena does not hire a single policeman, fireman, regular day-time school teacher, meter-reader, or any other type of employee for the utilities; no, not even a janitor or elevator boy in the City Hall."[94]

Stone v. Board of Directors of Pasadena

During the 1930s, black women in the Pasadena NAACP branch spearheaded a new effort to force the city to integrate the Brookside Plunge. This time, Edna Griffin, Ruby McKnight Williams, and other women represented a new leadership closely linked to the middle class in ways the Negro Taxpayers and Voters Association could not have been two decades earlier. The Great Migration had resulted in a much larger and more diverse black population in Southern California; black professionals had established businesses and offices throughout Southern California. Griffin's position as a medical doctor garnered tremendous respect from her peers, as did Williams's prior experience as a teacher and position as a City of Pasadena employee. In this second round of challenges, Pasadena's pool case attracted considerable attention from the lawyers of the NAACP's Legal Defense Fund, including Thurgood Marshall and Charles Hamilton Houston. The NAACP had also undergone extensive change in two decades. Houston had begun collecting data in the South to disprove the "separate but equal" doctrine, and the organization's campaign against lynching brought national visibility. A victory in the case *Murray v. Pearson* (requiring the University of Maryland to admit law student Donald Murray) in 1935 had earned accolades and young Thurgood Marshall was beginning to make a name for himself. The Pasadena branch, however, deserves the credit for mobilizing a group many thought to be complacent and untouched by Jim Crow: the black middle class in the richest city in the nation.

Mustering the community to fight the pool case again would not be easy, however. Although the local branch had won recognition from the national office for their membership drive in the 1920s, a number of issues caused conflict in Pasadena's black communities and the NAACP.[95] Both the Pasadena and Los Angeles chapters struggled to garner attention from the national office and recruit members in the 1930s. Not surprisingly, black citizens in Pasadena did not agree on the best way to address segregation, including, if, when, or how to support the NAACP. Edna Griffin recalled that "when I started with the NAACP. . . . people were afraid. They were just filled with fear. It [later] became a badge of honor to be in NAACP but it wasn't then."[96] Many church leaders, however, did support the NAACP's efforts to challenge segregation. Reverend W. D. Carter of Friendship Church organized a protest in 1929 to integrate the pools in the two high schools. This effort led to a new policy and black high school students were allowed to swim in the school pools.[97] The following year, the city agreed to revert back to their original policy at Brookside and allow people of color one day a week: International Day was reinstated.[98]

A group of college students were among the first to challenge the International Day policy at Brookside that decade. In 1934, three students petitioned the city with the help of the NAACP branch.[99] The city remained as committed to segregation as it had twenty years earlier when the pool opened. The city manager replied, "it is just not acceptable to the majority of Pasadena people to mix bathing and swimming at Brookside."[100] That year the NAACP branch president, Reverend J. C. McCorkle, worked to motivate the city's four hundred members to desegregate the pool, with the *Crisis* reporting on their efforts.[101] By the end of the decade, the branch had the case that could make a difference. It would not be easy finding volunteers for the lawsuit, however. As Dr. Griffin, who became president of the local chapter in 1939, remembered, "Those were treacherous times . . . everybody bowed his head." According to Griffin, Episcopal priest and former president of the Pasadena NAACP Alfred Wilkins was instrumental in finding the men who were named in the lawsuit. "He knew the young men," Griffin said, "and you had a time trying to find the young black to use for the suit. You had to be denied [access to the pool] to start the suit. He's the one that got these young men, all of them that's named there. And they went, and I think Father Wilkins was with them when they were denied and they stood up. They stood up."[102]

Griffin was president of the Pasadena NAACP when the branch filed a lawsuit against segregation at the Brookside Pool. (Courtesy of the Trigg family)

On June 11, 1939, Charles Stone, William J. Brock, W. H. Harrison, Frederick M. James Jr., Frederick D. Smith, and James Price attempted to gain admission to the Plunge on a day open to whites only.[103] The men were denied entrance. Nine days later they attempted the same and were similarly denied. The group filed suit against the Pasadena Board of Directors, the Superintendent of Parks, and employees at the plunge. The trial of *Stone v. Board of Directors of the City of Pasadena* began on September 13, 1939, in Los Angeles County Superior Court.

To argue Stone's case against the city, the local branch secured the services of attorney Thomas L. Griffith Jr., a member of the National Legal Committee (NLC) of the NAACP (predecessor of the Legal Defense Fund), and president of the Los Angeles branch since 1935. With Griffith representing them, the Pasadena branch had a high-profile lawyer and a charismatic figure leading their case. Edna Griffin worked closely with Griffith, who had a wide network of supporters across Southern California. The year after he was elected, the LA branch hosted a fund-raiser hosted by celebrity Jack Benny to support passage of the Costigan-Wagner antilynching bill. Hollywood connections helped, but for the Pasadena branch Griffith's knowledge of the Bath House Battle and his relationship with the national office mattered most. Griffith had already handled a string of desegregation battles throughout the 1930s, defending African Americans against restrictive covenants, police brutality, and discrimination in restaurants and other public places.[104] Griffith threw himself into the very demanding Pasadena Brookside case, while keeping in constant contact with Houston and Marshall. He knew if the Pasadena branch could win their case it would add to the arsenal of precedent-setting lawsuits Marshall and Houston needed as they prepared for *Brown v. Board of Education*.[105] The strategy for the case developed in concert with Griffin, the Pasadena Branch, and the national office. A series of collegial letters between Griffith, Houston, and Marshall shows the significance of the case for the NLC.[106] Although the NAACP would assist over a dozen cities with pool segregation cases, Pasadena's was one of its earliest and most protracted cases.[107]

In his argument, Griffith asked Superior Judge Clement D. Nye for a writ that would "compel the Board of Directors to open the pool to negroes every day in the week."[108] Griffith stressed first and foremost that African Americans were homeowners and paid taxes to the city and therefore were entitled to city services. The city vehemently denied that city funds were being used to maintain the pool. On September 15, 1939, during the trial in the Superior Court of Los Angeles County, Griffith called the city treasurer of Pasadena, B. H. Rhodes, to the stand to testify. Rhodes claimed that no taxes had been used for the upkeep of the pool and that it was, therefore self-sustaining. The city controller then gave identical testimony. City attorney H. P. Huls and the city engineer, W. F. Alworth, argued that the city's policies amounted to equal treatment given the population figures, citing that at the time there were 85,000 white people living in Pasadena and 4,000 black people.[109] In other words, the numbers showed that black people were getting a fair deal

Thomas L. Griffith Jr. was president of the Los Angeles branch of the NAACP when he became the attorney for the Brookside Pool case in 1939. Griffith worked closely with Dr. Edna Griffin, Thurgood Marshall, and Charles Hamilton Houston to formulate legal strategies. (Courtesy of the Southern California Library)

considering they made up less than 5 percent of the population. This fact, in addition to the argument that the pool was self-sustaining, constituted what the city believed was an airtight defense. The newspaper of record agreed, proclaiming "Park Plunge Support by Taxes Denied: Claim of Negroes Hit in Court." The paper revealed another concern of segregationists: the fear that if the city was forced to allow people of color to swim when whites did, the city would lose revenue. City attorney Huls noted in court that while the pool had been self-sustaining, he was certain that "if it opened to Negroes, business would slump with the result that tax money would be required to continue its operation."[110] Emphasizing the economic as well as the social costs of integration played well among the status-conscious white elite. Further, the economic argument masked the underlying concerns about contaminated and dangerous black bodies.

Griffith's strategy in the courtroom was to direct the judge's attention away from the question of which bodies swam together and back to the constitutional and judicial arguments that the NAACP pursued rigorously in cases across the country. Just as attorneys in Los Angeles had argued, Griffith emphasized the Civil Code of California and constitutional provisions that prohibited discrimination. But he could not leave bodies out of the argument. After all, the issue of bodies and sex had been raised by city attorney Huls, who had declared that "swimming offered the opportunity of certain intimacies like marriage."[111] Griffith pointed out that the six petitioners were "of clean and moral habits" and that their bodies were free of contagious or infectious diseases and "any physical or mental defect or disability such as to make his admission to and use of said bath houses and swimming pool inimical, harmful or detrimental to the health, welfare, or safety of other users."[112] None of this impressed Judge Nye, who ruled on January 3, 1940, in favor of the city. His explanation for the ruling was that the writ of mandate was "an improper remedy."

Most likely Griffith had anticipated such a decision. On March 8, 1940, he wrote Charles Hamilton Houston with details of the appeal process: "Dear Charlie: On March 5, I filed my transcript on appeal in the District Court of Appeal, Second District, at the California State Building, Room 1201, Los Angeles, California. The case number is now Civil Appellate 12593." The details mattered. The national office had thirty days to file its friend of the court brief. A flurry of correspondence between the national office and Griffith ensued, and Thurgood Marshall replied to Griffith the same day that the office had been "working steadily" on the *Stone* brief.[113] Marshall had recently taken charge of the legal operations at the NAACP office in New York, and while inundated with requests from local branches, he believed in the importance of nurturing these local cases and spent significant time on the Pasadena appeal. His keen legal mind and charismatic personality is evidenced in the series of letters he wrote to Griffith as they prepared the brief for the appeal. As the lawyers discussed strategies, one question weighing heavily was whether to seek damages versus mandamus action. Debates about whether to pursue mandamus action had been central to the NAACP as they prepared for school segregation cases; Marshall had won his first graduate case in a mandamus action.[114] In the Brookside case, Marshall and Griffith felt strongly that pursuing damages was not the right strategy, but they deliberated for a long time before deciding on that course of action.[115] The brief reflected Marshall's thinking on this question and argued that "Damages would perhaps do for the past, but they are not adapted to the future. The injury here is of a kind which is impossible to measure with any approach of certainty by damages."[116] In spite of Nye's decision, NAACP lawyers believed that asking for a writ of mandamus was the right legal strategy.

Dr. Edna Griffin proved a diligent president of the local branch during the legal proceedings, working tirelessly to raise money for the appeal, which was filed in January 1940. But again, this work was not without its challenges; black Pasadena was not united in the effort to launch the appeal. Writing to director of branches William Pickens in June 1940, she explained, "The swimming pool case has been appealed and we are now in the process of trying to raise the much needed money. We do not get the cooperation of many of the ministers, especially in our larger churches, to be frank, A.M.E., Friendship and Metropolitan Baptist. Our people are more filled with Churchitis and selfish ministers than we can seemingly break through. We shall continue to hammer on them."[117] Griffin's frustrations with black Pasadenans were matched by her equally painful encounters with the City of Pasadena Board of Directors. The chairman of the board was also president of the Pasadena Improvement Association, formed to enforce restrictive covenants or as Griffin put it, it was an organization "whose one purpose is to restrict all property to the Caucasian Group."[118] Fighting city hall, in this case, took tremendous organizational skill, money, and courage. In an interview forty years after the lawsuit, she recalled African Americans' tangible reasons for distancing themselves from the pool case: "The black man became fearful of his job. Some cut out from supporting [us]. I looked into this."[119] After investigating the claim of a local janitor, Griffin realized that Pasadena businesses were using scare tactics to prevent black workers from supporting the NAACP's case, a strategy that was repeated across the country to stop black citizens from joining civil rights organizations and the black freedom movement. White supremacists threatened Griffin herself as a result of leading the branch during the lawsuit.[120]

Griffin's work as a physician gave her firsthand experience with Pasadena's Jim Crow practices. She recalled treating a Mexican American family in her clinic: "About half the family was dark-skinned and about half was very light-skinned. And I noticed one of the darker-skinned boys was sitting on the front steps crying. When I asked him what was wrong he said he was crying because his older brother had gone to swim in the pool but he couldn't go."[121] Griffin remembered going to City Hall and "trying to reason" with the city directors. However, she and her fellow NAACP members suspected that the city would only desegregate the Brookside Plunge if forced to do so.

The appeal was heard on September 22, 1941, in the District Court of Appeals, Second District. The appellate judges concurred that a mandamus was the proper remedy for unlawful discrimination and reversed the judgment from the Superior Court of Los Angeles County. But the city commissioners of Pasadena would not give up. In 1942 the city tried again to deny blacks access to the pool, appealing to the California Supreme Court. The court denied the city a hearing, allowing the NAACP's victory to stand on appeal.[122] Rather than comply, the city closed the pool.[123] Edna Griffin remembered that the city claimed they had no chlorine. "There were other excuses," she said, "and after two years of the pool being closed, we went to the courts and forced them to reopen it."[124] The NAACP, with Griffin's leadership, filed an injunction and finally on June 7, 1947, the Brookside Plunge opened to the general public without racial restrictions. "They didn't open the pool until we forced it and then everybody was in there swimming: black, white, yellow, what have you," Griffin recalled.[125]

It seemed as though African Americans, Mexican Americans, and Asian Americans would finally be swimming at Brookside. But just as open access looked possible after the war, the city chose a new strategy: stop improvements and let the pool deteriorate. The *Star News* reported the situation in 1949 as follows: "Plunges at Brookside were permitted to lapse into a state of disuse following a court action some years ago filed by a group of Negro citizens who claimed that a policy of discrimination existed."[126]

The lessons of Brookside are many. First and foremost, it is a story that foretells the ongoing struggles against segregation. In this case, the legal "victory" mattered little, as the city allowed the pool to deteriorate and become inoperable. A traditional NAACP-led battle did not, in fact, desegregate the facility. By the end of the twentieth century, the pool had been resegregated. While it is noteworthy that the national office had its eye on this case and other pool cases, these cases could never be the ones that undid *Plessy v. Ferguson*, as the NAACP was not ready to take on lawsuits that brought up questions of bodies and interracial sex.[127] By not dealing with bodies, segregationists' fears were left to fester, and in many ways they prevailed in the ugly battles of school desegregation. The unsolved pool case foretold the problems with *Brown* and its enforcement. Finally, the history of Brookside pool belies California's reputation as a place out of Jim Crow's reach.

Epilogue

Remembering (and Forgetting) Jim Crow

For over thirty years, city attorneys, the Pasadena Board of Commissioners, and local citizens committed considerable resources to prevent African Americans, Mexican Americans, and Asian Americans from swimming in Pasadena's municipal pool. How this story is remembered or forgotten reveals much about the way the city chooses to see itself, the way histories of western segregation are erased, and the difference between memories of Jim Crow and official histories. Paying close attention to the sites of this remembering and forgetting tells us who values this story and why. As various versions of the history of the Brookside Plunge continue to circulate, it is crucial to understand this as a living history, one that still resonates with Pasadenans who consider it central to their experience of the city and the state. It is a story that has been packaged and sold. In written texts, oral histories, children's literature, and public monuments, the Brookside Plunge appears and disappears, and with it, the history of a central battle over western Jim Crow.

The interviews compiled within the oral history collection at the Pasadena Museum of History reveal stories of struggle, humiliation, victories, and defeats. The memories of Pasadena held by men and women who endured segregation recall discrimination in housing and employment and instances of police harassment. Black Pasadenans remember segregated schools and being rejected from the pool. Although the oral histories did not set out to capture the story of the Brookside Plunge, most of the interviews with people of color mention the pool and its history of segregation. Ray Bartlett, a friend of Jackie Robinson's since childhood, emphasized Pasadena's long history of discrimination. Eventually serving on the board of directors for the local YMCA, Bartlett told his interviewer that, when he started volunteering there in the 1950s, "we couldn't even go in the Y."[1] One of the first black police officers in the city, Bartlett recounts many incidents of poor treatment; he experienced "more problems from other officers" than from ordinary citizens. About the pool, Bartlett recalled "We finally got to go in there to swim one day a week. Of course the war came along." What Bartlett remembers is that once African Americans could finally swim in the pool, the war came and it was closed. The meager concessions offered by the city meant little whenever they occurred, and the pool, like the schools, jobs, and the police force, was riddled with racism.

One longtime Pasadena resident, engineer Tatsuo George Hayakawa, alluded to the erasure of the history of Brookside in his interview conducted by the Pasadena Heritage Oral History Project. In response to the innocuous question "what did you and your brothers do for fun as you were growing up?" he answered:

> Well, we did pretty much the same thing that everyone else did that were of our age. We played in the neighborhood. We used to play hide and seek. And we used to play marbles. We used to play most of the games that the children played in the Depression years. We certainly didn't play many of the games that the younger children play now because of so many things that are available to them. We used to go swimming in the summertime. When I tell people about this, they are shocked to learn that there was a period in Pasadena's history where non-Caucasian people were unable to attend the public plunge, as it was called in those days, at Brookside Park. And I have found since then that many other cities in Southern California had similar restrictions on people attending the plunge. And my recollection was that we could go on Tuesday, and that's when all of us went to the plunge at Brookside Park. That was our summer activities.[2]

Hayakawa prevents historical amnesia by telling anyone who will listen about the history of Brookside.

Pasadena's best-known sports hero, Jackie Robinson, does some heavy lifting in this process of remembering and forgetting segregation's past. Indeed, one of the ways the story of the Plunge surfaces and then disappears is through Robinson's memorialization. The city was and is anxious to claim him as a favorite son who developed into a talented athlete in its public schools. Robinson honed his athletic skills at John Muir Technical High School and then Pasadena Junior College (now Pasadena City College) in the 1930s. He first emerged as a star athlete in four sports at Muir: basketball, track and field, football, and baseball. Pasadena makes strategic use of the Robinson family and Jack in particular. Remembering and memorializing Robinson and connecting him to Pasadena allowed city boosters to claim his civil rights legacy and distance Pasadena from its Jim Crow past. For Robinson, however, his inability to swim at the Brookside Plunge is one of the most significant memories of his boyhood. Pasadena was then a place of deep and pervasive segregation and discrimination, the place where his athletic ambition and promise were marred by racism.

Robinson told the story of segregation and racism at the Plunge repeatedly in interviews and memoirs. In a 1949 interview with the *Washington Post*, he recalled that "during hot spells, you waited outside the picket fence and watched white kids splash around. I honestly think the officials didn't think the Negroes got as warm and uncomfortable as white people during the Pasadena heat." Other versions of Pasadena's racism appear in Robinson's published memoirs. "Pasadena regarded us as intruders," he wrote in his autobiography, *Baseball Has Done It*. "We saw movies from segregated balconies, swam in the municipal pool only on Tuesdays, and were permitted in the YMCA on only one night a week. Restaurant doors were slammed in our faces." Robinson did not mince words about the racial climate in the city: "In certain respects Pasadenans were less understanding than Southerners and even more openly hostile."[3] Like Ruby McKnight Williams, Robinson made public the message that Pasadena's color line was enforced and blacks were not welcome.

Robinson's stories about the Brookside Plunge often appear in children's literature about Robinson's life. In the Childhood of Famous Americans series, *Jackie Robinson: Young Sports Trailblazer* does not step lightly around Pasadena's history of Jim Crow. In this version of Jack's early years in California, the Robinson family experiences outright racial hatred: "if Mallie Robinson thought California was going to be a paradise, she was mistaken. As it turns out, African-Americans were treated no better in Pasadena than they had been in Georgia." Aimed at readers between eight and twelve years old, this version, like many of the other children's books about Robinson, teaches readers about racism and about facing adversity. When the Robinson family moves to the all-white Pepper Street, for example, the author recounts the terrorism they experienced this way: "One day a note appeared under the Robinson door threatening to burn the house down. . . . Nobody ever set the house on fire, but one night somebody put up a large cross on the lawn and ignited it. The Ku Klux Klan, a hate group, often did this to intimidate blacks, Jews, and other people it didn't like. It was a warning—get out!"[4] The Robinsons' confrontation with the KKK is not a story Pasadena promoters like telling. This story, while not recounted in every children's book about the sports hero, reveals that children may have more exposure to this aspect of Pasadena's history than grown-ups.[5]

Herb Dunn's *Jackie Robinson: Young Sports Trailblazer* foregrounds the swimming pool restrictions in its telling of Robinson's youth. The image of little Jack at the fence, outside a swimming pool with conspicuous signage to mark the Brookside Plunge, fills one page. As the story unfolds, Mallie Robinson takes the children to a picnic in Brookside Park on a hot summer day, the children play hide-and-seek, and Jackie "came to a big fence. . . . He looked through the fence and saw a huge swimming pool. Hundreds of kids were in it, splashing and laughing. Jackie didn't notice that all the children were white."[6] But as Robinson recounted the story numerous times, he was always aware of the color line, and he experienced Pasadena's discriminatory policies and practices from childhood onward.

Two incidents from his Pasadena years confirmed Robinson's recollection about racism practiced by the City of Pasadena officials. In 1939, the same year the Pasadena NAACP went back to court over the pool case, Jack's older brother Edgar was beaten and arrested by police at the city's Tournament of Roses Parade. Although Edgar had rented chairs to watch the show, when he attempted to reach in his pocket to get the receipt for the chairs, police knocked him down, giving him a black eye and bruised arms. The local hospital refused to treat his injuries and when Edgar tried to complain to the chief of police, he was told to get out "before you are clubbed on the head." Jack also experienced police harassment in Pasadena that year. When he and his friend Ray Bartlett were driving home from a softball game at Brookside Park, they were taunted by white drivers; Jack, as Bartlett recalled, refused to ignore the incident. After a crowd gathered, a policeman cited Jack for resisting arrest and hindering traffic and he was taken to jail. By then Jack had become extremely valuable to UCLA as a star athlete; with the help of UCLA staff and legal connections, he got off with a fine, which the university paid. Robinson's anger at the way Pasadena treated African Americans never subsided. As biographer Arnold Rampersad put it, Jack came to "loathe Pasadena."[7]

In addition to his career in major league baseball, Robinson was active in the civil rights movement. His status as a celebrity guaranteed press coverage, which Robinson used to draw attention to racial discrimination on and off the field. His 1964 autobiography opens with these words:

> The right of every American to first-class citizenship is the most important issue today.
>
> We Negroes are determined that our children shall enjoy the same blessings of democracy as white children. We are adamant: we intend to use every means at our disposal to smash segregation and discrimination wherever it appears.[8]

By the time these words appeared in print, Robinson had chaired fund-raising efforts for the NAACP, attended the 1963 March on Washington, and entertained numerous civil rights leaders, including Martin Luther King Jr. and Roy Wilkins at his home in Stamford, Connecticut. Robinson's commitment to civil rights was not without controversy; he criticized Paul Robeson during a 1949 House Un-American Activities Committee appearance (something he came to regret), and he was temporarily lulled by the empty promises of Dwight Eisenhower and Richard Nixon regarding their commitment to civil rights. A radical he was not. Yet the impact of Robinson's dedication to civil rights and especially his status as the first to break baseball's color line should not be underestimated; whether justified or not, the face of Jackie Robinson, for many Americans of a certain generation, was the face of integration. Robinson died of a heart attack in 1972 at the age of fifty-three; in 1984 he was posthumously awarded the Presidential Medal of Freedom, the nation's highest civilian honor.

After Robinson's death, City of Pasadena officials may have thought the troubles at Brookside swimming pool were behind them. However, the NAACP refused to let the policies and history of the Plunge be buried. In 1990, when the Pasadena City Board of Directors reviewed the new facility that replaced the Plunge, the Rose Bowl Aquatics Center (RBAC), the Pasadena branch of the NAACP came forward to tell the story of racial restrictions. Branch President John Kennedy spoke before the board to question the openness of RBAC and its promise to the city to make the facility available to minority youths, children who had not always had access to the Brookside swimming pool. At that point, the city had loaned the project $5 million to build the new center and provided as much as 75 percent of the construction costs. But citizens complained that despite promises of "public access," there had been "no effort to include people of color in pool activities" and there were "terrible lingering vibrations in the community."[9] Kennedy reminded the board that "approximately forty years ago the NAACP sued the City to open up the Brookside Plunge to all people," which the city responded to by draining and closing the pool. Kennedy continued: the NAACP then "forced the City to reopen the pool [in 1947] to all people regardless of race, religion, or national origin." The youngest person to ever become branch president (he was twenty-six when elected in 1987), Kennedy nevertheless had a keen sense of history and understood the power in this past. While acknowledging that times had indeed changed, he told the board that "a good part of the land in the area was commonly referred to as 'Nigger Canyon,' and . . . by enlightened people, 'Negro Canyon'."[10] Kennedy's history lesson helped people understand that while terms had changed between 1914 and 1990—RBAC was accused of being "exclusive," not segregated—the results were the same: a public facility, paid for by the city, which served residents from Pasadena's white neighborhoods.

That the city has dedicated a public park, a stadium, a community center, and a piece of public art to the Robinson family, which fought segregation locally and nationally, does not erase the city's history of segregation. In fact, claiming the Robinsons—especially Jackie—as its own served a vital purpose for the city. Rewriting the narrative of Jackie's relationship to Pasadena could be accomplished symbolically, if not in fact. A closer look at these memorials reveals Pasadena's erratic relationship to its own racial past, a relationship that embraces some aspects of its black history while obscuring other painful aspects. The history of the Brookside Plunge and other stories of Jim Crow and racial tensions are a part of the Robinsons' memories, and for some city residents they are the inspiration behind these memorials. But this history is not visible materially. Like the written record, the ways Jim Crow is remembered or forgotten in memorials reveals how the city, state, and nation narrate and erase the history and memories of Jim Crow. For Pasadena, the desire to paper over or forget the city's conviction to segregate coexists with a desire to celebrate individual triumph over racism (as opposed to an understanding of racism as systemic) by claiming the name and story of Jackie Robinson.

In November 1997 the city of Pasadena dedicated the Pasadena Robinson Memorial statue. By all accounts, Pasadena was late to the party: between 1985 and 2013, seven other Robinson statues were erected across the United States and in Canada, three of them finished before Pasadena announced its intention to erect one and five of them built before Pasadena's was fin-

Completed in 2002, the Robinson Memorial is across the street from the Pasadena City Hall. (Courtesy of the Library of Congress)

ished. In fact, Pasadena could have been first: shortly after Jackie died in 1972, Mack Robinson approached the city about building the first statue to honor his brother. The city refused, and UCLA claimed that honor. As of 2013, there were more statues of Jackie Robinson in North America than of any other U.S. baseball player.[11]

When Pasadena announced its intention to dedicate a sculpture to the Robinsons in 1997, the nation was in the middle of what scholar Erika Doss calls "memorial mania." The desire to erect memorials and thus "control particular narratives about the nation and its public" had become ubiquitous.[12] That same year also marked the fiftieth anniversary of Jackie Robinson joining the Brooklyn Dodgers, thereby breaking the color barrier in major league baseball. Although the timing of the dedication is understandable, the meaning of the sculpture's form and the story it tells are less clear. Completed in 2002, the memorial consisted of two enormous bronze sculptures of the heads of Jackie and Mack Robinson made by artists Ralph Helmick, John Outterbridge, and Stuart Schechter. The sculptures stand nine feet tall and tower over Centennial Square, a small park that lies across the street from the Pasadena City Hall, a focal point of the civic center. Their location — in the center of the city and at the site of local power — and their size make them impossible to ignore. Going about their daily routines, locals would find it difficult to avoid the city center: the main branch of the public library, the police headquarters, and the main post office are all clustered around the square. Even if you were not looking for them, the Robinson statues are hard to miss: each head weighs 2,700 pounds. The city's brochure about the statues explains their raison d'être: "The Robinson brothers' abilities, self-confidence and determination set the stage for others to overcome barriers. Both men led complex lives, contributing to the communities, serving as role models and working tirelessly for civil justice." The phrase "civil rights" is assiduously avoided. Pasadena is mentioned only once in the description: "Mack was raised and stayed in Pasadena, and his portrait eternally faces City Hall. Jackie, who left the city, faces east, toward Brooklyn and the location of his adult domiciles." The purpose of the sculptures, as spelled out in the brochure, is "to create empathy and intrigue, meditation and reflection."[13]

What narrative is the city projecting through this memorial? The placement of the two heads and the text about "adult domiciles" underscores that Jackie left Pasadena, and could be read as implying that his relationship to the city was troubling. Artist Ralph Helmick confirmed this in an interview; in order to "acknowledge Jackie's discomfort with his childhood experiences," he "deliberately pitched Jackie's head at a right-angle to Mack's, looking eastwards away from the city, as a reflection on his desire to leave."[14] This seems to leave the city itself blameless in Jackie's "discomfort." That may indeed have been the intention of the artists and the city in commissioning the work. The choice to portray only Jackie's head also distinguishes this statue from the seven others that, for the most part, show Robinson's entire frame. The brothers' athletic abilities are never mentioned or referenced in the style or text of the memorial. Since Mack Robinson was a medal-winning Olympian (he placed second to Jesse Owens in the 200-meter dash in Berlin in 1936), it seems an odd choice to disembody the brothers, unless the intent was for viewers to focus on their activities that were not sports-related. A study of Robinson statues finds that all of the other memorials participate in what they call "tolerance branding," that is, they attempt to associate their city with the idea of tolerance and racial justice.[15] Pasadena's memorial was not included in that study, but it seems clear that it is attempting to do the same thing, despite the family's experience with intolerance in the city and Jackie's in particular. And, in some ways, the city uses the memorial to erase that history. Viewers who know the history of the Robinsons may find this attempt at reconciliation problematic; other viewers may experience the memorial as uplifting and a sign that Pasadena is proud of its black history and citizens.

This is the only memorial to the Robinson family created by the City of Pasadena. The post office in northwest Pasadena, a predominantly African American part of the city, was renamed for Mack Robinson; but, as a local journalist points out, "that was a decision made by federal officials, not the city." A community center and park in northwest Pasadena were named after Jackie, but an editorial in the *Pasadena Weekly* notes that "these were all pre-existing structures."[16]

The effectiveness and meaning of civil rights memorials vary, but as one scholar explains, all "enact a dialectical tension between reconciliation and amnesia, conflicts resolved and simply reconfigured."[17] The same can be said for the Robinson memorial in Pasadena, although it does not claim to be a civil rights memorial. By publicly displaying the Robinsons, the city can lay claim to the popular national narrative about breaking down the color line. Segregation's history can be retold as a victorious story of individuals who "overcame barriers" and "worked tirelessly for civil justice," without referencing that many of these barriers were erected in Pasadena. While the sculptures reference a narrative of discrimination, that discrimination happened elsewhere, the nation that would not let Jackie Robinson play major league baseball. In this telling, the discrimination is "solved" when Jackie begins playing for the Dodgers in 1947 or when Mack wins his Olympic medal in 1936. The public history of the Robinsons is not about employment discrimination and domestic work. It is not about their brother Edgar being attacked by the police at the Rose Parade. It is certainly not a story of the city's persistent and often violent culture of Jim Crow and segregation. And it not a story about the Brookside Plunge. In fact, Southern California is the savior in this story: Pasadena raised the Robinsons in their public schools and had the good sense to encourage their athleticism. Los Angeles gets credit for nurturing Jackie Robinson's athletic ability at UCLA and in the Dodgers, even though when Jackie played for the team they were still in Brooklyn. In an analysis of the ways Americans remember acts of violence such as September 11 and the 1995 Oklahoma City bombing, Marita Sturken shows how the politics of memory "enable particular notions of innocent victimhood."[18] The history of segregation and the countless acts of violence committed to sustain it can be remembered in similar ways; Americans would rather portray Jim Crow as a history of innocent victims rather than as a history of deliberate acts of violence. This concept is readily apparent in the memorials and children's literature dedicated to Jackie Robinson's history.

Reading the history of the Brookside Plunge through Jackie Robinson is at once illuminating and troubling. The efforts of hundreds of black Californians and other people of color who fought segregation in public facilities become the story of a little brown boy at the chain link fence in the 1920s, or of a sports hero denied. Women's work as protesters in the long civil rights movement is erased. In spite of the fact that Edna Griffin and Ruby McKnight Williams fought segregation in Pasadena for over fifty years, their history is not part of the story of the Robinsons. As Barbara Ransby, Belinda Robnett, Kathryn Nasstrom, and others have noted, the erasure of women's leadership in the long civil rights movement obscures the messy process of organizing and has implications for the way the larger history is understood today.[19] The stories of Griffin and Williams highlight the length and significance of the Pasadena struggle and the difficulties organizers encountered. Without their histories, the pool struggle appears either as a few court cases—a simple legal history—or a history dominated by men (the men of the NTVA, Jack Robinson, and NAACP lawyers).

The Robinson family was not the only family with stories about Pasadena's segregation. Oral histories from Pasadenans are filled with stories of anger, sadness, and frustration, but also of men and women and children who made do and made different memories. Like black southerners, black westerners developed complicated strategies to resist and manipulate the intricacies of Jim Crow. For Williams and Griffin, resistance meant joining and leading the NAACP in a series of court cases against the wealthiest city in the nation, fighting discrimination in employment, restaurants, and hospitals. But other westerners chose different methods: some swam at the Plunge one day a week, others swam in the canyons or not at all until restrictions were lifted. The story of the Brookside Plunge and other public swimming pools across southern California reveal truths about Jim Crow that the nation would rather not dwell on. Segregation made deep inroads in the western landscape, and it shaped Pasadena's landscape, culture, and identity as a city. These traces of segregation and the legacy of Jim Crow can be found in oral histories, monuments, and memoirs. The dangers that swimming pools represented—as opposed to restaurants or movie theaters—inspired white Californians to hold the line and enforce segregation doggedly through city councils, the courts, eugenics organizations, and intimidation. Black Californians, like black southerners and Midwesterners, were afraid to lose their jobs if they joined the NAACP and local efforts to end segregation at swimming pools and parks. Forgetting Brookside is not possible for many people of color in Pasadena, and their memories make it that much harder to erase the history of western Jim Crow.

✳ ✳ ✳

Only twenty-five years after Ruby McKnight Williams, Edna Griffin, and their fellow freedom fighters finally secured the right to swim in Pasadena's public pool, the city's record of segregation became national news. It was not the Brookside struggle that was the focus of all the attention, however. The nation watched as the battle over the racial makeup of Pasadena's schools reached a crisis point. In 1970, Pasadena became the first school district outside the South to be ordered by federal courts to desegregate. The state that liked to see itself as progressive and forward-thinking, modern, and sophisticated had, again, shown itself to be a leader in the creation of color lines and the inequity that they ensured. While the revelation that Pasadena's students of color were receiving an inferior education struck many as newsworthy, for Williams and her cohort this was yesterday's news.

In the 1960s, Pasadena parents became increasingly frustrated by the city's refusal to implement the *Brown v. Board of Education* decision. When Jay Jackson Sr. sued the Pasadena Unified School District (PUSD) in 1961, he argued that his son was receiving an inferior education at Washington Junior High School, where most of the city's black students were forced to enroll.[20] Although the California Supreme Court ruled in Jackson's favor, confirming that the PUSD was encouraging segregation, little changed. When white flight exacerbated the situation, upsetting the racial balance at John Muir High School, a group of parents sued the school district. The lawsuit, *Spangler v. Pasadena City Board of Education*, filed in 1967, became a flashpoint for the school board, parents, teachers, and students, about segregation and bussing. When the U.S. District Court Judge Manuel Real ordered the public schools to comply with *Brown v. Board of Education* in 1970, the city had twenty-seven days to come up with a plan for compliance. The plan that they adopted involved busing white students across the Arroyo to nearby schools in African American neighborhoods. Opponents of integration mounted a fierce protest, adopting the slogan "Stop Forced Bussing."[21] The debate over integration dominated school politics and civic life for years to come. Many, however, remembered discrimination at Brookside Plunge and insisted the school crisis was not an aberration in the city's history; after all, the city's commitment to segregation began long before the 1960s. Revisiting the memories of the battle over Brookside became essential to many opponents of segregation. Despite their efforts, a certain amnesia seemed to attach itself to California's long history of Jim Crow.

Hiding behind a veil of liberalism and good intentions, California enforced racial hierarchies and segregation in ways that were sometimes bold—as in the case of the Short family murders—but oftentimes under the radar. White supremacy took many forms in the Golden State. This is a history that, as this book argues, runs broad and deep. Beginning with statehood and the blurring of lines between slavery and freedom, antiblack laws and customs have been a sturdy thread running through the state's history. Telling these stories of western Jim Crow brings to light hidden voices of enforcers of white supremacy as well as its resistors. Histories of white supremacy in the West have often been obscured beneath the more dramatic tales of the Jim Crow South. Why these histories remain submerged in the national imaginary is worth considering.

Stories of California's practices of segregation disappear due to region and habit; the West is not the place where these racialized practices have been most visible. In spite of ample scholarship that shows otherwise, the myth persists that Jim Crow originated in the South. This phenomenon has benefitted western states and skewed our understanding of the national invention and expression of Jim Crow. The price of this imaginary is serious: it prevents us from seeing the West as a creator of racialized hierarchies and regimes of white supremacy. We would be better served by a vision of the West that understands it as a region that not only borrowed certain practices of Jim Crow from southern states but also created new ones to fit its needs. We must be mindful of the ways racial formations morph and shift, blend across borders, and adapt to place and time.[22]

California pioneered ways of instilling segregation in its law, culture, and social formations. This process was not smooth, linear, or progressive. Nor did it always meet with success. As the histories of Delilah Beasley, Charlotta Bass, O'Day Short, and Ruby McKnight Williams make clear, black resistance to the color line was forceful and constant in the Golden State. Sometimes California showed the way to democracy. As the story of the Short family indicates, in the aftermath of World War II, a wide coalition of Japanese, Mexican, Catholic, and Jewish Americans, joined with other black and white Angelenos to fight for fair housing, equal employment, and racial justice.[23] Their efforts served as a model for the nation. Indeed, historian Mark Brilliant calls the state of this era a "civil rights frontier."[24] Yet to understand these heroic efforts at combatting racism, we must turn to the first century of statehood and examine the creation of the color lines that these citizens sought to eradicate. The establishment of racialized science, barriers in the housing market, and white-only public spaces were not new in 1940s California, as Ruby McKnight Williams fully appreciated. Her surprise when she arrived in Pasadena in the 1930s was not due to the fact that Jim Crow existed in the promised land, but that it was already so entrenched. California segregationists had, by the Great Depression, constructed a divided and demarcated state: signage and custom kept Mexican, Asian, and African Americans in certain neighborhoods and out of public and privately owned spaces. This was not appreciated—or accepted—in all quarters across the country, although the black press informed anyone who cared to know that the state championed the color line. But Pasadena and other cities across the state did not face the national scrutiny that southern cities would when they fine-tuned "separate but equal" in the twentieth century. Due partly to the scrutiny inspired by the *Brown* decision, southern schools would become among the most desegregated in the nation.[25] As attorney Loren Miller told an assembly of western governors in 1964, "more Negro children attend all-Negro schools in Los Angeles than in Jackson, Mississippi, and Little Rock, Arkansas, combined."[26] While city builders in the New South worried about attracting investors if they appeared too racially intolerant, Californians had little to fear on that score. Segregationists and white supremacists in the Golden State worked boldly to limit the lives of people of color. Their efforts closed off opportunities for housing, education, employment, and recreation for nonwhite citizens.

Towns up and down the state benefitted from a certain invisibility with regard to racialized practices. Even when California cities became infamous for perfecting Jim Crow's practices—like San Jose in 1933 or Los Angeles in 1946—the reputation never seemed to stick. The state had too much invested, literally and figuratively, in maintaining a reputation for progressive, forward-thinking, liberal policies for these events to be seen as little more than aberrations. Not until the 1965 Watts Rebellion and the creation of the Black Panther Party in 1966 would the state have an image problem vis-à-vis race relations. Into that problem walked a new kind of politics symbolized by Ronald Reagan and Richard Nixon; the New Right and the Moral Majority helped shift the racial rhetoric of the Golden State. Reframing the calls for racial and economic justice as riots and the new actors as thugs and hoodlums, the political leadership in the 1960s worked to erase the long history of racism and segregation that had shaped the Los Angeles and Oakland of the period. Making Jim Crow invisible became a political and economic imperative. Suppressing the historical memory of white supremacy in California was also a part of this legacy. Ironically, Ronald Reagan did not understand Allensworth as part of the history of Jim Crow and black nationalism when he authorized the building of the state park.

In its first century, California created systems of racial discrimination in the areas of housing, public recreation, education, and employment. The state attempted to control people of color, police the borders of racial intimacy, and stop desegregation in its tracks. In the twenty-first century, segregation works differently than it did one hundred years ago, but it remains insidious and powerful. Learning from past practices is essential as westerners face new forms of racial discrimination, containment, and violence.

Notes

Introduction

1. Ruby McKnight Williams, interview, no date, video, PMH Black History Collection.

2. Flamming, *Bound for Freedom*, 50.

3. Taylor, *In Search of the Racial Frontier*, 233.

4. *Crisis*, July 1913.

5. Mosley's series of detective fiction featuring Easy Rawlins unravels the complicated and segregated geography of Los Angeles. See, for example, Mosley, *Black Betty*.

6. Cox, "Evolution of Black Music"; Bryant et al., *Central Avenue Sounds*; Daniels, "LA Zoot"; Von Eschen, *Satchmo Blows Up the World*.

7. Among the scholars touting what Earl Lewis ("Expectations, Economic Opportunities, and Life") refers to as the West's "culture of expectations" is Albert Broussard (*Expectations of Equality*). Shirley Ann Wilson Moore provides a telling example of the ways black Californians exemplify this cultural phenomenon. See Moore, *To Place Our Deeds*.

8. Ruby McKnight Williams, interview by Sharon E. Girdner, April 9, 1999, transcript, PMH.

9. Holt, *Problem of Race*, 69.

10. *Ninth Census*, vol. 1 (Washington, D.C.: Government Printing Office, 1872), 5, https://www2.census.gov/library/publications/decennial/1870/population/1870a-04.pdf.

11. *Abstract of the Fourteenth Census of the United States* (Washington, D.C.), 98, https://www2.census.gov/library/publications/decennial/1920/abstract/abstract-1920-part2.pdf.

12. Gordon, *Ghostly Matters*.

13. Haley, *No Mercy Here*.

14. I see my work in conversation with feminist scholarship that challenges simple understandings of black women's work, race women, and respectability politics. See Cooper, *Beyond Respectability*.

15. See for example Pascoe, *What Comes Naturally*; Lee, *At America's Gates*; Sánchez, *Becoming Mexican American*; Molina, *Fit to Be Citizens?*; Bernstein, *Bridges of Reform*; Kurashige, *Shifting Grounds of Race*; Brilliant, *Color of America*.

16. See for example Molina, *How Race Is Made in America*.

17. On the diversity of the state population after the gold rush see, for example, Johnson, *Roaring Camp*; Rohrbough, *Days of Gold*; Holliday, *World Rushed In*.

18. *The Statutes of California Passed at the First Session of the Legislature*, ch. 99, *An Act Concerning Crimes and Punishments*, passed April 16, 1850, 3rd division, Who May Be a Witness in Criminal Cases, section 14, states: "No black or mulatto person, or Indian, shall be permitted to give evidence in favor of, or against, any white person. Every person who shall have one eighth part or more of Negro blood shall be deemed a mulatto, and every person who shall have one half or Indian blood shall be deemed an Indian" (San Jose: J. Winchester, 1850, 229–30).

19. Welke, "Rights of Passage"; Hudson, *Making of "Mammy Pleasant,"* ch. 3.

20. Larson, *Sex, Race, and Science*, 38.

21. Beasley, *Negro Trail Blazers of California*, 157.

22. A. Wood, *Lynching and Spectacle*, 213.

23. *California Eagle*, December 1, 1933, https://archive.org/details/la_caleagle
_reel14/page/n309.

24. U.S. Bureau of the Census, *Seventeenth Census*, vol. 2, part 5.

25. For scholarship on western segregation see, for example, Flamming, *Bound for Freedom*; Moore, *To Place Our Deeds*; Sides, *L.A. City Limits*; Broussard, *Black San Francisco*; Lemke-Santangelo, *Abiding Courage*; Taylor, *Forging of a Black Community*.

26. Kelley, *Race Rebels*.

27. I use the word *modern* here with caution. While I acknowledge it is often a sloppy, ahistorical term, here I reference a host of beliefs that are associated, sometimes wrongly, with California. I also acknowledge the false dichotomy of a backward South and a modern West. For studies that address California and modernism, see, for example, McGirr, *Suburban Warriors*.

28. The California Park Department in the 1970s conducted some forty interviews in preparation for the creation of the Colonel Allensworth State Park; these are archived in the CPDA. The second set of interviews is part of the Donated Oral Histories Collection, Special Collections, University of California, Los Angeles.

29. I am indebted to the pathbreaking work produced by the Duke University Center for Documentary Studies and its collection of interviews. See Chafe et al., *Remembering Jim Crow*.

30. Farnham, *California*, 327.

Chapter 1. Freedom Claims: Reconstructing the Golden State

1. On the meanings of drink in gold rush California, see Johnson, *Roaring Camp*, esp. ch. 3.

2. *Pacific Appeal*, September 7, 1872.

3. This decision was originally reported in the *Washington Chronicle*, August 28, 1872, and reprinted in *Pacific Appeal*, September 7, 1872. Judge William B. Snell decided the case in Police Court and the case involved William A. Foote who charged Sebastian Aman, a restaurant keeper with refusing to entertain him at the bar. The Washington, D.C., Police Court case of *Foote v. Aman* (case 2385) was immediately appealed by Sebastian Aman in the U.S. District Court for the District of Columbia as case 9420. The records of Aman's appeal are located in record group 21, Records of the United States District Court for the District of Columbia, entry 77, Criminal Case Files, 1863–1934, case file 9420, *District of Columbia v. Sebastian Aman*. Aman won his appeal.

4. *Pacific Appeal*, October 5, 1872.

5. On this point, see Clark, *Defining Moments*.

6. Cooper, *Beyond Respectability*.

7. Haley, *No Mercy Here*.

8. Esterovich, *Proceedings*, 3. See note 18 in the introduction. For antiblack testimony in civil cases, see *The Statutes of California Passed at the Second Session of the Legislature*, ch. 5, An Act to Regulate Proceedings in Civil Cases in the Courts of Justice of this State, passed April 29, 1851; title 11, Of Witnesses, and of the Manner of Obtaining Evidence; ch. 1, Of Witnesses, section 394. "The following persons shall not be witnesses: 4th. Negroes, or persons having one half or more Negro blood, in an action or proceeding to which a white person is a party" (Eugene Casserly, 1851, 113–14).

9. Taylor, *In Search of the Racial Frontier*, 83.

10. Farnham, *California*.

11. On the ways that free states crafted black codes, see, for example, Woodward, *Strange Career of Jim Crow*; Litwack, *North of Slavery*; Douglas, *Jim Crow Moves North*.

12. Quoted in Almaguer, *Racial Fault Lines*, 37. Almaguer argues that "although antiblack sentiment was widespread, white Californians were never drawn into the same frenzied competition with blacks as they were with the thousands of Chinese immigrants. . . . California's black population was never

allowed to effectively compete with European-American immigrants in the state and, consequently, were never perceived as the same formidable threat that other racialized groups posed for white men" (41). While this assessment of the labor market rings true, the evidence shows that European Americans did see black men as a threat even though African Americans could not compete with whites for jobs.

13. On the attempt to pass an anti-immigration law in 1850, see Hittell, *History of California*, 2:806. The California Assembly Journal index reports an introduction of an anti-immigration bill in 1851 by Mr. Merritt; the bill was referred to a select committee. See *Journals of the Legislature of the State of California at its Second Session* (Eugene Casserly, 1851), 1315–16, 1439–40. For the 1857 bill, which the House refused to pass, see *Journal of the Eighth Session of the Assembly of the State of California* (Sacramento: James Allen, 1857), 742, 811, 823–24. On the 1858 attempt, see *Journal of the Ninth Session of the Assembly of the State of California* (Sacramento: John O'Meara, 1858), 342, 408, 416–17, 444–45, 447, 462, 489, 500, 523, 525; and *Journal of the Ninth Session of the Senate of the State of California* (Sacramento: John O'Meara, 1858), 553, 661, 663–65.

14. Smith, *Freedom's Frontier*, 145, 2, 64.

15. Smith uses the manuscript census to meticulously determine the extent of the free black and slave populations. See *Freedom's Frontier*, appendix. Rudolph Lapp claims there were up to three hundred slaves working in the mines in the early 1850s and up to six hundred slaves involved in the Gold Rush. Lapp, *Blacks in Gold Rush California*, 65.

16. Smith, *Freedom's Frontier*, 244; Lapp, *Blacks in Gold Rush California*, 65.

17. These records were either destroyed in a fire or lost in the mail. Smith, *Freedom's Frontier*, 238.

18. Taylor, *In Search of the Racial Frontier*, 76. The black population in most western states rarely exceeded 1 percent of the population before the Civil War. In 1860, only California, the Indian Territories, and Texas had black populations totaling more than 1 percent of their total inhabitants (76).

19. Smith, *Freedom's Frontier*, 72.

20. Richard Blackett makes the point that to best understand what slaves thought of freedom we should look at what they *did*. Blackett, *Captive's Quest*, xiii.

21. Coleman, "African American Women," 103.

22. Moore, *Sweet Freedom's Plains*, 197–99.

23. Quoted in ibid., 199. See also Hayden, *Power of Place*, 151.

24. On Mason's philanthropic legacy, see Campbell, *Making Black Los Angeles*.

25. Smith, *Freedom's Frontier*, 131.

26. *In the Matter of Archy, On Habeas Corpus* (Supreme Court of California), 9 Cal. 147 (1858).

27. Lapp, "Negro Rights Activities," 11.

28. Smith, *Freedom's Frontier*, 77.

29. Campbell, *Making Black Los Angeles*, 45. One of Lee's attorneys, Edwin Crocker, was the brother of railroad magnate Charles Crocker, an avid anti-slavery advocate.

30. Blackett, *Captive's Quest*; Blackett, "Dispossessing Massa."

31. Esterovich, *Proceedings*, 3.

32. Bragg, "Anxious Foot Soldiers," 105.

33. The first convention acknowledged a resolution from Mrs. Alfred J. White thanking the business committee. The second convention thanks the ladies of San Francisco for financially supporting the first black newspaper in the state, the *Mirror*. At the third convention, it was announced that the women of Sacramento were organizing a fruit festival to raise funds for a new church building. See Esterovich, *Proceedings*, 24, 60, 80. Barbara Welke is not convinced that women influenced conventions in a significant way. See Welke, "Rights of Passage," 88. On gender and black conventions, see Horton, *Freedom's Yoke*.

34. Jones, *All Bound Up Together*, esp. ch. 2. Jones sees the 1840s as the high point of the woman question in black conventions, peaking in 1848 at the Cincinnati convention, where the delegates voted to embrace women's rights. In the 1850s, after the passing of the Fugitive Slave Law, Jones sees a turning away from the woman question.

35. Quoted in Jones, *All Bound Up Together*, 69.

36. *Constitution, By-Laws, and Act of Incorporation, Ladies' Union Beneficial Society*, February 1861, CHS.

37. Daniels, *Pioneer Urbanites*, 31.

38. Hunter, *To 'Joy My Freedom*.

39. Coleman, "African American Women," 111.

40. Campbell, *Making Black Los Angeles*, 53.

41. *Pacific Appeal*, April 12, 1862.

42. E. Brown, "Womanist Consciousness"; E. Brown, "Negotiating and Transforming the Public Sphere"; E. Brown, "To Catch the Vision of Freedom." Brown argues that women interpreted the civil and political rights of Reconstruction as belonging to women as well as men. For a different interpretation, see Barbara Welke, who argues that "in their quest for freedom and civic equality, black men and women pursued separate rights defined in the prevailing gendered-rights consciousness of the time as male or female" ("Rights of Passage," 74). Pleasant's case, among others, confirms that women interpreted the rights of Reconstruction as belonging to them; women and men did adopt gendered-rights language and strategies, but I am not convinced, as Welke is, that this is what guaranteed success in California's nineteenth-century civil rights movement.

43. *Elevator*, October 13, 1865.

44. D. Michael Bottoms sees this change in the testimony law as the undoing

of a biracial racial hierarchy that pitted all nonwhite groups against whites. See Bottoms, *Aristocracy of Color*, ch. 1. We can assume that "Mongolian" in this case refers to Asians who are not Chinese.

45. In addition to Brown, Turner, and Pleasant, William Bowen also filed lawsuits against San Francisco streetcar companies. See Welke, "Rights of Passage."

46. *Pleasants v. North Beach Mission Railroad*, California Reports 34, 586 (1868). See also Hudson, *Making of "Mammy Pleasant."*

47. *Pleasants v. NBMRR*, June 20, 1867, California State Archives.

48. E. Brown, "Womanist Consciousness"; B. Brown, "Negotiating and Transforming the Public Sphere"; Gilmore, *Gender and Jim Crow*; Rosen, *Terror in the Heart*.

49. The eclipse of black women's politics can be explained in part by a tendency to focus on the conventions and formal political activities, a focus that has obscured female activism. On this point see Bragg, "Anxious Foot Soldiers," 98.

50. U.S. Bureau of the Census, *Negro Population*, 43–44.

51. On this point, see Paddison, *American Heathens*.

52. Lawrence B. de Graaf notes that "as long as black students were denied entry to white schools in the West, black women were responsible for much of their education." De Graff, "Race, Sex, and Region," 295.

53. Bragg, "Anxious Foot Soldiers," 108.

54. Hendrick, *Education of Non-Whites*, 7.

55. Andrew Moulder, *Annual Report of the State Superintendent of Public Instruction* (1858), 14, San Francisco Public Library Archives.

56. On the career of Moulder, see Hendrick, "From Indifference to Imperative Duty."

57. Hendrick, *Education of Non-Whites*, 7.

58. Swett, *History*, 205.

59. Kennedy, *Population*, 598–99 (Recapitulation of the Tables of Population, Nativity, and Occupation-Population of the States and Territories By Color And Condition, With the Rate of Increase and Representation In Congress).

60. The term "Negroization of the Chinese" appeared first in Caldwell, "Negroization of the Chinese Stereotype." Aarim-Heriot, *Chinese Immigrants, African Americans*; see also McClain, "Chinese Struggle for Civil Rights."

61. On this point, see Wong, *Racial Reconstruction*; Paddison, *American Heathens*.

62. William Newby quoted in Lapp, *Blacks in Gold Rush California*, 104.

63. On the significance of Swett's election and the battle over segregated schools, see Bottoms, *Aristocracy of Color*, ch. 3.

64. "Have Negroes Been Taught and Classed on Terms of Equality in a Public School Under the Charge of Mr. John Swett?," 1862 newspaper clipping, Benjamin Ignatius Hayes Scrapbook, Bancroft Library.

65. Swett describes these handbills in his autobiography. See Swett, *Public Education in California*. See also Swett, *History*, 205.

66. Hendrick, *Education of Non-Whites*, 17.

67. Eugene H. Berwanger calls the Democratic victories in 1867 and 1869 "among the most stunning political reversals in the nation in the immediate postwar years." Berwanger, *West and Reconstruction*, 202.

68. Smith, *Freedom's Frontier*, 210. Smith further notes that while California was the only free state that did not ratify the Fourteenth Amendment in the 1860s, at least three other free states—New Jersey, Ohio, and Oregon—ratified the Fourteenth Amendment but rescinded ratification prior to 1870. See Smith, 287n10.

69. Many black citizens took comfort in the fact that Booth made his acceptance speech while residing in Mary Ellen Pleasant's boardinghouse. See Hudson, *Making of "Mammy Pleasant,"* 58.

70. *Pacific Appeal*, December 9, 1871.

71. On Republican parties and education, see Foner, *Reconstruction*, 469.

72. *Pacific Appeal*, September 2, 1871.

73. H. Davis, *We Will Be Satisfied*, 110.

74. *Sixth Biennial Report of the Superintendent of Public Instruction of the State of California, 1874–1875* (Sacramento: G. H. Springer, 1875), San Francisco Public Library.

75. *Pacific Appeal*, October 7, 1871.

76. Wollenberg, *All Deliberate Speed*, 14.

77. Lapp, *Afro-Americans in California*, 19. Lapp locates the beginning of this strategy in the convention in Stockton in November 1871: "the Chinese were not included in their request [for equal education] because the delegates felt that such a broadening of the campaign would ensure its defeat in the anti-Oriental atmosphere of nineteenth-century California" (19).

78. *Pacific Appeal*, February 24, 1872.

79. Low, *Unimpressible Race*.

80. Ibid., 26–27.

81. There were certainly exceptions to this sentiment. *Pacific Appeal* published an editorial in 1873 exposing "cruelty, murder" and "unjust oppression" in the treatment of Chinese. The article compared the cutting of queues in prison to making "Jews eat pork." *Pacific Appeal*, May 31, 1873.

82. *Pacific Appeal*, February 10, 1872.

83. "The Word 'White' in the California School Laws: Speech of Hon. J. F. Cowdery of San Francisco, in the House of Assembly, Sacramento, Cal., January 30, 1874," Bancroft Library.

84. On the use of racial science in the 1850s, see discussion of *People v. Hall* in Bottoms, *Aristocracy of Color*, 17–18.

85. *Pacific Appeal*, April 5, 1862. On the Gordon case, see Lapp, *Blacks in Gold Rush California*, 208–9; Mullen, *Dangerous Strangers*, 107. Mullen calls the Gordon case "the most notorious white-on-black homicide" in nineteenth-century San Francisco (107).

86. Mullen, *Dangerous Strangers*, 107.

87. The case is given substantive treatment in Wollenberg, *All Deliberate Speed*; and Hendrick, *Education of Non-Whites*; see also Broussard, *Black San Francisco*; Heizer and Almquist, *Other Californians*.

88. *Ward v. Flood* (1874), 48 Cal. 36.

89. H. Davis, *We Will Be Satisfied*, 124.

90. Bottoms, *Aristocracy of Color*, 123.

91. On the significance of parades and commemorations, see Clark, *Defining Moments*; S. White, "It Was a Proud Day"; Kachun, *Festivals of Freedom*.

92. Kachun, *Festivals of Freedom*, 123.

93. I do not mean to imply here that Emancipation Day festivities in former slave states were *only* celebratory. Southerners also used the occasion to offer harsh critiques of Reconstruction and the empty promises of politicians. On this point see Kachun, *Festivals of Freedom*. On the inability of the federal government to assure the promises of freedom after the Civil War, see, for example, Downs and Masur, *World the Civil War Made*.

94. On Sanderson see Lapp, "Jeremiah B. Sanderson"; Noel, "Jeremiah B. Sanderson"; Thurman, *Pioneers of Negro Origin*, 37–42.

95. *Pacific Appeal*, August 21, 1875.

96. Lapp, *Jeremiah B. Sanderson*, 329.

97. Kathleen Ann Clark reminds us that while this kind of commemoration "consistently emphasized male accomplishments" and stressed manhood rights, we should be careful not to de-emphasize the ways women participated and shaped such commemorations. "Marching in or cheering on a parade, voicing their opinions at a rally, engaging in prayer, selling their wares on a streetside corner, or singing and dancing into the night, women were visible — not always "respectable" — participants in patriotic and commemorative events." Clark, *Defining Moments*, 83.

98. *Elevator*, January 3, 1868.

99. *Elevator*, January 24, 1868.

100. Lapp, *Jeremiah B. Sanderson*, 328.

101. *Elevator*, January 24, 1868.

102. Ibid.

103. Haight had moved from the Republican to the Democratic Party to run as a Democrat for governor in 1867. On Haight's inflammatory racial rhetoric, see Bottoms, *Aristocracy of Color*.

104. "The Governors' Gallery, Henry Haight's Inaugural Address (December 5, 1867), posted in 2019 by California State Library, https://governors.library.ca.gov/addresses/10-Haight.html.

105. Aarim-Heriot, *Chinese Immigrants, African Americans*. See also Smith, *Freedom's Frontier*.

106. *San Francisco Daily Examiner*, August 1869, CHS.

107. Quoted in Johnsen, "Equal Rights."

108. While I appreciate that D. Michael Bottoms calls attention to the ways African Americans utilized racial hierarchies, specifically pointing out their superiority over Chinese, I take issue with his argument that "California's racial minorities did not mount a direct challenge to the intellectual foundations of white supremacy" (*Aristocracy of Color*, 29).

109. As cited in Richardson, *West from Appomattox*, 127.

110. On the competition between these newspapers, see Snorgrass, "Black Press"; H. Davis, *We Will Be Satisfied*.

111. *Elevator*, January 3, 1868.

112. Gaines, *Uplifting the Race*, 34–35.

113. Caddoo, *Envisioning Freedom*.

114. O. Lewis and Hall, *Bonanza Inn*.

115. Daniels, *Pioneer Urbanites*, 35.

116. *Pacific Appeal*, January 29, 1876.

117. Ibid.

118. Daniels, *Pioneer Urbanites*, 36. By January 1896, twenty years after the ball in question, Morton organized the emancipation proclamation celebration under the auspices of the Afro-American League, see *San Francisco Chronicle*, January 2, 1896.

119. *Elevator*, May 1, 1876.

120. *Pacific Appeal*, May 6, 1876.

121. H. Davis, *We Will Be Satisfied*, 47. Bell believed pressure should be brought to bear on the Democratic-controlled state legislature; Anderson believed that to be a futile strategy.

122. H. Davis, *We Will Be Satisfied*, 64–65.

123. *Pacific Appeal*, May 6, 1876.

124. Ibid.

125. Bederman, *Manliness and Civilization*.

126. *Pacific Appeal*, April 24, 1875.

127. Ibid.

128. Taylor, *In Search of the Racial Frontier*, 196.

129. Rogin, *Blackface, White Noise*, 40.

130. Saxton, *Rise and Fall*; Roediger, *Wages of Whiteness*; Lott, *Love and Theft*.

131. Berson, *San Francisco Stage*, 2:81.

132. Estavan, *San Francisco Theatre Research* 13:11.

133. Berson, *San Francisco Stage*, 1:63.

134. Kurutz, "Popular Culture," 291. San Francisco was not the only western city with a penchant for minstrelsy. Between 1864 and 1911, 149 minstrel troupes performed in Seattle, Washington. Hill and Hatch, *History of African American Theatre*, 117.

135. Estavan, *San Francisco Theatre Research*, 48.

136. Rodecape, "Tom Maguire," 291.

137. Berson, *San Francisco Stage*,1:31.

138. Ibid., 1:63.

139. Weiner, *Black Trials*, 215–31.

140. Stanley, "Slave Emancipation," 269, 271.

141. *Pacific Appeal*, January 8, 1876; Weiner, *Black Trials*, 218.

142. Quoted in Weiner, *Black Trials*, 221.

143. The first case, *U.S. v. Thomas Maguire*, 1366, was filed in the U.S. Circuit Court Ninth Circuit for the District of California sitting in San Francisco. The criminal information was filed on January 10, 1876, by U.S. Attorney Walter Van Dyke on behalf of Charles Green. The case itself doesn't mention how the court ruled, and the only verification that Green's case was lost appears in a January 20, 1876, *San Francisco Chronicle* article. According to this article, the date of the ruling in *U.S. v. Maguire* (in which Green's case was lost) was January 19, 1876. In addition, a second case cited as *U.S. v. Thomas Maguire*, 1367, U.S. Circuit Court Ninth Circuit for the District of California, was also presented and filed on January 10, 1876. This criminal information was again filed by U.S. Attorney Van Dyke but on behalf of George M. Tyler; similar to case 1366, case 1367 does not provide the court's adjudication. However, U.S. Attorney Van Dyke would file a second case on behalf of George M. Tyler on February 12, 1876, this time against Maguire's theater doorkeeper, Michael Ryan. Originally filed as case 1392 in the U.S. Circuit Court Ninth Circuit for the District of California, *U.S. v. Ryan* would be consolidated and become a part of the notable U.S. Supreme Court case *U.S. v. Stanley*, 109 U.S. 3 (1883), also known as the Civil Rights Cases.

144. Weiner, *Black Trials*, 221.

145. *Pacific Appeal*, February 13, 1876.

146. *San Francisco Examiner*, October 26, 1899.

147. *Wasp*, December 2, 1881.

148. Daniels, *Pioneer Urbanites*, 31.

149. On the significance of cultural venues as places where social power and racial hierarchies are made visible, see Berglund, *Making San Francisco American*, 225.

Chapter 2. "This Is Our Fair and Our State": Race Women, Race Men, and the Panama Pacific International Exposition

1. The best source for information about Beasley and her career is E. Brown, introduction; see also, E. Davis, *Lifting as They Climb*, 188–95; Crouchett, *Delilah Leontium Beasley*; Dillon, *Humbugs and Heroes*, 32–36.

2. For a discussion of black women's leadership, see Shaw, *What a Woman Ought to Be*.

3. Caddoo, *Envisioning Freedom*, 31–32.

4. Boisseau and Markwyn, *Gendering the Fair*, 2. See also Hudson, "This Is Our Fair"; Markwyn, *Empress San Francisco*.

5. Robert Rydell, *All the World's a Fair*, 209.

6. A. W. Hunton, "The Club Movement in California," *Crisis*, December 1912, 90. On Hunton, see Salem, *To Better Our World*.

7. W. E. B. Du Bois, "Colored California," *Crisis*, August 1913, 192–95.

8. Bunch, "Greatest State for the Negro."

9. De Graaf, "City of Black Angels"; De Graaf, "Race, Sex, and Region."

10. Quoted in Broussard, *Black San Francisco*, 39.

11. *Oakland Sunshine*, December 21, 1907.

12. Sides, *L.A. City Limits*, 17; Flamming, *Bound for Freedom*, 69.

13. Broussard, *Black San Francisco*, 76, 79.

14. Ibid., 77; see also Stokes, D. W. Griffith's *"The Birth of a Nation."*

15. Caddoo, *Envisioning Freedom*, 143.

16. Broussard, *Black San Francisco*, 77–78.

17. *Oakland Independent*, December 14, 1929.

18. On the global context of the fair, see Markwyn, *Empress San Francisco*, ch. 1.

19. Kline, *Building a Better Race*, 14.

20. On eugenicists at the fair, see Stern, *Eugenic Nation*.

21. Stern, *Eugenic Nation*, 180.

22. Rydell, *All the World's a Fair*, 224.

23. Todd, *Story of the Exposition*, 5:38–40.

24. Rydell, Findling, and Pelle, *Fair America*, 66.

25. Stern, *Eugenic Nation*, 55.

26. Quoted in Kline, *Building a Better Race*, 14.

27. Kline, *Building a Better Race*, 15. In a letter from Charles Davenport to Kellogg, Davenport claimed that only the American Academy of Science received more press coverage. Stern, *Eugenic Nation*, 55.

28. Pascoe, *What Comes Naturally*, 84–85.

29. *Crisis*, June 1913; see also April 1913.

30. Stern, *Eugenic Nation*, 114–15.

31. Larson, *Sex, Race, and Science*, 38–39.

32. Cooper, *Beyond Respectability*.

33. Most clubwomen in the West could be categorized as middle class, but Shirley Ann Wilson Moore makes the important point that working-class women contributed to California's club movement as well. Moore, "Your Life," 217.

34. Mitchell, *Righteous Propagation*, 80.

35. Ibid., 81. Mitchell notes that while the politics of respectability could be subversive when African Americans "decided not to allow stereotypes and insults to affect their own measure of self-worth," efforts to enforce respectability "could be oppressive for those black women, men, and children who opted to live by different standards" (81).

36. S. L. Mash to Chas. Moore, January 14, 1915, box 23, PPIE Records.

37. Mash is most likely referring to the fact that in 1893 the California Legislature passed a bill prohibiting racial discrimination in places of public accommodation.

38. Mash to Moore, January 14, 1915.

39. R. J. Taussig to S. L. Mash, February 6, 1915, box 23, PPIE Records.

40. S. L. Mash to Chas. Moore, February 13, 1915, box 23, PPIE Records.

41. Lentz-Smith, *Freedom Struggles*; C. Williams, *Torchbearers of Democracy*.

42. *Crisis*, March 1918, 240.

43. Beasley, *Negro Trail Blazers of California*, 303.

44. Wilson & Waters to James Rolph Jr., March 8, 1915, box 23, PPIE Records.

45. Ibid.

46. Wilson & Waters, March 24, 1915, box 23, PPIE Records.

47. *Crisis*, December 1915, 61.

48. Ackley, *San Francisco's Jewel City*, 341.

49. Beasley, *Negro Trail Blazers of California*, 303.

50. D. Lewis, *Small Nation of People*, 33.

51. Reed, *All the World*, 17.

52. Wells-Barnett, *Crusade for Justice*, 117; see also Massa, "Black Women."

53. Ida B. Wells, "To Tole with Watermelons," *Cleveland Gazette*, July 22, 1893, reprinted in Sklar and Dublin, *Women and Social Movements*.

54. Rydell, *Reason Why*, xxvi.

55. Quoted in Schechter, *Ida B. Wells-Barnett*, 97.

56. "Women at the World's Fair: The Lady Managers Explain Their Attitude," *New York Age*, October 24, 1891, reprinted in Sklar and Dublin, *Women and Social Movements*.

57. Manring, *Slave in a Box*.

58. Rydell, *Reason Why*, xviii.

59. The National Association of Colored Women formed in 1896. See Shaw, "Black Women"; Giddings, *When and Where I Enter*.

60. For the rare exception to this oversight, see E. Brown, introduction.

61. Wilson, *Negro Building*, 63.

62. Ibid.

63. As quoted in Lewis, 26.

64. Wilson, *Negro Building*, 111. See also Willis, "Sociologist's Eye."

65. Markwyn, *Empress San Francisco*, 108.

66. F. Wood, "Zone," 271. I thank journalist Dave Gilson for this citation and

his research on the African Dip. Gilson does not find evidence that African Americans were depicted inside the booth in the ethnic "dummies," but it is possible since they appeared in similar games at other fairs and carnivals. http://davegilson.com/african-dip.html.

67. *Oakland Sunshine*, March 27, 1915.

68. Ibid.

69. *Oakland Sunshine*, May 29, 1915.

70. *Western Outlook*, April 3, 1915.

71. Markwyn, *Empress San Francisco*, 125.

72. *Oakland Sunshine*, May 29, 1915.

73. *Oakland Sunshine*, June 5, 1915. *Oakland Sunshine*, August 28, 1915; *Oakland Sunshine*, June 5, 1915.

74. *San Francisco Chronicle*, June 11, 1915.

75. *Oakland Sunshine*, June 12, 1915.

76. *San Francisco Chronicle*, June 11, 1915.

77. *Oakland Sunshine*, June 5, 1915.

78. S. White, "It Was a Proud Day," 34.

79. Ibid., 48.

80. Terborg-Penn, *African American Women*; E. Brown, "Womanist Consciousness"; Higginbotham, *Righteous Discontent*.

81. For a discussion of the ways white women challenged male authority at the PPIE, see Markwyn, "Encountering 'Woman.'"

82. *Crisis*, November 1915, 35.

83. *Oakland Sunshine*, June 12, 1915.

84. Ackley, *San Francisco's Jewel City*, 208, 209.

85. *Oakland Sunshine*, November 6, 1915.

86. Quoted in Mitchell, *Righteous Propagation*, 123. Mitchell, *Righteous Propagation*, 136.

87. On the NAACP and children, see Bragg, "Marketing the Modern Negro"; English, *Unnatural Selections*. On the popularity of baby contests in California branches of the NAACP, see, for example, the records of the Pasadena branch. Part 1, box G-21, Branch Files, NAACP.

88. In November, the black newspaper *Western Outlook* bragged of black participation in the fair's San Francisco Day. But as Markwyn notes, the white papers again ignored the presence of African Americans. Markwyn, *Empress of San Francisco*, ch. 3.

89. *Oakland Sunshine*, June 19, 1915.

90. *Oakland Sunshine*, June 26, 1915.

91. See, for example, her discussion of the Civil War in *Oakland Sunshine*, June 26, 1915.

92. *Oakland Sunshine*, June 26, 1915.

93. Ibid.

94. *Oakland Sunshine*, July 17, 1915.

95. Ibid.

96. Ibid.

97. Broussard, *Black San Francisco*, 39.

98. *Oakland Sunshine*, December 11, 1915.

99. *Oakland Sunshine*, September 18, 1915.

100. Wilson, *Negro Building*, 130.

101. Des Jardins, *Women and the Historical Enterprise*.

102. Beasley, *Negro Trail Blazers of California*, n.p.

103. Charles E. Chapman, review of *The Negro Trail Blazers* and *Grizzley Bear* by Delilah L. Beasley (June 1919): n.p., Francis B. Loomis Papers.

104. Carter Woodson, review of *The Negro Trail Blazers* and *Grizzley Bear* by Delilah L. Beasley, *Journal of Negro History* 5 (January 1920): 128–29.

105. Ibid., 129.

106. Roger Streitmatter believes that Beasley borrowed the money from the Loomis's and took three years to pay it back, but Beasley's preface in NTB indicates that the Loomises were not the only financial benefactors. See Streitmatter, *Raising Her Voice*, 76; Beasley, *Negro Trail Blazers*, preface.

107. Delilah Beasley to Elizabeth Loomis, June 25, no year, Francis B. Loomis Papers.

108. E. Brown, introduction.

109. Moore, "Your Life," 221.

110. E. Brown, introduction.

111. *Oakland Tribune*, May 7, 13, and 17, 1925; May 19, 1925, B-23; March 29, 1925, X-8; May 10, 1925, B-2; May 24, B-3.

112. *Oakland Tribune*, May 17, 1925.

113. *Oakland Tribune*, May 8, 1927. As cited in Crouchett, *Delilah Leontium Beasley*, n.p.

114. Elsa Barkley Brown uncovered a series of letters that Beasley wrote to W. E. B. Du Bois in which she reveals that the *Oakland Tribune* supported her efforts to crusade against lynching. E. Brown, introduction, xlv, n.45.

Chapter 3. "The Best Proposition Ever Offered to Negroes in the State": Building an All-Black Town

1. Painter, *Exodusters*, 149, 116, 108, 207, 108.

2. Henry Singleton, interview, transcript, no date, Allensworth Collection, CPDA. Because this collection contains three interviews with Henry Singleton, whenever possible I note the interviewer and/or the date of the interview.

3. Singleton interview. Three sets of oral histories—all conducted in the 1970s and 1980s—contain vivid recollections of life in the town. One set is

preserved as the Allensworth Collection, CPDA; the second set was conducted by Eleanor Ramsey ("Allensworth"); the third is in the Donated Oral Histories Collection, UCLA.

4. Singleton interview.

5. Singleton interview, transcript, March 23, 1977, Allensworth Collection, CPDA.

6. Singleton interview, transcript, p. 6, tape 1, side 2, no date, Allensworth Collection, CPDA.

7. Painter, *Exodusters*, 119.

8. On the subject of California's all-black towns, see Beasley, *Negro Trail Blazers of California*, 157. Beasley mentions the all-black towns of Furlong Tract and Albia in addition to Allensworth. Hamilton, *Black Towns and Profit*. Hamilton mentions the towns of Bowles, Victorville, and Abilia. See also McBroome, "Harvests of Gold." On rural black townships in the San Joaquin Valley, see Eissinger, *African Americans*.

9. See Hamilton, *Black Towns and Profit*.

10. Singleton interview, transcript, March 23, 1977, 2, Allensworth Collection, CPDA.

11. *Visalia Times Delta* (no date), clippings file, Allensworth Collection, Tulare County Library.

12. Exodusters to Oklahoma also migrated multiple times. Kendra T. Field argues that we should understand these post-emancipation experiences as "unbound migrations" that complicate our understanding of the methods and meanings of migration in African American history. Field, "No Such Thing as Stand Still."

13. Ruby McKnight Williams, interview by Sharon E. Girdner, April 9, 1999, transcript, p. 2, PHOHP.

14. One of Overr's friends, Joe Durel, said Overr "worked for a millionaire" in Pasadena. Joe Durel, interview by Eleanor Ramsey, transcript, Feb. 15, 1976, in Ramsey, "Allensworth," 9.

15. Beasley, *Negro Trail Blazers of California*, 154, 154, 157, 157.

16. Ramsey, "Allensworth," 25.

17. Royal, *Allensworth*, 4.

18. On the history of black towns, see Painter, *Exodusters*; Hamilton, *Black Towns and Profit*; Crockett, *Black Towns*; Stuckey, "Boley"; Slocum, "Black Towns"; and *The Black Towns Project* website (http://www.blacktownsproject.org/).

19. See, for example, Rhodes, *Mary Ann Shadd Cary*; Blackett, *Beating against the Barriers*; F. Miller, *Search for a Black Nationality*.

20. Hamilton, *Black Towns and Profit*, 1. See also Cha-Jua, *America's First Black Town*.

21. Hamilton, *Black Towns and Profit*, 153. According to Quintard Taylor,

black farmers in Oklahoma owned land valued at $11 million by 1900. Taylor, *In Search of the Racial Frontier*, 147.

22. On Singleton's settlements in Tennessee, see Painter, *Exodusters*, 113–16; on Mound Bayou, Mississippi, see Hamilton, *Black Towns and Profit*, 43–98. The other communities are listed in appendix 1 in Hamilton, *Black Towns and Profit*, 153–54.

23. On Allen Allensworth's "rags to riches" story, see Hamilton, *Black Towns and Profit*, 139; Royal, *Allensworth*, 1–4.

24. Alexander, *Battles and Victories*, 172, 191.

25. Ibid., 231.

26. In 1907 he preached on the "Five Manly Virtues" at the Memorial Baptist Church in Los Angeles. See *Los Angeles Herald*, May 12, 1907, CDNC.

27. Alexander, *Battles and Victories*, 219.

28. See, for example, Bederman, *Manliness and Civilization*; Gaines, *Uplifting the Race*; Jenkins and Hine, *Question of Manhood*.

29. Ramsey, "Allensworth," 19.

30. Quoted in Dobak and Phillips, *Black Regulars*, 117.

31. These black regulars were the first generation of African Americans to serve in a peacetime army. Dobak and Phillips, *Black Regulars*, vi.

32. Quoted in the *Cleveland Gazette*, May 7, 1898.

33. Dobak and Phillips, *Black Regulars*, 133.

34. *Cleveland Gazette*, August 2, 1890.

35. Fewer than 20,000 served as regulars in the U.S. Army between the Civil War and 1898. However, Dobak and Phillips argue that they were not always treated worse than white regulars. Dobak and Phillips, *Black Regulars*, intro.

36. *Cleveland Gazette*, April 22, 1905, and May 12, 1906.

37. *Los Angeles Herald*, August 1, 1906, CDNC.

38. For example, on June 20, 1908, the *Los Angeles Herald* reported that Allensworth was active in Republican Party politics, and gave a speech to ratify Taft's nomination.

39. See, for example, *California Eagle*, February 27, 1914.

40. Alexander, *Battles and Victories*, iii.

41. There are different theories about Allensworth's motivation to start the colony. Lonnie Bunch argues that Allensworth was motivated by racial uplift and the desire to counter eugenicist notions of black inferiority. Bunch, *Allensworth*. Hamilton claims this was a scheme about speculation, not race. See Hamilton, *Black Towns and Profit*.

42. *Indianapolis Freeman*, May 14, 1904.

43. *Indianapolis Freeman*, November 9, 1907.

44. *Washington Bee*, November 2, 1907.

45. *Indianapolis Freeman*, November 2, 1907. By December 1908, the Indianapolis *Freeman* seemed to be back on board supporting the endeavor and

published four articles in one month announcing the new town. (Dec. 5, 12, 26; Jan. 2, 1909).

46. Bunch, "Allensworth," 28.

47. *Los Angeles Herald* (July 16, 1908); Ramsey, "Allensworth," 16; Hamilton, *Black Towns and Profit*, 138.

48. Ramsey, "Allensworth," 44–46.

49. Harlan and Smock, *Booker T. Washington Papers*, 13:522–23.

50. McBroome argues that "Washington's support for all-black towns and land development schemes for economic self-sufficiency encouraged several African American entrepreneurs in California to participate in business ventures that they hoped would foster economic growth" ("Harvest of Gold," 149). Marne Campbell notes that Washington had his doubts about black Californians ability to farm the land, given the reliance on irrigation. Campbell, *Making Black Los Angeles*, 189.

51. Harlan and Smock, *Booker T. Washington Papers*, 13:522.

52. *Indianapolis Freeman*, December 12, 1908.

53. Singleton interview, transcript, p. 2, March 23, 1977, CPDA.

54. *Cleveland Gazette*, August 5, 1911.

55. *Tulare County Register*, August 6, 1908, Allensworth Collection, TCL.

56. Quoted in Hamilton, *Black Towns and Profit*, 142.

57. Perhaps by 1910 the retired colonel realized that his town was in trouble. In 1910 Allensworth considered the Back-to-Africa movement as a viable alternative to the race problem in California. Like his contemporaries enamored by Marcus Garvey, Allensworth joined other Angelenos at a lecture at the Tabernacle Baptist Church about an African colonization scheme, called the International Household African Missionary Association. More than 800 black Angelenos attended the lecture and Allensworth was elected treasurer of the new organization. *Los Angeles Herald* (November 21, 1910).

58. Royal, *Allensworth*, 61.

59. *California Eagle*, October 3, 1914.

60. The *Oakland Sunshine* reported that a white man was on trial for an undisclosed crime; "The writer is made to wonder what the negroes of this Black colony want with a white man there. Can they not buy their few canned goods from some negro? What's the use of colonizing and then let some straggling white, negro woman-loving man come in the colony, scoop up the poor Negroes' pennies, insult their women and laugh?" (October 2, 1915). On the economic dependency of all-black towns, see Cha-Jua, *America's First Black Town*.

61. Royal, *Allensworth*, 81.

62. In May 1912, the town published its own newspaper, the *Sentiment Maker*, though there is only one extant edition. It appears to have served primarily as a marketing tool. *Sentiment Maker*, May 15, 1912, Allensworth Collection, TCL.

63. *Sentiment Maker*, May 15, 1912.

64. *Indianapolis Freeman*, July 10, 1909, AAN.

65. McBroome, "Harvests of Gold."

66. *Sentiment Maker*, May 15, 1912, Allensworth Collection, TCL. Black towns in Oklahoma were also settled by Buffalo Soldiers. See Slocum, "Black Towns."

67. Durel interview, 4, 7. There is no record of how many retired Buffalo Soldiers settled in the town, but oral histories indicate that they were never in the majority.

68. Quoted in Royal, *Allensworth*, 16.

69. Singleton, interview by Kay Gibson, transcript, pp. 5–7, no date, CPDA.

70. A Kansas newspaper was much impressed by the election of Joshua Singleton as postmaster. *Topeka Plaindealer*, June 23, 1911.

71. *California Eagle*, October 3, 1914. It is possible that Charles Alexander worked for the *Eagle*. He is described as a newspaper man by Emory Tolbert. See Tolbert, *UNIA and Black Los Angeles*, 40.

72. The town also had its own fire department and women's auxiliary. *San Jose Mercury News*, December 15, 1912, AAN.

73. *Los Angeles Herald*, November 21, 1915, CDNC.

74. Tolbert, *UNIA and Black Los Angeles*, 42.

75. Royal, *Allensworth*, 63.

76. Rivers, *Hackett Family*, n.p.

77. On this point see Cooper, *Beyond Respectability*, ch. 2.

78. Royal, *Allensworth*, 90.

79. Cooper, *Beyond Respectability*, 12.

80. Ramsey, "Allensworth," 131.

81. Bunch was interviewed for Kelty, *Allensworth*.

82. Sadie Calbert, interview by S. J. Cullers, March 1, 1977, transcript, CPDA.

83. Rivers, *Hackett Family*.

84. Singleton interview by Gibson, p. 25. Joe Durel's mother was a midwife. See Durel interview.

85. Caitlin, "Black Utopia," 11.

86. *San Francisco Call*, June 19, 1899, CDNC. On black women and racial uplift, see, for example, Shaw, *What a Woman Ought to Be*; Mitchell, *Righteous Propagation*.

87. For a nuanced discussion of the connection between family and migration during slavery (including the Underground Railroad), see Camp, *Closer to Freedom*. Camp argues that assumptions about women's role in childbearing and childrearing have led historians to underestimate their mobility away from and resistance to slavery.

88. Sadie Calbert, interview by Alfred Ray, transcript, no date, CPDA.

89. Betty Rivers, "The First Baptist Church of Allensworth: A Contribution to Its History," California State Library (Sacramento: n.p., n.d.).

90. Royal, *Allensworth*, 48.

91. Ramsey ("Allensworth") and Beasley (*Negro Trail Blazers of California*) both claim that the school became the central social and political institution—not the churches.

92. Library Building Report, vertical file, TCL.

93. Beasley, *Negro Trail Blazers of California*, 154.

94. "Copy of Mrs. Allensworth's Address," Allensworth Collection, TCL.

95. *San Francisco Call*, August 10, 1907.

96. "Copy of Mrs. Allensworth's Address."

97. Ramsey, "Allensworth," 118–19.

98. Royal, *Allensworth*, 41–42.

99. Ibid., 42.

100. Bessie Herman Twaddle to Herman Clark, February 3, 1915, Allensworth Collection, TCL.

101. Assembly Bill 299 as reprinted in *California Eagle*, January 30, 1915.

102. *California Eagle*, January 30, 1915.

103. *Oakland Sunshine*, March 20, 1915.

104. *California Eagle*, January 30, 1915.

105. *California Eagle*, February 6, 1915.

106. *California Eagle*, April 3, 1915.

107. Allensworth's main church was the Second Baptist church in Los Angeles, but he had a small congregation in Monrovia. Interview with Allensworth J. Blodgett, Donated Oral Histories Collection, UCLA.

108. Royal, *Allensworth*, 87.

109. Allensworth J. Blodgett, interview by Mayme Clayton, June 26, 1970, transcript, Donated Oral Histories Collection, UCLA.

110. Beasley, *Negro Trail Blazers of California*, 155, 155, 156.

111. Ibid., 155.

112. Ramsey, "Allensworth," 60–63, quote on 62.

113. Quoted in ibid., 64. The *California Eagle* of Oct. 3, 1914, contains a promotional article about Allensworth in which they assure settlers that the "water tax" is fair and they should pay it.

114. Marjory Towns Patterson, interview by Kay Gibson, March 6, 1977, transcript, CSPA.

115. Royal, *Allensworth*, 63.

116. Sadie Calbert, interview by Alfred Ray, no date, transcript, CPDA.

117. Patterson interview. Elizabeth Payne McGhee, interview, transcript, no date, CPDA.

118. Ramsey, "Allensworth," 151, 153.

119. Between 1890 and 1920, most black women across the United States worked in agriculture or domestic service. But it was rare for black women to farm in the West; in 1910 there were only thirty black female farmers in the Mountain and Pacific states. Even accounting for census discrepancies, these

numbers mean black female farmers in Allensworth would have been anomalies. See de Graaf, "Race, Sex, and Region."

120. Ramsey, "Allensworth," 145.

121. Ibid., 149.

122. Ibid., 149. Payne's daughter, Elizabeth Payne McGhee, told her interviewer in the Park Service project, "We were poor. You can imagine with eight children, and a teacher's salary." McGhee interview.

123. Royal, *Allensworth*, 60. Blodgett interview. The principal industry of the valley would eventually become cotton.

124. *California Eagle*, October 3, 1914. On Johnson and her husband, see Royal, *Allensworth*, 55.

125. Phillips interview.

126. Ramsey, "Allensworth," 158. On his appointment as postmaster, see *California Eagle*, February 27, 1915.

127. Ramsey, "Allensworth," 156, 157, 157.

128. Royal, *Allensworth*, 52.

129. Ramsey states that "social conditions in the wider society precluded the most highly trained Allensworth pioneers, motivation notwithstanding, from finding employment commensurate with their skills" ("Allensworth," 144).

130. McWilliams, *California*; McWilliams, *Factories in the Field*.

131. Streshensky, "Dream Dies Hard," 54.

132. *Visalia Times Delta*, April 4, 1958, vertical file, TCL.

133. Ibid.

134. *Visalia Times Delta*, November 11, 1967, vertical file, TCL. See also *Visalia Times Delta*, June 20, 1967; *Visalia Times Delta*, February 13, 1968; *Visalia Times Delta*, March 7, 1968; *Los Angeles Times*, March 13, 1967, and April 17, 1968, all in vertical file, TCL. According to this article, the town's water had been contaminated with arsenic since its founding due to its location in the basin.

135. *Visalia Times Delta*, April 6, 1968, vertical file, TCL. Concerned local citizens and residents of the colony were successful in their efforts to raise $37,500 and they received a matching grant from the Farmers Home Association; they had to supply the labor to lay the pipes and install the purification systems in each home. The problems were not solved by the water purification system. By 1975 the water had dried up. See *Visalia Times Delta*, August 16, 1975, vertical file, TCL.

136. *Visalia Times Delta*, February 13, 1968, Allensworth Collection, TCL. See also *Visalia Times Delta*, March 7, 1968, TCL.

137. *El Macriado*, May 10, 1967, California State Library.

138. Jerilyn Oliveira, interview by author, January 16, 2010; Ramsey, "Allensworth," 65–68.

139. Oliveira interview.

140. Audience members told me this when I presented a paper on Pleasant at a conference at San Francisco State University in 1987.

141. James A. Lark, interview by Mayme Clayton, June 18, 1970, transcript, Donated Oral Histories Collection, UCLA.

142. *Visalia Times-Delta*, January 17, 2004, TCL.

143. *Tulare Advance Register*, February 28, 1970, TCL.

144. Allensworth file, NAACP/Bancroft Library.

145. California State Parks, *Allensworth: A Feasibility Study*, 5, Bancroft Library.

146. *Westways*, May 1991, 26, Allensworth Vertical File, LAPL.

147. *San Jose Mercury*, February 28, 1993, Allensworth Collection, TCL. This article mentions Gemelia Herring as one of the leaders of the movement to help the park.

148. *Visalia Times Delta*, July 10, 1999, TCL.

149. The *Los Angeles Times*, October 6, 2008, reports that 19 buildings were restored.

150. *USA Today*, January 21, 2007. The 2006 visitor figures are from this article.

151. *Los Angeles Times*, December 20, 2006.

152. *Los Angeles Times*, April 20, 2007. It appears that the dairy farmer, Sam Ethegaray, settled out of court and sold his land to the Parks Department.

153. *New York Times*, March 7, 2007.

154. See "Colonel Allensworth State Historic Park," California Department of Parks and Recreation, http://www.parks.ca.gov/?page_id=583. See also Bunch, "Allensworth Saga." Nicodemus, Kansas, is a national historic site managed by the National Park Service. Five buildings have been preserved. See "Nicodemus National Historic Site Kansas," National Park Service, http://www.nps.gov/nico/index.htm.

155. The Friends of Allensworth (see http://friendsofallensworth.com/) is the official organization dedicated to saving and improving the park; there are chapters throughout the state. They have started a Facebook page and many chapters have blogs.

Chapter 4. A Lesson in Lynching

1. Thomas Fleming, "A Lynching in San Jose," *Columbus Free Press*, December 2, 1998, accessed at Reflections on Black History, http://freepress.org/fleming/flemng63.html.

2. Ibid.

3. Ibid.

4. Fleming also worked briefly at the *Oakland Tribune*, where he inherited Delilah Beasley's column, "Activities among Negroes." Fleming's mother and sister both worked as domestics in the home of William Knowland, the son of

Tribune publisher Joseph Knowland. On Fleming, see Fleming and Millard, *In the Black World*.

5. A. Wood, *Lynching and Spectacle*, 213.

6. Goldsby, *Spectacular Secret*.

7. Faragher, *Eternity Street*, 2.

8. Gonzales-Day, *Lynching in the West*, 14–15. Placerville is also the site of the only historical marker in the state that memorializes the crime of lynching.

9. Arellano, *Vigilantes and Lynch Mobs*, 108. On Bancroft, see also Pfeifer, *Rough Justice*; Waldrep, *Many Faces of Judge Lynch*.

10. On Ida B. Wells, see Schechter, *Ida B. Wells-Barnett*; Bay, *To Tell the Truth*; McMurray, *To Keep the Waters*; Feimster, *Southern Horrors*; and Giddings, *Ida*. On Jesse Daniel Ames, see Hall, *Revolt against Chivalry*.

11. For an important discussion on the slippery nature of the term lynching, see Goldsby, *Spectacular Secret*, esp. ch. 1. See also Waldrep, *Many Faces of Judge Lynch*; and Waldrep, "War of Words."

12. National Association for the Advancement of Colored People, *Thirty Years of Lynching*.

13. Waldrep, *Many Faces of Judge Lynch*, 134.

14. Gonzales-Day, *Lynching in the West*, 43.

15. We cannot be sure that these are the same two victims in each of the studies. The NAACP study names Henry Planz, lynched in 1892, and an unknown victim lynched in 1904.

16. National Association for the Advancement of Colored People, *Thirty Years of Lynching*, 52.

17. Gonzales-Day, *Lynching in the West*, app. 1, 205–28.

18. W. White, *Rope and Faggot*, 232.

19. Gonzales-Day, *Lynching in the West*, 46, 27. According to Gonzales-Day, California's total number of 352 victims is nearer to Mississippi's record of 373 lynchings and more than the number of cases in Texas, which was 335. Instead of being ranked twenty-first, California's record of lynching becomes the sixth worst in the nation. Gonzales-Day acknowledges that the number of cases in other states would be "expanded by extending their lists back in time," but California's most turbulent years occurred before the dates used in conventional records of lynching (9–10). Gonzales-Day relied on newspaper accounts, published leaflets, first-person narratives, and lynching ephemera to document the state's history of lynching.

20. Gonzales-Day, *Lynching in the West*, app. 1. Gonzales-Day also found evidence of one African American man who was "legally lynched" in 1885 in San Francisco (235).

21. Folder 14, box C350, Part 1: Admin., NAACP/LoC.

22. The *Oakland Tribune*, where Beasley was a columnist, printed a banner headline after the attack, "Mob Balked in Lynching." Folder 14, box C350, Part 1: Admin., NAACP/LoC.

23. A. Wood, *Lynching and Spectacle*, 1.

24. For journalism that details the kidnapping, see *San Jose Mercury Herald*, esp. November 10–27, 1933; *Philadelphia Record*, November 28, 1933; *San Francisco Chronicle*, November 11, 17, 22, 25, and 26, 1933. For a partially dramatized account of the kidnapping and lynching, see Farrell, *Swift Justice*.

25. Farrell, *Swift Justice*, 47. The *San Francisco Chronicle* claimed that the kidnapping "called into action the greatest manhunting machinery ever set into motion in Northern California." November 11, 1933, Clippings File, Brooke Hart, CHS.

26. *San Jose Mercury Herald*, November 16, 1933.

27. *San Jose Mercury Herald*, November 17, 1933; November 19, 1933; and November 20 and 27, 1933.

28. Farrell, *Swift Justice*, 300. There were ten kidnappings in 1933, eighteen in 1934, twenty-six in 1935, thirty-one in 1936, thirty in 1937, thirty-seven in 1938.

29. The Charles Lindbergh baby was kidnapped in March 1932 and found nearby in May 1932. But Bruno Hauptman was not arrested until 1934, tried in January and February 1935, and executed for the kidnapping in 1936. When the Hart kidnapping took place, no one had been charged.

30. *San Jose Mercury Herald*, November 21, 1933.

31. Ibid.

32. *San Jose Mercury Herald*, November 18, 1933.

33. *San Jose Mercury Herald*, November 21, 1933.

34. Ibid.

35. *San Francisco Chronicle*, November 17, 1933, Clippings File, CHS.

36. See, for example, *San Francisco Chronicle*, November 17, 1933.

37. *San Francisco Chronicle*, November 17, 1933.

38. Quoted in Farrell, *Swift Justice*, 139.

39. *San Francisco Chronicle*, November 22, 1933. The men were indicted under the 1932 Lindbergh Act, which established federal jurisdiction in any kidnapping case where the victim was taken across state lines, extortion was attempted, or the U.S. mail was used. California had passed a "Little Lindbergh" law in 1933, effective only fifteen days before the Hart kidnapping. Farrell, *Swift Justice*, 19, 142.

40. *San Francisco Chronicle*, November 25, 1933.

41. Worthen, *Governor James Rolph*, 182.

42. *San Jose Mercury Herald*, November 27, 1933.

43. On the size and significance of lynch mobs, see Brundage, *Lynching in the New South*.

44. On November 27, 1933, the *San Jose Mercury Herald* claimed there were 5,000; *New York Times*, December 3, 1933, claimed there were 7,000; *Philadelphia Record*, November 28, 1933, and the *San Francisco Chronicle*, November 27, 1933, reported 10,000; and the *San Francisco Examiner* claimed there 15,000. Folder 15, box C350, Part 1: Admin., NAACP/LoC.

45. *New York Herald Tribune*, November 28, 1933, folder 15, Part I: Admin., C350, NAACP/LoC.

46. *Philadelphia Record*, November 28, 1933, folder 15, box C350, Part 1: Admin., NAACP/LoC.

47. *San Francisco Chronicle*, November 27, 1933. The *San Jose Mercury Herald* reported the governor saying "That was a fine lesson to the whole nation. There will be less kidnapping in the country now. They made a good job of it" (November 27, 1933).

48. *New York Times*, December 3, 1933, folder 15, box C350, Part 1: Admin., NAACP/LoC.

49. *New York Herald Tribune*, November 28, 1933, folder 15, box C350, Part 1: Admin., NAACP/LoC.

50. Ibid.

51. See, for example, *Philadelphia Inquirer*, November 28, 1933, folder 15, box C350, Part 1: Admin., NAACP/LoC.

52. *Nation* 137, no. 357 (December 13, 1933): 666. *California Eagle*, December 1, 1933.

53. *Pittsburgh Courier*, December 9, 1933, folder 16, box C350, Part 1: Admin., NAACP/LoC.

54. Dray, *At the Hands*, 335. Dray claims that in the late fall of 1933 "lynching dominated the headlines as at no other time in American history" (335).

55. *California Eagle*, December 1, 1933. *Washington Tribune*, December 7, 1933, folder 16, box C350, Part 1: Admin., NAACP/LoC.

56. *Chicago Defender*, December 2, 1933.

57. A. Wood, *Lynching and Spectacle*, 247. Wood notes that rioters stole cameras from journalists and "pushed a Paramount camera into the water" (247). On the Armwood lynching, see "Lynching—1933," folder 5, box C350, Part 1: Admin., NAACP/LoC. Armwood was lynched on October 18 after being accused of attacking an eighty-two-year-old white woman. See also folder 15, box C350, Part 1: Admin., NAACP/LoC.

58. *Willow Journal*, December 1, 1933, Rolph scrapbook, James Rolph Jr. Papers, CHS. *Byron Times*, December 6, 1933, Rolph scrapbook, James Rolph Jr. Papers.

59. *Washington Herald*, November 28, 1933, folder 15, box C350, Part 1: Admin., NAACP/LoC.

60. Farrell, *Swift Justice*, 271.

61. *Santa Paula Chronicle*, November 28, 1933, Rolph Scrapbook, James Rolph Jr. Papers.

62. *Pasadena Independent*, November 30, 1933, Rolph Scrapbook, James Rolph Jr. Papers.

63. *New York Times*, December 3, 1933, folder 15, box C350, Part 1: Admin., NAACP/LoC.

64. Zangrando, *NAACP Crusade*, 102.

65. *New Journal and Guide*, December 9, 1933.

66. On this point, see A. Wood, *Lynching and Spectacle*, 204.

67. National Association for the Advancement of Colored People, *Thirty Years of Lynching*, 8.

68. Feimster, *Southern Horrors*; M. Brown, *Eradicating This Evil*.

69. Hall, *Revolt against Chivalry*.

70. W. White, *Rope and Faggot*, 232.

71. Telegram, box C350, bolder 15, NAACP/Bancroft.

72. Walter White Memo, November 27, 1933, folder 15, box C350, NAACP/LoC.

73. Night Letter—Telegram, November 30, 1933, folder 15, box C350, NAACP/LoC.

74. Folder 16, box C350, NAACP/LoC.

75. *Pittsburgh Courier*, December 9, 1933, folder 16, box C350, NAACP/Bancroft. On the Los Angeles Forum, sometimes called the Los Angeles Sunday Forum, see Flamming, *Bound for Freedom*, 25–26.

76. See, for example, *Chicago Defender*, December 2, 1933.

77. *Plaindealer*, December 8, 1933, AAN.

78. *New York Herald Tribune*, November 28, 1933, folder 15, box C350, Part 1: Admin., NAACP/Bancroft. See also *Pittsburgh Courier*, December 9, 1933, folder 16, box C350, Part 1: Admin., NAACP/LoC.

79. Day Letter by Postal Telegraph Company, November 28, 1933, folder 15, box C350, Part 1: Admin., NAACP/LoC. *New York Times*, December 4, 1933, folder 16, box C350, NAACP/LoC.

80. *Baltimore Afro-American*, December 16, 1933. *New York Times*, December 4, 1933, folder 16, box C350, NAACP/LoC.

81. J. Miller, Pennybacker, and Rosenhaft, "Mother Ada Wright," 391.

82. *California Eagle*, December 1, 1933.

83. Ibid. On Bass and her association with the CP and the Scottsboro Boys, see Freer, "L.A. Race Woman." On African American communists, see Kelley, *Hammer and Hoe*.

84. K. Williams, *They Left Great Marks*, 183.

85. On rape and Scottsboro, see Hall, *Revolt against Chivalry*; and Hall, "Mind."

86. *New Republic*, December 13, 1933, 117. *Los Angeles Sentinel*, February 8, 1940. *Crisis* 40, no. 12 (December 1933): 269. For another discussion of Rolph and Hitler, see *Crisis*, January 1934.

87. *San Jose News*, July 13, 1933, quoted in Winter, "California's Little Hitlers."

88. Ruiz, *Cannery Women*, 49.

89. Starr, *California*, 206. Ruiz, 49–50. Starr notes that the Kern County sheriff deputized over 300 growers who acted as vigilantes and terrorized strikers (206).

90. *New Republic*, December 27, 1933, 188. See also McWilliams, *Factories in the Field*.

91. *New Republic*, December 27, 1933, 189. *Nation*, December 13, 1933, 666.

92. W. White, *Man Called White*, 166. N. Weiss, *Farewell*, 100.

93. *Crisis*, January 1934.

94. *Baltimore Afro-American*, December 23, 1933.

95. *California Eagle*, December 8, 1933.

96. *San Francisco Chronicle*, December 7, 1933; Farrell, *Swift Justice*, 264.

97. Farrell, *Swift Justice*, 269–70.

98. *Washington Tribune*, December 7, 1933; *Norfolk New Journal and Guide*, December 9, 1933. *Washington Tribune*, December 7, 1933.

99. Zangrando, *NAACP Crusade*, 114.

100. A. Wood, *Lynching and Spectacle*, 211.

101. Rushdy, *End of American Lynching*, 68.

102. Raiford, *Imprisoned in a Luminous Glare*, 32–34. Goldsby, *Spectacular Secret*, 250.

103. In 1930, local NAACP members in Marion, Indiana, blocked the distribution of lynching photos of Abe Smith and Tom Shipp, who had been murdered in their town on August 7. The photograph was, however, printed in the *Crisis* and captioned "Civilization in the United States, 1930." This photo inspired a long-lasting controversy. See Madison, *Lynching in the Heartland*; Apel and Smith, *Lynching Photographs*.

104. A. Wood, *Lynching and Spectacle*, 213.

105. The image of a lynched black man first appeared in the mainstream press in 1937. A. Wood, *Lynching and Spectacle*, 212.

106. Farrell, *Swift Justice*, 214.

107. A. Wood, *Lynching and Spectacle*, 215.

108. The mob photo was published in the *Los Angeles Times*, November 28, 1933, and the *New York American*, November 28, 1933, in addition to San Jose and Bay Area newspapers.

109. Farrell, *Swift Justice*, 250, 251.

110. Gonzales-Day, *Lynching in the West*, 115; Farrell, *Swift Justice*, 249–50; Allen, *Without Sanctuary*.

111. Apel, *Imagery of Lynching*, 93.

112. William Steig, cartoon, *Nation*, December 13, 1933.

113. *Time*, December 11, 1933, 15.

114. A. Wood, *Lynching and Spectacle*, 232–34.

115. Ibid., 196.

116. Ibid., 228.

117. Ibid., 223–24. The showing never happened, and Wood notes that even White thought it a "hare-brained scheme" (224); Zangrando, *NAACP Crusade*, 135.

118. W. White quoted in A. Wood, *Lynching and Spectacle*, 223.

119. A. Wood, *Lynching and Spectacle*, 231.

120. Ibid., 237.

121. See, for example, *Nation*, June 24, 1936, 821.

122. See, for example, *New York Times*, June 6, 1936, 21; *Amsterdam News*, June 6, 1936.

123. A. Wood, *Lynching and Spectacle*, 235.

124. *Los Angeles Sentinel*, November 5, 1936. *Los Angeles Sentinel*, October 29, 1936. *California Eagle*, November 6, 1936.

125. Delilah Beasley to William Pickens, January 26, 1931, folder 14, box C350, NAACP/LoC.

126. *Oakland Tribune*, December 3, 1933. *Oakland Tribune*, December 10, 1933. *Oakland Tribune*, December 10, 1933.

127. *Baltimore Afro-American*, June 16, 1934.

128. Ibid.

Chapter 5. Burning Down the House: California's Ku Klux Klan

1. M. Davis, *City of Quartz*, 398.

2. *Plaindealer*, December 28, 1945, AAN.

3. M. Davis, *City of Quartz*, 164. "Southland" refers to the Los Angeles area.

4. Mack, *Representing the Race*, 203. Mack explains that this is due, in part, to the crusading legal work of civil rights lawyer Loren Miller.

5. Brilliant, *Color of America*, 5.

6. Brilliant notes that as part of his southwestern strategy, "Reagan courted Mexican American voters by pitting bilingual education (which he supported) against school desegregation through busing (which he opposed)" (6).

7. Dallek, *Right Moment*.

8. MacLean, *Behind the Mask*, xi; Ibid., 10; Baker, *Gospel*, 8.

9. As discussed in ch. 2, protests against *The Birth of a Nation* in the state were significant. See Broussard, *Black San Francisco*, 77–81.

10. Lay, *Invisible Empire*, 11.

11. Jackson, *Ku Klux Klan*, 188.

12. Lay, *Invisible Empire*, 8.

13. McVeigh, *Rise of the Ku Klux Klan*, 15–16.

14. See Johnston, *Radical Middle Class*. Johnston makes the point that the strength of the Portland Klan over local politics has been exaggerated by some scholars.

15. Toy, "Robe and Gown," 154.

16. In a telling map of Klan activity in the 1920s, California is the only western state marked as "a center for violence." Chalmers, *Hooded Americanism*, frontispiece.

17. L. Moore, "Historical Interpretation." Many scholars trace this portrayal of the Klan to Mecklin, *Ku Klux Klan*.

18. Baker, *Gospel*, 10. On this point, see also Jackson, *Ku Klux Klan*.

19. Lay, *Invisible Empire*, 12. By 2004, when the second edition was published, Lay had qualms about the impact of such a portrayal of the KKK, writing in his new preface, "A problem with this more objective and dispassionate type of scholarship, however, is that it may fail to provide readers with a full appreciation of how mean-spirited the Klan movement was and thus why it was so ardently opposed" (xi).

20. Coltcochos, "Invisible Empire," 105, 105, 107, 111, 112. See Mecklin, *Ku Klux Klan*, 175.

21. Rhomberg, *No There There*, 62.

22. Feldman, *Politics, Society, and the Klan*, 9.

23. Chalmers, *Hooded Americanism*, 3.

24. U.S. Bureau of the Census, *Fourteenth Census*, vol. 3.

25. U.S. Bureau of the Census, *Fourteenth Census*; Jackson, *Ku Klux Klan*, 282.

26. U.S. Bureau of the Census, *Fourteenth Census*.

27. Varzally, *Making a Non-White America*, 33; Sánchez, *Becoming Mexican American*, 72–77.

28. Flamming, *Bound for Freedom*, 152.

29. Burton Ceruti to James Weldon Johnson, May 23, 1921, folder 11, box G-15, NAACP/LoC.

30. Walter White to Burton Ceruti, May 31, 1921, folder 11, box G-15, NAACP/LoC. NAACP records indicate that Ceruti's anti-Klan efforts were noticed by Klan members who by 1922 had "openly threatened" him and another member of the local NAACP board. Beatrice Thompson to Robert W. Bagnall, December 20, 1922, folder 11, box G-15, NAACP/LoC.

31. *California Eagle*, October 1, 1921. Charlotta Bass and her husband J. R. Bass refused to be silenced by the Klan, and their paper did more than fluster the Klan. In 1925 the California Ku Klux Klan sued the *California Eagle* in a criminal libel suit. The *Eagle* responded: "We ask no quarter from the Ku Klux Klan or any of its sympathizers. If to jail we must go for publishing, without malice such propaganda as we, in common with all fair-minded citizens, believe to be prejudicial to good government, we can go with a smile and feel that we are rendering a service for the protection of society"(May 29, 1925). The Klan lost the suit.

32. Ida B. Wells had used a similar strategy when she called on northern white men to ban lynching because it was the lawful and thus civilized thing to do, urging them to differentiate themselves from the southern savages who were on a lynching rampage in the 1890s. Bederman, *Manliness and Civilization*, ch. 2.

33. Cady, "Battle Transplanted," 53.

34. Ibid.

35. Nicolaides, *My Blue Heaven*, 163. Nicolaides details a series of open air meetings in suburbs like South Gate, Maywood (where Nathan Baker lived), and Lyngate. Some of the antipathy in these communities focused on African Americans, partly due to the concern over integration in the local schools. Local newspapers depicted crazed black men on an anti-white rampage. For a list of southern California towns with early chapters of the Klan, see Jackson, *Ku Klux Klan*, 189.

36. *Los Angeles Times*, April 24, 1922.

37. *Dallas Texas Morning News*, May 6, 1922, folder F18, box C313, NAACP/LoC; see also *Morning Olympian*, May 13, 1922, AHN.

38. See also *Los Angeles Times*, April 26, 1922; *San Jose Mercury News*, April 26, 1922, AHN.

39. *Los Angeles Times*, April 26, 1922; *Oregonian*, April 26, 1922, AHN.

40. *San Jose Mercury News*, April 27, 1922, AHN.

41. *Los Angeles Times*, April 27, 1922. See also Jackson, *Ku Klux Klan*, 190.

42. *Messenger*, June 1922, AAN.

43. *Los Angeles Times*, April 28, 1922. See also *Oregonian*, May 10, 1922, AHN. For a discussion of the Inglewood raid and its repercussions, see Flamming, *Bound for Freedom*, 204–5.

44. Jackson, *Ku Klux Klan*, 190, 282 n.5.

45. Ibid., 191.

46. *Los Angeles Times*, April 28, 1922.

47. *Crisis*, November 1922, 28.

48. Jackson, *Ku Klux Klan*, 190.

49. *Los Angeles Times*, April 27, 1922. See also *Bellingham Herald*, April 27, 1922, AHN.

50. *Los Angeles Times*, April 30, 1922.

51. Ibid.

52. Hernández, *City of Inmates*, 168–69. *California Eagle*, June 10, 1922.

53. Owens's visit is discussed in *California Eagle*, April 1, 1922; his articles appeared on May 13 and 20, June 10, and August 19, 1922.

54. *California Eagle*, May 13, 1922. *California Eagle*, May 20, 1922.

55. By 1927, Claude Hudson, president of the Los Angeles NAACP, would launch a campaign against the "increasing intrusion of police into black homes." Hernández, *City of Inmates*, 177.

56. *Los Angeles Times*, August 7, 1922; see also *Miami Herald*, June 8, 1922, AHN.

57. *Los Angeles Times*, May 15, 1922.

58. Ibid.

59. *Los Angeles Times*, August 7, 1922. *Los Angeles Times*, August 11, 1922. *Los Angeles Times*, August 16, 1922. *Los Angeles Times*, August 26, 1922.

60. Beatrice Thompson to Robert Bagnall, December 20, 1922, folder 12, box G-15, NAACP/LoC.

61. *Los Angeles Express*, December 11, 1922, folder 5, box C-315, NAACP/LoC; Jackson, *Ku Klux Klan*, 191.

62. *California Eagle*, October 28, 1922. Apostol, "District Attorney Thomas Lee Woolwine."

63. Flamming, *Bound for Freedom*, 206.

64. *Los Angeles Times*, January 15, 1923; Flamming, *Bound for Freedom*, 208.

65. Kurashige, *Shifting Grounds of Race*, 24.

66. Kelly Lytle Hernández shows that the LAPD arrested nearly one-tenth of the black population in Los Angeles between January 1925 and April 1927. Hernández, *City of Inmates*, 158.

67. *Riverside Enterprise*, July 25, 1924.

68. Ibid.

69. Interviews about the overlap between members of the Riverside Klan and the American Legion are included in a series about the Klan that appeared in the 1960s. See *Riverside Daily Press*, July 16, 1964.

70. *Riverside Enterprise*, July 25, 1924.

71. *Riverside Enterprise*, July 24, 1924.

72. MacLean, *Behind the Mask*, 98–99.

73. *Riverside Daily Press*, April 28, 1924.

74. *Riverside Enterprise*, January 6, 1925.

75. *Riverside Daily Press*, January 9, 1925.

76. On the junior order and masculinity, see Baker, *Gospel*, 116–19.

77. *Riverside Press-Enterprise*, July 13, 1964.

78. *Riverside Daily Press*, January 12, 1925, quoted in *Riverside Press-Enterprise*, July 13, 1964.

79. *Riverside Press-Enterprise*, July 13, 1964. These interviews were conducted by George Ringwald, a staff writer for the *Riverside Press-Enterprise*, as part of a series of articles he wrote for the newspaper on the Riverside Klan.

80. *Riverside Press-Enterprise*, July 13, 1964.

81. *Riverside Daily Press*, July 13, 1964.

82. *Riverside Press-Enterprise*, July 12, 1964.

83. Ibid. Because no membership records are available for Riverside, as there are for Anaheim, the relative strengths of the Klan in the two locales can only be estimated.

84. *Los Angeles Times*, November 9, 1927.

85. Curl, "Law Enforcement," 10.

86. Ibid., 12.

87. *Riverside Press-Enterprise*, July 13, 1964.

88. For a telling discussion of Evans and his vision, see Schultz, *Tri-Faith America*, ch. 1. Schultz notes that Evans found African Americans "too few in number to be truly threatening," and focused on the threat of new immigrants from Europe (18–19).

89. Chalmers, *Hooded Americanism*, 323; Jackson, *Ku Klux Klan*, 254.

90. Chalmers, *Hooded Americanism*, 320.

91. Kurashige, *Shifting Grounds of Race*, 135

92. Nash, *World War II*, 69.

93. Kurashige, *Shifting Grounds of Race*, 135.

94. U.S. Bureau of the Census, *Seventeenth Census*, vol. 2, part 5.

95. *Los Angeles Sentinel*, December 7, 1939.

96. *Plaindealer*, March 5, 1943, AAN. Hall, "Long Civil Rights Movement," 1244. On the significance of homeownership in California politics, see M. Davis, *City of Quartz*; McGirr, *Suburban Warriors*; Nicolaides, *My Blue Heaven*.

97. *California Eagle*, December 20, 1945.

98. Taylor, *In Search of the Racial Frontier*, 233.

99. In 1943, workers at Kaiser's Portland shipyard refused to pay dues to the Boilermaker's Union and Kaiser was obligated (through his contract with the union) to fire them. In the 1945 California Supreme Court Case, *Marinship v. James*, the union was forced to give the workers back their jobs and full membership in the union. Nash, *World War II*, 60. On the significance of the California Boilermakers, see Brilliant, *Color of America*, ch. 1. For a discussion of Kaiser and labor unions, see Mark J. Foster, *Henry J. Kaiser*, 79–80. About discrimination and shipyard workers in Los Angeles, see, for example, *California Eagle*, March 7, 1943, and June 13, 1944. On the boilermakers and the *Marinship* case, see Brilliant, *Color of America*, 15–27.

100. Nash, *World War II*, 59.

101. S. Moore, *To Place Our Deeds*, 52.

102. Nash, *World War II*, 59.

103. M. Davis, *City of Quartz*, 376; On Kaiser, see Dias, "Henry J. Kaiser"; Mark J. Foster, "Prosperity's Prophet."

104. Lotchin, *Fortress California*, 55.

105. Nash, *World War II*, 136.

106. M. Davis, *City of Quartz*, 396.

107. *California Eagle*, December 20, 1945.

108. Myra Tanner Weiss, *Vigilante Terror in Fontana: The Tragic Story of O'Day H. Short and his Family* (Los Angeles: Socialist Workers Party, 1946), 7; Bancroft Library.

109. *Plaindealer*, December 28, 1945, AAN.

110. Yamamoto, "Fire in Fontana."

111. *California Eagle*, December 20, 1945.

112. Ibid.; *Plaindealer*, December 20, 1945, AAN.

113. *California Eagle*, December 20, 1945.

114. *Plaindealer*, December 28, 1945.

115. *California Eagle*, December 20, 1945. *California Eagle*, January 3, 1946.

116. *Los Angeles Sentinel*, January 3, 1946.

117. Ibid.

118. M. Weiss, *Vigilante Terror in Fontana*, 12.

119. *Los Angeles Tribune*, January 19, 1946, AAN.

120. *Los Angeles Sentinel*, January 10, 1946.

121. *California Eagle*, January 3, 1946.

122. *California Eagle*, January 17, 1946.

123. *Los Angeles Sentinel*, January 24, 1946.

124. *Los Angeles Sentinel*, January 10, 1946.

125. *Los Angeles Sentinel*, January 31, 1946.

126. *California Eagle*, January 31, 1946.

127. *Los Angeles Tribune*, February 9, 1946, AAN.

128. Ibid.

129. M. Weiss, *Vigilante Terror in Fontana*, 6.

130. *California Eagle*, February 7, 1946.

131. Pascoe, *What Comes Naturally*, 205–23. The case, *Perez v. Sharp*, was a watershed in the history of legal challenges to miscegenation. See also Brilliant, *Color of America*, 106–14.

132. *California Eagle*, February 7, 1946.

133. *Los Angeles Sentinel*, February 14, 1946.

134. Bass, *Forty Years*, 136.

135. *Los Angeles Sentinel*, February 28, 1946. Shortly after this article was published in the *Sentinel*, the Fontana branch of the NAACP went into default. Folder 9, box C-13, NAACP/LoC.

136. In 1914, Bass and a "brigade of a hundred women" marched to the home of Mary Johnson, who was being harassed in her home in South Central Los Angeles. Bass, *Forty Years*, 95–114. See also Freer, "L.A. Race Woman," 616. The Communist Political Association, chaired by Pettis Perry, also stood in the frontlines of the fight against restrictive housing.

137. Bass, *Forty Years*, 101.

138. Ibid., 102.

139. Loren Miller provided the 80 percent figure in a 1946 article in the *Defender* (September 3, 1947). See also Hassan, *Loren Miller*; Klarman, *From Jim Crow to Civil Rights*, 261.

140. *California Eagle*, August 5, 1944.

141. Sides, *L.A. City Limits*, 40–43.

142. On the Sugar Hill case, see Kurashige, *Shifting Grounds of Race*, 162–63, 232–3; Sides, *L.A. City Limits*, 98–101.

143. Smemo, "Little People's Century," 1182.

144. *California Eagle*, January 25, 1945.

145. Bass, *Forty Years*, 102.

146. Harold Draper, *Jim Crow in Los Angeles* (Los Angeles: Worker's Party, 1946), 8, folder 6, box C-14, NAACP/LoC.

147. *Los Angeles Sentinel*, April 4, 1946.

148. *California Eagle*, May 16, 1946; Draper, *Jim Crow in Los Angeles*, 11.

149. Draper, *Jim Crow in Los Angeles*, 12.

150. *Monthly Report for May 1946*, NAACP/Bancroft, UCB.

151. *Los Angeles Citizens Must Stop the KKK* (pamphlet), no date, folder 12, carton 15, Carey McWilliams Papers, Bancroft; Draper, *Jim Crow in Los Angeles*, 18.

152. *Los Angeles Citizens*.

153. *California Eagle*, June 27, 1946.

154. *California Eagle*, June 6, 1946. The meeting was organized by the Mobilization for Democracy.

155. Dochuk, *From Bible Belt to Sunbelt*, 97.

156. Jeansonne, *Gerald L. K. Smith*, 99.

157. Quoted in Dochuk, *From Bible Belt to Sunbelt*, 108.

158. *Los Angeles Sentinel*, April 11, 1946.

159. Copy of Attorney General's Report, April 6, 1946, *Legal Challenges to Residential Segregation*, NAACP Papers, History Vault.

160. *Los Angeles Sentinel*, May 23, 1946.

161. Smemo, "Little People's Century," 1185.

162. Monthly Report for May 1946, carton 1, NAACP/Bancroft; Mike Davis also mentions Kenny's ban in association with the house burning in Fontana (*City of Quartz*, 401).

163. Guzman, Foster, and Hughes, *Negro Year Book 1947*, 218.

164. Walter White to Robert Kenny, May 17, 1946, folder 9, box B-83, NAACP/LoC.

165. *Negro Star* (Wichita, KS), April 19, 1946, AAN.

166. *Los Angeles Citizens*.

167. *Los Angeles Sentinel*, May 23, 1946.

168. *California Eagle*, June 20, 1946.

169. *California Eagle*, June 20, 1946; *Los Angeles Citizens*.

170. *California Eagle*, June 20, 1946.

171. *California Eagle*, June 27, 1946.

172. Postcard, no date, folder 12, carton 15, Carey McWilliams Papers.

173. Sides, *L.A. City Limits*, 102–3.

174. *California Eagle*, June 26, 1952.

175. Horne, *Fire This Time*, 26.

176. Althea Simmons to Eugene H. Kelly, April 9, 1965, *Staff: Althea Simmons, 1961–1965*, NAACP Papers, History Vault.

177. NAACP (West Coast Regional Branch) 1964 Report by Althea Simmons, Loren Miller Papers, Huntington Library.

Chapter 6. "The Only Difference between Pasadena and Mississippi Is the Way They're Spelled": Swimming in Southern California

1. *Pasadena Star News*, January 3, 1983.

2. Ibid. In another version of this story, she told the director that the only difference between Pasadena and Mississippi was the sunshine. *Los Angeles Times*, December 6, 1990.

3. Reid, *History of Pasadena*, 386; Flamming, *Bound for Freedom*, 21. On Mason and the Owens family, see also Hayden, *Power of Place*; Beasley, *Negro Trail Blazers of California*. There is some dispute about the naming of Negro Canyon; some locals believe it was named after the first black settler in Pasadena, Joseph Holmes. See Robin D. G. Kelley, *Research Report*, Black History Collection. Kelley conducted an exhaustive study of black Pasadena that remains at the Pasadena Museum of History. I thank him for talking with me about his research; without it this chapter would not be possible.

4. Reid, *History of Pasadena*, 386.

5. Charles Clay, "An Outstanding Pasadenan Overlooked." *Pasadena Star News*, clipping, no date, Black History Collection.

6. On NAACP strategy and the *Brown* decision, see Tushnet, *NAACP's Legal Strategy*. For studies that address NAACP strategy but do not focus exclusively on *Brown*, see Sullivan, *Lift Every Voice*; Pascoe, *What Comes Naturally*. Pascoe's discussion of miscegenation reveals the ways the NAACP avoided cases involving, sex, marriage, and bodies until after *Brown*.

7. Part 2, box 66, NAACP/LoC.

8. See, for example, Nasstrom, "Down to Now."

9. Green, "History of Pasadena," 36.

10. On Pasadena's early history, see Page, *Pasadena*.

11. Rolle, *California*, 374–75.

12. Green, "History of Pasadena," 37.

13. Lew-Williams, *Chinese Must Go*; Hernández, *City of Inmates*.

14. Frank Prince, interview by Earl F. Cartland, July 1947, PMH. In Cartland, "Study of Negroes." Prince's chronology that locates a better era for race relations in the nineteenth century has been criticized by James who disputes the idea that there was a "golden age" of race relations in the city of Pasadena. James, *Conspiracy of the Good*, 230–31. But other scholars have noted that conditions for African Americans in and around Los Angeles were indeed better before World War I than they would be after the war. See Kurashige, *Shifting Grounds of Race*; De Graaf, "City of Black Angels."

15. Prince said there were six families. Prince interview.

16. Lund, *Historic Pasadena*, 97. According to Kelley, the number is 245, not 218 as listed in the 1900 census (*Research Report*).

17. Benjamin McAdoo, interview, video, no date, PHOHP. Benjamin McAdoo, interview by Frances B. White, February 23, 1978, transcript, PHOHP.

18. William Prince, interview in Crimi, "Social Status," 49. Delilah Beasley claimed the Prince family was "interested in every movement for the best interests of the race." Beasley, *Negro Trail Blazers of California*, 132.

19. Lund, *Historic Pasadena*, 49.

20. Fogelson, *Bourgeois Nightmares*, 97.

21. Lund, *Historic Pasadena*, 47.

22. M. Davis, *City of Quartz*, 213, n.13.

23. James, *Conspiracy of the Good*, 31.

24. Federal Writers' Project, *California*, 247; see also Thorndike, *Your City*, 33, 36.

25. McWilliams, *California*, 86.

26. Shorr, "Thorns in the Roses," 522.

27. Beasley, *Negro Trail Blazers of California*, 143.

28. James claims that it is impossible to know how many African Americans lived in Pasadena at the end of the nineteenth century, but that "a handful of ex-slaves" lived in the Indiana Colony in the 1870s. James, *Conspiracy of the Good*, 271.

29. Prince interview by Cartland, 9–11.

30. *California Eagle*, January 2, 1915.

31. *Pasadena Daily News*, March 9, 1898, Black History Collection. *Pasadena Daily News*, October 19, 1898; Kelley, *Research Report*.

32. *Pasadena Daily News*, August 2, 1898. *Pasadena Daily News*, August 3, 1898. *Pasadena Daily News*, July 27, 1898.

33. *Pasadena Daily News*, August 3, 1903. On Prince, see *Prince Family History*, unpublished manuscript, Black History Collection.

34. *Pasadena Daily News*, August 20, 1903. James, *Conspiracy of the Good*, 239.

35. Kelley, *Research Report*.

36. James, *Conspiracy of the Good*, 238.

37. *Crisis*, August 1913, 193–94. Ibid., 194.

38. The plunge technically meant the diving board, but soon the words "pool" and "plunge" were used interchangeably to mean the pool at Brookside Park.

39. U.S. Department of Commerce, *General Statistics*, 82.

40. Ibid. These data only reflect information from cities of 30,000 or more. Pasadena was one of ten cities in the state to report data. It can be inferred, therefore, that Brookside had the most visitors of any pool in the state.

41. U.S. Department of Commerce, *General Statistics*, 63. The record at-

tendance at the Pasadena pool represents the popularity not only of sport but also of the new commercial leisure activities that would peak in the 1920s. On European Americans and leisure during this era, see Peiss, *Cheap Amusements*.

42. Wiltse, *Contested Waters*, 88.

43. Van Leeuwen, *Springboard in the Pond*, 165. According to Van Leeuwen, there were one million pools in Los Angeles by the 1950s.

44. Some interviewees remembered International Day as Tuesday. It changed to Tuesdays because, as Ruby McKnight Williams recalled, Tuesdays were typically the maid's days off. See James, *Conspiracy of the Good*, xviii.

45. Caro, *Power Broker*, 456–57, 512–14. According to Caro, Moses was determined to prevent racial mixing at "his" pools, and to that end, he kept the water at the Harlem pool unheated to deter black swimmers who he believed, didn't like cold water. Moses also supervised the building of 255 playgrounds, only one of which was in a black neighborhood (514).

46. Ruby McKnight Williams, interview, no date, videotape, Pasadena Oral History Project.

47. Robin D. G. Kelley was told by a black Pasadenan that "as far as she knows, they did not actually drain the pool every week." Kelley, *Research Report*.

48. Lund, *Historic Pasadena*, 50.

49. *Star News*, July 15, 1914. *Star News*, July 17, 1914. Tyler & Macbeth (law firm) to Honorable Board of City Commissioners of the City of Pasadena, July 29, 1914, Brookside Park Vertical File.

50. Hugh Macbeth, a graduate of Harvard Law School, would become one of the most prominent attorneys in Los Angeles. During World War II he defended the rights of Japanese Americans and challenged the legality of internment. See Flamming, *Bound for Freedom*, 50; Varzally, *Making a Non-White America*, 137.

51. Tyler & Macbeth to Board, July 29, 1914.

52. "Report of City Attorney," Brookside Park Vertical File. James points out that this interpretation of Ward was incorrect as the state had already overturned the school segregation clauses. James, *Conspiracy of the Good*, 245.

53. *Pasadena Daily News*, October 5, 1915.

54. Wiltse argues that, before World War II, segregation at municipal pools went unchallenged in the courts due to the cost of a lawsuit and the lack of attention these cases received from the national NAACP office (*Contested Waters*, 146).

55. *Pasadena Daily News*, August 20, 1914.

56. *Pasadena Star*, April 12, 1915.

57. *California Eagle*, December 4, 1915.

58. W. E. B. Du Bois, *Crisis*, August 1913; on Washington's visit, see *California Eagle*, March 21, 1914.

59. *Pasadena Star News*, September 4, 1994.

60. *California Eagle*, May 18, 1918.

61. Beasley, *Negro Trail Blazers of California*, 204.

62. See Bragg, "Marketing the Modern Negro." Bragg notes that most historians have believed Charles Payne's adage, "men led, but women organized" (28). Her study, however, documents that women were central to debates about the New Negro and shaped the organization as a whole. On gender and the black freedom struggle, see also Ransby, *Ella Baker*.

63. Cora J. Carter to R. W. Bagnall, October 2, 1925, folder 11, box G-21, part 1, Branch Files, NAACP/LoC.

64. On the politics of respectability, see Higginbotham, *Righteous Discontent*; Rhodes, "Pedagogies of Respectability."

65. Folder 11, box G-21, part 1, Branch Files, NAACP/LoC.

66. Stern, *Eugenic Nation*, 182.

67. "Human Sterilization Today," Human Betterment Foundation File, UCLA Special Collections. See also E. S. Gosney Papers, California Institute of Technology. On California and eugenics, see Stern, *Eugenic Nation*. Paul Popenoe became a well-known expert on marriage. Beginning in 1930, he founded (with Gosney's backing) and directed the American Institute of Family Relations in Hollywood dedicated to the reconstitution of the U.S. family in ways that dovetailed with Cold War ideology. His advice column for the *Ladies Home Journal* also garnered significant attention. On Popenoe, see Stern, *Eugenic Nation*, 179–204; Kline, *Building a Better Race*; James, *Conspiracy of the Good*, 123–26.

68. James, *Conspiracy of the Good*, 124. James claims that within five years, the HBF rivaled the Eugenics Record Office in Cold Spring Harbor, New York, as "the world's leading center of eugenic studies" (125).

69. The first public swimming pool in Riverside, called the Fairmont Park Plunge, opened in 1912, two years before Brookside Park plunge; it was understood that African Americans could only use the facilities on Thursdays. According to Lawrence B. de Graaf, a woman initiated the protest against the segregated pool. In 1920, Frank H. Johnson, president of the Riverside branch of the NAACP, sued the City of Riverside, the Park Board, and the mayor, after they refused to let his daughter use the bathhouse and the swimming pool. The Riverside case delivered an uneven victory at best; it was settled out of court in the NAACP's favor but did not result in a desegregated pool. When the City of Riverside settled out of court and the pool was technically desegregated, violence and intimidation kept the pool effectively segregated until a separate pool opened. On the Riverside case, see Percy Carter to James Weldon Johnson, November 13, 1921, part 1, Branch Files, NAACP/LoC; De Graaf, "Race, Sex, and Region," 293; Patterson, *Colony for California*, 299; Strickland, "Fairmount Park Episode," 21.

70. On segregated beaches in southern California, see de Graaf, "City of

Black Angels"; Jefferson, "African American Leisure Space"; Mark S. Foster, "In the Face of 'Jim Crow'"; Culver, "America's Playground."

71. Culver, "America's Playground," 428.

72. De Graff, "City of Black Angels," 348; Flamming, *Bound for Freedom*, 272.

73. De Graff, "City of Black Angels," 348.

74. Flamming, *Bound for Freedom*, 274–75. Flamming argues that after Hudson's victory, "racial restrictions on public beaches generally disappeared." (275) On Hudson's arrest, see Watson, "NAACP in California," 191.

75. Flamming, *Bound for Freedom*, 216.

76. Ibid., 217.

77. Ibid.

78. Ibid., 218.

79. *California Eagle*, February 27, 1931.

80. Scott Kurashige points out that protests against pools and recreational spaces were much more successful in Los Angeles than those against housing restrictions. Kurashige, *Shifting Grounds*, 32.

81. Flamming, *Bound for Freedom*, 217.

82. Coletta Clark interview, no date, video, Black History Collection.

83. Edna Banks, interview, no date, video, Black History Collection. Manuel Pineda, interview by Ruth Powell, February 7, 1984, transcript, PHM.

84. Ibid. Elbie J. Hickambottom, interview by Sarah Cooper, 2000, transcript, PHOHP.

85. Rampersad, *Jackie Robinson*, 21. According to Rampersad, "Jim Crow had been a feature of Pasadena almost from the start" (21). About its early settlement, he writes, "If Pasadena could now claim to be the Athens of southern California, its white citizens saw only one flaw in all this perfection: the presence of blacks" (22).

86. Williams, interview by Sharon E. Girdner, April 9, 1999, transcript, PHOHP.

87. Robnett, *How Long?* Robnett's concept of bridge leaders emphasizes the fact that although women may be excluded from traditional avenues of formal leadership such as church hierarchies, they often act as formal leaders of a movement organization during times of crisis (20).

88. Edna Griffin, interview by Robert Oliver, October 1984, transcript, Pasadena Oral History Project.

89. Ibid. On Griffin's medical career, see also Branson, *Let There Be Life*.

90. Ruby McKnight Williams, interview, no date, transcript, p. 23, Black History Collection.

91. *Pasadena Star News*, January 3, 1983.

92. *Los Angeles Times*, December 6, 1990.

93. Ibid.

94. *California Eagle*, November 7, 1924. *California Eagle*, August 1, 1940. Kelley argues that aside from the pool case, "the struggle to reverse the discriminatory hiring practices of the City of Pasadena has been the most significant civil rights movement [in the city]." By 1954, there were 1,653 city employees, only 88 of whom were African American. Most black employees worked as street cleaners and garbage truck drivers. In 1956 members of CORE and the NAACP organized a picket at City Hall to protest the city's hiring practices. Kelley, *Research Report.*

95. The LA NAACP branch struggled over accusations of communism. While there is not an extensive record of conflicts over communism in the Pasadena branch, at least one activist was denied membership because he was a member of the communist party. See Donald Clayton Wheeldin, interview by Meenakashi Chakraverti, December 20, 22, and 27, 1997, and January 5 and 10, 1998, transcript, PHM.

96. Edna Griffin, interview by Howard Shorr, 1991, taped recording, Huntington Library.

97. Shorr, "Thorns in the Roses," 525.

98. Ibid.

99. Ibid.

100. Ibid.

101. Daisy Lampkin, "California Campaigns for the NAACP," *Crisis*, July 1934, 210.

102. Griffin interview by Shorr.

103. Folder 2, box 66, part 2, NAACP/LoC.

104. Flamming, *Bound for Freedom*; Watson, "Crossing the Colour." In 1950, Griffith became the first black attorney ever admitted to the Los Angeles Bar Association; in 1953, Earl Warren appointed him to the Municipal Court; he was a Superior Court judge when he retired from the bench.

105. On Houston, see McNeil, *Groundwork.*

106. The NAACP's win of a swimming pool segregation case in Newton, Kansas, proved helpful in the Pasadena case. The appellate judges cited *Kern v. Commissioners of City of Newton* (1938) when they overturned the Superior Court's 1939 decision. See Calif. Appellate Reports 47 2d (1985), p. 753.

107. In addition to the cases in Pasadena and Newton, Kansas, the NAACP fought lawsuits related to segregated pools in St. Louis (MO; 1949–50), Warren (OH; 1946–49), New York (1945–47), New Jersey (1945–49), Pennsylvania (1948), and West Virginia (1940–48), among others. Box 66, part 22, NAACP/LoC.

108. "Park Plunge Support by Taxes Denied," *Pasadena Star News*, September 15, 1939. According to *Black's Law Dictionary*, mandamus is defined as "the name of a writ . . . which issues from a court of superior jurisdiction, and is directed to a private or municipal corporation, or any of its officers, or to an executive, administrative or judicial officer, or to an inferior court, command-

ing the performance of a particular act therein specified, and belonging to his or their public, official, or ministerial duty, or directing the restoration of the complainant to rights or privileges of which he has been illegally deprived" (*Black's Law Dictionary* 961, 6th ed., 1990).

109. "Park Plunge Support by Taxes Denied." See also "Park Plunge Trial Plaintiffs Rest," *Pasadena Star News*, September 14, 1939.

110. "Park Plunge Support by Taxes Denied."

111. *California Eagle*, July 27, 1939.

112. As cited in Calif. Appellate Reports 47 2d, p. 750.

113. Thomas Griffith Jr. to Charles Hamilton Houston, March 8, 1940, folder 2, box 66, part 2, NAACP/LoC.

114. Tushnet, *NAACP's Legal Strategy*, 51.

115. Marshall wrote on March 9: "On the question of adequate remedy of law being a bar to mandamus action. I seem to remember some cases on the question of damage suits not being a bar to mandamus action where the question will involve multiplicity of suits. There is also the question that this type of action is not aimed at seeking damages but rather to get actual performance of constitutional rights. I am still running both over in my mind and will write to you from time to time until I actually make up my mind on the point." Thurgood Marshall to Griffith, March 9, 1940, folder 2, box 66, part 2, NAACP/ LoC.

116. Rough Draft of Legal Brief, *Stone v. Board*, March 21, 1940, folder 2, box 66, part 2, NAACP/LoC.

117. Edna Griffin to William Pickens, June 13, 1940, folder 11, box C-17, part 2, Branch Files, NAACP/LoC. There is a discrepancy in dates of Griffin's presidency. The *Pasadena Star News* claims it was 1942–48, but she signs letters as president in 1940. *Los Angeles Times*, September 3, 1978.

118. Edna Griffin to NAACP National Office, July 16, 1941, folder 11, box C-17, part 2, Branch Files, NAACP/LoC. On the efforts of the Pasadena Improvement Association, see James, *Conspiracy of the Good*, 248–49.

119. Griffin interview by Oliver.

120. Griffin interview by Shorr.

121. *Los Angeles Times*, September 3, 1978.

122. *Pasadena Star News*, September 4, 1994.

123. This practice—of closing an institution that was legally required to be integrated—was not uncommon. Indeed, it would predominate as a strategy after *Brown v. Board of Education* when southern school districts closed schools rather than integrate them. Pasadena's pool closing preceded these school closings by a decade.

124. Griffin interview by Shorr.

125. Griffin interview by Shorr.

126. *Star News*, December 2, 1949.

127. On this question of NAACP strategy, see Pascoe, *What Comes Naturally*; Goluboff, *Lost Promise*.

Epilogue

1. Ray Bartlett, interview, no date, video, Black History Collection.

2. Tatsuo George Hayakawa, interview by Corrine Bergmann, June 29, 2005, transcript, PHOHP.

3. *Washington Post*, August 21, 1949. Robinson, *Baseball Has Done It*, 29.

4. Dunn, *Jackie Robinson*, 32, 34.

5. At last count, over a hundred books published about Jackie Robinson are classified as children's literature. Most of these books reference the history of discrimination and anti-black sentiment in Pasadena; and many mention the Plunge. See for example, Shorto, *Jackie Robinson*; Coombs, *Jackie Robinson*, 12. See also Ford, *Jackie Robinson*.

6. Dunn, *Jackie Robinson*, 36.

7. Rampersad, *Jackie Robinson*, 60, 65–66, 61. Robinson's views of Pasadena and its history of Jim Crow are reprised in Ken Burns's documentary of his life. Discrimination at the pool figures prominently. See Burns, *Jackie Robinson*.

8. Robinson, *Baseball Has Done It*, 22.

9. Steele, "Rose Bowl Aquatic Center."

10. Quoted in ibid.

11. Stride, Thomas, and Smith, "Ballplayer or Barrier Breaker," 2165.

12. Doss, *Memorial Mania*, 2.

13. *Pasadena Robinson Memorial*, ephemera (Pasadena: City of Pasadena Cultural Affairs Division, n.d.), in the author's possession.

14. Stride, Thomas, and Smith, "Ballplayer or Barrier Breaker," 2181.

15. Ibid., 2164–96.

16. "Robinson Family Way," *Pasadena Weekly*, April 19, 2007, https://pasadena weekly.com/robinson-family-way/. The *Pasadena Weekly* reported that "the other paper," the *Star News*, conducted a survey in April 2007 asking readers if the city had done enough to honor Jackie Robinson. The initial results, according to the *Weekly*, showed that 59 percent said yes. This editorial proposed renaming a street in the city for the family.

17. Gallagher, "Memory and Reconciliation," 304.

18. Sturken, *Tourists of History: Memory*, 4.

19. Robnett, *How Long?*; Nasstrom, "Down to Now"; Ransby, *Ella Baker*.

20. Loren Miller, Samuel Sheats, and A. L. Wirin represented the Jacksons. See box 42, Loren Miller Papers.

21. On the school crisis, see R. Smith et al., *Advocates for Change*; Lozano, "Brown's Legacy." See also Gray, "To Fight the Good Fight."

22. On this point see Miles, "Long Arm of the South."

23. See, for example, Bernstein, *Bridges of Reform*.

24. Brilliant, *Color of America*, 4.

25. Todd-Breland, *Political Education*, 23.

26. Loren Miller, "Civil Rights and State's Rights," 1964 Address to Western Governors, folder 8, box 29, Loren Miller Papers.

Bibliography

Archives and Manuscript Collections

African American Museum and Library at Oakland, Oakland Public Library
    Colored Women's Clubs Association Collection

The Bancroft Library, University of California, Berkeley
    Robert W. Kenny Papers
    National Association for the Advancement of Colored People, Region I
        records, 1942–1986 (bulk 1945–1977), BANC MSS 78/180 c (NAACP/
        Bancroft)
    Panama Pacific International Exposition Records (PPIE Records)
    J. B. Sanderson Papers
    John Swett Papers
    Carey McWilliams Papers

The California Historical Society (CHS), San Francisco
    American Civil Liberties Union of Northern California Records
    California League of Women Voters Papers
    James Rolph Jr. Papers

California State Library, Sacramento
    Allensworth Collection

California Park Department Archives (CPDA), Sacramento
    Allensworth Collection

Center for Bibliographical Studies and Research, University of California,
    Riverside
    California Digital Newspaper Collection (CDNC)

The Huntington Library
    Fletcher Bowron Papers
    Loren Miller Papers

Library of Congress
    National Association for the Advancement of Colored People Records,
        1842–1999 (bulk 1919–1991), MSS34140. Part 1: Administration. (NAACP/
        LoC)

Los Angeles Public Library
    Allensworth File

NewsBank
    America's Historical Newspapers (AHN)

Pasadena Museum of History Research Library and Archives
    Black History Collection
    Pasadena Oral History Project
    Pasadena Heritage Oral History Project (PHOHP, from 1996 onward)

Pasadena Public Library
    African American Vertical File
    Brookside Park Vertical File
    NAACP Vertical File

ProQuest
    NAACP Papers, History Vault

Readex
    African American Newspapers, 1827–1998 (AAN)

Riverside Public Library
    Ku Klux Klan Vertical File

San Francisco Public Library, San Francisco History Room
    Panama Pacific International Exposition Vertical Files

Southern California Library, Los Angeles
    Charlotta A. Bass Papers

Special Collections, Young Research Library, University of California, Los
    Angeles
    Donated Oral Histories Collection
    Extremist Literature Collection, Human Betterment Foundation Files
    Miriam Matthews Papers

Special Collections and University Archives, Stanford University
    Francis B. Loomis Papers

Tulare County Library (TCL), Visalia Branch
    Allensworth Collection

Bibliography

Selected Works

Aarim-Heriot, Najia. *Chinese Immigrants, African Americans, and Racial Anxiety in the United States, 1848–82.* Urbana: University of Illinois Press, 2003.

Ackley, Laura A. *San Francisco's Jewel City: The Panama Pacific International Exposition of 1915.* San Francisco: Heyday Books, 2015.

Alexander, Charles. *The Battles and Victories of Allen Allensworth.* Boston: Sherman, French, 1914.

Allen, James. *Without Sanctuary: Lynching Photography in America.* Santa Fe, NM: Twin Palms, 2000.

Almaguer, Tomás. *Racial Fault Lines: The Historical Origins of White Supremacy in California.* Berkeley: University of California Press, 1994.

Apel, Dora. *Imagery of Lynching: Black Men, White Women, and the Mob.* New Brunswick, NJ: Rutgers University Press, 2004.

Apel, Dora, and Shawn Michelle Smith. *Lynching Photographs.* Berkeley: University of California, 2007.

Apostol, Jane. "District Attorney Thomas Lee Woolwine: Stormy Petrel of Politics." *Southern California Quarterly* 87, no. 4 (winter 2005–6): 377–96.

Arellano, Lisa. *Vigilantes and Lynch Mobs: A Narrative of Community and Nation.* Philadelphia: Temple University Press, 2012.

Baker, Kelly J. *Gospel According to the Klan: The KKK's Appeal to Protestant America, 1915–1930.* Lawrence: University Press of Kansas, 2011.

Bass, Charlotta A. *Forty Years: Memoirs from the Pages of a Newspaper.* Los Angeles: C. A. Bass, 1960.

Bay, Mia. *To Tell the Truth Freely: The Life of Ida B. Wells.* New York: Hill & Wang, 2009.

Beasley, Delilah L. *The Negro Trail Blazers of California.* Los Angeles: N.p., 1919.

Bederman, Gail. *Manliness and Civilization: A Cultural History of Gender and Race in the United States, 1880–1917.* Chicago: University of Chicago Press, 1995.

Berglund, Barbara. *Making San Francisco American: Cultural Frontiers in the Urban West, 1846–1906.* Lawrence: University Press of Kansas, 2007.

Bernstein, Shana. *Bridges of Reform: Interracial Civil Rights Activism in Twentieth-Century Los Angeles.* New York: Oxford University Press, 2011.

Berson, Misha. *The San Francisco Stage.* Vol. 1, *From Gold Rush to Golden Spike, 1849–1869.* Vol. 2, *From Golden Spike to Great Earthquake, 1869–1906.* San Francisco Performing Arts Library and Museum, 1989, 1992.

Berwanger, Eugene H. *The West and Reconstruction.* Urbana: University of Illinois Press, 1981.

Blackett, R. J. M. *Beating against the Barriers: The Lives of Six Nineteenth-Century Afro-Americans.* Ithaca, NY: Cornell University Press, 1986.

———. *The Captive's Quest for Freedom: Fugitive Slaves, the 1850 Fugitive Slave Law, and the Politics of Slavery.* New York: Cambridge University Press, 2018.

———. "Dispossessing Massa: Fugitive Slaves and the Politics of Slavery after 1850." *American Nineteenth Century History* 10, no. 2 (June 2009): 119–36.

Boisseau, T. J., and Abagail M. Markwyn, eds. *Gendering the Fair: Histories of Women and Gender at World's Fairs.* Urbana: University of Illinois Press, 2010.

Bottoms, Michael. *An Aristocracy of Color: Race and Reconstruction in California and the West, 1850–1890.* Norman: University of Oklahoma Press, 2013.

Bragg, Susan. "'Anxious Foot Soldiers': Sacramento's Black Women and Education in Nineteenth-Century California." In Taylor and Moore, *African American Women Confront the West,* 97–116.

———. "Marketing the Modern Negro: Race, Gender and the Culture of Activism in the NAACP, 1909–1941." PhD diss., University of Washington, 2007.

Branson, Helen Kitchen. *Let There Be Life: The Contemporary Account of Edna L. Griffin, M.D.* Pasadena: M. S. Sen, 1947.

Brilliant, Mark. *The Color of America Has Changed: How Racial Diversity Shaped Civil Rights Reform in California, 1941–1978.* New York: Oxford University Press, 2010.

Broussard, Albert S. *Black San Francisco: The Struggle for Racial Equality in the West, 1900–1954.* Lawrence: University Press of Kansas, 1993.

———. *Expectations of Equality: A History Black Westerners.* Wheeling, IL: Harlan Davidson, 2012.

Brown, Elsa Barkley. Introduction. In Delilah L. Beasley, *The Negro Trail Blazers of California,* xv–xlviii. New York: Macmillan, 1997 reissue.

———. "Negotiating and Transforming the Public Sphere: African American Political Life in the Transition from Slavery to Freedom," *Public Culture* 7 (1994): 107–46.

———. "To Catch the Vision of Freedom: Reconstructing Southern Black Women's Political History, 1865–1880." In *African American Women and the Vote, 1837–1965,* edited by Ann Gordon et al., 66–99. Amherst: University of Massachusetts Press, 1997.

———. "Womanist Consciousness: Maggie Lena Walker and the Independent Order of Saint Luke." *Signs* 14 (spring 1989): 610–33.

Brown, Mary Jane. *Eradicating This Evil: Women in the Anti-Lynching Movement.* New York: Garland, 2000.

Brundage, W. Fitzhugh. *Lynching in the New South: Georgia and Virginia, 1880–1930.* Urbana: University of Illinois Press, 1993.

Bryant, Clora, et al., eds. *Central Avenue Sounds: Jazz in Los Angeles.* Berkeley: University of California Press, 1998.

Bunch, Lonnie G. "Allensworth: The Life, Death, and Rebirth of an All-Black Community." *Californians* 5, no. 6 (November/December 1986): 26–33.

———. "The Allensworth Saga as Public History." *OAH Newsletter* 16, no. 4 (November 1988): 4–5.

———. "'The Greatest State for the Negro': Jefferson L. Edmonds, Black Propagandist of the California Dream." In de Graff, Mulroy, and Taylor, *Seeking El Dorado*, 129–48.

Burns, Ken, prod. *Jackie Robinson.* TV miniseries. Aired April 11–12, 2016, on PBS. Florentine Films and WETA, 2016. 240 min.

Caddoo, Cara. *Envisioning Freedom: Cinema and the Building of Modern Black Life.* Cambridge, MA: Harvard University Press, 2014.

Cady, Daniel. "A Battle Transplanted: Southern California's White Churches, Black Press, and the 1920's Ku Klux Klan." *Journal of the West* 48, no. 2 (spring 2009): 50–57.

Caitlin, Robert A. "Black Utopia: The Development of Allensworth, California, USA, 1908–1930." *Planning History: Bulletin of the International Planning History Society* 23, no. 3 (2001): 5–14.

Caldwell, Dan. "The Negroization of the Chinese Stereotype in California," *Southern California Quarterly* 53, no. 2 (1971): 123–31.

Camp, Stephanie M. H. *Closer to Freedom: Enslaved Women and Every Resistance in the Plantation South.* Chapel Hill: University of North Carolina Press, 2004.

Campbell, Marne L. *Making Black Los Angeles: Class, Gender, and Community, 1850–1917.* Chapel Hill: University of North Carolina Press, 2016.

Caro, Robert A. *The Power Broker: Robert Moses and the Fall of New York.* New York: Alfred A. Knopf, 1974.

Cartland, Earl F. "A Study of Negroes Living in Pasadena." MA thesis, Whittier College, 1948.

Chafe, William, et al., *Remembering Jim Crow: African Americans Tell about Life in the Segregated South.* New York: New Press, 2001.

Cha-Jua, Sundiata Keita. *America's First Black Town: Brooklyn, Illinois, 1830, 1915.* Urbana: University of Illinois Press, 2000.

Chalmers, David M. *Hooded Americanism: The First Century of the Ku Klux Klan, 1865–1965.* New York: Doubleday, 1965.

Clark, Kathleen Ann. *Defining Moments: African American Commemoration and Political Culture in the South, 1863–1913.* Chapel Hill: University of North Carolina Press, 2005.

Coleman, Willi. "African American Women and Community Development in California, 1848–1900." In de Graff, Mulroy, and Taylor, *Seeking El Dorado*, 98–125.

Coltcochos, Christopher N. "The Invisible Empire and the Search for Orderly Community: The Ku Klux Klan in Anaheim, California." In Lay, *Invisible Empire*, 97–120.

Coombs, Karen Mueller. *Jackie Robinson: Baseball's Civil Rights Legend.* Springfield, NJ: Enslow, 1997.

Cooper, Brittany. *Beyond Respectability: The Intellectual Thought of Race Women.* Urbana: University of Illinois Press, 2017.

Cox, Bette Yarbrough. "The Evolution of Black Music in Los Angeles, 1890–1955." In de Graff, Mulroy, and Taylor, *Seeking El Dorado,* 259–78.

Crimi, James. "The Social Status of the Negroes Living in Pasadena, California." Master's thesis, University of Southern California, 1941.

Crockett, Norman. *The Black Towns.* Lawrence: Regents Press of Kansas, 1979.

Crouchett, Lorraine J. *Delilah Leontium Beasley: Oakland's Crusading Journalist.* El Cerrito, CA: Downey Place, 1990.

Culver, Lawrence. "America's Playground: Recreation and Race." In *A Companion to Los Angeles,* edited by William Deverell and Greg Hise, 421–37. Malden, MA: Wiley Blackwell, 2010.

Curl, Alan. "Law Enforcement, Politics and Prohibition." *Journal of the Riverside Historical Society* 3 (February 1999): 10–17.

Dallek, Matthew. *The Right Moment: Ronald Reagan's First Victory and the Decisive Turning Point in American Politics.* New York: Free Press, 2000.

Daniels, Douglas Henry. "LA Zoot: Race "Riot," The Pachuco, and Black Music Culture," *Journal of African American History* (winter 2002): 98–118.

———. *Pioneer Urbanites: A Social and Cultural History of Black San Francisco.* Philadelphia: Temple University Press, 1980.

Davis, Elizabeth Lindsey. *Lifting as They Climb.* Washington, DC: National Association of Colored Women, 1933.

Davis, Hugh. *"We Will Be Satisfied with Nothing Less: The African American Struggle for Equal Rights in the North during Reconstruction.* Ithaca, NY: Cornell University Press, 2011.

Davis, Mike. *City of Quartz: Excavating the Future in Los Angeles.* New York: Random House, 1990; reprinted 1992 by Verso.

De Graaf, Lawrence B. "Race, Sex, and Region: Black Women in the American West, 1850–1920." *Pacific Historical Review* 49 (May 1980): 285–313.

———. "The City of Black Angels: Emergence of the Los Angles Ghetto, 1890–1930." *Pacific Historical Review* 39, no. 3 (August 1970): 323–52.

De Graff, Lawrence B., Kevin Mulroy, and Quintard Taylor, eds. *Seeking El Dorado: African Americans in California.* Seattle: University of Washington Press, 2001.

Des Jardins, Julie. *Women and the Historical Enterprise in America: Gender, Race, and the Politics of Memory, 1880–1945.* Chapel Hill: University of North Carolina Press, 2003.

Dias, Ric A. "Henry J. Kaiser: Can-do Capitalist, 'Government Entrepreneur,' and Western Booster." *Journal of the West* 42, no. 4 (fall 2003): 54–62.

Dillon, Richard. *Humbugs and Heroes: A Gallery of California Pioneers.* New York: Doubleday, 1970.

Dobak, William, and Thomas Phillips. *The Black Regulars.* Norman: Oklahoma University Press, 2001.

Dochuk, Darren. *From Bible Belt to Sunbelt: Plain-Folk Religion, Grassroots Politics, and the Rise of Evangelical Conservatism.* New York: Norton, 2011.

Doss, Erika. *Memorial Mania: Public Feeling in America.* Chicago: University of Chicago Press, 2010.

Douglas, Davison M. *Jim Crow Moves North: The Battle Over Northern School Segregation, 1865–1954.* Cambridge: Cambridge University Press, 2005.

Downs, Gregory P., and Kate Masur, eds. *The World the Civil War Made.* Chapel Hill: University of North Carolina Press, 2015.

Dray, Philip. *At the Hands of Persons Unknown: The Lynching of Black America.* New York: Random House, 2002; Modern Library edition, 2003.

Dunn, Herb. *Jackie Robinson: Young Sports Trailblazer.* New York: Simon & Schuster/Aladdin Paperbacks, 1999.

Edwards, Laura. *Gendered Strife and Confusion: The Political Culture of Reconstruction.* Urbana: University of Illinois Press, 1997.

Eissinger, Michael. "African Americans in the Rural San Joaquin Valley, California: Colonization Efforts and Townships." MA thesis, CSU Fresno, 2008.

English, Daylanne K. *Unnatural Selections: Eugenics in American Modernism and the Harlem Renaissance.* Chapel Hill: University of North Carolina Press, 2004.

Esterovich, Adam S., ed. *Proceedings of the First State Convention of the Colored Citizens of the State of California (1855, 1856, 1865).* San Francisco: R & E Research Associates, reprint 1969.

Estavan, Lawrence, ed. *San Francisco Theatre Research.* Vol. 13, *Minstrelsy.* San Francisco: Works Progress Administration, 1939.

Faragher, John Mack. *Eternity Street: Violence and Justice in Frontier Los Angeles.* New York: Norton, 2016.

Farnham, Eliza. *California: In-Doors and Out.* New York: Dix, Edwards, 1856.

Farrell, Harry. *Swift Justice: Murder and Vengeance in a California Town.* New York: St. Martin's Press, 1992.

Federal Writers' Project of the Works Progress Administration of Northern California. *California: A Guide to the Golden State.* New York: Hastings House, 1939.

Feimster, Crystal. *Southern Horrors: Women and the Politics of Rape and Lynching.* Cambridge, MA: Harvard University Press, 2009.

Field, Kendra T. "'No Such Thing as Stand Still': Migration and Geopolitics in African American History." *Journal of American History* 102, no. 3 (December 2015): 693–718.

Flamming, Douglas. *Bound for Freedom: Black Los Angeles in the Age of Jim Crow*. Berkeley: University of California, 2005.

Fleming, Thomas C., and Max Millard. *In the Black World: Thomas Fleming, 1907–1932*. San Francisco: Max Millard, 2011.

Fogelson, Robert M. *Bourgeois Nightmares, Suburbia, 1870–1930*. New Haven, CT: Yale University Press, 2005.

Foner, Eric. *Reconstruction: America's Unfinished Revolution, 1863–1877*. New York: Harper & Row, 1988.

Ford, Carin T. *Jackie Robinson: All I Ask Is That You Respect Me as a Human Being*. Springfield, NJ: Enslow, 2005.

Foster, Mark J. *Henry J. Kaiser: Builder in the Modern American West*. Austin: University of Texas Press, 1989.

———. "Prosperity's Prophet: Henry J. Kaiser and the Suburban/Consumer Culture of 1930–1950." *Western Historical Quarterly* (April 1986): 165–84.

Foster, Mark S. "In the Face of 'Jim Crow': Prosperous Blacks and Vacations, Travel, and Outdoor Leisure, 1890–1945." *Journal of Negro History* 84, no. 2 (spring 1999): 130–49.

Freer, Regina. "L.A. Race Woman: Charlotte Bass and the Complexities of Black Political Development in Los Angeles." *American Quarterly* 56, no. 3 (September 2004): 607–32.

Gaines, Kevin K. *Uplifting the Race: Black Leadership, Politics, and Culture in the Twentieth Century*. Chapel Hill: University of North Carolina Press, 1996.

Gallagher, Victoria J. "Memory and Reconciliation in the Birmingham Civil Rights Institute," *Rhetoric and Public Affairs* 2, no. 2 (summer 1999): 303–20.

Giddings, Paula. *Ida: A Sword among Lions, Ida B. Wells-Barnett and the Campaign against Lynching*. New York: Harper Collins, 2008.

———. *When and Where I Enter: The Impact of Black Women on Race and Sex in America*. New York: Bantam Books, 1984.

Gilmore, Glenda. *Gender and Jim Crow: Women and the Politics of White Supremacy in North Carolina, 1896–1920*. Chapel Hill: University of North Carolina Press, 1996.

Goldsby, Jacqueline. *A Spectacular Secret: Lynching in American Life and Literature*. Chicago: University of Chicago Press, 2009.

Goluboff, Risa L. *The Lost Promise of Civil Rights*. Cambridge, MA: Harvard University Press, 2007.

Gonzales-Day, Ken. *Lynching in the West, 1850–1935*. Durham, NC: Duke University Press, 2006.

Gordon, Avery F. *Ghostly Matters: Haunting and the Sociological Imagination*. Minneapolis: University of Minnesota Press, 2008.

Gray, Julie Salley. "'To Fight the Good Fight:' The Battle Over Control of the Pasadena City Schools, 1969–1979." *Essays in History* 37, no. 1 (1995).

Green, Perry M. "A History of Pasadena." In *A Southern California Paradise* (in the Suburbs of Los Angeles): Being a Historic and Descriptive Account of Pasadena, San Gabriel, Sierra Madre, and La Cañada, edited by R. W. C. Farnsworth. Pasadena, CA: R. W. C. Farnsworth, 1893.

Guzman, Jessie Parkhurst, V. C. Foster, and W. H. Hughes. Negro Year Book 1947: A Review of Events Affecting Negro Life, 1941–1946. New York: W. H. Wise, 1947.

Hale, Grace Elizabeth. Making Whiteness: The Culture of Segregation in the South, 1890–1940. New York: Random House/Vintage, 1998.

Haley, Sarah. No Mercy Here: Gender, Punishment, and the Making of Jim Crow Modernity. Chapel Hill: University of North Carolina Press, 2016.

Hall, Jacquelyn Dowd. "The Long Civil Rights Movement and the Political Uses of the Past." Journal of American History (March 2005): 1233–63.

———. "'The Mind that Burns in Each Body': Women, Rape, and Racial Violence." In Powers of Desire: The Politics of Sexuality, edited by Ann Snitow, Christine Stansell, and Sharon Thompson, 328–49. New York: Monthly Review Press, 1983.

———. Revolt against Chivalry: Jesse Daniel Ames and the Women's Campaign against Lynching. New York: Columbia University Press, 1979.

Hamilton, Kenneth Marvin. Black Towns and Profit: Promotion and Development in the Trans-Appalachian West, 1877–1915. Urbana: University of Illinois Press, 1991.

Harlan, Louis R., and Raymond W. Smock, eds. The Booker T. Washington Papers. 14 vols. Urbana: University of Illinois Press, 1977–89.

Hassan, Amina Loren Miller: Civil Rights Attorney and Journalist. Norman: University of Oklahoma Press, 2015.

Hayden, Dolores. The Power of Place: Urban Landscapes as Public History. Cambridge: MIT Press, 1995.

Heizer, Robert F., and Alan J. Almquist. The Other Californians: Prejudice and Discrimination under Spain, Mexico, and the United States to 1920. Berkeley: University of California Press, 1971.

Hendrick, Irving G. The Education of Non-Whites in California, 1849–1970. San Francisco: R & E Research Associates, 1977.

———. "From Indifference to Imperative Duty: Educating Children in Early California." California History (summer 2000): 226–49.

Hernández, Kelly Lytle. City of Inmates: Conquest, Rebellion, and the Rise of Human Caging in Los Angeles, 1771–1965. Chapel Hill: University of North Carolina Press, 2017.

Higginbotham, Evelyn Brooks. Righteous Discontent: The Women's Movement in the Black Baptist Church, 1880–1920. Cambridge: Harvard University Press, 1983.

Hill, Errol G., and James V. Hatch, A History of African American Theatre. New York: Cambridge University Press, 2003.

Hittell, Theodore H. *History of California.* 4 vols. San Francisco: N. J. Stone, 1885–97.

Holliday, J. S. *The World Rushed In: The California Gold Rush Experience.* New York: Simon & Schuster, 1981.

Holt, Thomas. *The Problem of Race in the Twenty-First Century.* Cambridge, MA: Harvard University Press, 2000.

Horne, Gerald. *Fire This Time: The Watts Uprising and the 1960s.* Charlottesville: University Press of Virginia, 1995.

Horton, James O. *Freedom's Yoke: Gender Conventions among Free Blacks in Free People of Color: Inside the African American Community.* Washington, DC: Smithsonian Institution Press, 1993.

Hudson, Lynn M. *The Making of "Mammy Pleasant": A Black Entrepreneur in Nineteenth-Century San Francisco.* Urbana: University of Illinois Press, 2003.

———. "This Is Our Fair and Our State: African Americans and the Panama-Pacific International Exposition." *California History* 87, no. 3 (2010): 26–45.

Hunter, Tera W. *"To 'Joy My Freedom": Southern Black Women's Lives and Labors after the Civil War.* Cambridge, MA: Harvard University Press, 1997.

Jackson, Kenneth. *The Ku Klux Klan in the City, 1915–1930.* New York: Oxford University Press, 1967.

James, Michael E. *Conspiracy of the Good: Civil Rights and the Struggle for Community in Two American Cities, 1875–2000.* S.L.: Peter Lang, 2008.

Jeansonne, Glen. *Gerald L. K. Smith: Minister of Hate.* New Haven, CT: Yale University Press, 1988.

Jefferson, Allison Rose. "African American Leisure Space in Santa Monica: The Beach Sometimes Known as the Inkwell, 1900s–1960s," *Southern California Quarterly* 91, no. 2 (summer 2009): 155–89.

Jenkins, Ernestine, and Darlene Clark Hine, eds. *A Question of Manhood: A Reader in U.S. Black Men's History and Masculinity.* Vol. 2. Bloomington: Indiana University Press, 2001.

Johnsen, Leigh Dana. "Equal Rights and the 'Heathen Chinee': Black Activism in San Francisco, 1865–1875." *Western Historical Quarterly* 11, no. 1 (January 1980): 57–68.

Johnson, Susan Lee. *Roaring Camp: The Social World of the California Gold Rush.* New York: Norton, 2000.

Johnston, Robert D. *The Radical Middle Class: Populist Democracy and the Question of Capitalism in Progressive Era Portland, Oregon.* Princeton, NJ: Princeton University Press, 2003.

Jones, Martha S. *All Bound Up Together: The Woman Question in African American Public Culture, 1830–1900.* Chapel Hill: University of North Carolina Press, 2007.

———. *Birthright Citizens: A History of Race and Rights in Antebellum America.* Cambridge: Cambridge University Press, 2018.

Kachun, Mitchell Alan. *Festivals of Freedom: Memory and Meaning in African American Emancipation Celebrations, 1808–1915*. Amherst: University of Massachusetts Press, 2003.

Kantrowitz, Stephen. *More than Freedom: Fighting for Black Citizenship in a White Republic, 1829–1889*. New York: Penguin, 2012.

Kelley, Robin D. G. *Hammer and Hoe: Alabama Communists during the Great Depression*. Chapel Hill: University of North Carolina Press, 1990.

———. *Race Rebels: Culture, Politics, and the Black Working Class*. New York: Free Press, 1994.

Kelty, James C., dir. *Allensworth: A Piece of the World*. 2003. James Kelty & Associates. Distributed by California Department of Parks and Recreation. DVD.

Kennedy, Joseph C. G. *Population of The United States in 1860 Compiled from the Original Returns of The Eighth Census*. Washington, DC: Government Printing Office, 1864.

Klarman, Michael J. *From Jim Crow to Civil Rights: The Supreme Court and the Struggle for Racial Equality*. New York: Oxford University Press, 2004.

Kline, Wendy. *Building a Better Race: Gender, Sexuality, and Eugenics from the Turn of the Century to the Baby Boom*. Berkeley: University of California, 2001.

Kurashige, Scott. *The Shifting Grounds of Race: Black and Japanese in the Making of Multiethnic Los Angeles*. Princeton, NJ: Princeton University Press, 2008.

Kurutz, Gary F. "Popular Culture on the Golden Shore." *California History* 79, no. 3 (summer 2000): 280–315.

Lapp, Rudolph. *Afro-Americans in California*. San Francisco: Boyd & Fraser, 1979.

———. *Blacks in Gold Rush California*. New Haven, CT: Yale University Press, 1977.

———. "Jeremiah B. Sanderson: Early California Negro." *Journal of Negro History* 53, no. 4 (1968): 321–33.

———. "Negro Rights Activities in Gold Rush California." *California Historical Society Quarterly* 45 (March 1966): 3–20.

Larson, Edward J. *Sex, Race, and Science: Eugenics in the Deep South*. Baltimore, MD: Johns Hopkins University Press, 1996.

Lay, Shawn, ed. *The Invisible Empire in the West: Toward a New Appraisal of the Ku Klux Klan in the 1920s*. 1st ed. Urbana: University of Illinois Press, 1992. 2d ed., 2004.

Lee, Erika. *At America's Gates: Chinese Immigration during the Exclusion Era, 1882–1943*. Chapel Hill: University of North Carolina Press, 2003.

Lemke-Santangelo, Gretchen. *Abiding Courage: African American Migrant Women and the East Bay Community*. Chapel Hill: University of North Carolina Press, 1996.

Lentz-Smith, Adriane. *Freedom Struggles: African Americans and World War I*. Cambridge, MA: Harvard University Press, 2009.

Lewis, David Levering, and Deborah Willis. *A Small Nation of People: W.E.B. Du Bois and African American Portraits of Progress*. New York: HarperCollins, 2003.

Lewis, Earl. "Expectations, Economic Opportunities, and Life in the Industrial Age: Black Migration to Norfolk, Virginia, 1910–1945." In *The Great Migration in Historical Perspective: New Dimensions of Race, Class, and Gender*, edited by Joe Trotter Jr., 22–24. Bloomington: Indiana University Press, 1991.

Lewis, Oscar, and Carroll D. Hall. *Bonanza Inn: America's First Luxury Hotel*. New York, 1939.

Lew-Williams, Beth. *The Chinese Must Go: Violence, Exclusion, and the Making of the Alien in America*. Cambridge, MA: Harvard University Press, 2018.

Litwack, Leon. *North of Slavery: The Negro in the Free States, 1790–1860*. Chicago: University of Chicago Press, 1961.

———. *Trouble in Mind: Black Southerners in the Age of Jim Crow*. New York: Knopf, 1998.

Lotchin, Roger W. *Fortress California, 1910–1961: From Warfare to Welfare*. 2d ed. Urbana: University of Illinois Press, 2002.

Lott, Eric. *Love and Theft: Blackface Minstrelsy and the American Working Class*. New York: Oxford, 1993.

Low, Victor. *The Unimpressible Race: A Century of Educational Struggle by the Chinese in San Francisco*. San Francisco: East/West Publishing, 1982.

Lozano, Rosina A. "Brown's Legacy in the West: Pasadena Unified School District's Federally Mandated School Desegregation." *Southwestern University Law Review* 36, no. 2 (2007): 257–85.

Lund, Anne Scheid. *Historic Pasadena: An Illustrated History*. San Antonio: Historical Publishing Network, 1999.

Mack, Kenneth W. *Representing the Race: The Creation of the Civil Rights Lawyer*. Cambridge, MA: Harvard University Press, 2012.

MacLean, Nancy. *Behind the Mask of Civility: the Making of the Second Ku Klux Klan*. New York: Oxford University Press, 1994.

Madison, James H. *A Lynching in the Heartland: Race and Memory in America*. New York: Palgrave/St. Martin's Press, 2001.

Manring, M. M. *Slave in a Box: The Strange Career of Aunt Jemima*. Charlottesville: University Press of Virginia, 1998.

Markwyn, Abigail M. *Empress San Francisco: The Pacific Rim, the Great West, and California at the Panama-Pacific International Exposition*. Lincoln: University of Nebraska Press, 2014.

———. "Encountering 'Woman' on the Fairgrounds of the 1915 Panama-Pacific Exposition," In *Gendering the Fair: Histories of Women and Gender at World's*

Fairs, edited by T. J. Boisseau and Abigail M. Markwyn, 169–86. Urbana: University of Illinois Press, 2010.

Massa, Ann. "Black Women in the White City." *Journal of American Studies* (Great Britain) 8 (1974): 319–37.

McBroome, Dolores. "Harvests of Gold: Boosterism, Agriculture, and Investment in Allensworth and Little Liberia." In de Graff, Mulroy, and Taylor, *Seeking El Dorado*, 149–80.

McClain, Charles. "The Chinese Struggle for Civil Rights in Nineteenth Century America: The First Phase, 1850–1870." In *Chinese Immigrants and American Law*, edited by Charles McClain Jr., 157–96. New York: Garland, 1994.

———. *In Search of Equality: The Chinese Struggle against Discrimination in Nineteenth-Century America*. Berkeley: University of California Press, 1996.

McGirr, Lisa. *Suburban Warriors: The Origins of the New American Right.* Princeton, NJ: Princeton University Press, 2001.

McMurray, Linda O. *To Keep the Waters Troubled: The Life of Ida B. Wells.* New York: Oxford University Press, 1998.

McNeil, Genna Rae. *Groundwork: Charles Hamilton Houston and the Struggle for Civil Rights.* Philadelphia: University of Pennsylvania Press, 1983.

McVeigh, Rory. *The Rise of the Ku Klux Klan: Right-Wing Movements and National Politics.* Minneapolis: University of Minnesota Press, 2009.

McWilliams, Carey. *California: The Great Exception.* 1949; Santa Barbara: Peregrine Smith, 1979.

———. *Factories in the Field: The Story of Migratory Farm Labor in California.* Boston: Little, Brown, 1939.

Mecklin, John Moffatt. *The Ku Klux Klan: A Study of the American Mind.* New York: Harcourt Brace, 1924.

Miles, Tiya. "The Long Arm of the South." *Western Historical Quarterly* 43, no. 3 (autumn 2012): 274–81.

Miller, Floyd J. *The Search for a Black Nationality: Black Emigration and Colonization, 1787–1863.* Urbana: University of Illinois Press, 1975.

Miller, James A., Susan D. Pennybacker, and Eve Rosenhaft. "Mother Ada Wright and the International Campaign to Free the Scottsboro Boys, 1931–1934." *American Historical Review* 106, no. 2 (April 2001): 387–430.

Mitchell, Michele. *Righteous Propagation: African Americans and the Politics of Racial Destiny after Reconstruction.* Chapel Hill: University of North Carolina Press, 2004.

Molina, Natalia. *Fit to Be Citizens? Public Health and Race in Los Angeles, 1879–1939.* Berkeley: University of California Press, 2006.

———. *How Race Is Made in America: Immigration, Citizenship, and the Power of Racial Scripts.* Berkeley: University of California Press, 2014.

Moore, Leonard J. "Historical Interpretation of the 1920s Klan: The Traditional View and Recent Revisions." In Lay, *Invisible Empire*, 17–38.

Moore, Shirley Ann Wilson. *Sweet Freedom's Plains: African Americans on the Overland Trails, 1841–1869*. Norman: University of Oklahoma Press, 2016.

———. *To Place Our Deeds: The African American Community in Richmond, California, 1910–1963*. Berkeley: University of California Press, 2000.

———. "'Your Life Is Really Not Just Your Own': African American Women in Twentieth-Century California." In De Graff, Mulroy, and Taylor, *Seeking El Dorado*, 210–46.

Mosley, Walter. *Black Betty: An Easy Rawlins Mystery*. New York: Washington Square Press, 2002.

Mullen, Kevin. *Dangerous Strangers: Minority Newcomers and Criminal Violence in the Urban West*. New York: Palgrave-Macmillan, 2009.

Nash, Gerald D. *World War II and the West: Reshaping the Economy*. Lincoln: University of Nebraska Press, 1990.

Nasstrom, Kathryn. "Down to Now: Memory, Narrative, and Women's Leadership in the Civil Rights Movement in Atlanta, Georgia." *Gender and History* (April 1999): 113–44.

National Association for the Advancement of Colored People. *Thirty Years of Lynching in the United States, 1889–1918*. New York: NAACP, 1919; Arno, 1969.

Nicolaides, Becky M. *My Blue Heaven: Life and Politics in the Working-Class Suburbs of Los Angeles, 1920–1965*. Chicago: University of Chicago Press, 2009.

Noel, Jana. "Jeremiah B. Sanderson: Educator and Organizer for the Rights of 'Colored Citizens' in Early California." *Journal of Negro Education* 74, no. 2 (spring 2005): 151–58.

Paddison, Joshua. *American Heathens: Religion, Race, and Reconstruction in California*. Berkeley: University of California Press, 2012.

Page, Henry Markham. *Pasadena: Its Early Years*. Los Angeles: L. L. Morrison, 1964.

Painter, Nell Irvin. *Exodusters: Black Migration to Kansas After Reconstruction*. New York: Alfred A. Knopf, 1976.

Pascoe, Peggy. *What Comes Naturally: Miscegenation Law and the Making of Race in America*. New York: Oxford University Press, 2009.

Patterson, Tom. *A Colony for California: Riverside's First Hundred Years*. Riverside, CA.: Museum Press, 1991.

Payne, Charles. *I've Got the Light of Freedom: The Organizing Tradition of the Mississippi Freedom Struggle*. Berkeley: University of California Press, 2007.

Peiss, Kathy Lee. *Cheap Amusements: Working Women and Leisure in Turn-of-the-Century New York*. Philadelphia: Temple University Press, 1986.

Pfeifer, Michael J. *Rough Justice: Lynching and American Society, 1874–1947*. Urbana: University of Illinois Press, 2004.

Raiford, Leigh. *Imprisoned in a Luminous Glare: Photography and the African*

American Freedom Struggle. Chapel Hill: University of North Carolina Press, 2011.

Rampersad, Arnold. *Jackie Robinson: A Biography*. New York: Alfred A. Knopf, 1997.

Ramsey, Eleanor Mason. "Allensworth: A Study in Social Change." PhD diss., UC Berkeley, 1977.

Ransby, Barbara. *Ella Baker and the Black Freedom Movement: A Radical Democratic Vision*. Chapel Hill: University of North Carolina Press, 2005.

Reed, Christopher Robert. *All the World Is Here: The Black Presence in the White City*. Bloomington: Indiana University Press, 2000.

Reid, Hiram A. *History of Pasadena*. Pasadena, CA: Pasadena History Company, 1895.

Rhodes, Jane. *Mary Ann Shadd Cary: The Black Press and Protest in the Nineteenth Century*. Bloomington: Indiana University Press, 1998.

———. "Pedagogies of Respectability: Race, Media, and Black Womanhood in the Early 20th Century." *Souls* 18, nos. 2–4 (April–December 2016): 203–14.

Rhomberg, Chris. *No There There: Race, Class, and Political Community in Oakland*. Berkeley: University of California Press, 2004.

Richardson, Heather Cox. *West from Appomattox: The Reconstruction of America after the Civil War*. New Haven, CT: Yale University Press, 2007.

Rivers, Betty. *The Hackett Family in Allensworth*. Sacramento: California Department of Parks and Recreation, n.d.

Robinson, Jackie. *Baseball Has Done It*. Edited by Charles Dexter. Philadelphia: J. B. Lippincott, 1964.

Robnett, Belinda. *How Long? How Long? African-American Women in the Struggle for Civil Rights* New York: Oxford University Press, 1997.

Rodecape, Lois Foster. "Tom Maguire: Napoleon of the Stage." *California Historical Society Quarterly* (December 1941): 289–314.

Roediger, David R. *The Wages of Whiteness: Race and the Making of the American Working Class*. New York: Verso, 1991.

Rogin, Michael *Blackface, White Noise: Jewish Immigrants in the Hollywood Melting Pot*. Berkeley: University of California Press, 1996.

Rohrbough, Malcolm J. *Days of Gold: The California Gold Rush and the American Nation*. Berkeley: University of California Press, 1997.

Rolle, Andrew F. *California: A History*. 2d ed. New York: Thomas Y. Crowell, 1969.

Romano, Renee C., and Leigh Raiford, eds. *The Civil Rights Movement in American Memory*. Athens: University of Georgia Press, 2006.

Rosen, Hannah. *Terror in the Heart of Freedom: Citizenship, Sexual Violence, and the Meaning of Race in the Postemancipation South*. Chapel Hill: University of North Carolina Press, 2009.

Royal, Alice C. *Allensworth, the Freedom Colony: An African American Township.* Berkeley, CA: Heyday Books, 2008.

Ruiz, Vicki L. *Cannery Women, Cannery Lives: Mexican Women, Unionization, and the California Food Processing Industry, 1930–1950.* Albuquerque: University of New Mexico Press, 1987.

Rushdy, Ashraf H. A. *The End of American Lynching.* New Brunswick, NJ: Rutgers University Press, 2012.

Rydell, Robert. *All the World's a Fair: Visions of Empire at American International Expositions, 1876–1916.* Chicago: University of Chicago Press, 1984.

Rydell, Robert, John E. Findling, and Kimberly D. Pelle, eds. *Fair America: World's Fairs in the United States.* Washington, DC: Smithsonian Institution Press, March 2000.

Salem, Dorothy. *To Better Our World: Black Women in Organized Reform, 1890–1920.* New York: Carlson, 1990.

Sánchez, George J. *Becoming Mexican American: Ethnicity, Culture, and Identity in Chicano Los Angeles, 1900–1954.* New York: Oxford University Press, 1993.

Saxton, Alexander. *The Rise and Fall of the White Republic: Class Politics and Mass Culture in Nineteenth-Century America.* New York: Verso, 1990.

Schechter, Patricia A. *Ida B. Wells-Barnett and American Reform, 1880–1930.* Chapel Hill: University of North Carolina Press, 2001.

Schultz, Kevin M. *Tri-Faith America: How Catholics and Jews Held Postwar America to its Protestant Promise.* New York: Oxford University Press, 2011.

Shaw, Stephanie J. "Black Women and the Creation of the National Association of Colored Women." In *"We Specialize in the Wholly Impossible": A Reader in Black Women's History,* edited by Darlene Clark Hine, Wilma King, and Linda Reed, 433–47. New York: Carlson, 1995.

——. *What A Woman Ought to Be and to Do: Black Professional Women Workers During the Jim Crow Era.* Chicago: University of Chicago Press, 1996.

Shorr, Howard. "Thorns in the Roses: Race Relations and the Brookside Plunge Controversy in Pasadena, California, 1914–1947." In *Law in the Western United States,* edited by Gordon Morris Bakken, 522–28. Norman: University of Oklahoma Press, 2000.

Shorto, Russell. *Jackie Robinson and the Breaking of the Color Barrier.* Brookfield, CT: Millbrook, 1991.

Sides, Josh. *L.A. City Limits: African American Los Angeles from the Great Depression to the Present.* Berkeley: University of California Press, 2003.

Sklar, Kathryn Kish, and Thomas Dublin, eds., *Women and Social Movements in the United States, 1600–2000.* N.p.: Alexander Street, a Proquest Company, 2019.

Slocum, Karla. "Black Towns and the Civil War: Touring Battles of Race, Nation, and Place." *Souls: A Critical Journal of Black Politics, Culture and Society* 19, no. 1 (January–March 2017).

Smemo, Kristoffer. "The Little People's Century: Industrial Pluralism, Economic Development, and the Emergence of Liberal Republicanism in California, 1942–1946." *Journal of American History* 101, no. 4 (March 2015): 1166–89.

Smith, Rebecca, Elaine Zorbas, Abby Delman, Charlotte Krontiris, and Pasadena Heritage Oral History Project. *Advocates for Change: Oral History Interviews on the Desegregation of Pasadena Unified School District.* [Pasadena:] Pasadena Heritage, 2007.

Smith, Stacey L. *Freedom's Frontier: California and the Struggle Over Unfree Labor, Emancipation, and Reconstruction.* Chapel Hill: University of North Carolina Press, 2013.

Snorgrass, William J. "The Black Press in the San Francisco Bay Area." *California History* 60, no. 4 (1981–82): 306–17.

Stanley, Amy Dru. "Slave Emancipation and the Revolutionizing of Human Rights." In *The World the Civil War Made,* edited by Gregory P. Downs and Kate Masur, 269–303. Chapel Hill: University of North Carolina Press, 2015.

Starr, Kevin. *California: A History.* New York: Random House, 2005.

Steele, Gerda. "Rose Bowl Aquatic Center." *Pasadena Journal,* December 21, 1990, 4.

Stern, Alexandra Minna. *Eugenic Nation: Faults and Frontiers of Better Breeding in Modern America.* 2d ed. Berkeley: University of California Press, 2016.

Stokes, Melvyn. *D. W. Griffith's "The Birth of a Nation": A History of the Most Controversial Motion Picture of All Time.* London: Oxford University Press, 2008.

Streitmatter, Roger. *Raising Her Voice: African American Women Journalists Who Changed History.* Lexington: University Press of Kentucky, 1994.

Streshensky, Shirley. "The Dream Dies Hard for a Black Utopia." *Preservation* (July/August 1999): 53–59.

Strickland, Sue. "Fairmount Park Episode." *Journal of the Riverside Historical Society* 5 (February 2001): 21–27.

Stride, Christopher, Ffion Thomas, and Maureen M. Smith. "Ballplayer or Barrier Breaker: Branding through the Seven Statues of Jackie Robinson." *International Journal of the History of Sport* 31, no. 17 (2014): 2164–96.

Stuckey, Melissa N. "Boley, Indian Territory: Exercising Freedom in the All-Black Town." *Journal of African American History* 102, no. 4 (fall 2017): 492–516.

Sturken, Marita. *The Tourists of History: Memory, Kitsch, and Consumerism from Oklahoma City to Ground Zero.* Durham, NC: Duke University Press, 2007.

Sullivan, Patricia. *Lift Every Voice: The NAACP and the Making of the Civil Rights Movement.* New York: New Press, 2009.

Swett, John. *History of the Public School System of California.* San Francisco: A. L. Bancroft, 1876.

———. *Public Education in California: Its Origin and Development, with Personal Reminiscences of Half a Century.* New York: American Book, 1911.

Taylor, Quintard. *The Forging of a Black Community: Seattle's Central District from 1870 through the Civil Rights Era.* Seattle: University of Washington Press, 1994.

———. *In Search of the Racial Frontier: African Americans in the American West, 1528–1990.* New York: Norton, 1998.

Taylor, Quintard, and Shirley Ann Wilson Moore, eds. *African American Women Confront the West, 1600–2000.* Norman: University of Oklahoma Press, 2003.

Terborg-Penn, Rosalyn. *African American Women in the Struggle for the Vote, 1860–1920.* Bloomington: Indiana University Press, 1998.

Thorndike, E. L. *Your City.* New York: Harcourt, Brace, 1937.

Thurman, Sue Bailey. *Pioneers of Negro Origin.* R & E Research Associates, 1952, 2nd ed. 1971.

Todd, Frank Morton. *The Story of the Exposition: Being the Official History of the International Celebration held at San Francisco in 1915 to Commemorate the Discovery of the Pacific Ocean and Construction of the Panama Canal.* New York: G. P. Putnam's Sons, Knickerbocker Press, 1921.

Todd-Breland, Elizabeth. *A Political Education: Black Politics and Education Reform in Chicago since the 1960s.* Chapel Hill: University of North Carolina, 2018.

Tolbert, Emory J. *The UNIA and Black Los Angeles: Ideology and Community in the American Garvey Movement.* Los Angeles: Center for Afro-American Studies, 1980.

Toy, Eckard V. "Robe and Gown: The Ku Klux Klan in Eugene, Oregon in the 1920s." In Lay, *Invisible Empire*, 153–84.

Tushnet, M. V. *The NAACP's Legal Strategy against Segregated Education, 1925–1950.* Chicago: University of Chicago Press, 1987.

U.S. Bureau of the Census. *Fourteenth Census of the United States Population: 1920.* Washington, DC: Government Printing Office, 1923.

———. *Negro Population in the United States, 1790–1915.* Washington, DC: Government Printing Office, 1918.

———. *Seventeenth Census of the United States, 1950.* Washington, DC: Government Printing Office, 1952.

U.S. Department of Commerce. *General Statistics of Cities Including Recreation, Swimming Pools, Etc., 1916.* Washington, DC: Government Printing Office, 1917.

van Leeuwen, Thomas A. P. *The Springboard in the Pond: An Intimate History of the Swimming Pool.* Cambridge, MA: MIT Press, 1998.

Varzally, Allison. *Making a Non-White America: Californians Coloring Outside Ethnic Lines, 1925–1955.* Berkeley: University of California Press, 2008.

Von Eschen, Penny. *Satchmo Blows Up the World: Jazz Ambassadors Play the Cold War*. Cambridge, MA: Harvard University Press, 2004.

Waldrep, Christopher. *The Many Faces of Judge Lynch: Extralegal Violence and Punishment in America*. New York: Palgrave Macmillan, 2002.

———."War of Words: The Controversy Over the Definition of Lynching, 1899–1940," *Journal of Southern History* 66, no. 1 (February 2000): 75–100.

Watson, Jonathan. "Crossing the Colour Lines in the City of Angels: The NAACP and the Zoot-Suit Riot of 1943." *University of Sussex Journal of Contemporary History* 4 (2002): 1–10.

———. "The NAACP in California, 1914–1950." In *Long Is the Way and Hard: One Hundred Years of the NAACP*, edited by Kervern Verney and Lee Sartain, 185–200. Fayetteville: University of Arkansas Press, 2009.

Weiner, Mark S. *Black Trials: Citizenship from the Beginnings of Slavery to the End of Caste*. New York: Alfred A. Knopf, 2004.

Weiss, Nancy J. *Farewell to the Party of Lincoln: Black Politics in the Age of FDR*. Princeton, NJ: Princeton University Press, 1983.

Welke, Barbara. "Rights of Passage: Gendered-Rights Consciousness and the Quest for Freedom, San Francisco, California, 1850–1870." In Taylor and Moore, *African American Women Confront the West*, 73–93.

Wells-Barnett, Ida B. *Crusade for Justice: The Autobiography of Ida B. Wells*. Chicago: University of Chicago Press, 1970.

White, Shane. "'It Was a Proud Day': African Americans, Festivals, and Parades in the North, 1741–1834." *Journal of American History* (June 1994): 13–50.

White, Walter. *A Man Called White*. New York: Arno Press, 1969.

———. *Rope and Faggot: A Biography of Judge Lynch* (New York: Knopf, 1929; Arno, 1969).

Williams, Chad L. *Torchbearers of Democracy: African American Soldiers in the World War I Era*. Chapel Hill: University of North Carolina Press, 2010.

Williams, Kadida E. *They Left Great Marks on Me: African American Testimonies of Racial Violence from Emancipation to World War I*. New York: New York University Press, 2012.

Willis, Deborah. "The Sociologist's Eye: W.E.B. Du Bois and the Paris Exposition." In D. Lewis and Willis, *Small Nation of People*, 51–78.

Wilson, Mabel O. *Negro Building: Black Americans in the World of Fairs and Museums*. Berkeley: University of California Press, 2012.

Wiltse, Jeff. *Contested Waters: A Social History of Swimming Pools in America*. Chapel Hill: University of North Carolina Press, 2007.

Winter, Ella. "California's Little Hitlers." *New Republic*, December 17, 1933, 188–90.

Wollenberg, Charles. *All Deliberate Speed: Segregation and Exclusion in California Schools, 1855–1975*. Berkeley: University of California Press, 1977.

Wong, Edlie. *Racial Reconstruction: Black Inclusion, Chinese Exclusion, and the Fictions of Citizenship*. New York: New York University Press, 2015.

Wood, Amy Louise. *Lynching and Spectacle: Witnessing Racial Violence in America, 1890–1940*. Chapel Hill: University of North Carolina Press, 2009.

Wood, Fremont. "'The Zone' with Its Sixty-five Acres of Fun." *American Building Association News* (Chicago: 1915).

Woodward, C. Vann. *The Strange Career of Jim Crow*. New York: Oxford University Press, 1955.

Worthen, James. *Governor James Rolph and the Great Depression in California*. Jefferson, NC: McFarland, 2006.

Yamamoto, Hisaye. "A Fire in Fontana." *Rafu Shimpo*, December 21, 1985.

Zangrando, Robert L. *The NAACP Crusade against Lynching, 1909–1950*. Philadelphia: Temple University Press, 1980.

Index

LYNN M. HUDSON is an associate professor of history at the University of Illinois at Chicago. She is the author of *The Making of "Mammy Pleasant": A Black Entrepreneur in Nineteenth-Century San Francisco.*

The University of Illinois Press
is a founding member of the
Association of University Presses.

———————————————————————

Composed in 10.5/14 Electra
with Scala Sans display
by Jim Proefrock
at the University of Illinois Press
Manufactured by Sheridan Books, Inc.

University of Illinois Press
1325 South Oak Street
Champaign, IL 61820-6903
www.press.uillinois.edu